DATA ANALYTICS FOR SOCIAL MICROBLOGGING PLATFORMS

Hybrid Computational Intelligence for
Pattern Analysis and Understanding Series

DATA ANALYTICS FOR SOCIAL MICROBLOGGING PLATFORMS

Series Editors

SIDDHARTHA BHATTACHARYYA

NILANJAN DEY

SOUMI DUTTA
Department of Computer Application and Science
Institute of Engineering & Management (IEM)
Kolkata, India

ASIT KUMAR DAS
Department of Computer Science and Technology
IIEST Shibpur
Howrah, India

SAPTARSHI GHOSH
Department of Computer Science and Engineering
Indian Institute of Technology, Kharagpur
Kharagpur, India

DEBABRATA SAMANTA
Department of Computer Science
CHRIST (Deemed to be University)
Bangalore, India

ACADEMIC PRESS

An imprint of Elsevier

Academic Press is an imprint of Elsevier
125 London Wall, London EC2Y 5AS, United Kingdom
525 B Street, Suite 1650, San Diego, CA 92101, United States
50 Hampshire Street, 5th Floor, Cambridge, MA 02139, United States
The Boulevard, Langford Lane, Kidlington, Oxford OX5 1GB, United Kingdom

Notices

Knowledge and best practice in this field are constantly changing. As new research and experience
broaden our understanding, changes in research methods, professional practices, or medical
treatment may become necessary.

Practitioners and researchers must always rely on their own experience and knowledge in
evaluating and using any information, methods, compounds, or experiments described herein. In
using such information or methods they should be mindful of their own safety and the safety of
others, including parties for whom they have a professional responsibility.

To the fullest extent of the law, neither the Publisher nor the authors, contributors, or editors,
assume any liability for any injury and/or damage to persons or property as a matter of products
liability, negligence or otherwise, or from any use or operation of any methods, products,
instructions, or ideas contained in the material herein.

ISBN: 978-0-323-91785-8

For information on all Academic Press publications
visit our website at https://www.elsevier.com/books-and-journals

Publisher: Mara Conner
Editorial Project Manager: Franchezca A. Cabural
Production Project Manager: Punithavathy Govindaradjane
Cover Designer: Christian Bilbow

Working together
to grow libraries in
developing countries

www.elsevier.com • www.bookaid.org

Typeset by VTeX

I, Dr. Soumi Dutta, dedicate the book to my parents, daughter, brother, husband, friends, colleagues, and all my teachers.

I, Dr. Asit Kumar Das, dedicate the book to my wife, son, parents, friends, and colleagues.

I, Dr. Saptarshi Ghosh, dedicate the book to my wife, parents, friends, colleagues, and all my teachers.

I, Dr. Debabrata Samanta, dedicate the book to my parents Mr. Dulal Chandra Samanta, Mrs. Ambujini Samanta, my elder sister Mrs. Tanusree Samanta, brother-in-law Mr. Soumendra Jana and daughter Ms. Aditri Samanta.

Contents

PART 2 Microblogging dataset applications and implications

About the authors

Dr. Soumi Dutta is Associate Professor at the Institute of Engineering & Management,Saltlake, India. She has completed her PhD in Engineering at IIEST, Shibpur. She received her B.Tech (IT) and M.Tech (CSE) as a Gold medalist from MAKAUT. She is certified as Publons Academy Peer Reviewer, 2020 and Certified Microsoft Innovative Educator, 2020. Her research interests include data mining, online social network data analysis, and image processing. She has published 50 conference and journal papers with publishing houses like Springer, IEEE, IGI Global, and Taylor & Francis. She has contributed five book chapters published by Taylor & Francis Group and IGI Global. She is peer reviewer and TPC member of different international journals. She was editor of the CIPR-2020, CIPR-2019, IEMIS-2018, IEMIS-2020, CIIR-2021,IEMIS-2022 and special issues in IJWLTT. She is a member of several technical functional bodies such as IEEE, ACM, IFERP, MACUL, SDIWC, Internet-Society, ICSES, ASR, AIDASCO, USERN, IRAN, and IAENG. She has published six patents and one Indian Copyright. She has delivered more than 30 keynote talks at different international conferences.

Dr. Asit Kumar Das works as a Professor in the Department of Computer Science and Technology, Indian Institute of Engineering Science and Technology, Shibpur, Howrah, West Bengal, India. He has published more than 100 research papers in various international journals and conference proceedings, 1 book, and 4 book chapters. He has worked as a member of the Editorial/Reviewer Board of various international journals and conferences. He has shared his research experiences in many workshops and conferences as an invited lecturer in various institutes in India. He has acted as the general chair, program chair, and advisory member of committees of many international conferences. His research interests include data mining and pattern recognition in various fields, including bioinformatics, social networks, text mining, audio and video data analysis, and medical data analysis. He has already guided ten PhD students and is currently guiding six PhD students.

Dr. Saptarshi Ghosh is Assistant Professor at the Department of Computer Science and Engineering, Indian Institute of Technology Kharagpur,

India. His primary research interests include social network analysis, legal analytics, and algorithmic bias and fairness. His research is interdisciplinary and uses techniques from machine learning, natural language processing, information retrieval, computational social science, and complex network theory. He heads the Max Planck Partner Group at IIT Kharagpur, which focuses on algorithmic bias and fairness. He received his PhD in computer science from IIT Kharagpur in 2013. He was a Humboldt Postdoctoral Research Fellow at the Max Planck Institute for Software Systems (MPI-SWS), Germany.

Dr. Debabrata Samanta is presently working as Associate Professor in the Department of Computer Science, CHRIST (Deemed to be University), Bangalore, India. He obtained his Bachelors in Physics (Honors) from Calcutta University, Kolkata, India. He obtained his MCA from the Academy of Technology, under WBUT, West Bengal. He obtained his PhD in Computer Science and Engineering from the National Institute of Technology, Durgapur, India, in the area of SAR image processing. He is keenly interested in interdisciplinary research and development and has experience spanning fields of SAR image analysis, video surveillance, heuristic algorithms for image classification, deep learning frameworks for detection and classification, blockchain, statistical modeling, wireless ad hoc networks, natural language processing, and V2I communication. He has successfully completed six consultancy projects. He has received an Open Access Publication fund. He has received funding under the International Travel Support Scheme in 2019 for attending a conference in Thailand. He is the owner of 21 patents (3 Indian patents designed, 2 Australian patents granted, 16 Indian patents published) and 2 copyrights. He has authored and coauthored over 189 research papers in international journals (SCI/SCIE/ESCI/Scopus) and conference proceedings published by publishing houses including IEEE, Springer, and Elsevier. He has received the "Scholastic Award" at the 2nd International conference on Computer Science and IT application, CSIT-2011, Delhi, India. He is a coauthor of 13 books and the coeditor of 11 books. He has presented various papers at international conferences and received Best Paper awards. He has authored and coauthored eight book chapters. He also serves as acquisition editor for Springer, Wiley, CRC, Scrivener Publishing, and Elsevier. He is a Professional IEEE Member, an Associate Life Member of the Computer Society of India (CSI), and a Life Member of the Indian Society for

Technical Education (ISTE). He has been a convener, keynote speaker, session chair, cochair, publicity chair, publication chair, advisory board member, and technical program committee member for many prestigious international and national conferences. He was invited speaker at several institutions.

Preface

This book focuses on microblogging sites, which have opened up a variety of new opportunities for communication, as well as new obstacles. Spammers and other types of users who upload dangerous content on microblogging sites are becoming more prevalent as the services become more popular. As a result, it is critical to screen spam posts from such sites. The abundance of information provided on microblogging services is a second difficulty. On Twitter, for example, more than 500 million posts (tweets) are published per day on average. Users are experiencing information overload as a result of the vast amount of information that is submitted. As a result, strategies for organizing information must be developed. The goal of this work is to create strategies for dealing with the two practical difficulties mentioned above: screening out hazardous content and organizing information on microblogging sites. We believe this book will be both instructive and provocative. We believe it will move the data analysis community forward, allowing each user to study various queries, applications, and future arrangements in order to make safe and secure plans for everybody. It also focuses on theory and methods in related disciplines such as intelligent information filtering and organization systems for social microblogging sites.

Acknowledgments

This work would not have been possible without close cooperation with many people who were always there when we needed them the most. We take this opportunity to acknowledge them and extend our sincere gratitude for helping us make this book a reality.

We would like to acknowledge the distinguished researcher Dr. Tanmoy Chakraborty, with whom we have coauthored a publication. We feel very fortunate as he has provided us with valuable suggestions.

We would also like to acknowledge Vibhash Chandra and Kanav Mehra of IIEST Shibpur, with whom we have coauthored several publications.

We are highly thankful to the director of IEM, Kolkata, Dr. Satyajit Chakraborti, and the Head of the Department of Computer Science and Application, Dr. Abhishek Bhattacharya, for their invaluable advices and moral support which transformed our work. We also acknowledge the invaluable support provided by our colleagues.

On our journey we had some other wayfarers, whose support is unforgettable because of their loving disposition and who are now our friends.

Finally, we would like to acknowledge the people who mean the world to us: our parents, brothers, sisters, and children. We cannot imagine a life without their love and blessings. Thank you all for showing faith in us and giving us the liberty to choose what we desire. We consider ourselves the luckiest in the world to have such supportive families, standing behind us with their love and support. We express our great pleasure, sincere thanks, and gratitude to the people who significantly helped, contributed, and supported the completion of this book. Our sincere thanks go to Fr. Benny Thomas, Professor in the Department of Computer Science and Engineering, CHRIST (Deemed to be University), Bengaluru, Karnataka India, for his continuous support, advice, and cordial guidance from the conception to the completion of this book.

Dr. Soumi Dutta
Associate Professor, Department of Computer Application and Science,
Institute of Engineering & Management (IEM), Kolkata, India
Dr. Asit Kumar Das
Professor, Department of Computer Science and Technology,
IIEST Shibpur, Howrah, India

Dr. Saptarshi Ghosh
Assistant Professor, Department of Computer Science and Engineering,
Indian Institute of Technology, Kharagpur, Kharagpur, India
Dr. Debabrata Samanta
Associate Professor, Department of Computer Science, CHRIST
(Deemed to be University), Bangalore, India

About the book

The goal of this book is to discuss important computational techniques in the domain of microblogging datasets, such as pattern recognition, machine learning, data mining algorithms, rough set and fuzzy set theory, evolutionary computations, combinatorial pattern matching, and efficient data mining techniques, including clustering and classification. This book provides a comprehensive explanation of microblog datasets as a field that is focused on information, data, and knowledge in the context of natural language processing.

Chapter 1 states that Tumblr, Twitter, and Sina Weibo are three of the most popular online social microblogging platforms today. Microblogging platforms have become popular communication tools because they allow for fast information exchange. Every day, these sites generate massive amounts of data as a result of commercial, intellectual, and social activities. This crowdsourced data can be used for fraud detection, market analysis, spam posts, spam detection, categorization or grouping of users based on their behavior, customer retention, and extraction of crucial news, as well as production control and scientific discovery. Microblog data is rapidly being used to build real-time search engines and recommendation systems, as well as services that mine and summarize public reaction to events. Microblogging sites, in addition to having a wide range of applications, also present a number of challenges in terms of exploitation of crowdsourced data, such as the need to filter out potentially harmful content uploaded by spammers and the need to organize the voluminous data. The purpose of this book, as stated in the next section, is to provide ways for dealing with these two challenges.

Chapter 2 provides a review of the literature on a number of themes. Filtering undesired information (e.g., spam), clustering, and summarization are three commonly used strategies to achieve information filtering and organization. Prior to clustering and summarization, attribute selection and dimensionality reduction are critical tasks. Because of the growing and diverse nature of microblog vocabulary, attribute selection plays an increasingly important role in data analysis. Attribute selection increases the generation of summarization, grouping, and classification procedures as well as reducing the dimension of the large dataset. The state-of-the-art attribute selection methods are explored in this section. Without any prior knowledge, cluster analysis looks for patterns in a collection to detect similarity across objects (i.e., unsupervised). Clustering is particularly important in the analysis of microblog data. Various standard clustering algorithms are briefly reviewed in this section. This section also covers related issues such as cluster quality evaluation measures and cluster validation. Automatic document summarization is a well-known problem in the field of information retrieval. Hundreds to thousands of microblogs (tweets) are routinely posted on Twitter during an emergency, making it impossible to read through each tweet individually. As a result, summarizing emergency microblogs has become a major research area in recent years. Some off-the-shelf extractive summarization algorithms are explored in this chapter. This chapter analyzes many publications that have employed attribute selection, summarization, and clustering approaches in the domain of online social microblogging sites, in addition to analyzing these methods in general.

Chapter 3 states that some of the most prominent microblogging services are Twitter, Facebook, and LinkedIn. On the Twitter microblogging site, which is one of the most popular websites on the Internet today, millions of users post real-time messages (tweets) on a variety of topics. Popular content on Twitter (i.e., content that is widely discussed) can be used for a variety of purposes on any given day, including content suggestion, marketing, and commercial campaigns. One of the most exciting characteristics of Twitter is its real-time nature: at any given time, millions of Twitter users are giving their thoughts on a wide range of topics or incidents/events occurring across the world. As a result, Twitter content is particularly useful for acquiring real-time information on a variety of topics. This section covers the dataset that was used in a number of experiments in the book. Twitter provides an API for gathering many types of data, including streams of tweets published through the website, user profile information, and so on. Twitter, in particular, provides a 1% random sample of all tweets published on the Twitter website worldwide. This chapter provides the reader with a quick rundown of the experimental dataset that was used to evaluate the various data analytics methodologies described in the book.

Chapter 4 discusses that spammers are increasingly targeting online social network (OSN) sites, placing dangerous content on them as their popularity grows. Spam posts and spam accounts must consequently be filtered from OSNs. Several prior attempts to categorize spam on OSNs used a number of criteria to distinguish spam from legitimate entities. The purpose of this chapter is to improve spam categorization by developing a method for selecting attributes that enables for a fewer number of attributes to be discovered, resulting in better classification. We explicitly apply rough set theory concepts to construct the attribute selection method. On five different spam classification datasets spanning a variety of OSNs, the suggested methodology's performance is compared to that of numerous baseline feature selection approaches. We discovered that the suggested strategy selects a smaller attribute subset than baseline procedures for the majority of datasets, but produces better classification performance than the other methods.

In Chapter 5, it is discussed that crowdsourced textual data from social media sites like Twitter, in particular, has emerged as a valuable source of real-time information on current events such as geopolitical events, natural and man-made disasters, and so on. During emergency situations, microblogging networks, particularly Twitter, have become vital sources of real-time situational information. During an emergency, hundreds to thousands of microblogs (tweets) are routinely posted on Twitter, making it hard to go through each one individually. As a result, summarizing microblogs written during emergency situations has been a major research topic in recent years. Extractive summarizing algorithms have been developed to generate summaries of text in general and microblogs in particular. A few studies have looked into the utility of various summarizing algorithms on microblogs. Rather than attempting to create a new summary algorithm in this chapter, we examine if existing off-the-shelf summarizing systems may be coupled to provide better-quality summaries than any of the separate algorithms. This chapter covers a variety of supervised and unsupervised techniques. Unsupervised methods divide the tweets identified by the underlying algorithms into groups based on some measure of tweet similarity and then selects one tweet from each group. Algorithms using this method seek to find the most important tweets while avoiding redundancy in the final summary. Based on the rankings evaluated by several base methods and the performance of the base approaches throughout a training set, the supervised ensemble technique attempts to learn a ranking of tweets according to significance. The goal is to integrate multiple ranks to improve tweet ranking (for inclusion in the final summary). Experiments are carried out on microblogs related to four recent disasters, motivated by the relevance of microblog summaries during crisis situations. It is shown that the proposed ensemble methods can combine the outputs of many different base approaches to provide summaries that are superior to any of the basis algorithms.

In Chapter 6, it is discussed that with millions of users posting hundreds of millions of tweets per day, Twitter is one of the most popular social networking services on the internet. Twitter is now largely considered as one of the most popular and fastest-growing communication platforms, and it is frequently used to stay up to date on current events and news items. While keyword matching might help you find tweets about a specific event or news stories fast, many of the tweets will have semantically identical content. It is difficult for a user to stay on top of an event or a news story if he/she needs to read all of the tweets that provide the same or redundant information. As a result, having effective methods for summarizing a large number of tweets is advantageous. We present a graph-based strategy for summarizing tweets in this chapter, in which a graph is first constructed based on tweet similarity, and then community recognition algorithms are used to cluster comparable tweets. Finally, a representative tweet from each cluster is picked for inclusion in the summary. Tweet semantic similarity is determined by a variety of factors, including WordNet synset-based features. Sumbasic, an existing summarization program, performs worse than the proposed method.

In Chapter 7, it is stated that Twitter, a microblogging platform, is one of the most widely used online communities today. During a major event, such as a disaster, a large number of tweets are instantly posted on Twitter. Because the information is posted too fast to follow for anyone, it must be categorized in order to be used effectively. Because many of the tweets created during an event are highly similar, clustering or grouping similar tweets is a good approach for minimizing the amount of information provided. Clustering, on the other hand, is difficult due to the small size and chaotic nature of tweets. In this chapter, we suggest a new tweet clustering strategy that combines two approaches: classic clustering with K-means and evolutionary clustering with genetic algorithms. We demonstrate that the proposed methodology outperforms existing clustering methods using a dataset of actual tweets gathered during a recent crisis event.

In Chapter 8, we discuss how the growing popularity of microblogging provides a varied platform for the general population to use as a communication medium. Every day, thousands of posts on any trending or non-trending topic are published as microblogs. A high number of messages are uploaded during any important event, such as a natural disaster, an election, or a sporting event like the IPL or the world cup. Because the rapid sending of messages causes information overload, clustering or grouping comparable messages is an effective approach for reducing it. Due to the small size and noisy nature of messages, grouping microblog data is tough. Incrementally huge data is another clustering challenge. Therefore, this chapter proposes a novel clustering approach for microblogs that integrates feature selection techniques. The proposed method has been evaluated on a range of experimental datasets and compared to a number of current clustering algorithms. All proposed methods outperform other methods.

Chapter 9 shows microblogging services like Twitter have risen to prominence as the preferred mode of public communication in recent years. Individual users can easily receive hundreds of microblogs (tweets) per day if they are mildly involved on Twitter. Furthermore, a large number of tweets contain virtually the same content as a result of retweeting and reposting. People may be overburdened by these vast amounts of repetitive data, and no user can effectively assimilate so much information. Under these circumstances, it is necessary to develop methodologies to deal with the data overburden. One of the most effective strategies to manage Twitter's data overflow is to combine semantically similar tweets into groups, with the goal of showing only a few tweets from each group to each user. Multiple graph clustering algorithms based on dimensionality reduction for clustering microblogs are presented in this chapter. Through experiments on four different microblog datasets, it is demonstrated that the suggested clustering approaches outperform various established clustering algorithms.

Chapter 10 explores the fundamental goal of this book: to create efficient algorithms for information filtering and organization on social microblogging platforms. This final chapter highlights the book's accomplishments and suggests research directions. During unique situations such as natural and man-made disasters, information organization is vital. Thousands of tweets are published every hour during such disasters, and because a timely reaction is essential, responders (such as relief workers) must acquire a quick summary of the information posted. The summarizing and grouping algorithms described in this book are applied to microblogs generated during numerous emergency scenarios, keeping this criterion in mind. The experiments show that the offered procedures are effective. It should be noted that the book's chapters have employed a wide range of methodologies from numerous fields, including rough set theory, complex network analysis, evolutionary algorithms, ensemble algorithms, and other mathematical and statistical methods.

PART 1

Introduction of intelligent information filtering and organization systems for social microblogging sites

CHAPTER 1

Introduction to microblogging sites

1.1 Introduction

Researchers in the domain of data mining are working on the expansion of new interesting facts extracting knowledge from microblog data. Microblogging sites have grown in popularity as real-time information sources, and all the information is very unstructured by nature, so data mining plays a significant role in filtering and organization of information to represent the knowledge in a simpler form. So, data mining can be termed as computational hybridization of techniques in disciplinary and interdisciplinary research for finding interesting facts by analyzing huge data. In recent times, online social media has played an important role in our daily life. Millions of users send real-time messages (tweets) on various topics of interest on the Twitter microblogging site, which is one of the most popular websites on the Internet today. On a given day, popular content on Twitter (i.e., content that is discussed by a large number of people) can be used for a variety of reasons, including content suggestion and marketing and commercial campaigns. One of the most intriguing aspects of Twitter is its real-time nature: at any given moment, millions of Twitter users are sharing opinions on a variety of themes or incidents/events taking place across the world. As a result, Twitter material is extremely valuable for gathering real-time news on a range of issues.

This information and knowledge gained through social activities can be exploited for applications ranging from fraud detection [1], market analysis [2], spam posts [3], detection of spammers [4], classification of users according to their behavior [5], summarization [6], identification of important news [7], and science exploration to customer retention and production control [8]. The microblogging site has become a popular tool for finding information on the internet. Along with the variety of applications, microblogging sites also introduce a number of obstacles in exploiting crowdsourced data, including the requirement to filter out dangerous content uploaded by spammers and the necessity to organize the profusion of data. This book aims to develop methodologies for addressing these

Data Analytics for Social Microblogging Platforms
https://doi.org/10.1016/B978-0-32-391785-8.00012-3

two challenges, as explained in the next section. The huge amounts of information exchanges open up several challenges to the researchers for information filtering and organization on online social microblogging sites. The research is designed to apply data mining techniques [9] on microblog datasets so that the relevant challenges of online social media can be served. As a result, data mining is crucial in pattern recognition due to the vast and increasing nature of the dataset.

1.2 Online social networking sites

Users may conduct dialogs, exchange data or expertise, and produce content through social networking, which is based on online development on a communication medium. The use of technology to build and maintain personal and business ties is known as social networking [10]. This is accomplished through the usage of social media platforms like Facebook, Instagram, and Twitter. These websites enable individuals and businesses to connect with one another in order to create connections and share information, ideas, and messages [11]. Family members who live far away might use personal social networking sites like Facebook to stay in touch. They may exchange images and information about what is going on in their lives. People can also connect with people who share their interests (especially strangers). Individuals can connect with one another through groups, lists, and hashtags [12,13]. Sentiment analysis, question answering, intelligent assistance, and other cutting-edge natural language processing (NLP) applications require a large amount of data. This vast amount of data can be sent directly into the machine learning model. Almost all text-based applications require considerable textual input preprocessing, such as the construction of embedding vectors from scratch with a word frequency counter. This necessitates a substantial amount of effort and time. To remedy this, transfer learning methods are presently used for all complicated preprocessing operations. Text preprocessing is a technique for cleaning up text data before feeding it to a machine learning model. Text data comprises a wide range of noise, including emotions, punctuation, and text capitalized differently. Because machines cannot understand language, they want numbers; this is merely the beginning of the issues we will confront. As a result, we must devise a method for converting text to numbers that is both quick and efficient. In every machine learning project, data cleaning or preprocessing is just as important as model creation. Human language is too complex to deal with; hence, text data is one of the most unstructured sorts of data available. Have you ever wondered how Alexa, Siri, and Google Assistant interpret, respond to, and comprehend human language? NLP is a technique that works in the background and allows for considerable text preparation before any response. The most important text preparation procedures that you will need to know if you are going to work with text data will be covered in this class.

Marketers frequently utilize social media to raise brand awareness and build brand loyalty. Social media marketing aids in the promotion of a brand's voice and content by making it more accessible to new customers and more identifiable to existing ones. A frequent Twitter user, for example, may discover about a firm for the first time through a news feed and decide to purchase a product or service. The higher the number of individuals who are exposed to a company's brand, the better are its prospects of attracting and maintaining new consumers. Marketers make advantage of social media to boost conversion rates [14]. Building a following gives you access to new, current, and old consumers, as well as the opportunity to communicate with them. Using social media to share blog entries, photographs, videos, or comments encourages followers to react, visit the company's website, and become clients.

Almost every product or service you use is supported by a social media-savvy firm. It is difficult to think of a significant organization that does not use social media to promote, advertise, and market themselves. Using social media for business is not only a wonderful idea, but it is also required if you want to flourish in the corporate world. Here we discuss two firms that are doing it correctly. Individuals and companies are connected through social networking because it allows them to exchange information, ideas, and messages. Companies also utilize social media to build brand awareness, market products and services, and respond to consumer questions and concerns [15,16].

Big brands like Facebook, Instagram, Facebook Messenger, and Twitter are among the most popular social media platforms. In the United States, these are the most popular social networking sites. Pinterest, Tumblr, Snapchat, TikTok, and YouTube are among the others. Another popular site that connects professionals with coworkers, business contacts, and employers is LinkedIn. Individuals utilize social networks because they allow them to form relationships with people they would not otherwise be able to meet. When utilized for public relations, marketing, and advertising, it may also enhance corporate productivity [17].

1.3   Advantages and disadvantages of social networking

Individuals and companies can be affected by social networking in both good and bad ways. As a result, it is critical to assess the benefits and drawbacks of utilizing these social networking platforms [18].

Advantages

As previously said, social networking helps people to stay in touch with family and friends with whom they would otherwise be unable to communicate due to distance or just lose touch. People can also form new relationships by connecting with others who have similar interests [19].

It also enables businesses to connect with both new and existing customers. They may also utilize social media to generate, advertise, and raise brand recognition through it. Client feedback and reviews are very important to them. The more positive reviews a firm receives, the more valuable its brand authority becomes. This results in increased sales and a higher search engine ranking. As a result, social networking may assist in establishing a brand's legitimacy, credibility, and trustworthiness [20].

Disadvantages

Misinformation spreads quickly on social media and may spread like wildfire. After 2012, this became increasingly common. Rumors travel quicker than facts. According to one research, disinformation is 70% more likely to be disseminated on Twitter than genuine information [21].

Social media networking may have a negative influence on businesses just as much as traditional networking. On social media, brand criticism can spread swiftly. For a company's public relations (PR) staff, this may be a nightmare. Despite the fact that social networking is free, creating and maintaining a corporate page takes many hours each week. The costs of those hours rapidly pile up. Before a social media marketing strategy generates a significant return on investment (ROI), businesses require a large number of followers. For example, sending a post to 15 followers has a different impact than sending it to 15,000 followers [22].

1.4   Microblogging sites

Microblogging is a type of short-form broadcasting that aids in keeping up with the act of blogging. Compared to normal blogging, each microblog helps to showcase smaller material. Microblogging sites abound on the internet, allowing users to share photographs, information, video links, and other media. Each microblogging website is significant and optimized for search engine optimization. These services encourage high-quality link development by allowing users to express their thoughts in a few words or a phrase that may be connected to a variety of other websites currently operating on the internet. Microblogs are short (under 300 words) blog postings that include photos, GIFs, links, infographics, videos, and audio snippets. Despite the fact that the word "microblogging" is new, the practice is not. Many of us are microblogging without even realizing it. Let us illustrate this with an example. You make an instructional video or publish a whitepaper based on research. You write a brief synopsis that covers the major points and include an embedded link to the resource while uploading it. That is a microblog, right there! It is like a hybrid of instant chatting and regular blogging. News updates, memes, quotations, event highlights, user-generated material, and infographics are the most prevalent kinds of content posted via microblogs. Most microblogs include photos or animated graphics, since 78% of marketers believe that visual content is effective in boosting interaction.

- **Benefits of microblogging**

  Microblogging has received increasing attention from the marketing community. The incentive is impossible to pass up: write and publish succinct content and get immediate results. But, before we get into the technical aspects of microblogging, let us take a look at why you need to microblog at scale in the first place.

- **Reduced effort**

  In the same amount of time it takes to write one long-form piece of content, you may write many microblog entries. Creating long-form blogs several times a day is neither creatively nor practically feasible. Microblog postings, on the other hand, just take a few moments to compose and publish. Microblogging provides a good ROI, which is a great motivator for small businesses and brands. They may save money on content generation while increasing their profits.

- **Always-on strategy**

  The secret to successful content marketing is consistency. Brands that publish regularly receive a higher level of engagement. Such companies are consumers' go-to resources for fast satisfaction. Microblogs allow firms to communicate with their customers 24 hours a day, seven days a week. A short tweet, for example, might disseminate information more effectively than a long blog post or press release.

- **Mobile friendliness**

  Consumers today are enamored with their mobile gadgets. They check their phones every 12 minutes, with 40% checking them within the first five minutes of waking up. Microblogging sites such as Pinterest and Twitter are gaining popularity because they are available as useful smartphone apps that current customers like using. Brands may reach a large audience and get awareness by microblogging on these platforms.

  A free microblogging sites list, which is designed to enhance referral as well as organic traffic for any site, has been given online as a joy to site owners who are operating a fresh and comparatively younger setup. It is considered a significant aspect of the search engine optimization (SEO) off-page method, along with off-page actions, that work towards boosting a certain site in the search engine result page. The top microblogging sites list for 2020 is available online to help users choose the finest places to submit their material and implement successful SEO tactics for site promotion.

  A range of microblogging sites provide site owners with a large list of benefits and are equipped with the most up-to-date SEO tools like as Alex Rank, Page Rank, and others. People all across the world are using these sites to upload the most recent information about their brands. Many bloggers and SEO service providers utilize Microblogging Sites 2020 to submit material and produce high PR backlinks that can be shared as URLs for blog posts and web pages. Thanks to these sites that rotate strong social sharing signals such as pins, tweets, shares, likes, and many more, many sites are doing a wonderful job on search engines and have gained a high rating.

1.4.1 The best microblogging site list includes the following names

- **Twitter** – This is the no. 1 microblogging website that fetches visits from a maximum number of users and gets countless page views.
- **Pinterest** – This portal allows users to post photos along with text to entertain the followers.
- **Tumblr.com** – This site gives site owners a platform to post their blog URLs to get instant traffic and improve site ranking in search engines.
- **Dipity** – This is another site for microblogging that fetches decent publicity and popularity.
- **Plurk** – This site also helps in generating high-quality traffic through microblogging and motivates bloggers to share new blog posts regularly. It also facilitates posting of photos and videos by the users.

- **Flattr** – This site has gained great scores for being a poplar SEO platform owing to its high PR and domain authority.
- **Yammer** – This is a site that offers a strong platform for private/social professionals.
- **Plerb** – Apart from the microblogging sites like Twitter, Plerb has carved a distinct place for itself by offering web pages with great page ranks and eight links.

This chapter aims to develop methodologies for addressing some practical challenges that are faced in effectively utilizing the information posted on microblogging sites for developing information systems. This section describes the challenges that are targeted in this chapter. The chapter focuses on following information mining for filtering and organizing online social microblog data to extract meaningful information effectively and efficiently.

1.5 Information of social microblogging sites

Microblogging systems allow bloggers to share any type of material or point of view on social media platforms such as Twitter. Microblogging is a means of exchanging information in order to promote your blog. Twitter is an excellent example of a best microblogging site that includes external links to a certain group. Microblogging also focuses on linking people in social media, allowing for the exchange of messages and postings as well as instant chat. We have compiled a list of the best free microblogging sites that can help you improve your search engine rankings.

- **Twitter:** The most popular microblogging site is Twitter, which is ranked first among all sites. Twitter is the most popular social media platform, with users ranging from ordinary people to celebrities and politicians.
- **Tumblr:** Tumblr is a great place to post photos, videos, links, and articles, among other things. It is one of the greatest free microblogging platforms available. This platform allows bloggers to immediately submit their URLs, which minimizes traffic and improves SEO through Google searches.
- **Scoop.it:** Scoop.it is a popular social bookmarking and microblogging service with a high user rating. Scoop.it is a software firm situated in San Francisco, California that specializes in content marketing. Scoop.it is a content curation service that the firm runs, and also sells content marketing tools to businesses.

- **Pinterest:** Bloggers are encouraged to publish photographs along with writing or information that reaches subscribers on this site. Pinterest is an online and mobile application startup that manages a software system for discovering content on the Internet, mostly through photographs, but also through GIFs and videos on a smaller scale.
- **Flattr:** This site is the most popular in terms of SEO and has the most domain ownership. Flattr is a microdonation subscription service headquartered in Sweden that allows users to pay a monthly fee to support their favorite websites and producers.
- **Reddit:** This site is capable of increasing the popularity and views of its postings, making it a rising microblogging site. Reddit is a social news aggregation, web content rating, and discussion website based in the United States. Registered members upload links, text entries, and photographs to the site, which are subsequently voted up or down by other users.
- **Yammer:** This site is a great place for social and private groups of professionals to promote their services and goods. Yammer is a freemium workplace social networking tool that allows employees to communicate privately.
- **Meetme:** Meetme's blog allows users to meet new people and also offers an online chat feature. Quepasa Corporation was a social media technology firm established in the United States that catered to Latino audiences all over the world.
- **VK:** VK is a Russian social networking and microblogging platform. It is available in a variety of languages, but Russian-speaking users find it particularly appealing.
- **Apsense:** Apsense is a prominent social networking service that allows individuals to interact with one another and exchange photographs, videos, and articles. Apsense aids in the branding and popularization of your company.

Recently, microblogging has become one of the most popular phenomena facilitated by disruptive platforms for communication i.e., online social media [23]. During important social events such as elections, cricket matches, the world cup, disasters (floods, earthquakes), etc., millions of users share their valuable opinions in microblogs. There are several popular microblogging sites such as Twitter, Weibo, Tumblr, etc., where colossal amounts of new information are created every day as a result of economic, political, academic, and social activities. Thus the microblog plays an important role in content and opinion mining, news propagation, recommendations, product marketing, surveys, notification, and political campaigns. Apart from useful information, spammers also target these platforms to spread malicious content such as shortened URLs, abusive words, etc., due to the popularity of microblogging sites. Researchers analyze these real-time data.

1.6 Challenges in using microblogging sites

As a source of information on current events such as sociopolitical events, sporting events, natural disasters, and a variety of topics of interest, the use of social microblogging services is increasing. As a result, techniques for assisting users in utilizing such information systems must be devised. This book focuses on two major issues that must be addressed in order to achieve this goal.

(1) **Filtering harmful information**: The quality of material shared on online social media varies greatly, ranging from critical real-time information on a number of issues provided by influential sources to various sorts of malevolent content such as spam, hate speech, and so on. Spam posts, in particular, are a serious issue on social media platforms like Twitter. As a result, one of the issues is identifying spam posts and persons responsible for this.

(2) **Organizing the information**: On social microblogging sites, a significant amount of information is shared on a regular basis. Twitter, for example, receives approximately 500 million tweets every day. Even from the perspective of a single user, a moderately engaged user of Twitter can effortlessly receive hundreds of tweets per day in his or her timeline. Information overload occurs as a result of the abundance of content, and no user can process it all. Addressing the issue of information overload is thus a new challenge. As a result, information organization strategies are needed.

In this book, we discuss methodologies to address the two problems stated above. Most of the experiments described in this book are performed on Twitter (https://twitter.com), the most popular microblogging service nowadays. Before describing the methodologies developed in this book, we would like to give a brief contextual description of the Twitter microblogging site. In this book, some methodologies are developed to address the two problems stated above. Most of the experiments in this book are performed on the Twitter microblogging site (https://twitter.com). Before describing the methodologies developed in this book, the background of the Twitter microblogging site is briefly described.

1.7 Background of the Twitter microblogging site

The microblogging service Twitter (https://twitter.com) is one of the most widely used platform for discovering real-time data on the Web. Since Twitter was launched in 2006, it has attracted a lot of attention from both the general public and research communities. Recent estimates suggest that Twitter has 314 million active users. Every day over 500 million tweets (short text-based posts of up to 140 characters called "tweets" are sent). This vast amount of user-generated content makes Twitter an important source for real-time news, especially during events such as political elections, sociopolitical revolutions, and natural disasters.

Every Twitter user has a user account with a profile page that contains basic information about them. Users can speak with one another in real-time by sending short messages, and they can establish a social network by following other users. If a user u discovers another thought-provoking user v, then u can subscribe to v (according to Twitter vocabulary, u can "follow" v), and all tweets written by v will be made accessible to u in real-time.

People employ acronyms, make spelling mistakes, and use emoticons and other characters that express particular meanings because of the nature of this microblogging service (rapid and short communications). Following someone on Twitter means being subscribed to another Twitter as a follower. Followers are people who receive others' tweets if someone follows him/her. Few terminologies regarding tweets are defined below:

Tweet: A tweet (also known as microblog) is a user-posted status update message. Tweets are limited to 140 characters and can include specific keywords (known as hashtags), URLs, and other information.

Hashtags: By utilizing a hashtag (#), certain words in a tweet can be emphasized. Hashtags are best utilized to identify topics that are trending at the moment. For example, during the 2018 FIFA World Cup, most frequently applied hashtags were #WorldCup, #Russia2018, and so on. A few samples of tweets with hashtags are depicted in Fig. 1.1.

Trending topics or "trends": If a term (hashtag) appears in a high number of tweets over time, it may appear in the list of Trending Subjects, which are the most prevalent topics on Twitter at a certain time. Twitter announces a collection of trending topics on a regular basis (e.g., every day),

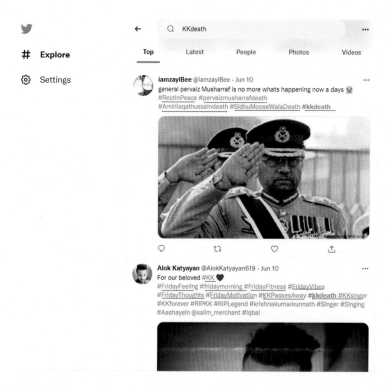

Figure 1.1 Sample tweets containing hashtags.

allowing users to easily follow tweets about these popular topics. Fig. 1.2 provides an example of a set of topics that are trending in Twitter at a certain point in time.

Hundreds of millions of people use Twitter these days, not only to chat with friends, but also to share content on a variety of themes. A huge amount of data – over 500 million tweets – is posted on Twitter every single day. This content is being used for many applications, ranging from search and recommendation to analyzing public opinion and gathering situational information during natural calamities. During the first hour after the Germanwings plane accident on March 24, 2015, 60 thousand messages with the hashtag #Germanwings were submitted on Twitter. During the 2012 hurricane Sandy in the United States, the official Twitter account reported that between October 27 and November 1, individuals sent almost 20 million tweets about the disaster using the phrases "hurricane" and "sandy," as well as the hashtags "#hurricane" and "#sandy" [24].

This enormous posting of data is the reason of information overload.

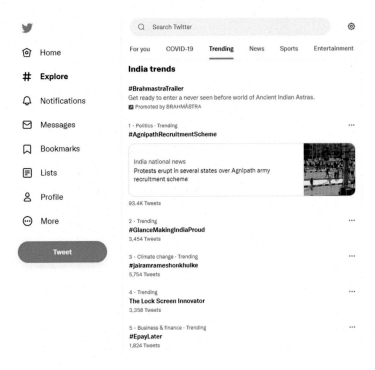

Figure 1.2 Twitter's trending topics at a given period in time.

Due to its growing popularity, Twitter has attracted the focus of not only legitimate users, but also spammers that make malicious use of social networks, popular keywords, and hashtags [25].

Compared to legitimate users, spammers post much less information about their locations and personal descriptions in their profiles.

The massive data publishing on Twitter provides microblog users with a popular platform for information transmission and collection. A substantial percentage of online social network (OSN) users make their content public (e.g., 90% on Twitter), allowing researchers and businesses to collect and analyze data on a wide scale. Twitter provides large data samples using the Twitter API (https://dev.twitter.com). Registered users can read and post tweets, but unregistered users can only read them. Due to this easy access to huge amounts of data, market analysis, identification of spammers, fraud detection, spam messages, extraction of vital news, customer retention, characterization or grouping of users based on their profession for scientific discoveries, and production control are just a few of the applications that Twitter is used for. The ease of accessing large amounts of data has also made the Twitter microblogging site popular among researchers studying social networks and information systems. There are several practical problems in social microblogging sites where data mining can be used, such as spam detection, sentiment analysis, summarization of document streams, predicting trending topics, feature or attribute reduction, and clustering of single and multiple documents.

1.8 Motivation of research

Twitter is a preeminent microblogging platform, where users can post facts, stories, or anything else. It is a website where users may find information about different events or news stories. For crisis scenarios such as the Iran protests or the Mumbai terror attacks, these microblogging services are a vital source of information and news updates. Every second, millions of tweets are published on Twitter. Twitter makes information retrieval easier by using hashtags, which are also labeled as non-trending or trending. Search results always show all pertinent tweets matched with the supplied term in backward chronological order. Tweets are typically shorter and written casually, for example, with abbreviations and colloquial vocabulary.

As stated in Section 1.6, the motivation of this book is to address the two practical problems of filtering out malicious information and organizing information. In this section the motivation is further described in more detail.

1.8.1 Information filtering

Microblogging systems allow bloggers to share any type of material or point of view on social media platforms such as Twitter. Microblogging is a means of exchanging information in order to promote your blog. Twitter is an excellent example of a best microblogging site that includes external links to a certain group. Microblogging also focuses on linking people through social media, allowing for the exchange of messages and postings as well as instant chat.

Twitter data is increasingly being utilized to create real-time search and recommendation systems, as well as services that mine and summarize reactions of the general populace to events. Such services are naturally targeted by spammers who post microblogs (tweets) containing malicious URLs. The spam problem in Twitter has been observed to be much more critical compared to spam on the general Web, primarily due to the real-time nature of information consumption on microblogging sites, where standard approaches like blacklists are too slow for real-time spam filtering [26]. As a result, it is critical to design mechanisms to filter out malicious tweets and malicious user accounts from the results returned by these services. While there has been lot of research towards countering spam on Twitter, most prior works have attempted to detect spammer accounts. In this book, we focus on the problem of spam classification based on individual tweets. The problem of filtering individual spam tweets is even more challenging than filtering spam accounts, because the minimal context information in an individual 140-character tweet makes it difficult to identify spam signals. Additionally, given the rapid rates at which tweets are posted (hundreds per second), spam filtering of tweets/user accounts needs to be performed in real-time. To this end, a rough set theory-based attribute selection algorithm is described for refining classification of spams – the motivation being that only a few well-selected attributes will enable the classification to be both fast and accurate.

1.8.2 Information organization

As previously said, a typical user receives hundreds of tweets every day from his/her followers, and the majority of users are unable to read them all. Furthermore, many of the tweets include extremely similar material as a result of retweeting and reposting. People may experience information overload as a result of this redundant information. Mechanisms for dealing with overabundance of data must be devised in this scenario:

(i)   similar tweets can be grouped together into relevant sub-groups, such that the user only sees a few tweets from each cluster, and

(ii)   the information can be summarized to generate a brief overview of the information.

The book's goal is to provide approaches for these activities, such as summarizing twitter streams so that a quick overview of a news article can be received by reading the summary. In this situation, clustering comparable tweets is an effective technique to reduce the user's information burden. So, clustering is considered here to organize information posted on social microblogging sites during an important event, for example a natural disaster, for effective utilization. Hence methodologies for organizing the information are required.

Summarizing tweets is another important task for reducing information overload and generating a quick summary of the topic. Summarization has been the most difficult tasks for researchers due to the irrelevant and brief character of tweets. One of the motivations for the clustering task is to summarize tweets, where comparable tweets are classified into single clusters and a summary is formed by picking significant tweets from each cluster.

Due to the huge popularity, Twitter is targeted by spammers who post microblogs (tweets) containing malicious URLs. Hence, it is necessary to develop mechanisms to filter out malicious tweets from the results returned by these services. In this book, we focus on real-time classification of spam tweets, which is a challenging problem due to the minimal amount of information in an individual tweet and the extremely high rates at which tweets are posted (several thousands per second). The objective of this study is to develop an attribute selection method for spam classification to distinguish spam and legitimate post in real-time.

Attribute selection

Attribute selection is a significant process in machine learning and data mining. The objective of this process is to identify a minimal subset of attributes to improve the performance of the subsequent mining process. In recent times, several research challenges have been tackled in different domains, such as data mining, machine learning, bioinformatics, pattern recognition, etc. Attribute selection removes the unrelated, redundant, and less important attributes from high-dimensional datasets and selects a significant optimal subset of most important attributes from the original set of attributes without sacrificing any valuable information. It improves the performance of the learning algorithms, reduces the computational cost, and provides better understanding of the datasets.

(A) Attribute selection algorithm

In attribute selection methods, a training dataset is required to analyze the significance of the attributes in order to make a decision about which attribute subset to select. A huge number of attribute selection algorithms have been proposed in the literature [27], which are broadly classified as filter methods and wrapper methods. Based on feature ranking, filter methods [28] identify optimal features, whereas wrapper methods use a learning algorithm to search feature subsets and test the performance of every subset of features. Therefore, the best performance is selected finally.

In attribute selection methods, a training dataset is required to analyze the significance of the attributes in order to make a decision about which attributes to select. A huge number of attribute selection algorithms have been proposed in the literature, which are broadly classified as filters method and wrapper methods. Based on feature ranking, filters method identify optimal features, whereas wrapper methods use a learning algorithm to search features and test the performance of every subset of features. Therefore, the best performance is selected finally.

(B) Attribute selection evaluation

To compare the performance of various attribute selection strategies, standard measures are considered such as precision (P), recall (R), accuracy (A), and the F-measure (F).

1.8.3 Clustering

Clustering is an unsupervised learning method which partitions the objects in such a way that objects in a group are similar and objects of two different groups are dissimilar to each other. For better clustering outcome, it is required to have high coupling within cluster objects and more dissimilarity between the clusters. In online social media, clustering has a great impact due to the huge volume of the datasets. An effective way to reduce the information load on the user is to cluster similar posts (messages), so that the user might see only few posts in each cluster. So, clustering is considered here to organize information, posted on social microblogging sites during an important event for effective utilization.

Clustering is a machine learning–based unsupervised learning strategy. The inferences are generated from datasets that do not have a labeled output variable in the unsupervised learning approach. It is a type of exploratory data analysis that lets us look at multivariate datasets. Clustering is the process of grouping datasets into a specified number of clusters with comparable features among the data points inside each cluster. Clusters are made up of data points that are grouped together in such a way that the space between them is kept to a minimum. To put it another way, clusters are areas with a high density of related data points. It is often used to analyze a data collection, locate interesting data among large datasets, and draw conclusions from it. The clusters are usually observed in a spherical shape. However, this is not required; the clusters can be any shape. In this chapter, you will learn about clustering and other data science principles. The way the clusters are produced is determined based on the sort of algorithm we choose. Because there is no criterion for good clustering, the conclusions that must be derived from the datasets are also dependent on the user.

(A) Clustering algorithms

Clustering may be divided into two categories: hard clustering and soft clustering. One data point can only belong to one cluster in hard clustering.

In soft clustering, however, the result is a probability likelihood of a data point belonging to each of the predefined groups.

Density-based clustering

Clusters are produced using this approach depending on the density of the data points represented in the data space. Clusters are locations that become dense as a result of the large amount of data points that reside there. The data points in the sparse area (the region with the fewest data points) are referred to as noise or outliers. These approaches allow for the creation of clusters of any form. Examples of density-based clustering methods include the following:

DBSCAN (Density-Based Spatial Clustering of Applications with Noise)

The distance metric and criterion for a minimum number of data points are used by DBSCAN to group data points together. It requires two inputs: the Eps value and minimum points. The Eps value shows how near data points should be in order to be deemed neighbors. To regard the region as dense, the condition for minimum points should be completed.

OPTICS (Ordering Points to Identify Clustering Structures)

It works in a similar way to DBSCAN, but it addresses one of the latter's flaws: the inability to generate clusters from data of variable density. It also takes into account two other parameters: core distance and reachability distance. By selecting a minimal value for core distance, it is possible to determine if a data point is core or not. The value of the distance metric used to calculate the distance between two data points is called reachability distance. One thing to keep in mind concerning the reachability distance is that if one of the data points is a core point, its value is undefined.

1.8.3.1 HDBSCAN (Hierarchical Density-Based Spatial Clustering of Applications with Noise)

HDBSCAN is a density-based clustering algorithm that converts the DB-SCAN approach to a hierarchical clustering algorithm.

Hierarchical clustering

Based on distance measurements, hierarchical clustering groups (the agglomerative approach, also known as bottom-up approach) or divides (the divisive approach, also known as top-down approach) the clusters. Each data point in agglomerative clustering functions as a cluster at first, and then the clusters are grouped one by one. The antithesis of agglomerative, divisive, starts with all of the points in one cluster and splits them to make other clusters. These algorithms generate a distance matrix for all existing clusters and connect them together based on the linkage criteria. A dendrogram is used to show the grouping of data points. There are several sorts of connections:

- Single linkage: The distance between two clusters is the smallest distance between points in those two clusters in single linkage.
- Complete linkage: The distance between two clusters is the largest distance between points in those two clusters in complete linkage.
- Average linkage: In average linkage, the distance between two clusters is equal to the average distance between every point in one cluster and every point in the other.

Fuzzy clustering
The assignment of data points to any of the clusters is not crucial in fuzzy clustering. A single data point can be assigned to many clusters. It gives the likelihood of a data point belonging to each of the clusters as the result. Fuzzy c-means clustering is one of the techniques used in fuzzy clustering. This algorithm is similar to K-means clustering in terms of procedure, but it differs in terms of the parameters used in the calculation, such as the fuzzifier and membership values.

Partitioning clustering
This is one of the most popular methods for creating clusters among analysts. Clusters are partitioned depending on the properties of the data points in partitioning clustering. For this clustering procedure, we must provide the number of clusters to be produced. These clustering algorithms use an iterative procedure to allocate data points between groups depending on their distance from one another. The following algorithms fit within this category:

K-means clustering
One of the most extensively used methods is K-means clustering. Based on the distance metric used for clustering, it divides the data points into K clusters. The user is responsible for determining the value of K. The distance between the data points and the cluster centroids is determined. The cluster is awarded to the data point that is closest to the cluster's centroid. It computes the centroids of those clusters again after each iteration, and the procedure is repeated until a predetermined number of iterations have been finished or the centroids of the clusters have not changed after

each iteration. It is a time-consuming approach since it calculates the distance between each data point and the centroids of all the clusters at each iteration. This makes implementing the same for large datasets harder.

PAM (partitioning around medoids)

The K-medoid algorithm is another name for this approach. It works in a similar way to the K-means clustering method, with the exception of how the cluster's center is assigned. The cluster's medoid must be an input data point in PAM; however, this is not true in K-means clustering since the average of all data points in a cluster may not be an input data point.

CLARA (Clustering Large Applications)

CLARA is a modification of the PAM method that reduces computing time to improve performance for huge datasets. To do so, it chooses a random chunk of data from the entire dataset to serve as a representation of the real data. It uses the PAM algorithm to analyze several samples of data and selects the best clusters after several rounds.

Grid-based clustering

In grid-based clustering, the dataset is represented as a grid structure which is comprised of grids (also called cells). The overall approach in the algorithms of this method differs from the rest of the algorithms. They are more concerned with the value space surrounding the data points rather than the data points themselves. One of the greatest advantages of these algorithms is its reduction in computational complexity. This makes it appropriate for dealing with humongous datasets. After partitioning the datasets into cells, it computes the density of the cells which helps in identifying the clusters. A few algorithms based on grid-based clustering are as follows:

- STING (Statistical Information Grid Approach): The dataset is partitioned recursively and hierarchically in STING. Each cell is subdivided further into a distinct number of cells. It records the statistical measurements of the cells, making it easier to respond to requests in a short amount of time.
- WaveCluster: Wavelets are used to represent the data space in this approach. The data space generates an n-dimensional signal that aids in cluster identification. Lower-frequency and high-amplitude components of the signal suggest that the data points are concentrated. The algorithm recognizes these locations as clusters. The cluster boundaries are represented by the regions of the signal where the frequency is high.
- CLIQUE (Clustering in Quest): CLIQUE is a clustering technique that combines density-based and grid-based clustering. Using the Apri-

ori principle, it separates the data space and identifies the sub-spaces. It determines the clusters by calculating the cell densities.

In data mining, cluster analysis is a statistical tool to gain insight into the distribution of data to observe characteristics of each cluster. The clustering approach, which is used popularly, can be categorized into three basic types: the partitioning method [29], the hierarchical method [30], and the density-based method [31]. Apart from these, several graph-based methods are also available such as community detection algorithms. In the partitioning method [32], the entire dataset is grouped into K clusters, where each object must belong to exactly one group. In the hierarchical clustering method, the dataset is hierarchically decomposed into clusters based on bottom-up (agglomerative) and top-down (divisive) approaches. The bottom-up approach starts with all data objects in individual clusters. Then nearest or similar clusters are merged until single clusters are formed that combine all the data objects. The top-down approach starts with all data objects assigned into a single cluster and repetitively performs splits until each data object forms a single cluster. Both methods may be terminated earlier based on some desirable termination criteria depending on the application. On the other hand, to figure out non-linear structures, density-based clustering [31] is widely used, which partitions the objects based on density of the neighborhood region of the objects. The method is also very important for outlier detection.

(B) Cluster evaluation

Detection of outliers in datasets is an advantage of clustering techniques which has drawn the attention of researchers to categorize experimental data into several groups based on different levels of similarities. Different clustering algorithms provide different set of clusters and none is the best for all types of datasets. So cluster validation is very important before applying the algorithm for a given dataset. For cluster validation, various cluster evaluation algorithms are popularly used [33], such as the DB index, the DUNN index (D), Calinski–Harabasz index (CH), the I-index (I), and the Silhouette index (S). These validity indices evaluate the goodness of the clusters by quantifying association distributions, entropies of the partition, compactness of clusters, and so on.

Summarization is a mining process to identify import information from a large dataset which can sum up all the content of the dataset. The incremental and huge nature of online social media datasets motivates researchers to focus on the microblog summarization method. This process can generate two different types of summary – abstractive and extractive. Abstractive summary represents the precise review of the dataset, which does not directly include the dataset content exactly, whereas extractive summary [34] yields a subset of the original dataset, which represents the most important information. On such sites, microblogs are usually posted so rapidly and in such large volumes that it is not feasible for human users to go through all the posts. In such scenario, summarization of microblogs is an important task.

Anyone may be a publisher on the internet. Restaurant/movie/book reviews, blogs, status updates, and other forms of information are being published on a regular basis. Traditional print media (newspapers, periodicals, technical journals, and white papers) can also be found online. Even if restricted to one domain, keeping track of current papers is hard. Here is where text summary comes in handy. The most significant information is usually contained in a summary, which is generated automatically by algorithms. The reader and the communication goals should both be considered while writing the summary. It may also assist the reader in determining whether the original content is worth reading in its entirety. The summary can also aid information retrieval by improving document indexing. When compared to a human-written summary, an automated summary is frequently less prejudiced.

News headlines, student outlines, movie trailers, meeting minutes, biographies for resumes or obituaries, abridged versions of books, newsletter production, financial research, patent research, legal contract analysis, tweeting about new content, chatbots that answer questions, and email summaries are all examples of text summarization. Some entries in Google Search's search results are accompanied with auto-generated summaries. This might be accomplished through the use of a knowledge graph by Google. The majority of Google's summarizing methods are entity-centric. Timelines and events regarding entities are included in the summarization process. Long medical notes covering dietary recommendations for pregnant women are written by doctors. Pregnant women found it much simpler to grasp when these were condensed to brief, clear summaries.

Extractive summarizing involves extracting phrases from the source text and reproducing them verbatim in the summary. The program reads the text and provides a summary, sometimes employing new words and sentences, using abstractive summarization. Extractive summarization is more data-driven and less time-consuming, and it frequently produces superior results. Humans use abstractive summarization to summarize text, but it is difficult for algorithms since it requires semantic representation, inference, and natural language production. Text extracts are frequently used in abstractive summarization. Sentences are rated and the ones with the highest scores are chosen for extraction. Word frequencies, placement heuristics, sentence similarity, rhetorical connections, and semantic roles are all possible scoring factors.

To pick relevant summary material, an intermediate representation is usually employed. The goal of topic representation is to identify the text's important points. Summarization has used topic words, word frequencies (including TF-IDF), clustering, LSA, and LDA. A feature set is used to rank and choose sentences using indicator representation. Graph-based approaches and machine learning are examples of this approach.

1.9 Challenges and requirements of multi-document summarization

Content selection, information ordering, and sentence realization are the same essential processes in the multi-document summarizing (MDS) pipeline as they are in the single-document summarization (SDS) pipeline. MDS, on the other hand, has certain distinct challenges:

- **Redundancy:** A single document has significantly less redundancy than a set of texts that are topically related. Similar sentences should not be repeated in the summary. Maximum marginal relevance (MMR) is a grading method that penalizes phrases that are too similar.
- **Temporal ordering:** A series of news stories may be reporting on the progress of a situation. They should be ordered appropriately in the summary, with subsequent developments taking precedence over previous ones.
- **Cohesion and coreference:** Both are critical for information organization. When cohesiveness requires a certain ordering, it might lead to coreference issues, such as when a person's truncated name appears before their full name.
- **Compression ratio:** When more compression is required, summarization becomes more challenging.

Similar papers and passages may be grouped together in MDS. The summary should offer enough context and the appropriate degree of depth. It is possible to report factual discrepancies between papers. Finally, users should be able to filter out extraneous content, explore deeper into sources through attribution, and compare related portions across texts.

(A) Summarization algorithm

Automatic text summarization is a technique to generate relevant information from a huge data source. Recently several groups have focused on this area. Different types of summarization algorithms have been proposed by researchers, including:

(1) Clusterrank [35] (CR),
(2) COWTS [36] (CW),
(3) Frequency Summarizer [37] (FS),
(4) LexRank [38] (LR),
(5) LSA [39] (LS),
(6) LUHN [40] (LH),
(7) Mead [41] (MD),
(8) SumBasic [42] (SB),
(9) SumDSDR [43] (SM).

These algorithms generally estimate an importance score for each textual unit in the input (e.g., sentence in a document or a tweet in a set of tweets) and include the textual units in the summary in decreasing the order of this score, until a predefined length of the summary is reached.

(B) Summarization evaluation

Using standard statistical results such as precision (P), recall (R), accuracy (A), and the F-measure (F), performance of the summarization methodology can be evaluated. Apart from this, the performance of the different algorithms can be evaluated using the standard Recall-Oriented Understudy for Gisting Evaluation (ROUGE) measure. It is effectively a set of metrics to calculate automatic summarization of texts as well as reference summaries (baseline-generated or human-produced). It works by comparing an automatically produced summary or baseline reference summaries. Due to the informal nature of microblog datasets, the recall and F-measure of the ROUGE-2 and ROUGE-L variants are considered.

1.10 Contributions of this research

Nowadays, online social networking sites such as Twitter and Facebook have become the most popular communication tool for rapid information exchange. Vast amounts of new information and data are generated everyday through economic, academic, political, and social activities. The information and knowledge gained through social activities can be used to meet different research challenges/problems which need to be solved in order to cater to the applications. Researchers focus on different data analysis tasks on microblog datasets, such as fraud detection, i.e., detection of spammers and spam posts, extraction of important news, market analysis, customer retention, opinion mining, summarization of document streams, predicting trend analysis, and clustering.

This book focuses primarily on the following two problems:

1) **Information filtering:** Attribute selection to improve spam classification of microblogs and user-accounts on social networking sites.

2) **Information organization:** Clustering of microblogs and summarization of microblogs.

The contributions made in the book on the above-mentioned problems are summarized in the rest of this section.

1.10.1 Attribute selection for spam classification

Spammers get access to online social microblogging sites as they become more popular, and they publish destructive stuff on the platforms. As a result, spam accounts and spam messages from OSNs must be filtered out. The goal of this research is to increase spam categorization by creating an attribute selection method that allows for the identification of a smaller collection of attributes, resulting in improved classification.

For attribute selection, a graph-based technique built on rough set theory principles is proposed as follows:

(i) Rough set theory is well known for its benefits in attribute selection – it can only work with the original data and there is no need for external information or training, and no assumptions about the data are required; furthermore, rough set theory is appropriate for analyzing both quantitative and qualitative attributes [44,45].

(ii) To depict attribute correlations or dependencies, a graph-based paradigm is used. Most past attempts at attribute selection for spam detection have ignored attribute mutual dependencies, potentially resulting in highly connected attributes being included in the reduced set. The graph-based technique is offered to address this flaw: when an attribute is included in the reduced attribute set, connected attributes can be simply deleted from the graph, resulting in further attribute set reduction.

For attribute/feature selection, we suggested a graph-based mechanism based on rough set theory. The following are the reasons for our approach. Rough set theory is well known for its various advantages for feature selection, including the ability to operate simply with the original data and the lack of reliance on external information or training. There is no need to make any assumptions about the data. Furthermore, rough set theory is appropriate for analyzing quantitative as well as qualitative characteristics [44,45]. Second, feature correlations or dependencies are represented using a graph-based approach. Most previous attempts at attribute selection for spam detection have ignored mutual dependencies between attributes, which may result in highly correlated features being included in the reduced set. This limitation is intended to be overcome by the graph-based methodology: by including a feature in the reduced feature set, correlated features can be easily removed from the graph, resulting in further feature set reduction.

To demonstrate the efficacy and efficiency of the proposed algorithm of attribute selection, the method is applied over five datasets, four of which are collected from previous works on spam classification on online social microblogging sites, and the other one is collected from the microblog site.

Dataset 1 – Benevenuto et al. [46] created a dataset of 1065 Twitter user profiles with 62 attributes that they divided into two categories: non-spammers and spammers. The classification is dependent on 62 criteria that capture a variety of user account features.

Dataset 2 – Benevenuto et al. also prepared this dataset [47] and they created a 60-attribute dataset to categorize three sorts of online video network users: spammers, users who are legitimate, and content promoters. The dataset consists of 60 features, including video attributes (that capture unique properties of the films posted by each user), social connection features (derived from video response interactions), and individual user behavior attributes.

Dataset 3 – The focus of this dataset, collected by Costa et al. [48], is on "tip spam" in location-based social networks. There are 2762 instances in the dataset, two classes (non-spam and spam), and 41 attributes.

Dataset 4 – Costa et al. [49] created this dataset, which is comparable to the one above for spam (in location-based social networks). This dataset, however, is larger, with 7076 instances and 60 attributes.

Dataset 5 – This dataset has been prepared for the experiment to tell the difference between spam and authentic tweets in microblogs.

The proposed algorithm's performance is compared with that of various baseline attribute selection methodologies, such as correlation-based feature selection (CFS), consistency subset evaluation (CON), Information Gain (InfoGain), chi squared, and community detection. The experiment is performed with several classifiers – a radial basis function (RBF) network, naive Bayes, LWL, logistic regression, decision table, Logit Boost, random tree, and OneR. The performance of the spam classification based on selected attributes is illustrated using standard evaluation criteria such as recall, precision, the F-measure, and accuracy. For the majority of datasets, the proposed algorithm identifies a narrower subset of attributes than that identified by baseline approaches but still provides better classification performance than that obtained by considering all features and feature subsets chosen by baseline approaches. The suggested technique could be particularly beneficial in circumstances where very quick yet accurate classification is required, such as spam filtering in real-time of twitter streams. Twitter now receives over 500 million tweets every day,[1] implying that millions of messages must be categorized per second. The proposed algorithm for selection of attributes can be used in this case to ensure quick classification.

Because CFS is the most direct rival to the suggested approach, the statistical significance of variations in performance between the two methods is determined using the T-test (parameterized) and the Wilcoxon rank sum test (Non-parameterized). It can be determined that the projected approach chooses a subset of features where the number of attributes is smaller than that for other attribute selection approaches, which results in greater classification performance too.

1.10.2 Microblog clustering

As previously noted, the massive amount of repetitive data uploaded on social microblogging sites causes users to experience information overload. One of the most successful ways to manage information overload is to cluster semantically comparable tweets into groups where each group contains only a few tweets. In this book, a number of clustering algorithms is proposed in a potential way of organizing large sets of microblogs.

In this book, we propose a number of clustering algorithms as a potential way of organizing large sets of microblogs.

Tweets are clustered using different types of clustering methods, and their performances are compared to determine the optimal set of clusters. A novel clustering approach presented in this book combines two different

[1] http://www.internetlivestats.com/twitter-statistics/.

clustering algorithms – a traditional K-means approach and an evolutionary approach, i.e., a genetic algorithm (GA)-based clustering approach. A graph-based clustering algorithm, namely the Infomap [50] community detection algorithm, has also been used for cluster analysis [51]. A clustering algorithm based on latent Dirichlet allocation (LDA) [52] is another significant approach proposed in the book to increase the clustering proficiency due to the presence of the attribute selection mechanism. Also, a novel algorithm is proposed for clustering microblogs using several graph clustering methods based on dimensionality reduction.

One situation where organization of microblogs is especially useful is during an emergency/disaster event. At such times, large numbers of microblogs are posted at rapid rates, and because timing is crucial in such situations, it is very important to group similar microblogs into news stories so that the relief workers can quickly get an overview of the situation. With this motivation, we perform our experiments on tweets posted during some such disaster events, such as bomb explosions. With this motivation, the experiments are performed on tweets posted during some of the disaster events, such as when Hyderabad was hit by a series of bomb explosions [53] and the shooting incident at Sandy Hook Elementary School in the USA [54]. During the following emergency situations, tweets are considered:

1. **HDBlast** – Hyderabad, India, was hit by two bomb explosions [53].
2. **SHShoot** – An assailant killed 20 children and 6 adults at Sandy Hook Elementary School in Connecticut, USA [54].
3. **UFlood** – India's Uttaranchal state was devastated by devastating floods and landslides [55].
4. **THagupit** – Typhoon Hagupit, a powerful typhoon, hit the Philippines [56].

The tweets are gathered using the Twitter API's [57] keyword-based matching feature. The terms "Hyderabad," "blast," and "bomb," for example, were used to find tweets concerning the Hyderabad bombings, while the phrases "Sandyhook" and "shooting" were used to find tweets about the Sandy Hook Elementary School massacre. We examine the first 5000 tweets in chronological order for each occurrence. We now briefly discuss the three clustering algorithms developed in this book.

1.10.2.1 Graph-based clustering algorithm

This technique (proposed in [51]) uses the graph clustering algorithm Infomap [50] to identify clusters from microblogging data. In this method, a *weighted similarity graph* is first constructed, where the weight of an edge between two nodes reflects the similarity between the matching pair of tweets, and each different tweet is regarded a node/vertex of the graph. Semantic similarity and term-level similarity are used to assess the similarity of tweets. Cosine similarity, Levenshtein distance, frequency of common hashtags, user names, and URLs are examples of term-level similarity, whereas semantic similarity denotes WordNet Synset Similarity [58]. The community detection algorithm Infomap is then used to cluster similar tweets using the tweet similarity network. Hidden patterns and related groups of information in tweets are detected using unsupervised learning models in this suggested approach.

1.10.2.2 *Genetic algorithm-based tweet clustering*

For microblogs, a unique clustering approach that combines GA with a classical clustering algorithm (K-means) has been proposed [59]. After preprocessing the data, a collection of unique terms is determined, and a document-term matrix is created, with the rows representing individual tweets and the columns representing distinct terms. The elements in the matrix are either 1 or 0, with 1 indicating the presence of a term in a tweet and 0 indicating its absence. To use GA, a population of 100 chromosomes with binary strings chosen at random is first created. An individual projection matrix is obtained as a projection from the document-term matrix to estimate the fitness value of each chromosome in the population. Then, using the fitness value determined for each chromosome, the projected data has been clustered using K-means. The typical steps of GA – selection, crossover, and mutation – are then performed. The GA is iterated until it converges, and the best-fit solutions are merged to determine which chromosomes should be included in the final population. Final clustering of the tweets is picked as the clustering that corresponds to the fittest chromosome in the final population. There are two parameters of the proposed algorithm – (i) the number of clusters and (ii) the weight factor w that determines the relative significance between the goodness of a chromosome and the length of the chromosome. It shows the performance of clustering of the proposed methodology for different choices of the two parameters, for one of the datasets (UFlood). The best performance is displayed in boldface for each metric. When the procedure is run until the GA has completed 100 iterations, the optimal clustering is obtained using five or six clusters and a weight factor of $w = 0.1$. As a result, when comparing the proposed methodology to other approaches, the appropriate options (which produce the greatest performance of the proposed methodology) are employed.

1.10.2.3 Clustering based on feature selection

The inclusion of a feature selection process in this technique seeks to maximize clustering efficiency (proposed in [60]). The dataset is used to discover intra-document topics using LDA, a topic modeler. After the dataset is preprocessed, to identify distinct terms or words, tweets are tokenized. Finally, a document-term matrix is created from the preprocessed dataset, with the rows representing individual tweets and the columns representing distinct terms. A document-term matrix is created from the preprocessed dataset, with the rows representing tweets and the columns denoting distinct terms. The p-values for each individual phrase are then calculated using Bayes' theorem. The document-term matrix is then reformed based on the new reduced corpus, using Shannon's theorem to eliminate terms that offer less information than the average. The LDA method is then used to identify a set of key features or phrases. The average Hamming distance for each subject is then calculated using the average distance between all tweet vectors in the document-feature matrix, resulting in a topic-feature matrix. Every tweet is assigned to a certain topic or category using a greedy technique. Individual tweets are tagged to the topic (cluster) with the Hamming distance between the tweet and the topic being less than or equal to the average distance.

1.10.2.4 Clustering using dimensionality reduction techniques

In this study, multiple graph clustering techniques formed on dimensionality reduction are projected for clustering microblogs. The first step is to preprocess the data, including (i) removing numerals, URLs, emails, special characters, and user mentions and (ii) stemming. Then, dimensionality reduction is carried out using LDA and thresholding with average TF-IDF scores of distinct terms. Then a tweet similarity graph is generated where each tweet is represented as a node or a point and the weight of the edge between every pair of tweets represents the similarity score between the tweets. Diverse types of measures are used to compute the similarity between tweets (for constructing the tweet similarity graph), such as text similarity, Word2Vec Vector similarity, Doc2Vec Vector similarity, and so on. Then, groups of similar nodes (tweets) are identified using several graph clustering approaches such as detecting connected components, community detection, etc.

1.10.2.5 Comparative analysis

The results of the various clustering techniques proposed in this book were compared. The performances of the various clustering algorithms developed in this book are compared to demonstrate their effectiveness. To this aim, the Davies–Bouldin index (DB), the Calinski–Harabasz index (CH), the Dunn index (D), the Silhouette index (S), the Xie–Beni index (XB), and the I-index (I) are used to assess the quality of clustering. For the Calinski–Harabasz index (CH), the Silhouette index (S), the I-index (I), and the Dunn index (D), higher values suggest better clustering performance, while for the Davies–Bouldin index (DB) and the Xie–Beni index (XB), lower values indicate better clustering performance [33].

To determine the best clustering algorithm for tweet clustering, the proposed approaches are compared to classical methods of clustering such as density-based clustering, hierarchical clustering, and K-means, as well as among themselves. It is discovered that the clustering method that is dimensionality reduction-based outperforms the feature selection-based clustering algorithm for the majority of the measures, while the dimensionality reduction-based clustering method outperforms the feature selection-based clustering method for some of the measures.

As unsupervised clustering is problematic, graph-based clustering is suitable for categorization of data where no prior information is available about the number of clusters. We find that the dimensionality reduction-based clustering method outperforms the others on the majority of the measures. In this approach, apart from dimensionality reduction, graph-based clustering approaches are also followed, whereas the attribute selection-based clustering algorithm performs better for some of the measures. The GA-based clustering technique also performs reasonably well; however, this approach is not suitable for large datasets because of the large processing time.

1.10.3 Summarization of OSN data (Twitter data)

Along with clustering, summarization is an effective method for organizing information. The topic of automatic summarization of documents is well known in the field of information retrieval, and several strategies have been developed to solve it [61]. Many of these algorithms have also been used for microblog summarization [62]. Instead of attempting to develop a new summarization algorithm, in this book we investigate whether existing summarization algorithms can be combined to produce higher-quality summaries.

1.10.3.1 Motivation of ensemble summarization

Nine extractive summarization techniques are chosen in this section – ClusterRank [35], COWTS [36], Frequency Summarizer, LexRank [38], LSA [39], Luhn [40], Mead [41,63], SumBasic [42], and DSDR [43] – and all of them have been executed on the same set of microblogs. The summaries created by different algorithms from the same set of tweets have relatively little overlap. Similar patterns can be seen across all of our datasets. Based on various parameters, different summarization algorithms are likely to determine the relative relevance of tweets, resulting in different summaries that highlight different aspects of the input dataset. Because of the wide variation in the set of tweets chosen by different summarization algorithms, we developed ensemble techniques that aggregate the perspectives of numerous base algorithms to provide summaries that outperform the summaries produced by any of the base algorithms.

1.10.3.2 Proposed ensemble summarization algorithms

This book proposes two ensemble schemes: an unsupervised scheme and a supervised scheme, which combine the predictions of several extractive summarization algorithms to generate summaries that outperform any of the base algorithms. A number of libraries and methods are used to solve NLP-related problems. A regular expression (re) is the most commonly used library for text cleaning. Natural language activities such as stopword removal, named entity recognition, part of speech tagging, and phrase matching are performed using the next-level libraries NLTK and spacy. NLTK is an out-of-date library that beginners can use to practice NLP techniques. Spacy is the most recently published library with the most complex approaches, and it is typically used in the production environment. Therefore, we advise the reader to study both libraries and get to know their strengths.

(1) An ensemble graph-based *unsupervised* summarization algorithm, En-GraphSumm, groups the tweets chosen by the base algorithms into groups based on some measure of tweet similarity and then chooses one tweet from every group. The approach tries to pick key tweets while eliminating redundancy in the final summary in this way.

(2) An *supervised* ensemble summarization algorithm attempts to learn a tweet rating based on the rankings computed by various base algorithms and the performance of the base algorithms across a training set of tweets. The goal is to incorporate several tweet rankings and learn how to better rank tweets (for inclusion in the final summary).

The performances of these two proposed ensemble summarization techniques are compared with several existing methods using two standards ROUGE Recall scores, namely ROUGE-L and ROUGE-2. It is observed that the proposed unsupervised ensemble algorithm, EnGraph-Summ scheme, performs better than all those base algorithms as shown in Chapter 5. In Chapter 6 the Rouge scores are demonstrated for the summaries produced by multiple supervised ensemble algorithms. Some of the supervised ensemble algorithms also perform better than all the base summarization algorithms.

It makes sense, because for various NLP tasks, certain words that are highly distinctive in nature, such as names, brands, and product names, as well as some noise characters, such as html leftouts, must be eliminated. We also use word length as a criterion for eliminating terms that are either too short or too long.

When the base algorithms are used as features, the RankBoost L2R algorithm works somewhat better, whereas the RandomForest L2R algorithm performs better when text-based features are utilized. Note that this is one of the first studies on ensemble summarizing that we are aware of, and we expect that it will pave the way for a number of subsequent studies, similar to the successful use of ensemble approaches for clustering and classification.

1.11 Conclusion

Microblog data is rapidly being used to create recommender systems and real-time search, as well as services that mine and summarize reactions of the general populace to events. As a result of commercial, intellectual, and social activities, massive amounts of data are generated on these sites every day. This crowdsourced data can be used for fraud detection, market analysis, spam posts, spam detection, categorization or grouping of users based on their behavior, customer retention, and extraction of important news, as well as production control and scientific discovery. Microblog data is increasingly being used to build real-time search engines and recommendation systems, as well as services that mine and summarize public reactions to events. In addition to a wide range of applications, microblogging sites offer a number of challenges to exploit crowdsourced data, such as the need to filter out potentially harmful content submitted by spammers and the need to organize the voluminous data. The purpose of this book is to provide ways for dealing with these two challenges, as stated in the next section.

This encourages researchers to use filtering and organization to effectively mine data. The phrase "information mining" refers to the computer process of detecting patterns in large datasets in order to get knowledge using difficult approaches such as data analysis.

References

[1] M. Kirlidog, C. Asuk, A fraud detection approach with data mining in health insurance, in: World Conference on Business, Economics and Management (BEM-2012), Antalya, Turkey, May 4–6 2012, Procedia – Social and Behavioral Sciences 62 (2012) 989–994, https://doi.org/10.1016/j.sbspro.2012.09.168, http://www.sciencedirect.com/science/article/pii/S1877042812036099.

[2] F.-R. Gabriel, M.-J. Margaret, I.-D.A. Pere, Applying data mining techniques to stock market analysis, in: D. Yves, D. Frank, C.J. M, B. Javier, C. Rafael, C. Emilio, F.-R. Florentino, J.V. J, P. Pawel, C. Andrew (Eds.), Trends in Practical Applications of Agents and Multiagent Systems, Springer Berlin Heidelberg, Berlin, Heidelberg, 2010, pp. 519–527.

[3] D. Soumi, G. Sujata, D. Ratnadeep, D.A. Kumar, G. Saptarshi, Attribute selection for improving spam classification in online social networks: a rough set theory-based approach, Social Network Analysis and Mining 8 (1) (2018) 7, https://doi.org/10.1007/s13278-017-0484-8.

[4] P. Mayank, R. Vadlamani, Text and data mining to detect phishing websites and spam emails, in: B.K. Panigrahi, P.N. Suganthan, S. Das, S.S. Dash (Eds.), Swarm, Evolutionary, and Memetic Computing, Springer International Publishing, Cham, 2013, pp. 559–573.

[5] N. Azam, Jahiruddin, M. Abulaish, N.A.H. Haldar, Twitter data mining for events classification and analysis, in: 2015 Second International Conference on Soft Computing and Machine Intelligence (ISCMI), 2015, pp. 79–83.

[6] S. Dutta, V. Chandra, K. Mehra, A.K. Das, T. Chakraborty, S. Ghosh, Ensemble algorithms for microblog summarization, IEEE Intelligent Systems 33 (3) (2018) 4–14, https://doi.org/10.1109/MIS.2018.033001411.

[7] Y. Peilin, F. Hui, L. Jimmy, Anserini: enabling the use of lucene for information retrieval research, in: Proceedings of the 40th International ACM SIGIR Conference on Research and Development in Information Retrieval, SIGIR '17, ACM, New York, NY, USA, 2017, pp. 1253–1256, http://doi.acm.org/10.1145/3077136.3080721.

[8] M. Chidozie, B. David, S. Nurul, A data-driven methodology for agent based exploration of customer retention, in: Proceedings of the 20th International Symposium on Distributed Simulation and Real-Time Applications, DS-RT '16, IEEE Press, Piscataway, NJ, USA, 2016, pp. 108–111.

[9] I. Mohammadnoor, S. Fadi, N. Ali, Data mining techniques in social media: a survey, Neurocomputing 214 (2016) 654–670.

[10] S. Goswami, A.K. Das, Determining maximum cliques for community detection in weighted sparse networks, Knowledge and Information Systems 64 (2) (2022) 289–324, https://doi.org/10.1007/s10115-021-01631-y.

[11] A. Mukherjee, S. Bhattacharyya, K. Ray, B. Gupta, A.K. Das, A study of public sentiment and influence of politics in COVID-19 related tweets, in: A.K. Das, J. Nayak, B. Naik, S. Dutta, D. Pelusi (Eds.), Computational Intelligence in Pattern Recognition, Springer, Singapore, 2022, pp. 655–665.

[12] P. Das, A.K. Das, Convolutional neural networks-based sentence level classification of crime documents, in: A.K. Das, J. Nayak, B. Naik, S. Dutta, D. Pelusi (Eds.), Computational Intelligence in Pattern Recognition, Springer, Singapore, 2022, pp. 65–73.

[13] A. Das, D. Pal, C. Mallick, A.K. Das, An unsupervised COVID-19 report summarizer for developing smart healthcare system, in: A.K. Das, J. Nayak, B. Naik, S. Dutta, D. Pelusi (Eds.), Computational Intelligence in Pattern Recognition, Springer, Singapore, 2022, pp. 157–168.

[14] C. Mallick, S. Das, A.K. Das, Evolutionary algorithm based summarization for analyzing COVID-19 medical reports, in: J. Nayak, B. Naik, A. Abraham (Eds.), Understanding COVID-19: The Role of Computational Intelligence, in: Studies in Computational Intelligence, Springer International Publishing, Cham, 2022, pp. 31–58.

[15] S. Chattopadhyay, T. Basu, A.K. Das, K. Ghosh, L.C.A. Murthy, Towards effective discovery of natural communities in complex networks and implications in e-commerce, Electronic Commerce Research 21 (4) (2021) 917–954, https://doi.org/10.1007/s10660-019-09395-y.

[16] M. Basu, S.D. Bit, S. Ghosh, Utilizing microblogs for optimized real-time resource allocation in post-disaster scenarios, Social Network Analysis and Mining 12 (1) (2021) 15, https://doi.org/10.1007/s13278-021-00841-0.

[17] P. Bhattacharya, S. Paul, K. Ghosh, S. Ghosh, A. Wyner, DeepRhole: deep learning for rhetorical role labeling of sentences in legal case documents, Artificial Intelligence and Law (Nov. 2021), https://doi.org/10.1007/s10506-021-09304-5.

[18] K. Hazra, T. Ghosh, A. Mukherjee, S. Saha, S. Nandi, S. Ghosh, S. Chakraborty, Sustainable text summarization over mobile devices: an energy-aware approach, Sustainable Computing: Informatics and Systems 32 (2021) 100607, https://doi.org/10.1016/j.suscom.2021.100607, https://www.sciencedirect.com/science/article/pii/S2210537921000950.

[19] A. Mandal, K. Ghosh, S. Ghosh, S. Mandal, A sequence labeling model for catchphrase identification from legal case documents, Artificial Intelligence and Law (Jul. 2021), https://doi.org/10.1007/s10506-021-09296-2.

[20] M. Basu, K. Ghosh, S. Ghosh, Information retrieval from microblogs during disasters: in the light of IRMiDis task, SN Computer Science 1 (1) (2020) 61, https://doi.org/10.1007/s42979-020-0065-1.

[21] R. Mandal, S. Dutta, R. Banerjee, S. Bhattacharya, R. Ghosh, S. Samanta, T. Saha, City traffic speed characterization based on city road surface quality, in: J.M.R.S. Tavares, P. Dutta, S. Dutta, D. Samanta (Eds.), Cyber Intelligence and Information Retrieval, Springer, Singapore, 2022, pp. 515–524.

[22] D. Samanta, S. Dutta, M.G. Galety, S. Pramanik, A novel approach for web mining taxonomy for high-performance computing, in: J.M.R.S. Tavares, P. Dutta, S. Dutta, D. Samanta (Eds.), Cyber Intelligence and Information Retrieval, in: Lecture Notes in Networks and Systems, Springer, Singapore, 2022, pp. 425–432.

[23] V. Arnaboldi, A. Passarella, M. Conti, R.I. Dunbar, Chapter 1 - introduction, in: V. Arnaboldi, A. Passarella, M. Conti, R.I. Dunbar (Eds.), Online Social Networks, Computer Science Reviews and Trends, Elsevier, Boston, 2015, pp. 1–7, http://www.sciencedirect.com/science/article/pii/B9780128030233000011.

[24] H. Wang, E.H. Hovy, M. Dredze, The hurricane sandy twitter corpus, in: AAAI Workshop: WWW and Public Health Intelligence, 2015.

[25] S. Surendra, S. Aixin, An analysis of 14 million tweets on hashtag-oriented spamming★, Journal of the Association for Information Science and Technology 68 (7) (2017) 1638–1651, https://doi.org/10.1002/asi.23836.

[26] G. Chris, T. Kurt, P. Vern, Z. Michael, @spam: the underground on 140 characters or less, in: Proceedings of ACM Conference on Computer and Communications Security (CCS), 2010, pp. 27–37.

[27] Y. Li, B. Shen, Research on sentiment analysis of microblogging based on lsa and tf-idf, in: 2017 3rd IEEE International Conference on Computer and Communications (ICCC), 2017, pp. 2584–2588.

[28] J. Suto, S. Oniga, P.P. Sitar, Comparison of wrapper and filter feature selection algorithms on human activity recognition, in: 2016 6th International Conference on Computers Communications and Control (ICCCC), 2016, pp. 124–129.

[29] P. Dhara, M. Ruchi, S. Ketan, A comparative study of clustering data mining: techniques and research challenges, IJLTEMAS iii (2014) 67–70.

[30] S. Patel, S. Sihmar, A. Jatain, A study of hierarchical clustering algorithms, in: 2015 2nd International Conference on Computing for Sustainable Global Development (INDIACom), 2015, pp. 537–541.

[31] S. Vivek, H.N. Bharathi, Study of density based algorithms, International Journal of Computer Applications 69 (2013) 1–4.

[32] C. Marie, K. Vanessa, S. Jérôme, A partitioning method for the clustering of categorical variables, in: H. Locarek-Junge, C. Weihs (Eds.), Classification as a Tool for Research, Springer Berlin Heidelberg, Berlin, Heidelberg, 2010, pp. 91–99.

[33] Y. Liu, Z. Li, H. Xiong, X. Gao, J. Wu, Understanding of internal clustering validation measures, in: 2010 IEEE International Conference on Data Mining, 2010, pp. 911–916.

[34] M. N, G. Chitrakala, A survey on extractive text summarization, 2017, pp. 1–6.

[35] G. Nikhil, F. Benoit, K. Riedhammer, D. Hakkani-Tur, Clusterrank: a graph based method for meeting summarization, in: INTERSPEECH, ISCA, 2009, pp. 1499–1502.

[36] R. Koustav, G. Subham, G. Pawan, G. Niloy, G. Saptarshi, Extracting situational information from microblogs during disaster events: a classification-summarization approach, in: Proc. ACM CIKM, 2015.

[37] Text summarization with NLTK, https://tinyurl.com/frequency-summarizer, 2014.

[38] E. Günes, R.D. R, Lexrank: graph-based lexical centrality as salience in text summarization, Journal of Artificial Intelligence Research 22 (1) (2004) 457–479.

[39] G. Yihong, L. Xin, Generic text summarization using relevance measure and latent semantic analysis, in: SIGIR, 2001, pp. 19–25.

[40] L.H. P, The automatic creation of literature abstracts, IBM Journal of Research and Development 2 (2) (1958) 159–165.

[41] R.D. R, H. Eduard, M. Kathleen, Introduction to the special issue on summarization, Computational Linguistics 28 (4) (2002) 399–408.

[42] A. Nenkova, L. Vanderwende, The impact of frequency on summarization, Tech. Rep., Microsoft Research, 2005.

[43] H. Zhanying, C. Chun, B. Jiajun, W. Can, Z. Lijun, C. Deng, H. Xiaofei, Document summarization based on data reconstruction, in: Proc. AAAI Conference on Artificial Intelligence, 2012, pp. 620–626.

[44] S.R. W, S. Andrzej, Rough set methods in feature selection and recognition, Pattern Recognition Letters 24 (6) (2003) 833–849.

[45] C. Yaile, A. Delia, B. Rafael, Feature selection algorithms using rough set theory, in: Proceedings of IEEE International Conference on Intelligent Systems Design and Applications, 2007, pp. 407–411.

[46] B. Fabrício, M. Gabriel, R. Tiago, A. Virgílio, Detecting spammers on Twitter, in: Proceedings of Collaboration, Electronic Messaging, Anti-Abuse and Spam Conference (CEAS), 2010.

[47] F. Benevenuto, T. Rodrigues, J. Almeida, M. Goncalves, V. Almeida, Detecting spammers and content promoters in online video social networks, in: IEEE INFOCOM Workshops 2009, 2009, pp. 1–2.

[48] H. Costa, F. Benevenuto, L.H. de Campos Merschmann, Detecting tip spam in location-based social networks, in: Proceedings of the 28th Annual ACM Symposium on Applied Computing (SAC), 2013.

[49] H. Costa, L.H. de Campos Merschmann, F. Barth, F. Benevenuto, Pollution, bad-mouthing, and local marketing: the underground of location-based social networks, Elsevier Information Sciences 279 (2014) 123–137.

[50] Infomap - community detection, http://www.mapequation.org/code.html.

[51] S. Dutta, S. Ghatak, M. Roy, S. Ghosh, A.K. Das, A graph based clustering technique for tweet summarization, in: Reliability, Infocom Technologies and Optimization (ICRITO) (Trends and Future Directions), 2015, pp. 1–6.

[52] D.M. Blei, A.Y. Ng, M.I. Jordan, Latent Dirichlet allocation, Journal of Machine Learning Research 3 (2003) 993–1022, http://dl.acm.org/citation.cfm?id=944919.944937.

[53] Hyderabad blasts – Wikipedia, http://en.wikipedia.org/wiki/2013_Hyderabad_blasts, February 2013.

[54] Sandy Hook Elementary School shooting – Wikipedia, http://en.wikipedia.org/wiki/Sandy_Hook_Elementary_School_shooting, December 2012.

[55] North India floods – Wikipedia, http://en.wikipedia.org/wiki/2013_North_India_floods, June 2013.

[56] Typhoon Hagupit – Wikipedia, http://en.wikipedia.org/wiki/Typhoon_Hagupit, December 2014.

[57] REST API Resources, Twitter Developers, https://dev.twitter.com/docs/api.

[58] Wordnet – a lexical database for English, http://wordnet.princeton.edu/.

[59] S. Dutta, S. Ghatak, S. Ghosh, A.K. Das, A genetic algorithm based tweet clustering technique, in: Computer Communication and Informatics (ICCCI), 2017, pp. 1–6.

[60] D. Soumi, G. Sujata, D. Asit, M. Gupta, D. Sayantika, Feature selection based clustering on micro-blogging data, in: International Conference on Computational Intelligence in Data Mining (ICCIDM-2017), 2017, pp. 885–895.

[61] V. Gupta, G.S. Lehal, A survey of text summarization extractive techniques, Journal of Emerging Technologies in Web Intelligence 2 (3) (2010) 258–268.

[62] S. Mackie, R. McCreadie, C. Macdonald, I. Ounis, Comparing algorithms for microblog summarisation, in: CLEF, in: Lecture Notes in Computer Science, vol. 8685, Springer, 2014, pp. 153–159.

[63] R. Dragomir, A. Timothy, B.-G. Sasha, B. John, Ç. Arda, D. Stanko, D. Elliott, H. Ali, L. Wai, L. Danyu, O. Jahna, Q. Hong, S. Horacio, T. Simone, T. Michael, W. Adam, Z. Zhu, MEAD - a platform for multidocument multilingual text summarization, in: Proceedings of the Fourth International Conference on Language Resources and Evaluation (LREC'04), European Language Resources Association (ELRA), 2004, http://www.lrec-conf.org/proceedings/lrec2004/pdf/757.pdf.

CHAPTER 2

Literature review on data analytics for social microblogging platforms

2.1 Introduction

We present a literature survey of several concepts related to the problems addressed in this book. To address the problems of information filtering and organization, some frequently used techniques are filtering out unwanted information (e.g., spam), clustering, and summarization. Attribute selection and dimensionality reduction [1] are important steps before clustering and summarization. The increasing and varied nature of microblog vocabulary enhances the role of attribute selection in data analysis. Attribute selection not only reduces the dimension of huge datasets, it also improves the production of summarization, clustering, and classification processes. The state-of-the-art attribute selection methods are discussed.

Cluster analysis [2] looks for patterns in the dataset to identify similarity among the objects without any prior knowledge (i.e., unsupervised). Clustering is important especially for microblog data analysis [3]. Various standard clustering algorithms are briefly discussed [4]. Some related topics like evaluation measures for cluster quality and cluster validation [5] are also discussed.

In the field of information retrieval, automatic document summarization is a well-known issue. During an emergency, hundreds to thousands of microblogs (tweets) are typically posted on Twitter, thus personally reading through each tweet is not practicable. As a result, summarizing microblogs made during emergency situations has become a popular research topic in recent years. Some off-the-shelf extractive summarization algorithms are discussed here.

Apart from discussing attribute selection, summarization, and clustering methods in general, this section also reviews several works that have applied these methods in the domain of online social microblogging sites (OSMs).

Data Analytics for Social Microblogging Platforms
https://doi.org/10.1016/B978-0-32-391785-8.00013-5

2.2 Attribute selection and its application in spam detection

The recent popularity of dimensionality reduction in big data analysis has attracted the focus of researchers. Attribute selection can be useful for a wide variety of tasks, including clustering and classification. Here is an example scenario where attribute selection can be used (and has been used in this chapter).

Spammers that upload dangerous content on OSMs are targeting the sites as they become more popular. As a result, it is critical to filter spam accounts and spam messages from OSMs. Several prior attempts to classify spam on OSMs employed a range of criteria to distinguish between spam and lawful entities. The selection of a small subset of attributes that can speed up the classification process while maintaining (or even increasing) the classification production of the original collection of attributes is an important step in attribute-based classification [6]. The work [7] explores scalability of various classifiers for tweet classification, which shows the utility of attribute selection for speeding up the classification. In this chapter, an attribute selection methodology is proposed to make spam tweet classification more scalable and efficient by reducing the number of features [8].

Apart from attribute selection, there are different types of attribute ranking methods, e.g., information gain, chi squared, and so on. These ranking methods rank all the attributes according to the relevance score of each attribute. A fixed number of attributes with the highest rank or a variable number of attributes with rank above a predetermined threshold value are selected for attribute selection. The remainder of this section provides an overview of various approaches for selecting and ranking attributes [9,10].

2.2.1 Attribute selection methods

An attribute selection method considers a given training dataset in order to make a decision about which attribute (or feature) subset to select. Many researchers have proposed feature selection algorithms. These are discussed in the following sections.

2.2.1.1 Filter method

The filter method [11–13] is employed to select the best attribute subset using an attribute ranking function. Each attribute receives a relevance score from the ranking function. Naturally, the higher the rating of an attribute, the more relevant it is. A fixed number of attributes with the greatest rank or a variable number of attributes with a rank threshold greater than a

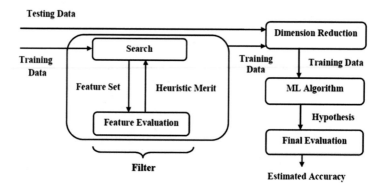

Figure 2.1 Filter feature selection method.

predetermined value are picked. Fig. 2.1 demonstrates the filter method's basic capability for attribute selection.

One of the fundamental drawbacks of filtering approaches is that, rather than considering attribute correlation, they look at each attribute separately. It is possible that the two attributes are ineffective in classification on their own, but when combined, they become valuable [14].

2.2.1.2 Wrapper method

The wrapper method [15,16] uses a learning algorithm to search attribute subsets and tests production of every subset of attributes. Thus, the best performing subset of attributes is determined [17]. If there are n attributes in total, 2^n possible subsets are to be searched, which is an NP-hard problem. Using a heuristic function, the search space is reduced in order to enhance the production of the wrapper algorithms. Fig. 2.2 shows the basic functionality of the wrapper method. The disadvantage of the wrapper method is that it tends to be computationally exhaustive and the use of a heuristic function to improve the search space can be ad hoc.

2.2.1.3 Other attribute selection algorithms

In machine learning and data mining, selecting attributes (or features) is a crucial step. In the context of a classification challenge, the purpose of attribute selection is to discover a minimal subset of attributes in order to speed up the classification process and improve classification production [18]. A wide range of attribute selection strategies have been given in the literature [19]. The majority of these algorithms rely on statistical measurements to evaluate a potential subset of qualities at each iteration; these

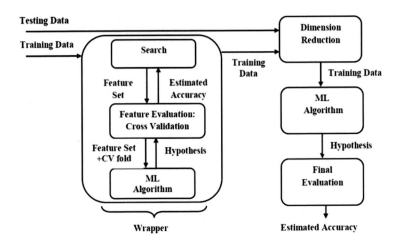

Figure 2.2 Wrapper feature selection method.

methods are known as filter methods [20]. The bulk of the suggested filter algorithms are supervised, which means they assume the training set's class labels are available [21].

However, certain unsupervised techniques have been proposed, such as employing attribute similarity [22] or graph-based clustering of attributes [23]. Wrapper approaches, on the other hand, use the production of a classifier as the assessment criterion for determining the goodness of a proposed subset of characteristics [16].

Some of the most widely used attribute selection approaches are based on rough set theory [24–27], a mathematical tool for dealing with imprecision, ambiguity, and vagueness [28,29]. Attribute selection algorithms based on rough sets are simply filtering methods that aim to discover an ideal subset of the original attribute set [30]; this optimal subset is referred to as a reduct. Remember that obtaining an ideal subset of attributes is an NP-hard problem that can be solved using algorithms like incremental hill climbing and ant colony optimization [25,26].

2.2.2 Spam detection

This section provides an attribute selection algorithm for better spam categorization in online social networks (OSNs), as described previously. Prior work on spam identification in OSMs, as well as current algorithms for attribute selection for spam detection, are briefly addressed in this section.

2.2.2.1 Spam detection in OSM

Similar to spam in the Web [31] and email [32,33], spammers have been targeting OSNs such as Facebook, Youtube, and Twitter [34–36]. A vast number of initiatives have been taken to prevent spam in various online systems, including OSNs; refer to [37,38] for surveys on such efforts. According to a recent study, spam transmitted through OSMs like Twitter is significantly more powerful (i.e., gets much greater click-through rates) than spam sent via spam emails. As a result, it is not surprising that many scholars have developed techniques to combat spam in OSMs [35].

There have been several attempts towards classifying user accounts of spammers [39–42], as well as spam posts [43,44]. We describe some of these studies in brief. In [39], the authors proposed a classification approach for detecting spammer accounts and non-spammer accounts. Their approach correctly classified around 96% of non-spammers and 70% of spammers. This work also identified the most significant attributes for spam detection in Twitter [45]. In [40], the authors analyzed the behavioral and structural differences between spammers and legitimate users in Twitter. This work identified several strategies adopted by spammers to spread spam contents, while evading detection by the Twitter spam tracking system. In [41] and [42], the authors designed *social honeypots* for harvesting spam profiles in OSN communities. Using the harvested spam accounts, profile features of spammers and legitimate Twitter users were analyzed, such as content, social contacts, posting patterns, user behavior over time, followers/following dynamics, and so on. These profile features were considered to design machine learning-based classifiers to detect spammers with a high accuracy rate. In [42] – a later work by the same authors as [41] – the authors designed 60 honeypots on Twitter to harvest 36,000 spammers and an automatic spam classifier was also proposed. This research demonstrated a detailed study of the harvested Twitter users which included several aspects such as user behavior over time, analysis of link payloads, and followers/following network dynamics. The proposed approach results in a set of attributes such as user demographics, follower/following social graph, user behavior, and properties of the tweet content, which can be used to investigate the usefulness of instinctive content and for polluter identification [46,47].

Some other works focused on detecting suspicious/malicious URLs posted on social media. In [43], the authors proposed a classifier to detect suspicious URLs. In this work, correlated redirect chains of URLs are identified from Twitter. Subsequently, URL features are extracted and these features are used further for classification. The classifier identifies the correlated URLs which redirect chains using the frequently shared URLs. Similarly, in [44], the authors proposed a real-time URL spam filtering system. This research shows several differences between spam that targets email and spam on Twitter. It can be noted that the feature selection algorithm developed in this chapter can be used with any of the above-mentioned works to improve classification accuracy [48].

2.2.2.2 Attribute selection for spam detection

Important features for spam detection have also been selected using attribute selection algorithms, particularly in the domains of web spam and email spam. Jaber et al. [31], for example, highlighted the value of attribute selection in web spam detection. To choose attributes for an email spam classification system, Zhang et al. [32] used a wrapper-based particle swarm optimization technique.

However, there have been few attempts to choose relevant criteria for spam identification in OSNs in a systematic manner [39,49]. To the best of our knowledge, only two previous studies have attempted to uncover crucial attributes for recognizing spam user accounts in Twitter and Facebook. Both studies used the well-known information gain and chi squared (X2) statistical metrics [50] to rank the traits, and then considered the top attributes based on these rankings. Furthermore, Ahmed et al. [49] investigated the drop in classification production by eliminating one characteristic at a time, identifying the most essential attributes whose removal results in the greatest decline in classification production [51].

2.2.3 Contributions of this chapter

One of the contributions of this chapter is to propose an attribute selection mechanism for improving spam classification in OSMs. Though similar attempts have been made in the past, it is evident from the above discussion that in the attribute selection methodologies in [39,49], the mutual reliance among the selected attributes was neglected, making it difficult to measure the overall quality of the selected attribute set. For example, two attributes that score highly independently according to a statistical metric may be highly dependent on each other, resulting in no new information being received if both of these traits are included in the selected set.

The algorithm suggested in this chapter aims to improve attribute selection methodology by taking into account attribute interdependencies. To describe the dependency among the attributes, a graph theoretic approach was utilized, and then a greedy algorithm was used to choose an optimal subset of nodes (attributes) from the graph [52].

2.3 Summarization with various methods

Twitter and other microblogging sites have become vital sources of real-time information on current events, such as sociopolitical upheavals, natural and man-made disasters, and so on. Microblogging sites are critical sources of situational information, particularly during emergency situations such as catastrophes [53]. Microblogs are typically uploaded so quickly and in such enormous quantities during such occurrences that human users are unable to read them all. In this situation, it is vital to summarize the microblogs (tweets) and provide informative summaries to those attempting to respond to the tragedy. This section gives an overview of document summarization in general and document summarization for microblogs in particular.

2.3.1 Automatic document summarization

Automatic document summarization is a well-known problem in information retrieval, with numerous algorithms proposed to solve it. Surveys on summarizing methods are recommended to the reader [54,55]. Information retrieval, text comprehension, question answering, and other natural language processing (NLP) applications can all benefit from the output of the automatic text summarization technique.

There are two sorts of summarization methods: abstractive and extractive. Abstractive algorithms aim to generate summaries by paraphrasing sections of the input data, whereas extractive algorithms attempt to generate summaries by extracting specified elements of the input data (e.g., certain sentences that are judged relevant) [56]. A large number of the algorithms proposed in the literature are extractive in nature [54]. A large number of automatic text summarization algorithms have been proposed in the literature [57–68]. We briefly describe a few of these algorithms.

In [57], the authors proposed several portable text summarization techniques that are language-independent and easily ported between different natural languages. In a concept named *holistic summarization*, both the text being summarized and the resulting summary are visually perceived holistically. The fitness of the summary is semantically assessed with veneration to the original text. In the work [58], the authors investigated several automatic summarization techniques and their evaluation strategies. The work [59] proposed a text summarization algorithm to compute lexical chains in a text, merging several robust knowledge sources using the Wordnet semantic dictionary. In [63], the authors focused on automatic text summarization based on supervised learning approaches. The work [64] developed a novel summarization method based on sentence extraction. The chapter [60] discusses major issues of automatic text summarization, such as corpus-based methods, evaluation approaches, etc.

Luhn suggested an approach that uses surface data such as word frequency to automatically extract technical publications [66]. The TextRank algorithm [67] is a graph-based strategy that uses the PageRank algorithm [69] to construct an adjacency matrix that finds the most highly scoring phrases based on keywords in a document. A summarization algorithm based on TOPIC [70] was proposed, taking into account hierarchical text graphs from an input document. For multi-document summarizing, Kupiec employed supervised learning and statistical approaches using a collection of 188 scientific documents and their related human-created summaries [71]. In the SCISOR system, a conceptual summarizing technique was suggested that selected elements of a concept graph built from Down Jones newswire reports [72]. In the MEAD algorithm, a sentence's centrality is measured with respect to the general subject of the document cluster or, in the case of single document summarization, in connection to a single document [73]. Notable algorithms were created for SumBasic content summarizing. MEAD [68] is a prominent multi-document multilingual summarizing platform that includes different summary methods and criteria for analyzing multi-document summaries. While most of the studies mentioned above focused on English text, there have also been works on summarization of non-English text. For instance, the authors in [61] proposed an automatic summarization approach for Swedish text, based on recognizing named entities in order to classify proper nouns. Again, in [62], the authors focused on evaluation of automatic text summarization methods and tools for Swedish text. In [65] the author proposed a system named SweNam, which focused on development, training, and evaluation of a Swedish named entity tagger based on machine learning techniques.

2.3.2 Summarization of microblogs

With the rise in popularity of microblogs as a source of information, a variety of summarizing algorithms tailored to microblogs have lately been developed. Microblog summarizing is a multi-document summary problem by definition. However, by interpreting the input set of microblogs as a single document, techniques for single-document summarizing can be used.

Microblog summarization presents some unique issues, owing to the small size of individual microblogs and the loud, informal style of microblogs, which make interpreting semantic similarity challenging.

Several research studies have proposed algorithms for tweet summarization. Xu et al. used a graph-based approach [74] for automatic tweet summarization. Arkaitz et al. attempted real-time event summarization [75] via sub-event identification from tweets and tweet selection. Chang et al. [76] proposed a context summarization approach on Twitter, applying user influence models. Yajuan et al. [77] also proposed a Twitter topic summarization algorithm by ranking tweets using social influence and content quality. Becker et al. [78] considered graph centrality measures such as centroid, degree, and LexRank to identify event content from huge tweet datasets. While most of the algorithms listed above are designed to summarize a group of tweets in a static format, a few approaches for summarizing tweet streams in real-time have recently been developed [79–82]. Shou et al. [80], for example, suggest a technique that involves clustering comparable tweets first and then picking a few representative tweets from each cluster and rating them according to importance using a graph-based approach (LexRank) [83]. Olariu [81] suggested a graph-based abstractive summarization system based on the extraction of bigrams from tweets, which are referred to as graph-nodes. Graph-based approaches for summarizing tweets have also been proposed by some other authors [74,84]. Other research has developed methods for analyzing microblogs posted during certain events [85–89]. In [85], the authors proposed a summarizing technique for tweets posted during sporting events, using a sentence ranking method to extract relevant information for any important moment in the event. In [86], the authors proposed a summarization method for microblogs during sporting events, circumnavigating spam and conversational posts. The work [87] proposed a summarization technique for event-specific tweets, based on learning the underlying hidden state representation of the event via hidden Markov models. The work [88] proposed a document stream summarization technique, which shows good results on microblogs posted during sports matches. In [89], the authors proposed a graph-based summarization technique to identify important tweets related to trending topics, from among the set of tweets returned by Twitter based on keyword-based search. Osborne et al. [90] proposed a real-time event tracking system considering greedy summarization.

Several recent studies have focused on the summary of news items and tweets issued during emergency situations [91–93]. The work [92], in particular, suggested a classification–summarization technique for extracting and analyzing situational data from tweet streams. To optimize for the presence of specific crucial terms (called "content words") in the summary, an approach based on integer linear programming was used. Mehta et al. [94] offer an extractive summarization strategy that combines earlier approaches to make significant improvements.

2.3.3 Microblog summarizing with comparative study

There have been a few major studies comparing different microblog summarizing techniques [95,96]. For four microblog datasets, Mackie et al. [96] compared the production of 11 summarization techniques. A random baseline, temporal approaches (e.g., those that rank tweets by time), ways based on phrase statistics such as TF-IDF (tfIDFSum, TFIDFSum), and approaches based on term statistics, novelty, and cohesion are among the 11 summarization methods [97]. Inouye et al. [95] compared extractive summarization algorithms for Twitter posts.

In [98] a hybrid TF-IDF-based method and a clustering-based algorithm were examined for selecting tweets to produce summaries from a given set. These algorithms' results are compared against summaries created manually (golden standard) and summaries created by eight different summarizers, including random, most recent, MEAD, TextRank, LexRank, cluster, hybrid TF-IDF, and SumBasic. Efficiency is measured in terms of recall, precision, and the F-score using the ROUGE automatic summarization tool and the MTurk human evaluator approach. The results of the comparison revealed that frequency-based summarizers (hybrid TF-IDF and SumBasic) produce the best ROUGE F-score [55].

2.3.4 Summarization validation

The following is a conventional approach for evaluating the quality of summarization generated by an algorithm. Human annotators create golden standard summaries, which are then compared against the algorithm-generated summaries. ROUGE scores are computed to quantify the production of a summarization algorithm [99], which range in [0, 1]. ROUGE is the industry standard. The quality of the summaries can be assessed using the recall scores of the (i) ROUGE-1, (ii) ROUGE-2, and (iii) ROUGE-L versions.

These scores indicate what percentage of the golden standard summaries' (i) unigrams, (ii) bigrams, and (iii) longest matching sequence of words are covered by the algorithms' summaries. It should be noted that summarization is essentially a subjective process, with different human annotators summarizing the same dataset in different ways. Hence, it is customary to employ multiple human annotators to generate golden standard summaries.

2.3.5 Contributions of this section

It is evident from the above discussion that a huge number of summarization algorithms already exist, not only for general text summarization, but also for specific microblog summarization. This chapter takes a different approach to microblog summarization – instead of trying to propose a new summarization algorithm, it is investigated whether multiple existing algorithms can be combined to produce summaries that are better (i.e., achieve higher ROUGE scores) than what any of the individual algorithms generate. Specifically, one of the important contributions of this chapter is to propose ensemble summarization algorithms that can combine the summaries generated by different extractive base algorithms to generate summaries better than any of the base summaries.

2.4 Cluster analysis of microblogs

Cluster analysis is an important data mining technique [100,101] that is widely used in many fields. Clustering is the method to identify groups of homogeneous objects (which are placed in the same groups) and heterogeneous objects (which are placed in different groups). A good clustering method produces high-quality clusters [102] with low inter-cluster similarity and high intra-cluster similarity. This section gives an overview of the different broad approaches for clustering and discusses applications of clustering specifically in the context of OSMs.

2.4.1 Clustering algorithms

There are different broad approaches for clustering, such as partition-based, hierarchical-based, density-based, and graph-based approaches. Applications and evaluations of different clustering algorithms for the analysis of microblog datasets obtained from several OSN sites are described in [103]. Some commonly used clustering algorithms are discussed below.

2.4.1.1 Partition-based clustering

Given a dataset of n objects, a partitioning method [104] constructs k ($k \leq n$) clusters disjoint to each other. The program divides the data into k groups that must all meet the following criteria: (1) There must be at least one object in each group and (2) each object must belong to only one group (hard clustering). In general, the algorithms employ an iterative relocation strategy based on an objective function that aims to increase partitioning by transferring objects from one cluster to another. The general criterion for good partitioning is that objects belonging to the same group are close to each other, whilst objects belonging to other clusters are far apart. There are several kinds of other criteria [105] for judging the quality of clusters. Partition-based clustering methods [106] need to be modified for datasets with difficult shapes of clusters. Some common partition-based clustering methods are described below.

(A) K-means clustering

The K-means clustering algorithm is one of the most common unsupervised learning algorithms [107,108]. It follows a simple iterative method to cluster a dataset into k clusters, where k is set a priori. The first step is to define k centers, one for each cluster. These centers should be positioned intelligently, because different locations may lead to different results. So the better choice is to place them at the maximum possible distance apart from each other. The next step is to consider each object belonging to a given dataset and associate it to the nearest center. When no object is pending, the first step is finished and an early clustering is done. At this point, k new centers are computed by calculating means of the k clusters obtained in the earlier step, and these new centers are set as centers of the clusters. After these k new centers are obtained, a new binding has to be done between the same objects and the nearest new centroid. During execution of the loop, k centers modify their position step by step until the algorithm converges.

Unfortunately, for any particular dataset, there is no general theoretical method for determining the necessary number of clusters. Comparing the results of numerous executions with varying k values and selecting the best one based on a set of criteria is a straightforward approach. However, one must exercise caution because, by definition, raising k results in reduced error function values, but larger k values also raise the risk of overfitting [109].

(B) K-medoids clustering

Because an object with an unusually large value can significantly alter the distribution of objects in the discovered clusters, the K-means clustering algorithm is sensitive to outliers. Instead of using the mean value of the items in a cluster, the most centrally situated object in the cluster is utilized as a point of reference in the K-medoids approach. As a result, object partitioning can still be done using the principle of minimizing the sum of dissimilarities between each item and its associated point of reference.

In the presence of noise and outliers, the K-medoids approach has been found to be more robust than the K-means method, because a medoid is less influenced by outliers or other extreme values than a mean [110].

However, K-medoid processing is more expensive than the K-means technique. The user must supply the value of K, the number of clusters, in both approaches. Partitioning around medoids (PAM) [111], a common K-medoids partitioning algorithm, works well for low-volume datasets but fails to scale well for large datasets.

(C) Partitioning methods in large databases

To deal with huge datasets, a sampling-based method called Clustering LARge Applications (CLARA) [112] might be utilized. CLARA's concept is that instead of considering the entire collection of items, a tiny subset of the original objects is chosen as the dataset's representations. PAM [111] is then used to pick medoids from the representatives. If the sample is chosen at random, it should be fairly representative of the original dataset. The representative items (medoids) chosen are likely to be similar to those chosen from the entire dataset. CLARA extracts several samples from the dataset, applies PAM [111] to each sample, and outputs the best clustering result. As a result, CLARA is capable of handling larger datasets than PAM. Each iteration is $O(ks2 + k(n - k))$ in complexity, where s, k, and n are the sample size, number of clusters, and total number of objects, respectively.

A K-medoids approach called Clustering Large Applications based upon RANdomized Search (CLARANS) [112] has also been developed to increase the quality and scalability of CLARA. This method combines the sampling technique with PAM; however, it is not limited to a single sample at a specific time. CLARANS represents a sample with some randomness in each phase of the search, whereas CLARA has a fixed sample at every step of the search. The clustering approach can be described as a network search in which each node represents a potential solution, such as a set of K-medoids.

2.4.1.2 Hierarchical clustering

According to the proximity matrix, hierarchical clustering algorithms group the items of a given dataset into a hierarchical structure. A dendrogram is commonly used to represent the results of hierarchical clustering [113,114]. The dendrogram's root node represents the entire dataset, whereas each leaf node is treated as an item. The height of the dendrogram usually reflects the distance between each pair of clusters or objects, or a cluster and an object, and the intermediate nodes describe the extent to which the objects are proximate to each other. By cutting the dendrogram at various levels, clustering can be obtained. Each attribute's relevance is determined by the ranking mechanism. The higher the rank, the more important the attribute. A fixed number of attributes with the greatest rank is chosen, or a variable number of attributes above a predetermined rank threshold is chosen. Most previous attempts to choose attributes for spam detection have overlooked reciprocal connections between attributes, potentially resulting in a smaller set of highly related attributes. The suggested graph-based solution addresses this flaw: when an attribute is included in the reduced attribute set, connected attributes can be easily deleted from the graph, resulting in a further reduction of the attribute set.

Agglomerative methods and divisive methods are the two types of hierarchical clustering algorithms. Agglomerative clustering begins with N clusters, each of which contains exactly one object. Then, a series of merge procedures are performed, culminating in all items being placed in the same group. In machine learning and data mining, selecting attributes (or features) is a crucial step. The goal of attribute selection in the context of a classification problem is to identify a minimal subset of attributes to speed up the classification process and enhance classification performance. In the literature, a vast variety of attribute selection methods have been presented. The greedy algorithm starts by selecting an important MSG node (attribute). In-degree, weighted in-degree (where in-degree of a node is the sum of connections related to that node), betweenness centrality, eigenvalue centrality, PageRank, and other graph centrality measures can be used to identify the significance of nodes in a graph. Studies were carried out using a range of centrality measures, and it was observed that the simple in-degree metric yielded the best results for the proposed methodology. Divisive clustering, on the other hand, works in the other direction. The entire dataset is assigned to a cluster in the first stage, and then the items are divided one by one until all clusters are singletons.

For a cluster with N objects, there are $(2^{(N-1)} - 1))$ possible two-subset divisions, which are very expensive in computation, and not commonly used in practice.

In recent years, with the requirement for handling large-scale datasets in data mining and other fields, many new hierarchical clustering techniques such as CURE [115], ROCK [116], Chameleon [117], and BIRCH [118] have appeared and greatly improved the clustering results. Though divisive clustering is not commonly used in practice, some of its applications can be found in [119]. Two divisive clustering algorithms, namely MONA and DIANA, are described in [119].

2.4.1.3 Density-based clustering

Density-based clustering methods [120] have been applied to discover clusters with arbitrary shapes. Typically these clusters are dense regions of objects in the space of datasets that are separated by regions of low density (representing noise). Two popular density-based spatial clustering techniques are DBSCAN and DENCLUE [121].

DBSCAN

In geographical datasets with noise, the algorithm creates areas with adequate high density into clusters and identifies clusters of arbitrary shape. It defines a cluster as a maximum set of density-connected objects and looks for clusters by inspecting every object in the dataset's *in*-neighborhood. A new cluster is produced with p as the core object if the *in*-neighborhood of an item p contains more objects than a threshold. Then DBSCAN gathers directly density-reachable items from the core objects iteratively, which may result in the merging of a few density-reachable clusters. When no additional points can be added to any of the clusters, the operation ends. DBSCAN's computational complexity is $O(n\log n)$ if a spatial index is employed, where n is the number of items; otherwise, it is $O(n^2)$. The user-defined parameters have an impact on the algorithm.

DENCLUE

DENCLUE is a clustering algorithm based on a collection of density distribution functions:

(i)   Each data object's control can be explicitly modeled using an "influence function," a mathematical function that represents the impact of a data point on its surroundings.

(ii)   A data space's overall density can be characterized logically as the sum of all data objects' influence functions.

(iii)   Clusters can then be statistically identified by locating density attractors, which are nearby maxima of the overall density function.

Compared to other clustering algorithms, the DENCLUE approach has various advantages:

(i)   It has a solid mathematical foundation and generalizes other clustering methods, such as partition-based, hierarchical, and locality-based methods.

(ii)   For datasets with a lot of noise, it offers good grouping properties.

(iii)   In high-dimensional datasets, it allows for a succinct mathematical description of arbitrarily formed clusters.

(iv)   Grid cells are used to store information about grid cells that include data points. It organizes these cells into a tree-based access structure, making it much faster than some popular techniques, such as DBSCAN.

The approach, on the other hand, necessitates careful selection of the density parameter and the noise threshold, as these factors can have a substantial impact on the quality of the clustering solutions.

2.4.1.4 Graph clustering algorithms

Clustering (also known as community detection in the context of graphs) methods for graphs/networks are designed to locate communities based on the network topology, such as tightly connected groups of nodes. Before performing the community detection algorithm in graph-based clustering, the data is represented by a graph. Edge weight in the graph can be calculated using a variety of similarity measures. A community is formed when nodes in a network are of the same type. Intra-community edges are the edges that connect the nodes within a community. Inter-community edges are nodes that connect nodes from different communities. In Fig. 2.3, a small graph depicts intra-community and inter-community edges between distinct communities. The following sections explain two prominent graph-based clustering algorithms.

The researchers utilized a variety of community discovery tools, including the Louvain algorithm [122] and Infomap [123].

(1) Louvain method: Blondel, Lambiotte, and Lefebvre (2008) [122] of the University of Louvain created the Louvain technique for community detection, which is a method for detecting functioning communities from massive networks. The Louvain community detection method is made up of two processes that repeat themselves. The first phase is a "greedy" task

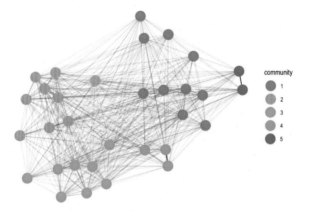

Figure 2.3 Community structure in a graph showing intra-community edges and inter-community edges.

of assigning nodes to communities, with a preference for neighborhood improvements. The second stage is a coarse-grained reorganization of the networks discovered in the first step. These two stages are performed until there are no more measured quality expanding network reassignments possible.

The Louvain strategy optimizes for "modularity" in the same way as previous methods, but in a fraction of the time, allowing for the analysis of far bigger systems. In this method, modularity is defined as a ratio of the density of edges inside communities to the density of edges outside communities in the range of $[-1, 1]$. Heuristic techniques are employed to maximize this modularity value so that the best possible groupings of nodes in a network can theoretically be produced. Small communities are first discovered by locally maximizing the modularity value, after which each microcommunity is grouped into a single node and the process is repeated.

(2) Infomap method: Rosvall and Bergstrom's Infomap is another famous community discovery algorithm (2008) [123]. It improves the map equation, which achieves a balance between the difficulty of data compression and the problem of recognizing and retrieving essential patterns or structures within the data. The Louvain community finding approach is closely followed by this algorithm. Each node is assigned to its own module at first. The nodes are then transferred to neighboring modules in a random sequential manner, resulting in the greatest reduction of the map equation. If no move leads to a further reduction of the map equation, the node remains in its original place. The method is done until the map equation can no longer be decreased in a different random sequential order each time. Finally, the network is rebuilt, with the lowest-level modules producing nodes at that level and nodes being joined into modules in the same way that previous-level nodes were. This hierarchical network rebuilding is continued until the map equation can no longer be lowered. Both undirected and directed graphs can be used with Infomap. Infomap returns a list of non-overlapping communities (node-set partitions) as well as a decimal value that represents the total flow in that node.

Thus, there are a wide variety of clustering algorithms, as is evident from the discussion above. It is a natural question as to which algorithm performs the best on a certain dataset. To answer this question, first some measures for cluster validation/evaluation need to be decided. The next section discusses some commonly used cluster validation measures.

2.4.2 Cluster validation indices

There are many approaches to quantify the quality of clusters. Jain and Dubes called the difficulty of determining the number of clusters "the fundamental problem of cluster validity" [124]. Clustering methods divide a dataset's items into a set of sub-groups. Although the number of clusters k is known for some applications, it is unknown in the vast majority of cases and must be calculated only from the item itself. Many clustering techniques use k as an input parameter, and it goes without saying that the quality of the resulting clusters is heavily influenced by the estimation of k.

Cluster validation is the measurement of a cluster's goodness in comparison to others formed by clustering algorithms with various parameter values, which is an essential topic in cluster analysis [5].

Several cluster validation measures, like compactness, connectedness, separation, and combinations, take a clustering method and the underlying dataset as the input and employ information intrinsic to the dataset to review the quality of the clusters. Some of these cluster validation measures are discussed below.

(A) Compactness
Compactness is a measure of how widely objects inside a cluster are scattered. It assesses the compactness or homogeneity of clusters, with intracluster variance being the most common indicator. The measurement of maximum or average pairwise intra-cluster distances and maximum or average center-based similarities and the use of graph-based approaches are all options for determining intra-cluster homogeneity.

(B) Connectedness

Connectedness is analyzed determine how well a given partitioning agrees with the concept of connectedness, that is, to what extent a partitioning considers local density and groups items in the data space with their nearest neighbors.

(C) Separation

Separation is a metric that indicates how far apart certain clusters are from one another. For example, the average weighted inter-cluster distance is a partitioning rating in which the distance between two separate clusters is measured as the distance between cluster centroids or as the shortest distance between items belonging to different clusters.

(D) Combinations of the above measures

The above measures can be combined to measure cluster quality considering multiple aspects. Combinations of compactness and separation are particularly popular, as the two classes of measures show an opposite tendency. Thus, a number of measures assess both inter-cluster separation and intra-cluster homogeneity and calculate a final score as the linear or non-linear combination of the two measures. Some of these cluster validation measures are discussed below.

Davies–Bouldin validity index: The Davies–Bouldin index (DBIndex) [125] is a function that equals the sum of intra-cluster scatter divided by inter-cluster separation. Let $U = \{X_1, X_2, X_3, X_4, \ldots, X_k\}$ be the k-cluster obtained by a clustering algorithm. To measure the goodness of the cluster U, the DBIndex is calculated as follows:

$$\text{DBIndex}(U) = \frac{1}{K} \sum_{i=1}^{k} \max_{i=j} \left\{ \frac{\Delta(X_i) + \Delta(X_j)}{\delta(X_i, X_j)} \right\}. \qquad (2.1)$$

Here, $\Delta(X_i)$ is the intra-cluster distance in X_i, i.e., the distance between the farthest objects in cluster X_i, and $\delta(S, T)$ is the inter-cluster distance of X_i and X_j, i.e., the distance between X_i and X_j.

Dunn's validity index: The Dunn index (D) [126] estimates intra–cluster compactness using the smallest pairwise distance between objects in distinct clusters as the inter-cluster separation and the maximum diameter among all clusters. The Dunn validation index (DN) is determined using Eq. (2.2) for every partition of clusters, where X_i denotes the i-th cluster. Here, $d(X_i, X_j)$ is the distance between clusters X_i and X_j, $d'(X_1)$ is the intra-cluster distance of cluster X_1, and k is the number of clusters. The aim of this measure is to minimize the intra-cluster distances and maximize the inter-cluster distances. As a result, the number of clusters that maximizes D_N is considered the optimal number, where

$$D = \min_{1 \leq i \leq k} \left\{ \min_{1 \leq j \leq k; i \neq j} \left\{ \frac{d(X_i, X_j)}{\max_{1 \leq l \leq k}(d'(X_l))} \right\} \right\}. \tag{2.2}$$

I-index: As illustrated in Eq. (2.3), the I-index [127] evaluates separation based on the maximum distance between cluster centers and compactness based on the sum of distances between objects and their cluster center:

$$I(k) = \left(\frac{1}{k} \cdot \frac{\sum_j \| x_j - \bar{c} \|_2}{\sum_{k=1}^{K} \sum_{j \in c_k} \| x_j - \bar{c} \|_2} \cdot \max_{i,j}^{K} \| (c_i - c_j) \| \right)^p. \tag{2.3}$$

Here the power p is a constant, which normally is set to be 2.

CH-index: The Calinski–Harabasz (CH) index [128] assesses cluster validity using the average sum of squares between and within clusters:

$$CH = \frac{traceB/(K-1)}{traceW/(N-K)}, \tag{2.4}$$

$$traceB = \sum_{k=1}^{K} | C_k | \| \overline{C_k} - \bar{x} \|^2, \tag{2.5}$$

$$traceW = \sum_{k=1}^{K} \sum_{i=1}^{K} w_{k,i} \| \overline{x_i} - \overline{C_k} \|^2, \tag{2.6}$$

where N is the number of objects in the dataset, K is the number of clusters ($K \in N$), W is the squared differences of all objects in a cluster from their respective cluster center, and B is the error sum of squares between distinct clusters (inter-cluster). The index's most notable feature is that, on the one hand, trace W will begin with a rather big value. As the number of clusters K approaches the ideal clustering solution in $K*$ groups, the value should fall dramatically due to increasing cluster compactness. When the optimal solution is reached, an increase in compactness and, as a result, a drop in value may occur; however, this decrease should be noticeably reduced. Trace T, on the other hand, should act in the opposite way, increasing in value as the number of clusters K grows, but relaxing in its rise if K is greater than $K*$. The optimal number of clusters is determined by the CH-index's maximum value.

Silhouette index: The Silhouette index (S) [129] assesses clustering performance using the pairwise difference between inter- and intra-cluster distances. Eq. (2.7) shows how the Silhouette index (S) is calculated for k clusters:

$$S = \frac{1}{k} \sum_{i=1}^{k} \frac{b_i - a_i}{max(a_i, b_i)}, \tag{2.7}$$

where a_i is the average dissimilarity of the i-th item to all other objects in the same cluster and b_i is the average dissimilarity of the i-th object to all objects in the nearest cluster. From Eq. (2.7), we can deduce that $-1 \leq SC \leq 1$. If the Silhouette value is close to 1, the sample is considered "well clustered" and assigned to the correct cluster. If the Silhouette value is close to 0, the sample may be assigned to the cluster closest to it, and the sample will be equally far from both. If the Silhouette value is close to -1, the sample is "misclassified" and placed in the middle of the clusters. As a result, the number of clusters with the highest SC-index value is considered the optimal number.

XB-index: The Xie–Beni (XB) index [130] is a fuzzy clustering index that takes advantage of compactness and separation. The compactness-to-separation ratio is taken into account by XB. Eq. (2.8) is a mathematical expression for the XB-index for a given dataset X and a partition with K clusters:

$$XB(K) = \frac{V_c(K)/N}{V_s(K)} = \frac{\sum_{n=1}^{N} \sum_{k=1}^{K} u_{k,n}^m \parallel x_n - c_k \parallel^2}{NX \min_{i,j} \parallel c_i - c_j \parallel}, \tag{2.8}$$

where $V_c(K)$ represents the compactness measure when the dataset is grouped into K clusters, which is given by $\sum_{n=1}^{N} \sum_{k=1}^{K} u_{k,n}^m \parallel x_n - c_k \parallel^2$, where $c_k = \sum_{n=1}^{N} u_{k,n}^m x_n / \sum_{n=1}^{N} u_{k,n}^m$ is the centroid of the k-th cluster. The degree of separation between clusters is represented by $Vs(K)$. In general, the best clustering performance for the dataset X is obtained by solving $\min k \in [2, N-1] XB(K)$.

2.4.3 Clustering in online social microblogging sites

In recent times, there have been many research works on clustering microblogs (tweets) and other entities in ONS [131]. For instance, Mathioudakis et al. [132] used bursty keywords and their co-occurrences to propose an algorithm to identify the trending topics, which employed clustering of tweets. Michelson et al. [133] offered an innovative method for determining a user's subject interest that makes use of Wikipedia as a knowledge basis. To identify real-world incidents from Twitter, Hila et al. [134] proposed an algorithm based on clustering. To categorize emerging topics on Twitter, Cataldi et al. [135] created topic-graphs based on phrase frequency and user authority, and then the topic-graphs were clustered. Hill et al. [136] highlighted how social network-based clusters can capture homophily, as well as the prospect that a network-based attribute method could not only capture homophily but also be utilized instead of demographic traits to assess user behavior similarity, maintaining user privacy.

For clustering comparable tweets [137], Kang et al. presented an affinity propagation technique. Cheong [138] used an unsupervised self-organizing feature map as a machine learning-based clustering approach to find intratopic user and message clusters on Twitter. As a complementary step to text classification, Thomas et al. [139] suggested an efficient text classification system based on semi-supervised clustering. The method was more accurate than the similarity measure for text processing, which was used to calculate distance. Yang and Leskovec [140] suggested a clustering method based on propagation of temporal patterns. Karypis et al. [117] devised a hierarchical clustering approach based on dynamic modeling that takes into account cluster dynamic modes and adaptive merging decisions. Natural clusters of varied shapes and sizes can be discovered using this method, based on the differences in clustering models. It features a two-phase structure that was created with the help of several graph representations that are appropriate for diverse application domains [141]. For clustering tweets, Dueck et al. presented an affinity propagation technique. Rangrej et al. [142] published a study comparing the production of three clustering algorithms – K-means, affinity propagation, and singular value decomposition – in grouping short text documents.

For clustering microblog data, some researchers have used graph-based techniques [143]. Dutta et al. [84] suggested a clustering technique for tweets that also conducts summarization, based on a graph-based community discovery approach. A graph-based approach known as TextRank algorithm [67] is used to discover the most highly ranked sentences based on keywords in a document, where ranks are determined by the PageRank algorithm. For the dataset of Down Jones newswire stories, a notion of concept graph has been developed in the SCISOR system [73] to construct conceptual summarization. Many previous publications have employed genetic algorithms for clustering, including clustering data from OSNs [144,145]. Adel et al. [146] suggested a Twitter data grouping method based on a cellular genetic algorithm. Hajeer et al. [147] proposed employing genetic algorithms to perform graph-based grouping. As previously noted, several procedures for clustering texts have been tested, including traditional methods such as K-means as well as evolutionary approaches such as genetic algorithms [148,149]. Ramage et al. [150] employed labeled latent Dirichlet allocation (LDA) to topically cluster tweets in a different way. Aside from clustering, Gencet et al. employed a Wikipedia-based classification strategy to categorize tweets using semantic distance as a classification metric to compare distances between Wikipedia sites. Soumi et al. [151] suggested a method to categorize microblogging data using a genetic algorithm. In a separate paper, Soumi et al. [152] suggested a feature selection-based clustering technique that can improve clustering effectiveness.

2.5 Conclusion

As discussed earlier in this section, there have been a lot of studies of clustering in OSMs, including microblogs. In this chapter, a number of clustering algorithms are developed and applied on tweets, with a particular motivation. One of the most important uses of clustering is in organizing tweets posted during emergency events (e.g., natural and man-made disasters such as floods, typhoons, and terror attacks). During such events, thousands of tweets can be posted per hour, and since time is critical, it is necessary for those responding to the emergency to get a quick overview of the situation. In this scenario, clustering the tweets posted is an effective way to organize the information.

This chapter discussed a number of clustering approaches – including graph-based approaches, genetic algorithm-based approaches, topic modeling (LDA)-based approaches, and approaches based on dimensionality reduction – and a comparative study of how different approaches perform on tweets posted during a variety of emergency events.

References

[1] N. Sharma, K. Saroha, Study of dimension reduction methodologies in data mining, in: International Conference on Computing, Communication Automation, May 2015, pp. 133–137.
[2] Manish Verma, Mauly Srivastava, Neha Chack, Atul Kumar Diswar, Nidhi Gupta, A comparative study of various clustering algorithms, in: Data Mining, International Journal of Engineering Research and Applications (IJERA), 2012, pp. 1379–1384.

[3] A. Magdy, M.F. Mokbel, Microblogs data management and analysis, in: 2016 IEEE 32nd International Conference on Data Engineering (ICDE), May 2016, pp. 1440–1443.

[4] Saxena Amit, Prasad Mukesh, Gupta Akshansh, Bharill Neha, Patel Om Prakash, Tiwari Aruna, Er Meng Joo, Ding Weiping, Lin Chin-Teng, A review of clustering techniques and developments, Neurocomputing 267 (C) (December 2017) 664–681.

[5] Y. Liu, Z. Li, H. Xiong, X. Gao, J. Wu, Understanding of internal clustering validation measures, in: 2010 IEEE International Conference on Data Mining, Dec 2010, pp. 911–916.

[6] X. Huosong, L. Jian, The research of feature selection of text classification based on integrated learning algorithm, in: 2011 10th International Symposium on Distributed Computing and Applications to Business, Engineering and Science, Oct 2011, pp. 20–22.

[7] G. Lin, N. Sun, S. Nepal, J. Zhang, Y. Xiang, H. Hassan, Statistical Twitter spam detection demystified: performance, stability and scalability, IEEE Access 5 (2017) 11142–11154.

[8] Swati Goswami, Asit Kumar Das, Determining maximum cliques for community detection in weighted sparse networks, Knowledge and Information Systems 64 (2) (February 2022) 289–324.

[9] Anjishnu Mukherjee, Souparno Bhattacharyya, Kinjal Ray, Balraj Gupta, Asit Kumar Das, A study of public sentiment and influence of politics in COVID-19 related tweets, in: Asit Kumar Das, Janmenjoy Nayak, Bighnaraj Naik, Soumi Dutta, Danilo Pelusi (Eds.), Computational Intelligence in Pattern Recognition, Springer, Singapore, 2022, pp. 655–665.

[10] Priyanka Das, Asit Kumar Das, Convolutional neural networks-based sentence level classification of crime documents, in: Asit Kumar Das, Janmenjoy Nayak, Bighnaraj Naik, Soumi Dutta, Danilo Pelusi (Eds.), Computational Intelligence in Pattern Recognition, Springer, Singapore, 2022, pp. 65–73.

[11] Andrew Hall Mark, Correlation-based feature selection for machine learning, Technical report, The University of Waikato, Hamilton, New Zealand, 06 2000.

[12] Wang Suge, Li Deyu, Wei Yingjie, Li Hongxia, A feature selection method based on Fisher's discriminant ratio for text sentiment classification, in: Liu Wenyin, Luo Xiangfeng, Wang Fu Lee, Lei Jingsheng (Eds.), Web Information Systems and Mining, Springer Berlin Heidelberg, Berlin, Heidelberg, 2009, pp. 88–97.

[13] Zhu Xiangxin, Liao Shengcai, Lei Zhen, Liu Rong, Z. Li Stan, Feature correlation filter for face recognition, in: Lee Seong-Whan, Z. Li Stan (Eds.), Advances in Biometrics, Springer Berlin Heidelberg, Berlin, Heidelberg, 2007, pp. 77–86.

[14] Singhal Vanika, Singh Preety, Correlation based feature selection for diagnosis of acute lymphoblastic leukemia, in: Proceedings of the Third International Symposium on Women in Computing and Informatics, WCI '15, ACM, New York, NY, USA, 2015, pp. 5–9.

[15] Kohavi Ron, Wrappers for Performance Enhancement and Oblivious Decision Graphs, PhD thesis, Stanford University, Stanford, CA, USA, 1996, UMI Order No. GAX96-11989.

[16] Ron Kohavi, George H. John, Wrappers for feature subset selection, Artificial Intelligence 97 (1) (1997) 273–324, Relevance.

[17] Ankur Das, Debdatta Pal, Chirantana Mallick, Asit K. Das, An unsupervised COVID-19 report summarizer for developing smart healthcare system, in: Asit Kumar Das, Janmenjoy Nayak, Bighnaraj Naik, Soumi Dutta, Danilo Pelusi (Eds.), Computational Intelligence in Pattern Recognition, Springer, Singapore, 2022, pp. 157–168.

[18] Chirantana Mallick, Sunanda Das, Asit Kumar Das, Evolutionary algorithm based summarization for analyzing COVID-19 medical reports, in: Janmenjoy Nayak,

Bighnaraj Naik, Ajith Abraham (Eds.), Understanding COVID-19: The Role of Computational Intelligence, in: Studies in Computational Intelligence, Springer International Publishing, Cham, 2022, pp. 31–58.

[19] M. Dash, H. Liu, Feature selection for classification, Intelligent Data Analysis 1 (1997) 131–156.

[20] Hosseinzadeh Mehdi Aghdam, Ghasem-Aghaee Nasser, Basiri Mohammad Ehsan, Text feature selection using ant colony optimization, Expert Systems with Applications 36 (3, Part 2) (2009) 6843–6853.

[21] Swarup Chattopadhyay, Tanmay Basu, Asit K. Das, Kuntal Ghosh, Late C.A. Murthy, Towards effective discovery of natural communities in complex networks and implications in e-commerce, Electronic Commerce Research 21 (4) (December 2021) 917–954.

[22] Mitra Pabitra, C.A. Murthy, S.K. Pal, Unsupervised feature selection using feature similarity, IEEE Transactions on Pattern Analysis and Machine Intelligence 24 (3) (2002) 301–312.

[23] Bandyopadhyay Sanghamitra, Bhadra Tapas, Pabitra Mitra, Maulik Ujjwal, Integration of dense subgraph finding with feature clustering for unsupervised feature selection, Pattern Recognition Letters 40 (2014) 104–112.

[24] M. Zhang, J.T. Yao, A. Rough, Sets based approach to feature selection, in: Proceedings of IEEE Annual Meeting of the Fuzzy Information, 2004, pp. 1313–1317.

[25] Lian-Yin Zhai, Li-Pheng Khoo, Sai-Cheong Fok, Feature extraction using rough set theory and genetic algorithms – an application for the simplification of product quality evaluation, Computers & Industrial Engineering 43 (4) (2002) 661–676.

[26] Chen Yumin, Miao Duoqian, Wang Ruizhi, A rough set approach to feature selection based on ant colony optimization, Pattern Recognition Letters 31 (3) (2010) 226–233.

[27] Xin Guan, Qiang Guo, Jing Zhao, Zheng chao Zhang, An attribute reduction algorithm based on rough set, information entropy and ant colony optimization, in: Proceedings of IEEE International Conference on Signal Processing, 2010, pp. 1313–1317.

[28] Z. Pawlak, Rough sets: basic notion, International Journal of Computer & Information Sciences 11 (5) (1982) 344–356.

[29] Zdzislaw Pawlak, Rough set theory and its applications to data analysis, Cybernetics and Systems 29 (7) (1998) 661–688.

[30] Skowron Andrzej, Rauszer Cecylia, The discernibility matrices and functions in information systems, in: Roman Słowinski (Ed.), Intelligent Decision Support. Handbook of Applications and Advances of the Rough Set Theory, in: Theory and Decision Library, vol. 11, Kluwer Academic Publishers, 1992, pp. 331–362.

[31] Karimpour Jaber, A. Noroozi Ali, Abadi Adeleh, The impact of feature selection on web spam detection, International Journal of Intelligent Systems and Applications 4 (9) (Aug 2012) 61–67.

[32] Zhang Yudong, Wang Shuihua, Wu Lenan, Spam detection via feature selection and decision tree, Advanced Science Letters 5 (2) (2012) 726–730.

[33] Tseng Chi-Yao, Sung Pin-Chieh, Chen Ming-Syan, Cosdes: a collaborative spam detection system with a novel e-mail abstraction scheme, IEEE Transactions on Knowledge and Data Engineering 23 (5) (May 2011) 669–682.

[34] Gao Hongyu, Hu Jun, Wilson Christo, Li Zhichun, Chen Yan, Y. Zhao Ben, Detecting and characterizing social spam campaigns, in: Proceedings of the ACM SIGCOMM Internet Measurement Conference, IMC, Dec 2000.

[35] Grier Chris, Thomas Kurt, Paxson Vern, Zhang Michael, @spam: the underground on 140 characters or less, in: Proceedings of ACM International Conference on Computer and Communications Security (CCS), 2010, pp. 27–37.

[36] F. Benevenuto, T. Rodrigues, J. Almeida, M. Goncalves, V. Almeida, Detecting spammers and content promoters in online video social networks, in: IEEE INFOCOM Workshops 2009, April 2009, pp. 1–2.

[37] Heymann Paul, Koutrika Georgia, Garcia-Molina Hector, Fighting spam on social web sites: a survey of approaches and future challenges, IEEE Internet Computing 11 (2007) 36–45.

[38] Caruana Godwin, Li Maozhen, A survey of emerging approaches to spam filtering, ACM Computing Surveys 44 (2) (Feb 2012) 9:1–9:27.

[39] Benevenuto Fabrício, Magno Gabriel, Rodrigues Tiago, Almeida Virgílio, Detecting spammers on Twitter, in: Proceedings of Collaboration, Electronic Messaging, Anti-Abuse and Spam Conference (CEAS), July 2010.

[40] Yardi Sarita, Romero Daniel, Schoenebeck Grant, M. Boyd Danah, Detecting spam in a Twitter network, First Monday 15 (1) (Jan 2010) 1–13.

[41] Lee Kyumin, Caverlee James, Webb Steve, Uncovering social spammers: social honeypots + machine learning, in: Proceedings of ACM International Conference on Research and Development in Information Retrieval (SIGIR), 2010, pp. 435–442.

[42] Lee Kyumin, Eoff Brian David, Caverlee James, Seven months with the devils: a long-term study of content polluters on Twitter, in: Lada A. Adamic, Ricardo A. Baeza-Yates, Scott Counts (Eds.), ICWSM, The AAAI Press, 2011.

[43] Lee Sangho, Kim Jong, WarningBird: a near real-time detection system for suspicious URLs in Twitter stream, IEEE Transactions on Dependable and Secure Computing 10 (3) (May 2013) 183–195.

[44] Thomas Kurt, Grier Chris, Ma Justin, Paxson Vern, Song Dawn, Design and evaluation of a real-time url spam filtering service, in: Proceedings of the 2011 IEEE Symposium on Security and Privacy, SP '11, IEEE Computer Society, Washington, DC, USA, 2011, pp. 447–462.

[45] Moumita Basu, Sipra Das Bit, Saptarshi Ghosh, Utilizing microblogs for optimized real-time resource allocation in post-disaster scenarios, Social Network Analysis and Mining 12 (1) (December 2021) 15.

[46] Paheli Bhattacharya, Shounak Paul, Kripabandhu Ghosh, Saptarshi Ghosh, Adam Wyner, DeepRhole: deep learning for rhetorical role labeling of sentences in legal case documents, Artificial Intelligence and Law (November 2021).

[47] Krishnandu Hazra, Tanmoy Ghosh, Avirup Mukherjee, Sujoy Saha, Subrata Nandi, Saptarshi Ghosh, Sandip Chakraborty, Sustainable text summarization over mobile devices: an energy-aware approach, Sustainable Computing: Informatics and Systems 32 (December 2021) 100607.

[48] Arpan Mandal, Kripabandhu Ghosh, Saptarshi Ghosh, Sekhar Mandal, A sequence labeling model for catchphrase identification from legal case documents, Artificial Intelligence and Law (July 2021).

[49] Ahmed Faraz, Abulaish Muhammad, A generic statistical approach for spam detection in Online Social Networks, Computer Communications 36 (10–11) (2013) 1120–1129.

[50] Yang Yiming, O. Pedersen Jan, A comparative study on feature selection in text categorization, in: Proceedings of the International Conference on Machine Learning (ICML), 1997, pp. 412–420.

[51] Moumita Basu, Kripabandhu Ghosh, Saptarshi Ghosh, Information retrieval from microblogs during disasters: in the light of IRMiDis task, SN Computer Science 1 (1) (January 2020) 61.

[52] Ratna Mandal, Soumi Dutta, Rupayan Banerjee, Sujoy Bhattacharya, Ritusree Ghosh, Sougata Samanta, Tiyasa Saha, City traffic speed characterization based on city road surface quality, in: João Manuel R.S. Tavares, Paramartha Dutta, Soumi Dutta, Debabrata Samanta (Eds.), Cyber Intelligence and Information Retrieval, Springer, Singapore, 2022, pp. 515–524.

[53] Imran Muhammad, Castillo Carlos, Diaz Fernando, Vieweg Sarah, Processing social media messages in mass emergency: a survey, ACM Computing Surveys 47 (4) (June 2015) 67:1–67:38.

[54] Vishal Gupta, Gurpreet Singh Lehal, A survey of text summarization extractive techniques, IEEE Journal of Emerging Technologies in Web Intelligence 2 (3) (2010) 258–268.

[55] Das Dipanjan, F.T. Martins André, A survey on automatic text summarization, Literature Survey for the Language and Statistics II course at CMU 4 (2007) 192–195.

[56] Salton Gerard, Automatic Text Processing: the Transformation, Analysis, and Retrieval of Information by Computer, Addison-Wesley Longman Publishing Co., Inc., Boston, MA, USA, 1989.

[57] Martin Hassel, Resource Lean and Portable Automatic Text Summarization, PhD thesis, KTH, Numerical Analysis and Computer Science, NADA, 2007, QC 20100712.

[58] Karen Spärck Jones, Automatic summarising: the state of the art, Information Processing & Management 43 (6) (November 2007) 1449–1481.

[59] Regina Barzilay, Michael Elhadad, Using lexical chains for text summarization, in: Proceedings of the ACL/EACL 1997 Workshop on Intelligent Scalable Text Summarization, 1997, pp. 10–17.

[60] Inderjeet Mani, Advances in Automatic Text Summarization, MIT Press, Cambridge, MA, USA, 1999.

[61] Martin Hassel, Exploitation of named entities in automatic text summarization for Swedish, in: Proceedings of NODALIDA 03 - 14th Nordic Conference on Computational Linguistics, May 30-31 2003, 2003.

[62] Hassel Martin, Evaluation of Automatic Text Summarization - a practical implementation, Licentiate thesis, Department of Numerical Analysis and Computer Science, Royal Institute of Technology, Stockholm, Sweden, May 2004.

[63] Inderjeet Mani, Mark T. Maybury, Automatic summarization, in: Association for Computational Linguistic, 39th Annual Meeting and 10th Conference of the European Chapter, Companion Volume to the Proceedings of the Conference: Proceedings of the Student Research Workshop and Tutorial Abstracts, July 9-11, 2001, Toulouse, France, 2001, p. 5.

[64] Chikashi Nobata, Satoshi Sekine, Hitoshi Isahara, Ralph Grishman, Summarization system integrated with named entity tagging and (ie) pattern discovery, in: Proceedings of the Third International Conference on Language Resources and Evaluation, LREC 2002, May 29-31, 2002, Las Palmas, Canary Islands, Spain, 2002.

[65] Hercules Dalianis, Erik Astrom, Erik Åström, Swenam-a Swedish named entity recognizer its construction, training and evaluation, 2001.

[66] H.P. Luhn, The automatic creation of literature abstracts, IBM Journal of Research and Development 2 (2) (April 1958) 159–165.

[67] Brin Sergey, Page Lawrence, The anatomy of a large-scale hypertextual web search engine, Computer Networks and ISDN Systems 30 (1–7) (April 1998) 107–117.

[68] Dragomir R. Radev, Timothy Allison, Sasha Blair-Goldensohn, John Blitzer, Arda Çelebi, Stanko Dimitrov, Elliott Drábek, Ali Hakim, Wai Lam, Danyu Liu, Jahna Otterbacher, Hong Qi, Horacio Saggion, Simone Teufel, Michael Topper, Adam Winkel, Zhu Zhang, MEAD - a platform for multidocument multilingual text summarization, in: Proceedings of the Fourth International Conference on Language Resources and Evaluation, LREC 2004, May 26-28, 2004, Lisbon, Portugal, 2004.

[69] Lawrence Page, Sergey Brin, Rajeev Motwani, Terry Winograd, The Pagerank Citation Ranking: Bringing Order to the Web, November 1999, Previous number = SIDL-WP-1999-0120.

[70] U. Reimer, U. Hahn, Text condensation as knowledge base abstraction, in: Artificial Intelligence Applications, 1988, Proceedings of the Fourth Conference on, Mar 1988, pp. 338–344.

[71] Kupiec Julian, Pedersen Jan, Chen Francine, A trainable document summarizer, in: Proceedings of the 18th Annual International ACM SIGIR Conference on Research and Development in Information Retrieval, SIGIR '95, ACM, New York, NY, USA, 1995, pp. 68–73.

[72] Debabrata Samanta, Soumi Dutta, Mohammad Gouse Galety, Sabyasachi Pramanik, A novel approach for web mining taxonomy for high-performance computing, in: João Manuel R.S. Tavares, Paramartha Dutta, Soumi Dutta, Debabrata Samanta (Eds.), Cyber Intelligence and Information Retrieval, Lecture Notes in Networks and Systems, Springer, Singapore, 2022, pp. 425–432.

[73] Lisa F. Rau, Paul S. Jacobs, Uri Zernik, Information extraction and text summarization using linguistic knowledge acquisition, Information Processing & Management 25 (4) (1989) 419–428.

[74] Xu Wei, Grishman Ralph, Meyers Adam, Ritter Alan, A preliminary study of tweet summarization using information extraction, in: Proceedings of the Workshop on Language Analysis in Social Media, Association for Computational Linguistics, 2013, pp. 20–29.

[75] Zubiaga Arkaitz, Spina Damiano, Martinez Raquel, Fresno Victor, Real-time classification of Twitter trends, Journal of the Association for Information Science and Technology 66 (3) (2015) 462–473.

[76] Chang Yi, Wang Xuanhui, Mei Qiaozhu, Liu Yan, Towards Twitter context summarization with user influence models, in: Proceedings of the Sixth ACM International Conference on Web Search and Data Mining, WSDM '13, ACM, New York, NY, USA, 2013, pp. 527–536.

[77] Yajuan Duan, Zhimin Chen, Furu Wei, Zhou Ming, Shum Heung-Yeung, Twitter topic summarization by ranking tweets using social influence and content quality, in: Proceedings of the 24th International Conference on Computational Linguistics, 2012, pp. 763–780.

[78] Becker Hila, Naaman Mor, Gravano Luis, Selecting quality Twitter content for events, 2011.

[79] Arkaitz Zubiaga, Damiano Spina, Enrique Amigó, Julio Gonzalo, Towards real-time summarization of scheduled events from Twitter streams, in: Proceedings of the 23rd ACM Conference on Hypertext and Social Media, HT '12, ACM, New York, NY, USA, 2012, pp. 319–320.

[80] Shou Lidan, Wang Zhenhua, Chen Ke, Chen Gang, Sumblr: continuous summarization of evolving tweet streams, in: Proceedings of the 36th International ACM SIGIR Conference on Research and Development in Information Retrieval, SIGIR '13, ACM, New York, NY, USA, 2013, pp. 533–542.

[81] Andrei Olariu, Efficient online summarization of microblogging streams, in: Proc. EACL (Short Paper), 2014, pp. 236–240.

[82] Z. Wang, L. Shou, K. Chen, G. Chen, S. Mehrotra, On summarization and timeline generation for evolutionary tweet streams, IEEE Transactions on Knowledge and Data Engineering 27 (2015) 1301–1314.

[83] Gunes Erkan, Dragomir R. Radev, LexRank: graph-based lexical centrality as salience in text summarization, in: Artificial Intelligence Research, vol. 22, 2004, pp. 457–479.

[84] Soumi Dutta, Sujata Ghatak, Moumita Roy, Saptarshi Ghosh, Asit Kumar Das, A graph based clustering technique for tweet summarization, in: Reliability, Infocom Technologies and Optimization (ICRITO) (Trends and Future Directions), Sept 2015, pp. 1–6.

[85] Nichols Jeffrey, Mahmud Jalal, Drews Clemens, Summarizing sporting events using Twitter, in: Proc. ACM International Conference on Intelligent User Interfaces (IUI), 2012, pp. 189–198.

[86] Gillani Mehreen, U. Ilyas Muhammad, Saleh Saad, S. Alowibdi Jalal, Aljohani Naif, S. Alotaibi Fahad, Post summarization of microblogs of sporting events, in: Proc. International Conference on World Wide Web (WWW) Companion, 2017, pp. 59–68.

[87] Deepayan Chakrabarti, Kunal Punera, Event summarization using tweets, in: Proc. 6th AAAI Int. Conf. on Weblogs and Social Media, 2011, pp. 340–348.

[88] Takamura Hiroya, Yokono Hikaru, Okumura Manabu, Summarizing a document stream, in: Clough Paul, Foley Colum, Gurrin Cathal, J.F. Jones Gareth, Kraaij Wessel, Lee Hyowon, Mudoch Vanessa (Eds.), Advances in Information Retrieval, Springer Berlin Heidelberg, Berlin, Heidelberg, 2011, pp. 177–188.

[89] Muhammad Asif Hossain Khan, Danushka Bollegala, Guangwen Liu, Kaoru Sezaki, Multi tweet summarization of real-time events, in: Proceedings of the 2013 International Conference on Social Computing, SOCIALCOM '13, Washington, DC, USA, 2013, pp. 128–133.

[90] Osborne Miles, Moran Sean, McCreadie Richard, Von Lunen Alexander, Sykora Martin, Cano Elizabeth, Ireson Neil, Macdonald Craig, Ounis Iadh, He Yulan, Jackson Tom, Ciravegna Fabio, O'Brien Ann, Real-time detection, tracking, and monitoring of automatically discovered events in social media, in: Proceedings of 52nd Annual Meeting of the Association for Computational Linguistics: System Demonstrations, Association for Computational Linguistics, 2014, pp. 37–42.

[91] Chris Kedzie, Kathleen McKeown, Fernando Diaz, Predicting salient updates for disaster summarization, in: Proceedings of the 53rd Annual Meeting of the Association for Computational Linguistics and the 7th International Joint Conference on Natural Language Processing (Volume 1: Long Papers), Association for Computational Linguistics, 2015, pp. 1608–1617.

[92] Rudra Koustav, Ghosh Subham, Goyal Pawan, Ganguly Niloy, Ghosh Saptarshi, Extracting situational information from microblogs during disaster events: a classification-summarization approach, in: Proc. ACM CIKM, 2015.

[93] Nguyen Minh-Tien, Kitamoto Asanobu, Nguyen Tri-Thanh, Tsum4act: a framework for retrieving and summarizing actionable tweets during a disaster for reaction, in: Cao Tru, Lim Ee-Peng, Zhou Zhi-Hua, Ho Tu-Bao, Cheung David, Motoda Hiroshi (Eds.), Advances in Knowledge Discovery and Data Mining, Springer International Publishing, Cham, 2015, pp. 64–75.

[94] Parth Mehta, Prasenjit Majumder, Effective aggregation of various summarization techniques, Information Processing & Management 54 (2) (2018) 145–158.

[95] Stuart Mackie, Richard McCreadie, Craig Macdonald, Iadh Ounis, Comparing algorithms for microblog summarisation, in: CLEF, in: Lecture Notes in Computer Science, vol. 8685, Springer, 2014, pp. 153–159.

[96] I. Inouye David, K. Kalita Jugal, Comparing Twitter summarization algorithms for multiple post summaries, in: Proc. IEEE SocialCom / PASSAT, 2011, pp. 298–306.

[97] K. Kevin Dela Rosa, R. Rushin Shah, B. Bo Lin, A. Anatole Gershman, R. Robert Frederking, Topical clustering of tweets, in: Proc. of the ACM SIGIR: SWSM (2011), 2011, pp. 298–306.

[98] P. Sharifi Beaux, I. Inouye David, K. Kalita Jugal, Summarization of Twitter microblogs, Computer Journal (2013), bxt109.

[99] Chin-Yew Lin, ROUGE: a package for automatic evaluation of summaries, in: Proc. Workshop on Text Summarization Branches Out, ACL, 2004, pp. 74–81.

[100] H.A. Madni, Z. Anwar, M.A. Shah, Data mining techniques and applications, a decade review, in: 2017 23rd International Conference on Automation and Computing (ICAC), Sept 2017, pp. 1–7.

[101] P. Hailong, Z. Hui, L. Wanglong, M. Ying, The research on the improved ant colony text clustering algorithm, in: 2017 IEEE 2nd International Conference on Big Data Analysis (ICBDA), March 2017, pp. 323–328.

[102] Bhatnagar Vikas, Majhi Ritanjali, Jena Pradyot Ranjan, Comparative performance evaluation of clustering algorithms for grouping manufacturing firms, Arabian Journal for Science and Engineering 43 (Aug 2017) 4071–4083.

[103] S. Baillargeon, S. Hallé, C. Gagné, Stream clustering of tweets, in: 2016 IEEE/ACM International Conference on Advances in Social Networks Analysis and Mining (ASONAM), Aug 2016, pp. 1256–1261.

[104] C.H. Lee, C.H. Hung, S.J. Lee, A comparative study on clustering algorithms, in: 2013 14th ACIS International Conference on Software Engineering, Artificial Intelligence, Networking and Parallel/Distributed Computing, July 2013, pp. 557–562.

[105] Servia-Rodríguez Sandra, Vilas Ana, Díaz Redondo Rebeca, Pazos-Arias Jose, Comparing tag clustering algorithms for mining Twitter users' interests, in: 2013 International Conference on Social Computing, Sept 2013, pp. 679–684.

[106] Celebi M. Emre, Partitional Clustering Algorithms, Springer Publishing Company, Incorporated, 2014.

[107] Kanungo Tapas, M. Mount David, S. Netanyahu Nathan, D. Piatko Christine, Silverman Ruth, Y. Wu Angela, An efficient k-means clustering algorithm: analysis and implementation, IEEE Transactions on Pattern Analysis and Machine Intelligence 24 (7) (July 2002) 881–892.

[108] D. McNicholas Paul, Murphy Thomas Brendan, Model-based clustering of microarray expression data via latent Gaussian mixture models, Bioinformatics 26 (21) (2010) 2705–2712.

[109] V. Tetko Igor, J. Livingstone David, I. Luik Alexander, Neural network studies. 1. Comparison of overfitting and overtraining, Journal of Chemical Information and Computer Sciences 35 (5) (1995) 826–833.

[110] M.I. Petrovskiy, Outlier detection algorithms in data mining systems, Programming and Computer Software 29 (4) (Jul 2003) 228–237.

[111] Enbo Zhou, S. Mao, Mei Li, Zhenming Sun, Pam spatial clustering algorithm research based on cuda, in: 2016 24th International Conference on Geoinformatics, Aug 2016, pp. 1–7.

[112] Kobren Ari, Monath Nicholas, Krishnamurthy Akshay, McCallum Andrew, A hierarchical algorithm for extreme clustering, in: Proceedings of the 23rd ACM SIGKDD International Conference on Knowledge Discovery and Data Mining, KDD '17, ACM, New York, NY, USA, 2017, pp. 255–264.

[113] Dash Manoranjan, Petrutiu Simona, Scheuermann Peter, Efficient parallel hierarchical clustering, in: Danelutto Marco, Vanneschi Marco, Laforenza Domenico (Eds.), Euro-Par 2004 Parallel Processing, Springer Berlin Heidelberg, Berlin, Heidelberg, 2004, pp. 363–371.

[114] S. Das, A. Abraham, A. Konar, Automatic clustering using an improved differential evolution algorithm, IEEE Transactions on Systems, Man and Cybernetics. Part A. Systems and Humans 38 (1) (Jan 2008) 218–237.

[115] Sudipto Guha, Rajeev Rastogi, Kyuseok Shim, Cure: an efficient clustering algorithm for large databases, Information Systems 26 (1) (2001) 35–58.

[116] S. Guha, K. Shim, R. Rastogi, Rock: a robust clustering algorithm for categorical attributes, in: Proceedings 15th International Conference on Data Engineering (Cat. No. 99CB36337), Mar 1999, pp. 512–521.

[117] G. Karypis, Eui-Hong Han, V. Kumar, Chameleon: hierarchical clustering using dynamic modeling, Computer 32 (8) (Aug 1999) 68–75.

[118] Zhang Tian, Ramakrishnan Raghu, Livny Miron, Birch: an efficient data clustering method for very large databases, SIGMOD Record 25 (2) (June 1996) 103–114.

[119] L. Kaufman, P.J. Rousseeuw, Finding Groups in Data: an Introduction to Cluster Analysis, Wiley, 1990.

[120] SWare Vivek, H.N. Bharathi, Study of density based algorithms, International Journal of Computer Applications 69 (05 2013) 1–4.

[121] R. Prabahari, Dr.V. Thiagarasu, Density based clustering using Gaussian estimation technique, in: Density Based Clustering Using Gaussian Estimation Technique, vol. 2, 2015, pp. 4078–4081.

[122] X. Que, F. Checconi, F. Petrini, J.A. Gunnels, Scalable community detection with the Louvain algorithm, in: 2015 IEEE International Parallel and Distributed Processing Symposium, May 2015, pp. 28–37.

[123] Infomap - community detection, http://www.mapequation.org/code.html.

[124] K. Jain Anil, C. Dubes Richard, Algorithms for Clustering Data, Prentice-Hall, Inc., Upper Saddle River, NJ, USA, 1988.

[125] L. Davies David, W. Bouldin Donald, A cluster separation measure, IEEE Transactions on Pattern Analysis and Machine Intelligence 1 (2) (February 1979) 224–227.

[126] U. Maulik, S. Bandyopadhyay, Performance evaluation of some clustering algorithms and validity indices, IEEE Transactions on Pattern Analysis and Machine Intelligence 24 (12) (Dec 2002) 1650–1654.

[127] H. Cui, K. Zhang, Y. Fang, S. Sobolevsky, C. Ratti, B.K.P. Horn, A clustering validity index based on pairing frequency, IEEE Access 5 (2017) 24884–24894.

[128] R. Xu, J. Xu, D.C. Wunsch, A comparison study of validity indices on swarm-intelligence-based clustering, IEEE Transactions on Systems, Man and Cybernetics. Part B. Cybernetics 42 (4) (Aug 2012) 1243–1256.

[129] Rousseeuw Peter, Silhouettes: a graphical aid to the interpretation and validation of cluster analysis, Journal of Computational and Applied Mathematics 20 (1) (November 1987) 53–65.

[130] Muranishi Mai, Honda Katsuhiro, Notsu Akira, Xie-beni-type fuzzy cluster validation in fuzzy co-clustering of documents and keywords, in: Young Im Cho, Eric T. Matson (Eds.), Soft Computing in Artificial Intelligence, Springer International Publishing, Cham, 2014, pp. 29–38.

[131] A.K. Jain, M.N. Murty, P.J. Flynn, Data clustering: a review, ACM Computing Surveys 31 (3) (September 1999) 264–323.

[132] Mathioudakis Michael, Koudas Nick, Twittermonitor: trend detection over the Twitter stream, in: Proceedings of the 2010 ACM SIGMOD International Conference on Management of Data, SIGMOD '10, ACM, 2010, pp. 1155–1158.

[133] Michelson Matthew, A. Macskassy Sofus, Discovering users' topics of interest on Twitter: a first look, in: Proceedings of the Fourth Workshop on Analytics for Noisy Unstructured Text Data, AND '10, ACM, 2010, pp. 73–80.

[134] H. Becker, M. Naaman, L. Gravano, Beyond trending topics: real-world event identification on Twitter, in: Fifth International AAAI Conference on Weblogs and Social Media, 2011.

[135] Cataldi Mario, Di Caro Luigi, Claudio Schifanella, Emerging topic detection on Twitter based on temporal and social terms evaluation, in: Proceedings of the Tenth International Workshop on Multimedia Data Mining, MDMKDD '10, ACM, 2010, pp. 4:1–4:10.

[136] Hill Shawndra, Benton Adrian, Ungar Lyle, Macskassy Sofus, Chung Annie, H. Holmes John, A cluster-based method for isolating influence on Twitter, 2016.

[137] Brendan J. Frey, Delbert Dueck, Clustering by passing messages between data points, Science 315 (2007) 2007.

[138] Cheong Marc, C.S. Lee Vincent, A study on detecting patterns in Twitter intra-topic user and message clustering, in: ICPR, IEEE Computer Society, 2010, pp. 3125–3128.

[139] Thomas Anisha Mariam, M.G. Resmipriya, An efficient text classification scheme using clustering, Procedia Technology 24 (2016) 1220–1225.

[140] Yang Jaewon, Leskovec Jure, Patterns of temporal variation in online media, in: Proceedings of the Fourth ACM International Conference on Web Search and Data Mining, ACM, 2011, pp. 177–186.

[141] Dueck Delbert, Affinity propagation: clustering data by passing messages, PhD thesis, Citeseer, 2009.

[142] Rangrej Aniket, Kulkarni Sayali, Ashish V. Tendulkar, Comparative study of clustering techniques for short text documents, in: Proceedings of the 20th International Conference Companion on World Wide Web, ACM, 2011, pp. 111–112.

[143] Chao Zhang, Dongming Lei, Quan Yuan, Honglei Zhuang, Lance M. Kaplan, Shaowen Wang, Jiawei Han, Geoburst+: effective and real-time local event detection in geo-tagged tweet streams, ACM TIST 9 (3) (2018) 34:1–34:24.

[144] R.H. Sheikh, M.M. Raghuwanshi, A.N. Jaiswal, Genetic algorithm based clustering: a survey, in: 2008 First International Conference on Emerging Trends in Engineering and Technology, July 2008, pp. 314–319.

[145] Ujjwal Maulik, Sanghamitra Bandyopadhyay, Genetic algorithm-based clustering technique, Pattern Recognition 33 (9) (2000) 1455–1465.

[146] Adel Amr, E. El Fakharany, Badr Amr, Clustering tweets using cellular genetic algorithm, Journal of Computer Science 10 (01 2014) 1269–1280.

[147] Mustafa H. Hajeer, Alka Singh, Dipankar Dasgupta, Sugata Sanyal, Clustering online social network communities using genetic algorithms, CoRR, arXiv:1312.2237 [abs], 2013.

[148] C. Aggarwal Charu, Zhai ChengXiang, A survey of text clustering algorithms, in: Charu C. Aggarwal, ChengXiang Zhai (Eds.), Mining Text Data, Springer, 2012, pp. 77–128.

[149] Genc Yegin, Sakamoto Yasuaki, V. Nickerson Jeffrey, Discovering context: classifying tweets through a semantic transform based on Wikipedia, in: Proceedings of the 6th International Conference on Foundations of Augmented Cognition: Directing the Future of Adaptive Systems, FAC'11, Springer-Verlag, 2011, pp. 484–492.

[150] Ramage Daniel, T. Dumais Susan, Daniel J. Liebling, Characterizing microblogs with topic models, in: ICWSM, The AAAI Press, 2010.

[151] Soumi Dutta, Sujata Ghatak, Saptarshi Ghosh, Asit Kumar Das, A genetic algorithm based tweet clustering technique, in: Computer Communication and Informatics (ICCCI), Jan 2017, pp. 1–6.

[152] Dutta Soumi, Ghatak Sujata, Das Asit, Manan Gupta, Dasgupta Sayantika, Feature selection based clustering on micro-blogging data, in: International Conference on Computational Intelligence in Data Mining (ICCIDM-2017), Nov 2017, pp. 885–895.

CHAPTER 3

Data collection using Twitter API

3.1 Introduction

Microblogging sites such as Twitter, Facebook, LinkedIn are popular websites. The Twitter microblogging site is one of the most popular websites on the Web today, where millions of users post real-time messages (tweets) on different topics of interest. The content that becomes popular on Twitter (i.e., discussed by a large number of users) on a certain day can be used for a variety of purposes, including recommendation of popular content and marketing and advertisement campaigns. One of the most interesting features of Twitter is its real-time nature – at any given instance of time, millions of Twitter users are exchanging views on various topics or incidents/events that are happening currently in any corner of the world. Hence, the content posted in Twitter is very useful to gather real-time news on a variety of topics [1]. This section describes the dataset used in several experiments of the chapter work. The Twitter online social network (OSN) provides an API to collect different forms of data, including streams of tweets posted on the website and profile details of particular users. Especially, Twitter provides a 1% random sample of all tweets posted on the Twitter website worldwide [1].

3.2 Experimental dataset description

This chapter focuses on analysis of microblog datasets using data mining techniques – such as data preprocessing [2], clustering [3], spam classification [4], attribute selection [5], and summarization [6] of samples with the aim of making researchers aware of the benefits of such techniques when analyzing microblog datasets [7]. The datasets are used in different experiments described here.

3.2.1 Experimental dataset for cluster analysis and summarization

Millions of messages are posted everyday on microblogs during any emergency event, such as natural calamities, elections, sports events like IPL, the world cup, the Hyderabad bomb explosion, the Uttarakhand flood, and

Data Analytics for Social Microblogging Platforms
https://doi.org/10.1016/B978-0-32-391785-8.00014-7

the Sandy Hook shooting. During emergency events, thousands of tweets are posted in short durations of time, and since time is critical during such events, it is necessary to get a quick overview of the situation. In such scenario, an effective way to reduce the information load on the user is to cluster similar messages, so that the user might see only a few of the messages from each cluster. So, one of the primary applications of clustering is to reduce information overload during emergency events. When a lot of messages (such as tweets) are posted in short intervals of time, time is critical. Hence this chapter focuses on clustering of tweets posted during some specific emergency events [8].

The Twitter microblogging site is one of the most popular websites on the Web today, where millions of users post real-time messages (tweets) on different topics of their interest. The content that becomes popular on Twitter (i.e., discussed by a large number of users) on a certain day can be used for a variety of purposes, including recommendation of popular content and marketing and advertisement campaigns [9]. One of the most interesting features of Twitter is its real-time nature – at any given instance of time, millions of Twitter users are exchanging views on various topics or incidents/events that are happening currently in any corner of the world [8]. Hence, the content posted on Twitter is very useful to gather real-time news on a variety of topics.

This section describes the dataset used in several experiments of the chapter. The Twitter OSN provides an API5 to collect different forms of data, including streams of tweets posted on the website and profile details of particular users. Especially, Twitter provides a 1% random sample of all tweets posted on the Twitter website worldwide [10]. For experiments, relevant tweets are collected and posted during each event through the Twitter API [11] using keyword-based matching. For instance, the keywords "Hyderabad," "bomb," and "blast" were used to identify tweets related to the HDBlast event, while the keywords "Sandyhook" and "shooting" were used to collect tweets related to the SHShoot event [12]. Initially, the chronologically earliest 5000 tweets for each event are considered. It is known that tweets often contain duplicates and near-duplicates since the same information is frequently retweeted/reposted by multiple users [13].

Tweets are considered during the following emergency events.

1. **HDBlast** – Two bomb explosions in the city of Hyderabad, India [14].
2. **SHShoot** – An assailant killed 20 children and 6 adults at the Sandy Hook elementary school in Connecticut, USA [15].

Table 3.1 A sample dataset of the Uttarakhand flood.

Tweet ID	Tweets
1	58 dead, over 58,000 trapped as rain batters Uttarakhand, UP.may god save d rest.NO RAIN is a problem.RAIN is a bigger problem.
2	Heavy rains wreak havoc in Uttarakhand, flood warning in UP, Delhi http://t.co/WOrNLlbmOp.
3	Harbhajan Singh stuck in Uttarakhand rains, tweets he's fine http://t.co/q0tTeZCpiZ.
4	RT @BJPRajnathSingh: I appeal to all BJP workers in Uttarakhand to provide every possible help and relief to flood affected people.
5	RT @amitvkaushik: Uttarakhand flood. Helpline numbers are: 0135-2710335, 2710233.

3. **UFlood** – Devastating floods and landslides in the Uttaranchal state of India [16].
4. **THagupit** – A strong cyclone code-named Typhoon Hagupit hit Philippines [17].

Note that the selected events include both man–made and natural disasters occurring in various regions of the world. Hence, the vocabulary and linguistic style in the tweets can be expected to be diverse as well. A sample dataset of five tweets is shown in Table 3.1. The tweets are derived from a dataset of tweets posted during the floods in the Uttaranchal state of India in 2013 [18]. Hence, the vocabulary and linguistic style in the tweets can be expected to be diverse as well [8,19]. It is known that tweets often contain duplicates and near-duplicates since the same information is frequently retweeted/reposted by multiple users [13].

Generating golden standard clusters

To analyze the performance of clustering algorithms, a golden standard needs to be developed with which the clustering obtained by various algorithms will be compared. It is customary to obtain the golden standard clustering through human feedback [20]. Three human volunteers were asked to identify the different types of information contained in the tweets and to cluster/group the tweets according to the type of information [9]. The observations of each of the human volunteers were similar – they recognized five distinct types of information in the tweet datasets:

(1) tweets informing about casualties or damage to assets,
(2) tweets giving climate-related updates,
(3) tweets giving helpline-related information,

Table 3.2 Examples of tweets related to the Uttaranchal flood event. Tweets including five different types of information were identified by human volunteers.

Information type	Sample tweet text
Casualties Info	8 dead, 3700 pilgrims stranded as incessant rains batter Uttarakhand: Eight persons were killed on Sunday.
	100 houses collapse; 25 dead, over 50 missing as rain batters Uttarakhand http://t.co/m8zrc3PQub.
Climate Info	RT-ANI_news: In Uttarkashi *Uttarakhand*, flash floods triggered by heavy rains wash away houses along the river.
	RT-kirankhurana: 02/05 Destruction in Uttarakhand due to Heavy Rains:-joinAAP
Helpline info	RT-PIB_India: IAF launches operation 'Rahat' to help stranded pilgrims & tourists in Uttarakhand & HP.
	RT-rahulmanthattil: #Uttarakhand flood helpline numbers: 0135-2710334, 0135-2710335, 0135-2710233. Please share ! -annavetticad.
Public opinion	Prayers for Uttarakhand. Just shows you should never take life for granted.
	Irony: the relatives of the Kedarnath flood victims praying to the same gods that the victims had so devotedly gone to visit.
Political news	RT-IndiaSpeaksPR: Rahul Gandhi promises to reach out to the victims in Kedarnath once Congress confirms that it would be secular to do so.
	Seems CM Vijay Bahuguna has no time to utter a few words of comfort to the people of #Uttarakhand, who are dealing with life & death.#shame.

(4) conclusions of the general population, sympathy, and petitions for the influenced population, and

(5) news about government/political actions with respect to the disaster.

Table 3.2 shows examples of tweets of each type related to the UFlood event. Consequently, the golden standard (created by human volunteers) clusters the tweets in five groups.

3.2.2 Experimental dataset for attribute selection

To demonstrate the utility of the proposed attribute selection methodology, the methodology is applied over five different datasets, one of which is collected by us, and the other four are from prior works on spam classification on OSNs [10].

Table 3.3 Description of datasets from prior works, used to demonstrate utility of the proposed attribute selection algorithm.

Dataset ID	Instances	Attributes	Classes	Reference
Dataset 1	1065	63	non-spammers and spammers	[22]
Dataset 2	829	60	promoters, spammers, and legitimates	[23]
Dataset 3	2762	23	spam and non-spam	[25]
Dataset 4	7076	60	spam and non-spam	[26]

3.2.2.1 Datasets from prior works

The datasets collected from prior works on spam classification on OSNs are described here [21]. The datasets used here made are public by the following four studies. The datasets are also summarized in Table 3.3.

1. **Dataset 1** – Benevenuto et al. [22] prepared a dataset of 1065 user accounts on Twitter, classified into two classes – spammers and non-spammers. The classification is based on 62 attributes that capture various characteristics of the user accounts. The dataset file is in LibSVM input file format. Each line represents a user from our test collection. The attributes are listed below.
   - **(a)** Number of followers per followee
   - **(b)** Fraction of tweets replied
   - **(c)** Fraction of tweets with spam words
   - **(d)** Fraction of tweets with URLs
   - **(e)** Existence of spam words in the screen name
   - **(f)** Number of hashtags per number of words on each tweet (mean)
   - **(g)** Number of hashtags per number of words on each tweet (median)
   - **(h)** Number of hashtags per number of words on each tweet (min)
   - **(i)** Number of hashtags per number of words on each tweet (max)
   - **(j)** Number of URLs per number of words on each tweet (mean)
   - **(k)** Number of URLs per number of words on each tweet (median)
   - **(l)** Number of URLs per number of words on each tweet (min)
   - **(m)** Number of URLs per number of words on each tweet (max)
   - **(n)** Number of characters per tweet (mean)
   - **(o)** Number of characters per tweet (median)
   - **(p)** Number of characters per tweet (min)
   - **(q)** Number of characters per tweet (max)
   - **(r)** Number of hashtags per tweet (mean)
   - **(s)** Number of hashtags per tweet (median)
   - **(t)** Number of hashtags per tweet (min)

(u)   Number of hashtags per tweet (max)
(v)   Number of mentions per tweet (mean)
(w)   Number of mentions per tweet (median)
(x)   Number of mentions per tweet (min)
(y)   Number of mentions per tweet (max)
(z)   Number of numeric characters per tweet (mean)
(aa) Number of numeric characters per tweet (median)
(ab) Number of numeric characters per tweet (min)
(ac) Number of numeric characters per tweet (max)
(ad) Number of URLs on each tweet (mean)
(ae) Number of URLs on each tweet (median)
(af) Number of URLs on each tweet (min)
(ag) Number of URLs on each tweet (max)
(ah) Number of words per tweet (mean)
(ai) Number of words per tweet (median)
(aj) Number of words per tweet (min)
(ak) Number of words per tweet (max)
(al) Number of times the tweet has been retweeted (mean), counted by the presence of "RT @username" in the text
(am) Number of times the tweet has been retweeted (median), counted by the presence of "RT @username" in the text
(an) Number of times the tweet has been retweeted (min), counted by the presence of "RT @username" in the text
(ao) Number of times the tweet has been retweeted (max), counted by the presence of "RT @username" in the text
(ap) Number of followees
(aq) Number of followers
(ar) Number of tweets
(as) Number of followees of a user's followers
(at) Number of times mentioned
(au) Number of times the user was replied
(av) Number of times the user replied
(aw) Number of tweets of a user's followees
(ax) Time between posts (mean)
(ay) Time between posts (median)
(az) Time between posts (min)
(ba) Time between posts (max)
(bb) Number of posted tweets per day (mean)
(bc) Number of posted tweets per day (median)

(bd) Number of posted tweets per day (min)

(be) Number of posted tweets per day (max)

(bf) Number of posted tweets per week (mean)

(bg) Number of posted tweets per week (median)

(bh) Number of posted tweets per week (min)

(bi) Number of posted tweets per week (max)

(bj) Age of the user account

2. **Dataset 2** – This dataset was also prepared by Benevenuto et al. [23], to classify three types of users in online video networks – legitimate users, spammers, and content promoters [24]. The dataset contains 60 attributes consisting of video attributes (which capture specific properties of the videos uploaded by each user), attributes of the social relationships established between users (from video response interaction), and attributes capturing individual characteristics of user behavior. The dataset file is in LibSVM input file format. The attributes are listed below.

(a) Total number of views of all videos uploaded

(b) Total number of views of all video responses

(c) Total number of views of all responded videos

(d) Total duration of all videos uploaded

(e) Total duration of all video responses

(f) Total duration of all responded videos

(g) Total number of ratings of all videos uploaded

(h) Total number of ratings of all video responses

(i) Total number of ratings of all responded videos

(j) Total number of comments of all videos uploaded

(k) Total number of comments of all video responses

(l) Total number of comments of all responded videos

(m) Total number of times that all videos uploaded were added as favorite

(n) Total number of times that all video responses were added as favorite

(o) Total number of times that all responded videos were added as favorite

(p) Total number of honors of all videos uploaded

(q) Total number of honors of all video responses

(r) Total number of honors of all responded videos

(s) Total number of links of all videos uploaded

(t) Total number of links of all video responses

(u)   Total number of links of all responded videos

(v)   Average number of views of all videos uploaded

(w)   Average number of views of all video responses

(x)   Average number of views of all responded videos

(y)   Average duration of all videos uploaded

(z)   Average duration of all video responses

(aa) Average duration of all responded videos

(ab) Average number of ratings of all videos uploaded

(ac) Average number of ratings of all video responses

(ad) Average number of ratings of all responded videos

(ae) Average number of comments of all videos uploaded

(af) Average number of comments of all video responses

(ag) Average number of comments of all responded videos

(ah) Average number of times that all videos uploaded were added as favorite

(ai) Average number of times that all video responses were added as favorite

(aj) Average number of times that all responded videos were added as favorite

(ak) Average number of honors of all videos uploaded

(al) Average number of honors of all video responses

(am) Average number of honors of all responded videos

(an) Average number of links of all videos uploaded

(ao) Average number of links of all video responses

(ap) Average number of links of all responded videos

(aq) Clustering coefficient

(ar) Reciprocity

(as) User rank

(at) Betweenness

(au) Assortativity: in–in degree

(av) Assortativity: in–out degree

(aw) Assortativity: out–in degree

(ax) Assortativity: out–out degree

(ay) Number of responses posted

(az) Number of responses received

(ba) Number of friends

(bb) Number of videos watched

(bc) Number of videos uploaded

(bd) Number of videos added as favorite

(be) Number of subscriptions

(bf) Number of subscribers

(bg) Maximum number of videos uploaded in 24 hours

(bh) Average time between video uploads

3. **Dataset 3** – This dataset is about "tip spam" in location-based social networks. Prepared by Costa et al. [25], the dataset consists of 2762 instances, 41 attributes, and two classes (spam and non-spam). The dataset file is in Weka ARFF input file format. The attributes are listed below.

(a) Clicks on the link "This tip helped me"

(b) Clicks on the link "Report abuse"

(c) Number of places registered by the user

(d) Number of tips posted by the user

(e) Number of photos posted by the user

(f) Number of clicks on the place page

(g) Number of tips on the place

(h) Place rating

(i) Clicks on the link "Thumbs down"

(j) Clicks on the link "Thumbs up"

(k) Similarity score (average)

(l) Similarity score (max)

(m) Similarity score (min)

(n) Similarity score (median)

(o) Similarity score (standard deviation)

(p) Number of spam words and spam rules

(q) Number of capital letters

(r) Number of numeric characters

(s) Number of phone numbers on the text

(t) Number of email addresses on the text

(u) Number of URLs on the text

(v) Number of contact information on the text

(w) Number of words

(x) Number of words in capital

(y) Distance among all places reviewed by the user (average)

(z) Distance among all places reviewed by the user (max)

(aa) Distance among all places reviewed by the user (min)

(ab) Distance among all places reviewed by the user (median)

(ac) Distance among all places reviewed by the user (standard deviation)

(ad) Clustering coefficient

(ae) Reciprocity
(af) Number of followers (in–degree)
(ag) Number of followees (out–degree)
(ah) Number of followers per followee
(ai) Degree
(aj) Betweenness
(ak) Assortativity (in–in)
(al) Assortativity (in–out)
(am) Assortativity (out–in)
(an) Assortativity (out–out)
(ao) PageRank
(ap) Class (spam or non-spam)

4. **Dataset 4** – This dataset, also prepared by Costa et al. [26], is similar to the above one (on spam in location-based social networks). But this dataset is larger, consisting of 7076 instances and 60 attributes [18, 27]. The last attribute is the review class with additional information about the sub-classes of spam (i.e., "pollution," "bad-mouthing," "local marketing," and "non-spam"). The dataset file is in Weka ARFF input file format. The attributes are listed below.

(a) Clicks on the link "This tip helped me"
(b) Clicks on the link "Report abuse"
(c) Number of places registered by the user
(d) Number of tips posted by the user
(e) Number of photos posted by the user
(f) Number of clicks on the place page
(g) Number of tips on the place
(h) Place rating
(i) Clicks on the link "Thumbs down"
(j) Clicks on the link "Thumbs up"
(k) Similarity score (average)
(l) Similarity score (max)
(m) Similarity score (min)
(n) Similarity score (median)
(o) Similarity score (standard deviation)
(p) Number of distinct 1-gram
(q) Fraction of 1-gram
(r) Number of distinct 2-gram
(s) Fraction of 2-gram
(t) Number of distinct 3-gram

- **(u)** Fraction of 3-gram
- **(v)** Number of spam words and spam rules
- **(w)** Number of capital letters
- **(x)** Number of numeric characters
- **(y)** Number of phone numbers in the text
- **(z)** Number of email addresses in the text
- **(aa)** Number of URLs in the text
- **(ab)** Number of contact information in the text
- **(ac)** Number of words
- **(ad)** Number of words in capital
- **(ae)** Distance among all places reviewed by the user (average)
- **(af)** Distance among all places reviewed by the user (max)
- **(ag)** Distance among all places reviewed by the user (min)
- **(ah)** Distance among all places reviewed by the user (median)
- **(ai)** Distance among all places reviewed by the user (standard deviation)
- **(aj)** Number of offensive words in the text
- **(ak)** Value of "Has offensive word"
- **(al)** Clustering coefficient
- **(am)** Reciprocity
- **(an)** Number of followers (in-degree)
- **(ao)** Number of followees (out-degree)
- **(ap)** Number of followers per followee
- **(aq)** Degree
- **(ar)** Betweenness
- **(as)** Assortativity (in-in)
- **(at)** Assortativity (in-out)
- **(au)** Assortativity (out-in)
- **(av)** Assortativity (out-out)
- **(aw)** PageRank
- **(ax)** Number of different areas where the user posted a tip
- **(ay)** Tip focus of a user
- **(az)** Tip entropy of a user
- **(ba)** SentiWordNet
- **(bb)** Emoticons
- **(bc)** PANAS-t
- **(bd)** SASA
- **(be)** SenticNet
- **(bf)** Happiness index

(bg)   SentiStrength
(bh)   Combined-method
(bi)   Class 1 (spam or non-spam)
(bj)   Class 2 (pollution, bad-mouthing, local marketing, or non-spam)

3.2.2.2 Collected dataset of spam tweets

For the experiment Dataset 5 was prepared to distinguish spam and legitimate tweets posted on the Twitter OSN. A crawler was also designed using the Twitter API [11] to collect the 1% random sample of tweets provided publicly by Twitter over a duration of two days [28]. Out of all the tweets collected, focus was placed on tweets which contained URLs, since spam is always disseminated through URLs to spam websites. In total, 343,791 tweets were collected containing URLs. The next step was to identify spam tweets and legitimate tweets (i.e., preparing the golden standard) [29,30].

Identification of spam tweets

Spam tweets are identified as follows by checking whether any of the URL(s) contained in a tweet is *blacklisted*. Since tweets are restricted to 140 characters, URLs are almost always shortened; hence, all URLs contained in the tweets are expanded by following HTTP redirects, to get the final landing URL [18]. Finally, each URL was checked (both the shortened version contained in the tweet and the final landing URL) using a variety of spam blacklists – Google Safe Browsing [31], SURBL [32], Capture-HPC [33], and Spamhaus [34]. A tweet was considered to be spam if any of the URLs contained in it (or the expanded version of any of the URLs) was found to be blacklisted; otherwise the tweet was considered legitimate [35]. In total, 93,791 tweets were identified as spam, while the rest were considered legitimate [20].

Note that the dataset developed by the above methodology has a potential limitation – some of the tweets that are considered as legitimate may actually contain spam URLs which could not be detected by the blacklists used. However, given the large number of URLs posted every day on Twitter, it is infeasible to manually verify URLs; hence the use of blacklists is the only practical option, as also used by prior studies [36,37].

3.2.2.3 Attributes for spam vs. legitimate classification

A set of 23 attributes were extracted for each of the tweets in the labeled collection. These attributes, which are described in Table 3.4, can be broadly grouped into the following three categories:

Table 3.4 List of attributes for the spam tweets dataset (Dataset 5).

Sl.	Attribute name	Brief description
Tweet text-based attributes		
1	word count	Number of words in the tweet
2	unique character count	Number of unique characters in the tweet
3	digits count	Number of numerals in the tweet
4	hashtag count	Number of hashtags mentioned in tweet
5	hashtags per word	Number of hashtags/number of words
6	position of hashtag	Position of a hashtag in the tweet
7	swear words count	Number of swear words in the tweet
8	spam words in tweet count	Number of spam words in the tweet
URL-based attributes		
(in case tweet contains multiple URLs, mean over all URLs)		
9	URL count	Number of URL in the tweet
10	URLs per word	Number of URLs per word in the tweet
11	expanded URL length	Length of expanded URL
12	dot in expanded URL	Number of dots used in expanded URL
13	no. of sub-domains	Number of sub-domains
14	no. of redirections	Number of redirections
User profile-based attributes		
(based on the user u who posted the tweet)		
15	user follower count	Number of users who follow u
16	user followee count	Number of users whom u follows
17	followers per followee	Number of followers/number of followings
18	user listed count	Number of times u has been listed by other users
19	user status count	Number of tweet posted by a user
20	user bio exists	Boolean status of bio of a user account
21	spam words in bio count	Number of spam words in the bio of a Twitter account
22	users mentioned count	Number of times u has been mentioned by other users
23	age of account	Number of days between the day on which u's user account was created and the day on which the tweet is posted

- *Tweet text-based attributes* – These include general text-based attributes, such as the word count, unique character count, digit count, hashtag count per tweet, spam words in tweet count, and so on.
- *URL-based attributes* – These are properties of the URL(s) contained in the tweet. Note that the final landing URL is considered for extracting

these attributes (not the shortened version contained in the tweet) [38]. Also, in case a tweet contains multiple URLs, these attributes are averaged over all the URLs contained in the tweet [39].

- *User profile-based attributes* – Characteristics of the user account which posted the tweet. These attributes attempt to capture notions such as how popular the user is in the Twitter social network (number of followers, number of times listed), how active he/she is (number of followings, number of tweets posted), and how old the account is (age of account in days) [40].

To ensure *real-time* spam classification, only those attributes are considered which can be derived directly from the tweet streams provided by Twitter (only the URL-based attributes require few HTTP redirects to get the final landing URL from the shortened URL).

Note that the 23 attributes considered here are *not* an exhaustive set of all attributes that can be used for classifying spam and legitimate tweets. Only these attributes are considered in the work, because most of them can be extracted directly from the live tweet stream provided by Twitter. Only, the URL-based attributes require the expansion of the shortened URL(s) contained in the tweet, which requires a small number of HTTP redirects [20]. These features are focused, since they are likely to be used by systems which aim for real-time classification of spam tweets, and hence need to extract features from hundreds of millions of tweets in real-time [41]. Massive data flow pushes academics to mine information effectively through filtering and organization. The phrase "information mining" refers to the computer process of detecting patterns in large datasets in order to get knowledge using difficult approaches such as data analysis [42]. In the Knowledge Discovery in Databases (KDD) process, data mining is an analytical phase. In order to increase the quantity of new intriguing facts, data mining researchers are working on extracting new fascinating facts from microblog data. As microblogging sites have become essential sources of real-time information and all content is generally unstructured by nature, data mining plays an important role in filtering and organizing information to portray knowledge in a simpler manner [43].

It can be noted that prior attempts for spam classification on Twitter [22, 36] used several other attributes, which is intentionally avoided since they are difficult to obtain in real-time. For instance, attributes which are based on the tweeting history of the user who posted a tweet [22] – such as how many times a user's tweets has been retweeted or replied to or the time since the previous tweet was posted by the same user – are not considered, since it is infeasible to obtain the history of the user in real-time [21]. Similarly, it is *not* attempted to fetch the contents of the web page corresponding to the URL mentioned in the tweet (which can be used to measure the similarity between the tweet text and the contents of the web page [36]). However, if one has sufficient infrastructure to extract such attributes in real-time, then such attributes can also be used along with the ones stated above [24].

3.3 Data preprocessing

Sentiment analysis, question answering, smart help, and other cutting-edge natural language processing (NLP) applications need a massive volume of data. This massive quantity of information may be supplied straight into the machine learning model. Almost all text-based applications need extensive preprocessing of textual input, such as the creation of embedding vectors from scratch using a word frequency counter. This takes a significant amount of effort and time. Transfer learning methods are currently employed for all complicated preprocessing jobs to solve this [27]. A technique known as text preprocessing is used to clean up text data before feeding it to a machine learning model [44]. Text data contains a variety of noise, such as emotions, punctuation, and text with different capitalization. This is only the beginning of the difficulties we will face because machines cannot understand words; they require numbers. So we must find a fast and efficient way to transform text to numbers. Cleaning or preprocessing data is just as crucial as model construction in every machine learning endeavor. Text data is one of the most unstructured types of data accessible, and dealing with human language is too difficult [45]. Have you ever wondered how Alexa, Siri, and Google Assistant comprehend, interpret, and respond to human language? NLP is a technique that operates behind the scenes, allowing for extensive text preparation prior to any response [28]. This section will go through the most important text preparation techniques that you will need to know if you are going to work with text data.

In most online microblogging sites, text-based messages contain URLs, punctuation marks, user names, numbers, special characters (except emoticons), whitespaces, and so on. So, to work with microblog datasets, preprocessing is necessary due to the noisy nature. The preprocessing step includes removal of punctuation, repeating letters, additional white spaces, stopwords, user names, and special characters (except the "#" symbol, as the hashtag plays an important role in microblogging). The corpus is tokenized into words and tweets. The bag of words is formed after omitting the stopwords, i.e., words that do not provide meaning to the corpus are removed. To achieve the data preprocessing, the following steps are taken [38].

3.4 Removal of user names and URLs

Words that start with "@" refer to user annotation which does not contribute significant meaning in a dataset. Similarly, many users (mostly spammers) post various URLs in shortened format while posting in microblogs, so this unnecessary information can be removed to identify significant data for further analysis. Massive data flows encourage academics to use filtering and organization to effectively mine data. The phrase "information mining" refers to the computer process of detecting patterns in large datasets in order to gain knowledge using difficult data analysis techniques. KDD includes an analytical phase called data mining [45]. To increase the quantity of new intriguing facts, data mining researchers are working on extracting new fascinating facts from microblog data. As microblogging sites have become key sources of real-time information, and all content is largely unstructured by nature, so data mining plays a critical role in filtering and organizing of information to portray knowledge in a simpler manner.

Removal of stopwords
Stopwords are words which do not include vital significance to be used in a text for data analysis. So these words can be filtered out from the dataset to ignore vast amounts of unnecessary information. Stopwords are a group of words that are often used in a language. Stopwords in English include "a," "we," "the," "is," "are," and others. Stopwords are used to remove low-information terms from text so that we can focus on the crucial words instead. We have the option of creating a bespoke list of stopwords (depending on the use case) or using preset libraries [41].

Stemming
Stemming generally refers to a basic heuristic procedure that chops off the ends of words to accomplish this goal correctly most of the time, and comprises the removal of derivational affixes. Porter's algorithm (Porter, 1980) is one of the most popular and effective algorithm for stemming [46].

Removal of punctuation and non-textual characters
In this step all the non-textual characters and punctuation are removed.

Removal of repeating letters and additional white spaces
In this step all whitespace characters, including space and tabs with a blank space, and repeating letters are removed.

Lower casing

Lower casing is the most straightforward and the most frequently used text preparation method. Most text mining and NLP issues can be solved using this method. The main purpose is to convert the same words of different case into lower case the text such that "apple", "Apple" and "APPLE".

Rare word removal

This makes sense since some words that are particularly distinctive in nature, such as names, brands, and product names, as well as some noise characters, such as html leftouts, must be deleted for various NLP jobs. We also utilize word length as a criterion for deleting extremely short or extremely lengthy terms [41].

Spelling correction

Data from social media is always sloppy and contains spelling errors [47]. As a result, spelling correction is an important preprocessing step since it helps us avoid using numerous terms. Even if they are used in the same sense, "text" and "txt" will be considered as separate terms. The textblob library can help with this.

3.5 Converting emojis and emoticons to words

Emojis and emoticons are used to communicate emotions in sentiment analysis. As a result, eliminating them may not be the best option. To deal with NLP-based difficulties, a variety of libraries and algorithms are employed. For text cleaning, a regular expression (re) is the most often used library [48]. The next-level libraries NLTK and spacy [49] are used to perform NLP tasks such as stopword removal, named entity recognition, part of speech tagging, phrase matching, and so on. NLTK is an outdated library that novices may use to practice NLP methods. Spacy is the most recently published library with the most sophisticated approaches, and it is usually utilized in the production environment. Therefore we recommend readers to study both libraries and get to know their strengths [1,50].

3.6 Conclusion

Some of the most prominent microblogging services are Twitter, Facebook, and LinkedIn. On the Twitter microblogging site, which is one of the most popular websites on the Internet today, millions of users post real-time messages (tweets) on a variety of topics of interest. Popular content on

Twitter (i.e., content that is widely discussed) can be used for a variety of purposes on any given day, including content suggestion, marketing, and political campaigns. One of the most exciting characteristics of Twitter is its real-time nature: at any given time, millions of Twitter users are giving their thoughts on a wide range of topics or incidents/events occurring across the world. As a result, Twitter content is particularly useful for acquiring real-time information on a variety of topics. This section covers the dataset that was used in a number of the experiments in the book. Twitter's OSN provides an API for gathering many types of data, including streams of tweets published through the website and user profile information. Twitter, in particular, provides a 1% random sample of all tweets published on the Twitter website worldwide. This chapter provides a quick rundown of the experimental dataset that was used to evaluate the various data analytics methodologies described in the book.

References

[1] S. Goswami, A.K. Das, Determining maximum cliques for community detection in weighted sparse networks, Knowledge and Information Systems 64 (2) (2022) 289–324, https://doi.org/10.1007/s10115-021-01631-y.

[2] Z. Hua-Ping, Z. Rui-Qi, Z. Yan-Ping, M. Bao-Jun, Big data modeling and analysis of microblog ecosystem, International Journal of Automation and Computing 11 (2) (2014) 119–127, https://doi.org/10.1007/s11633-014-0774-9.

[3] S. Dutta, S. Ghatak, M. Roy, S. Ghosh, A.K. Das, A graph based clustering technique for tweet summarization, in: Reliability, Infocom Technologies and Optimization (ICRITO) (Trends and Future Directions), 2015, pp. 1–6.

[4] G. Yue, Z. Hanwang, Z. Xibin, Y. Shuicheng, Event classification in microblogs via social tracking, ACM Transactions on Intelligent Systems and Technology 8 (3) (2017) 35:1–35:14, https://doi.org/10.1145/2967502, http://doi.acm.org/10.1145/2967502.

[5] D. Soumi, G. Sujata, D. Ratnadeep, D.A. Kumar, G. Saptarshi, Attribute selection for improving spam classification in online social networks: a rough set theory-based approach, Social Network Analysis and Mining 8 (1) (2018) 7, https://doi.org/10.1007/s13278-017-0484-8.

[6] Gillani Mehreen, Ilyas Muhammad U, Saleh Saad, Alowibdi Jalal S, Aljohani Naif, Alotaibi Fahad S, Post summarization of microblogs of sporting events, in: Proceedings of the 26th International Conference on World Wide Web Companion, WWW '17 Companion, International World Wide Web Conferences Steering Committee, Republic and Canton of Geneva, Switzerland, 2017, pp. 59–68.

[7] M. Hasan, M.A. Orgun, R. Schwitter, A survey on real-time event detection from the Twitter data stream, Journal of Information Science 44 (4) (2017) 443–463, https://doi.org/10.1177/0165551517698564.

[8] A. Mukherjee, S. Bhattacharyya, K. Ray, B. Gupta, A.K. Das, A study of public sentiment and influence of politics in COVID-19 related tweets, in: A.K. Das, J. Nayak, B. Naik, S. Dutta, D. Pelusi (Eds.), Computational Intelligence in Pattern Recognition, Springer, Singapore, 2022, pp. 655–665.

[9] P. Das, A.K. Das, Convolutional neural networks-based sentence level classification of crime documents, in: A.K. Das, J. Nayak, B. Naik, S. Dutta, D. Pelusi (Eds.), Computational Intelligence in Pattern Recognition, Springer, Singapore, 2022, pp. 65–73.

[10] A. Das, D. Pal, C. Mallick, A.K. Das, An unsupervised COVID-19 report summarizer for developing smart healthcare system, in: A.K. Das, J. Nayak, B. Naik, S. Dutta, D. Pelusi (Eds.), Computational Intelligence in Pattern Recognition, Springer, Singapore, 2022, pp. 157–168.

[11] REST API Resources, Twitter Developers, https://dev.twitter.com/docs/api.

[12] A. Campan, T. Atnafu, T.M. Truta, J. Nolan, Is data collection through Twitter streaming api useful for academic research?, in: 2018 IEEE International Conference on Big Data (Big Data), 2018, pp. 3638–3643.

[13] T. Ke, A. Fabian, H. Claudia, G.-J. Houben, G. Ujwal, Groundhog day: near-duplicate detection on Twitter, in: Proc. Conference on World Wide Web (WWW), 2013.

[14] Hyderabad blasts – Wikipedia, http://en.wikipedia.org/wiki/2013_Hyderabad_blasts, February 2013.

[15] Sandy Hook Elementary School shooting – Wikipedia, http://en.wikipedia.org/wiki/Sandy_Hook_Elementary_School_shooting, December 2012.

[16] North India floods – Wikipedia, http://en.wikipedia.org/wiki/2013_North_India_floods, June 2013.

[17] Typhoon Hagupit – Wikipedia, http://en.wikipedia.org/wiki/Typhoon_Hagupit, December 2014.

[18] C. Mallick, S. Das, A.K. Das, Evolutionary algorithm based summarization for analyzing COVID-19 medical reports, in: J. Nayak, B. Naik, A. Abraham (Eds.), Understanding COVID-19: The Role of Computational Intelligence, Studies in Computational Intelligence, Springer International Publishing, Cham, 2022, pp. 31–58.

[19] S. Kumar, K.M. Carley, What to track on the Twitter streaming api? A knapsack bandits approach to dynamically update the search terms, in: 2019 IEEE/ACM International Conference on Advances in Social Networks Analysis and Mining (ASONAM), 2019, pp. 158–163.

[20] S. Chattopadhyay, T. Basu, A.K. Das, K. Ghosh, L.C.A. Murthy, Towards effective discovery of natural communities in complex networks and implications in e-commerce, Electronic Commerce Research 21 (4) (2021) 917–954, https://doi.org/10.1007/s10660-019-09395-y.

[21] M. Basu, S.D. Bit, S. Ghosh, Utilizing microblogs for optimized real-time resource allocation in post-disaster scenarios, Social Network Analysis and Mining 12 (1) (2021) 15, https://doi.org/10.1007/s13278-021-00841-0.

[22] B. Fabrício, M. Gabriel, R. Tiago, A. Virgílio, Detecting spammers on Twitter, in: Proceedings of Collaboration, Electronic Messaging, Anti-Abuse and Spam Conference (CEAS), 2010.

[23] F. Benevenuto, T. Rodrigues, J. Almeida, M. Goncalves, V. Almeida, Detecting spammers and content promoters in online video social networks, in: IEEE INFOCOM Workshops 2009, 2009, pp. 1–2.

[24] P. Bhattacharya, S. Paul, K. Ghosh, S. Ghosh, A. Wyner, DeepRhole: deep learning for rhetorical role labeling of sentences in legal case documents, Artificial Intelligence and Law (Nov. 2021), https://doi.org/10.1007/s10506-021-09304-5.

[25] H. Costa, F. Benevenuto, L.H. de Campos Merschmann, Detecting tip spam in location-based social networks, in: Proceedings of the 28th Annual ACM Symposium on Applied Computing (SAC), 2013.

[26] H. Costa, L.H. de Campos Merschmann, F. Barth, F. Benevenuto, Pollution, bad-mouthing, and local marketing: the underground of location-based social networks, Elsevier Information Sciences 279 (2014) 123–137.

[27] K. Hazra, T. Ghosh, A. Mukherjee, S. Saha, S. Nandi, S. Ghosh, S. Chakraborty, Sustainable text summarization over mobile devices: an energy-aware approach, Sustainable Computing: Informatics and Systems 32 (2021) 100607, https://doi.org/10.1016/j.suscom.2021.100607, https://www.sciencedirect.com/science/article/pii/S2210537921000950.

[28] A. Mandal, K. Ghosh, S. Ghosh, S. Mandal, A sequence labeling model for catchphrase identification from legal case documents, Artificial Intelligence and Law (Jul. 2021), https://doi.org/10.1007/s10506-021-09296-2.

[29] H. Efstathiades, D. Antoniades, G. Pallis, M.D. Dikaiakos, Distributed large-scale data collection in online social networks, in: 2016 IEEE 2nd International Conference on Collaboration and Internet Computing (CIC), 2016, pp. 373–380.

[30] A. Dwi Laksito, Kusrini, H. Sismoro, F. Rahmawati, M. Yusa, A comparison study of search strategy on collecting Twitter data for drug adverse reaction, in: 2018 International Seminar on Application for Technology of Information and Communication, 2018, pp. 356–360.

[31] Google Safe Browsing API, https://developers.google.com/safe-browsing/.

[32] SURBL, http://www.surbl.org/.

[33] Capture-HPC, https://projects.honeynet.org/capture-hpc/.

[34] The Spamhaus Project, http://www.spamhaus.org/.

[35] P. Ray, A. Chakrabarti, Twitter sentiment analysis for product review using lexicon method, in: 2017 International Conference on Data Management, Analytics and Innovation (ICDMAI), 2017, pp. 211–216.

[36] M.-R. Juan, A. Lourdes, Detecting malicious tweets in trending topics using a statistical analysis of language, Expert Systems with Applications 40 (8) (2013) 2992–3000.

[37] G. Hongyu, H. Jun, W. Christo, L. Zhichun, C. Yan, Y.Z. Ben, Detecting and characterizing social spam campaigns, in: Proceedings of the ACM SIGCOMM Internet Measurement Conference, IMC, Dec 2000.

[38] M. Basu, K. Ghosh, S. Ghosh, Information retrieval from microblogs during disasters: in the light of IRMiDis task, SN Computer Science 1 (1) (2020) 61, https://doi.org/10.1007/s42979-020-0065-1.

[39] K. Jitkajornwanich, C. Kongthong, N. Khongsoontornjaroen, J. Kaiyasuan, S. Lawawirojwong, P. Srestasathiern, S. Srisonphan, P. Vateekul, Utilizing Twitter data for early flood warning in Thailand, in: 2018 IEEE International Conference on Big Data (Big Data), 2018, pp. 5165–5169.

[40] S.H. Archana, S.G. Winster, Drugs categorization based on sentence polarity analyzer for Twitter data, in: 2016 Second International Conference on Science Technology Engineering and Management (ICONSTEM), 2016, pp. 28–33.

[41] R. Mandal, S. Dutta, R. Banerjee, S. Bhattacharya, R. Ghosh, S. Samanta, T. Saha, City traffic speed characterization based on city road surface quality, in: J.M.R.S. Tavares, P. Dutta, S. Dutta, D. Samanta (Eds.), Cyber Intelligence and Information Retrieval, Springer, Singapore, 2022, pp. 515–524.

[42] T. Jagić, L. Brkić, Hot topic detection using Twitter streaming data, in: 2020 43rd International Convention on Information, Communication and Electronic Technology (MIPRO), 2020, pp. 1730–1735.

[43] R. Compton, C. Lee, T.-C. Lu, L. De Silva, M. Macy, Detecting future social unrest in unprocessed Twitter data: "emerging phenomena and big data", in: 2013 IEEE International Conference on Intelligence and Security Informatics, 2013, pp. 56–60.

[44] D. Samanta, S. Dutta, M.G. Galety, S. Pramanik, A novel approach for web mining taxonomy for high-performance computing, in: J.M.R.S. Tavares, P. Dutta, S. Dutta, D. Samanta (Eds.), Cyber Intelligence and Information Retrieval, in: Lecture Notes in Networks and Systems, Springer, Singapore, 2022, pp. 425–432.

[45] R.D. Perera, S. Anand, K.P. Subbalakshmi, R. Chandramouli, Twitter analytics: architecture, tools and analysis, in: 2010 - MILCOM 2010 Military Communications Conference, 2010, pp. 2186–2191.

[46] P. Tatineni, B.S. Babu, B. Kanuri, G.R.K. Rao, P. Chitturi, C. Naresh, Post Covid-19 Twitter user's emotions classification using deep learning techniques in India, in: 2021 International Conference on Artificial Intelligence and Smart Systems (ICAIS), 2021, pp. 338–343.

[47] C.M. Yoshimura, H. Kitagawa, Tlv-bandit: bandit method for collecting topic-related local tweets, in: 2021 IEEE 4th International Conference on Multimedia Information Processing and Retrieval (MIPR), 2021, pp. 56–62.

[48] C. Wang, L. Marini, C.-L. Chin, N. Vance, C. Donelson, P. Meunier, J.T. Yun, Social media intelligence and learning environment: an open source framework for social media data collection, analysis and curation, in: 2019 15th International Conference on eScience (eScience), 2019, pp. 252–261.

[49] G.A. Sandag, A.M. Manueke, M. Walean, Sentiment analysis of Covid-19 vaccine tweets in Indonesia using recurrent neural network (rnn) approach, in: 2021 3rd International Conference on Cybernetics and Intelligent System (ICORIS), 2021, pp. 1–7.

[50] A. Nsouli, A. Mourad, D. Azar, Towards proactive social learning approach for traffic event detection based on Arabic tweets, in: 2018 14th International Wireless Communications Mobile Computing Conference (IWCMC), 2018, pp. 1501–1506.

PART 2

Microblogging dataset applications and implications

CHAPTER 4

Attribute selection to improve spam classification

4.1 Introduction

With the fast expansion of online social microblogging (OSM) activities, websites such as Twitter (https://twitter.com), Tumblr (http://www.tumblr.com), and Sina Weibo (https://weibo.com), spammers typically use these information systems to send communications containing dangerous content [1,2]. Despite the fact that the OSM authorities take many steps to combat spam (e.g., suspending or canceling spam accounts depending on reports generated by users), spam continues to be a significant concern to OSM users [3,4]. In fact, according to a recent study [3,4], spam transmitted through OSMs such as Twitter is far more powerful (i.e., receives much greater click-through rates from users) than spam spread through traditional means such as spam messages and emails. This point emphasizes the importance of creating an automated mechanism for detecting spam in OSMs [5].

Several academics have come across spam in OSMs, and the most widely acknowledged solution is to create a machine learning-based categorization system that can distinguish between spam and legal entities. To distinguish between spam and real user accounts, classifiers have been proposed (see, for example, [6–11]). On location-based social networks, there are both spam and legalized "tips" [12,13]. All of these earlier studies identified a collection of criteria for the spam classification problem, which were then used to train classification models [14]. The classifiers' performance is influenced by the attributes used.

A crucial role is played by attribute selection in attribute-based classification, which tries to identify a minimal subset of features to speed up the process of classification and achieve higher classification performance than the original set of attributes [15]. The goal of this chapter's study is to improve spam categorization techniques in OSMs by offering a new methodology for attribute selection. Rough set theory [16,17] concepts have been applied to measure the attribute dependencies. Subsequently, the dependencies among the attributes are modeled as a network graph

Data Analytics for Social Microblogging Platforms
https://doi.org/10.1016/B978-0-32-391785-8.00016-0

and then a greedy approach is used to identify the best selection of features from the generated graph [18].

The current strategy is described in the following paragraphs. Rough set theory is recognized to have a number of advantages for attribute selection: it can work with only original data and requires no external information or training; no data assumptions are required; and rough set theory can be used to evaluate both quantitative and qualitative data [19,20]. Second, the attribute correlations or dependencies are represented using a graph-based technique. Most past attempts at attribute selection for spam detection have ignored reciprocal correlations between attributes, potentially resulting in a reduced set of highly connected attributes. This flaw is addressed by the proposed graph-based approach, where correlated attributes can be readily deleted from the graph when an attribute is included in the reduced attribute set, resulting in a further reduction of the attribute set [21].

The suggested method is tested on five different spam datasets from various OSMs, and the results are compared to the performance of a number of standard attribute selection approaches. For the majority of datasets, the suggested methodology chooses an attribute subset that is narrower than what baseline methodologies achieve. The method also produces *better classification results* than using all of the attributes and subsets of attributes acquired by the baseline methods [22]. This technique could be particularly useful in instances when rapid yet accurate categorization is required, such as filtering of real-time spam twitter streams with hundreds of millions of tweets/posts per day [23].

The rest of the chapter is structured as follows. Section 4.2 describes a literature survey related to this work. Section 4.3 elaborately describes the proposed approach for attribute selection. The experimental datasets have been described in Section 4.4. Section 4.5 presents a comparative analysis of the proposed approach and other existing attribute selection approaches. The work is concluded in Section 4.6.

4.2 Literature survey

As stated earlier, this chapter proposes an attribute selection algorithm for improving spam classification in online social networks (OSN). In this section, prior work on spam detection in OSMs and existing algorithms for attribute selection for spam detection are reviewed in brief.

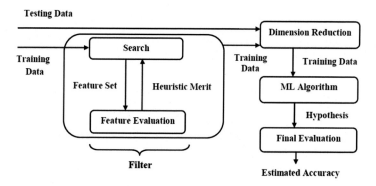

Figure 4.1 Filter feature selection method.

4.2.1 Attribute selection methods

An attribute selection method considers a given training dataset in order to make a decision about which attributes (or features) to select. Many researchers have proposed feature selection algorithms. These are discussed in the following sections.

4.2.1.1 Filter methods

Filter methods [24–26] employ an attribute ranking function to select the best attributes. The ranking function gives a relevance score of each attribute. Naturally, the more relevant the attribute, the higher its rank. Either a fixed number of attributes with the highest rank are selected or a variable number of attributes above a predetermined threshold value of the rank are selected [27]. Fig. 4.1 shows the basic functionality of filter methods for attribute selection.

One major limitation of filter methods is that, instead of considering the attribute correlation, such methods consider each attribute individually. It is possible that the two attributes are individually ineffective in classification, but taken together become useful [28].

4.2.1.2 Wrapper methods

Wrapper methods [29,30] use a learning algorithm to search attributes and test the performance of every subset of attributes. Thus, the best-performing subset of attributes is determined. If there are n attributes in total, 2^n possible subsets are to be searched, which is an NP-hard problem. Using a heuristic function, the search space is reduced in order to enhance the performance of the wrapper algorithms. Fig. 2.2 shows the basic functionality of wrapper methods. The disadvantage of wrapper methods is that they tend to be computationally exhaustive and the use of a heuristic function to improve the search space can be ad hoc [31].

4.2.1.3 Other attribute selection algorithms

Attribute (or feature) selection is a key process in machine learning and data mining. In the context of the classification problem, the objective of attribute selection is to identify a minimal subset of attributes to boost up the classification process and improve the classification performance. A large number of attribute selection algorithms have been proposed in the literature [15]. A majority of these algorithms are based on evaluating a candidate subset of attributes at each iteration, based on certain statistical measures; such methods are known as filter methods [32]. Most of the proposed filter methods are supervised, i.e., they assume availability of the class labels of the objects in the training set [33].

However, a few unsupervised algorithms have also been proposed, e.g., using similarity among attributes [34] or graph-based clustering of attributes [35]. On the other hand, another class of methods utilizes the performance of a classifier as the evaluation criteria for measuring the goodness of a candidate subset of attributes; such methods are called *wrapper methods* [30].

Some of the popular methodologies for attribute selection are based on *rough set theory*, which is a mathematical tool for handling imprecision, uncertainty, and vagueness [16,17]. Rough set-based attribute selection algorithms [36–39] are essentially filter methods, which attempt to find an optimal subset of the original attribute set; this optimal subset is known as a *reduct*. Recall that finding an optimal subset of attributes is an NP-hard problem [40]. Algorithms to find a minimal set of attributes include incremental hill climbing [37] and ant colony optimization [38].

4.2.1.4 Spam detection in OSM

Similar to spam in the Web [41] and email [42,43], spammers have been targeting OSNs such as Facebook, Youtube, and Twitter [44,3,10]. There have been a large number of efforts towards combating spam in various online systems including OSNs; refer to [1,2] for surveys on such efforts. Recent research [3] has shown that spam disseminated through OSMs like Twitter is much more potent (i.e., earns much higher click-through rates) compared to traditional means of disseminating spam such as spam emails.

Hence, it is natural that a large number of researchers have proposed mechanisms to counter spam in OSMs.

There have been several attempts towards classifying user accounts of spammers [9,6–8], as well as spam posts [45,46]. We describe some of these studies in brief. In [9], the authors proposed a classification approach for detecting spammer accounts and non-spammer accounts. Their approach correctly classified around 96% of non-spammers and 70% of spammers. This work also identified the most significant attributes for spam detection on Twitter. In [6], the authors analyzed the behavioral and structural differences between spammers and legitimate users on Twitter. This work identified several strategies adopted by spammers to spread spam contents, while evading detection by the Twitter spam tracking system. In [7] and [8], the authors designed *social honeypots* for harvesting spam profiles in OSN communities. Using the harvested spam accounts, profile features of spammers and legitimate Twitter users were analyzed, such as content, social contacts, posting patterns, user behavior over time, followers/following dynamics, and so on. These profile features were considered to design machine learning-based classifiers to detect spammers with high accuracy rates [47].

In [8] – a later work by the same authors as [7] – the authors designed 60 honeypots on Twitter to harvest 36,000 spammers and an automatic spam classifier was also proposed. This research demonstrated a detailed study of the harvested Twitter users which included several aspects such as user behavior over time, analysis of link payloads, and followers/following network dynamics. The proposed approach results in a set of attributes such as user demographics, follower/following graphs, user behavior, and properties of the tweet content, which can be used to investigate the usefulness of instinctive content and for polluter identification.

Some other works focused on detecting suspicious/malicious URLs posted on social media. In [45], the authors proposed a classifier to detect suspicious URLs. In this work, correlated redirect chains of URLs are identified from Twitter. Subsequently, URL features are extracted and these features are used further for classification. The classifier identifies the correlated URLs which redirect chains using the frequently shared URLs [48]. Similarly, in [46], the authors proposed a real-time URL spam filtering system. This research shows several differences between spam that targets email and spam on Twitter. It can be noted that the feature selection algorithm developed in this chapter can be used with any of the above-mentioned works to improve classification accuracy.

4.2.1.5 Attribute selection for spam detection

Attribute selection algorithms have also been used to select important attributes for spam detection, especially in the domains of *web spam* and *email spam*. For instance, Jaber et al. [41] demonstrated the benefits of attribute selection for web spam detection. Zhang et al. [42] used a wrapper-based particle swarm optimization technique to select attributes for an email spam classification system.

However, there have been very few attempts to systematically select important attributes for spam detection in OSNs. To the best of our knowledge, only two prior studies [9,49] attempted to identify important attributes for identifying spam user accounts on Twitter and Facebook. Both of these studies ranked the attributes based on the well-known information gain and chi squared (X2) statistical metrics [50], and then considered the top attributes according to these rankings. In addition, Ahmed et al. [49] checked the fall in classification performance by removing any one attribute at a time, and thus identified those attributes as most important whose removal leads to the highest reduction in classification performance [51].

4.3 Methodology for classification

The suggested attribute selection algorithm is described in this part, and it will be used to select the most relevant attributes for classification of spam. As previously indicated, the proposed methodology is based on rough set theory principles [16,17]. As a result, the rough set theory-based ideas that will be utilized to explain the technique are defined in this section.

4.3.1 Rough set theory fundamentals

Rough set theory considers every object in the universe of discourse to be some information (knowledge, data). Objects with similar information are indistinguishable. An elementary set is any set that contains all indistinguishable objects. The union of some elementary sets yields a crisp or exact set; otherwise, the set is rough (vague, imprecise). Vagueness is represented in rough set theory by a (rough) set's boundary area, which cannot be definitively identified or characterized [52]. A set's lower approximation comprises all things that positively belong to it, whereas its upper approximation contains all objects that might belong to it. The rough set's boundary region is defined by the difference between the upper and lower approximations. A brief description of some basic principles in rough set theory is given below, along with an example.

Table 4.1 This sample decision system consists of eight objects, four conditional attributes, and one decision (class) attribute.

Object ID	Conditional attributes				Decision ($\bar{d}$)
	$\bar{p}$	$\bar{q}$	$\bar{r}$	$\bar{s}$	
x_1	1	2	1	3	spam
x_2	1	1	1	1	legitimate
x_3	2	1	1	2	legitimate
x_4	3	3	1	1	spam
x_5	3	2	1	1	legitimate
x_6	3	3	1	3	legitimate
x_7	1	3	2	2	spam
x_8	2	1	2	3	legitimate

Decision system: A Decision system, also referred to as decision table, $\overline{DS} = (\overline{U}, \overline{A})$, can be written as a two-tuple, where $\overline{U}$ is a finite number of non-empty objects (referred as the *universe*) and $\overline{A} = \overline{C} \cup \{\bar{d}\}$ is a non-empty finite set of attributes, which consists of a group of $\overline{C}$ of *conditional attributes* and a decision or class attribute d. Every attribute $a \in \overline{A}$ defines an information function $f_a : \overline{U} \to \overline{V}_a$, where $\overline{V}_a$ is the set of attribute values a, represented as the attribute's domain.

Table 4.1 depicts a simple decision-making system comprised of eight different items (or tweets) $\bar{x}_1, \bar{x}_2, \dots, \bar{x}_8$, four conditional attributes $\overline{C} = \{\bar{p}, \bar{q}, \bar{r}, \bar{s}\}$, and a decision attribute $\bar{d}$.

Indiscernibility: For each pair of attributes $\overline{B} \subseteq \overline{A}$ in $\overline{DS} = (\overline{U}, \overline{A})$, an associated indiscernibility relation $IND(\overline{B})$ can be characterized as

$$\text{IND}(\overline{B}) = \{(\bar{x}, \bar{y}) \in \overline{U} \times \overline{U} \mid \forall a \in \overline{B}, f_a(\bar{x}) = f_a(\bar{y})\}. \tag{4.1}$$

If $(\bar{x}, \bar{y}) \in \text{IND}(\overline{B})$, this suggests that the objects $\bar{x}$ and $\bar{y}$ are indistinguishable from each other with respect to all the attributes in set $\overline{B}$, i.e., for each attribute, they have the same value in $\overline{B}$. As a result, these indistinguishable sets of objects constitute an indiscernibility relation, which is a term that can be used to describe the $\overline{B}$-indiscernibility relation, and the class of objects is represented by $[\bar{x}]_{\overline{B}}$.

The $\overline{B}$-relationship of indiscernibility is essentially a relationship of equivalence which accurately partitions the universe $\overline{U}$ of objects into a

Table 4.2 The decision system represented in Table 4.1. Left column – for each attribute, equivalence classes are induced by the indiscernibility relation. Right column – for each conditional property, equivalence classes are induced by the relative indiscernibility relation.

Equivalence classes for each attribute by the indiscernibility relation	Equivalence classes based on relative indiscernibility for each conditional attribute
$U_d = (\{\bar{x}_1, \bar{x}_4, \bar{x}_7\}, \{\bar{x}_2, \bar{x}_3, \bar{x}_5, \bar{x}_6, \bar{x}_8\})$	
$U_p = (\{\bar{x}_1, \bar{x}_2, \bar{x}_7\}, \{\bar{x}_3, \bar{x}_8\}, \{\bar{x}_4, \bar{x}_5, \bar{x}_6\})$	$U_{d/p} = (\{\bar{x}_1, \bar{x}_7\}, \{\bar{x}_3, \bar{x}_8\}, \{\bar{x}_2\}, \{\bar{x}_4\}, \{\bar{x}_5, \bar{x}_6\})$
$U_q = (\{\bar{x}_1, \bar{x}_5\}\{\bar{x}_2, \bar{x}_3, \bar{x}_8\}, \{\bar{x}_4, \bar{x}_6, \bar{x}_7\})$	$U_{d/q} = (\{\bar{x}_1\}, \{\bar{x}_5\}, \{\bar{x}_6\}, \{\bar{x}_4, \bar{x}_7\}, \{\bar{x}_2, \bar{x}_3, \bar{x}_8\})$
$U_r = (\{\bar{x}_1, \bar{x}_2, \bar{x}_3, \bar{x}_4, \bar{x}_5, \bar{x}_6\}, \{\bar{x}_7, \bar{x}_8\})$	$U_{d/r} = (\{\bar{x}_7\}, \{\bar{x}_8\}, \{\bar{x}_1, \bar{x}_4\}, \{\bar{x}_2, \bar{x}_3, \bar{x}_5, \bar{x}_6\})$
$U_s = (\{\bar{x}_1, \bar{x}_6, \bar{x}_8\}, \{\bar{x}_2, \bar{x}_4, \bar{x}_5\}, \{\bar{x}_3, \bar{x}_7\})$	$U_{d/s} = (\{\bar{x}_1\}, \{\bar{x}_3\}, \{\bar{x}_4\}, \{\bar{x}_7\}, \{\bar{x}_2, \bar{x}_5\}, \{\bar{x}_6, \bar{x}_8\})$

set of equivalence classes.[1] In terms of attributes, items belonging to the same equivalence class are indistinguishable from one another in $\bar{B}$. The partitioning of the universe $\bar{U}$ as stated by the $\bar{B}$-indiscernibility relation is referred to as $\bar{U}_{\bar{B}}$, and the partitioning's equivalence classes are labeled $[\bar{x}]_{\bar{B}}$. If set $\bar{B}$ contains a single attribute a, the partitioning is represented here as $\bar{U}_a$ and the equivalence classes as $[\bar{x}]_a$ (instead of $\bar{U}_{\{a\}}$ and $[\bar{x}]_{\{a\}}$, respectively). For instance, Table 4.1 shows that the objects $\bar{x}_4$ and $\bar{x}_6$ are indistinguishable with respect to the attributes $\bar{B} = \{\bar{p}, \bar{q}, \bar{r}\}$. Similarly, the objects $\bar{x}_7$ and $\bar{x}_8$ are indistinguishable with respect to the set of attributes $\bar{B} = \{\bar{r}\}$. Partitioning based on Table 4.1's indiscernibility relationship for each attribute in the decision system is represented in Table 4.2 (left column).

Reduct: Let $a \in B$ be an attribute, where $\bar{B} \subseteq \bar{A}$. The attribute a is termed *dispensable* in $\bar{B}$ if $\text{IND}(\bar{B}) = \text{IND}(\bar{B} - \{a\})$; if not, a is termed *indispensable* in $\bar{B}$. A set of attributes $\bar{B}$ is termed *independent* if each of them are essential. Any subset $\bar{B}'$ of $\bar{B}$ is termed as a *reduct* of $\bar{B}$ if $\bar{B}'$ is independent and $\text{IND}(\bar{B}') = \text{IND}(\bar{B})$. As a result, a reduct is a minimal subset of attributes that preserves the indiscernibility relation, allowing the same classification of universe objects as the entire set of attributes. There are often several subsets of attributes that are reducts of the entire set of attributes for a given decision system.

Calculating the reduct of a decision system is the most efficient technique to reduce the amount of characteristics while maintaining classification performance. Finding a minimal reduct, on the other hand, is an

---

[1] A binary relation $\bar{R} \subseteq \bar{U} \times \bar{U}$ is referred to as an equivalence relation if it is symmetric $((\bar{x}, \bar{y}) \in \bar{R}$ implies $(\bar{y}, \bar{x}) \in \bar{R})$, transitive $((\bar{x}, \bar{y}) \in \bar{R}$ and $(\bar{y}, \bar{z}) \in \bar{R}$ implies $(\bar{x}, \bar{z}) \in \bar{R})$, and reflexive $((\bar{x}, \bar{x}) \in \bar{R}, \forall \bar{x} \in \bar{U})$. The equivalence class of an object $\bar{x} \in \bar{U}$ contains all objects $\bar{y} \in \bar{U}$ such that $(\bar{x}, \bar{y}) \in \bar{R}$.

NP-hard issue [40]. As a result, many heuristic-based approaches to identify optimal subsets of qualities in a reasonable amount of time have been presented [37,38].

4.3.2 Attribute selection algorithm

A graph-based greedy strategy for detecting a reduct is proposed in this chapter. To examine the relationships between pairs of conditional variables and to visualize these relationships using a directed weighted graph, a modified version of the attribute indiscernibility relation was originally employed [53]. The nodes in this network are the conditional attributes, and the weight associated with the edge $\bar{j} \rightarrow \bar{i}$ denotes the dependence of attribute $\bar{j}$ over $\bar{i}$. Then, on the original graph's minimal spanning graph, a greedy node selection technique is used to choose a subset of nodes (attributes) that are likely to yield acceptable classification performance.

Relative indiscernibility: When it comes to a collection of conditional attributes $\bar{B} \subseteq (\bar{A} - \{\bar{d}\})$, a relationship of *relative indiscernibility* with respect to the decision attribute $\bar{d}$ is defined as follows:

$$
\begin{aligned}
\text{RIND}(\bar{B}) = \{(\bar{x}, \bar{y}) \& \in [\bar{x}]_{\bar{d}} \times [\bar{x}]_{\bar{d}}, \, \forall [\bar{x}]_{\bar{d}} \in \bar{U}_{\bar{d}} \\
\& \quad | \, \forall a \in \bar{B}, f_a(\bar{x}) = f_a(\bar{y})\},
\end{aligned}
\tag{4.2}
$$

where $[\bar{x}]_{\bar{d}} \in \bar{U}_{\bar{d}}$ are the equivalence classes of the partitioning $\bar{U}_{\bar{d}}$ according to the indiscernibility relation of the decision attribute d. If $(\bar{x}, \bar{y}) \in \text{RIND}(\bar{B})$, this implies that (i) the decision value of $\bar{x}$ and $\bar{y}$ is the same and (ii) $\bar{x}$ and $\bar{y}$ are indistinguishable with respect to the attribute set $\bar{B}$.

The relationship between relative invisibility and indiscernibility $\text{RIND}(\bar{B})$ is another equivalence relation that divides the universe $\bar{U}$ of objects into equivalence classes, each of which has the same decision class and is indistinguishable by attributes in B. Partitioning of $\bar{U}$ according to $\text{RIND}(\bar{B})$ is referred to as $\bar{U}_{\bar{d}/\bar{B}}$, and the equivalence classes of this relation are represented as $[\bar{x}]_{\bar{d}/\bar{B}}$.

If set $\bar{B}$ includes a single attribute a, as previously stated, the partitioning is represented as $\bar{U}_{\bar{d}/a}$ and the equivalence class as $[\bar{x}]_{\bar{d}/a}$ for simplicity. Table 4.2 (right column) demonstrates the partitioning of the decision system that is represented in Table 4.1, for each conditional attribute, according to the relative indiscernibility relationship.

Consider the following example to illustrate the distinctions between $IND(\bar{B})$ and $RIND(\bar{B})$. Table 4.2 represents that for the attribute $\bar{r}$, the objects $\bar{x}_7$ and $\bar{x}_8$ belong to $\bar{U}_{\bar{r}}$ (i.e., $IND(\bar{B})$ when $\bar{B} = \{\bar{r}\}$), as these objects are not able to be identified as different with respect to the attribute $\bar{r}$. So, with respect to the decision attribute, the objects $\bar{x}_7$ and $\bar{x}_8$ are distinguishable (see Table 4.1). As a result, $RIND(\overline{B})$ denotes discernibility for the attributes $\bar{x}_7$ and $\bar{x}_8$. So with respect to the decision attribute, the attributes $\bar{x}_7$ and $\bar{x}_8$ are divided into distinct classes in $\overline{U}_{\bar{d}/\bar{r}}$ (see Table 4.2).

Conditional attribute interdependence: The dependency of a given decision system is now measured among its conditional attributes. There are two conditional attributes $\bar{j}$ and $\bar{i}$. We let the partitions according to the relative indiscernibility relations of these attributes be $\overline{U}_{\bar{d}/\bar{j}} = \{[\bar{x}]_{\bar{d}/\bar{j}}\}$ and $\overline{U}_{\bar{d}/\bar{i}} = \{[\bar{x}]_{\bar{d}/\bar{i}}\}$. In terms of classification power, attribute $\bar{j}$ is similar to attribute $\bar{i}$ if they yield equal partitions of the objects based on their relative indiscernibility relations.

To determine the similarity of two partitions, several similarity measures have been tested, including metrics based on the Jaccard coefficient, normalized mutual information, and the F-measure (see [54] for details). The F-measure metric [54] was chosen for determining the similarity between the two partitions since it produced the best results in the classification experiments discussed later in this section. Traditionally, the F-measure has been used to compare two clusterings of a set of elements (analogous to partitions $\overline{U}_{\bar{d}/\bar{i}}$ and $\overline{U}_{\bar{d}/\bar{j}}$ in this case). Between two clusters, the F-measure (analogous to equivalence classes $[\bar{x}]_{\bar{d}/\bar{i}}$ and $[\bar{x}]_{\bar{d}/\bar{j}}$ in this case) calculates the harmonic average of the precision $\bar{p} = \frac{|[\bar{x}]_{\bar{d}/\bar{i}} \cap [\bar{x}]_{\bar{d}/\bar{j}}|}{|[\bar{x}]_{\bar{d}/\bar{j}}|}$ and the recall $\bar{r} = \frac{|[\bar{x}]_{\bar{d}/\bar{i}} \cap [\bar{x}]_{\bar{d}/\bar{j}}|}{|[\bar{x}]_{\bar{d}/\bar{i}}|}$ as

$$F([\bar{x}]_{\bar{d}/\bar{i}}, [\bar{x}]_{\bar{d}/\bar{j}}) = \frac{2 \cdot \bar{p} \cdot \bar{r}}{\bar{p} + \bar{r}}. \tag{4.3}$$

The F-measure accepts values ranging from 0 to 1, with 1 representing a perfect match and 0 representing no match [54]. The overall F-measure of the partition $\overline{U}_{\bar{d}/\bar{i}} = \{[\bar{x}]_{\bar{d}/\bar{i}}\}$ with the partition $\overline{U}_{\bar{d}/\bar{j}} = \{[\bar{x}]_{\bar{d}/\bar{j}}\}$ is then determined as the weighted sum of all equivalence classes' maximum F-measures in $\overline{U}_{\bar{d}/\bar{i}}$ with respect to the equivalence classes in $\overline{U}_{\bar{d}/\bar{j}}$, according to the following equation:

$$F(\overline{U}_{\bar{d}/\bar{i}}, \overline{U}_{\bar{d}/\bar{j}}) = \frac{1}{|\overline{U}|} \sum_{[\bar{x}]_{\bar{d}/\bar{i}} \in \overline{U}_{\bar{d}/\bar{i}}} |[\bar{x}]_{\bar{d}/\bar{i}}| \cdot \max_{[\bar{x}]_{\bar{d}/\bar{j}} \in \overline{U}_{\bar{d}/\bar{j}}} F([\bar{x}]_{\bar{d}/\bar{i}}, [\bar{x}]_{\bar{d}/\bar{j}}). \tag{4.4}$$

For every equivalence class $[\overline{x}]_{\overline{d}/\overline{i}}$ in $\overline{U}_{\overline{d}/\overline{i}}$, equivalence class $[\overline{x}]_{\overline{d}/\overline{j}} \in \overline{U}_{\overline{d}/\overline{j}}$ is computed which has the maximum F-measure with $[\overline{x}]_{\overline{d}/\overline{i}}$. The weighted sum of the F-measures is then calculated as $F([\overline{x}]_{\overline{d}/\overline{i}}, [\overline{x}]_{\overline{d}/\overline{j}})$, where the weight denotes the size of $[\overline{x}]_{\overline{d}/\overline{i}}$ (the universe's size is used to standardize the weighted sum). The F-measure specifies that attribute $\overline{i}$ is dependent on attribute $\overline{j}$. Precisely, $F(\overline{U}_{\overline{d}/\overline{i}}, \overline{U}_{\overline{d}/\overline{j}})$ denotes *how well the classification according to $\overline{i}$ can be deduced from the classification's knowledge according to $\overline{j}$.* It is worth noting that the F-measure is asymmetric, i.e., $F(\overline{U}_{\overline{d}/\overline{i}}, \overline{U}_{\overline{d}/\overline{j}})$ could differ from $F(\overline{U}_{\overline{d}/\overline{j}}, \overline{U}_{\overline{d}/\overline{i}})$.

In other words, the relationship between attribute $\overline{i}$ and attribute $\overline{j}$ may not be the same as the relationship between $\overline{j}$ and $\overline{i}$. Asymmetry is critical to examine since only one of two attributes with a high level of reliance would desire to be included in the reduct. Which attribute is included in the reduction will be determined by the asymmetric dependence.

Attribute dependency graph: A directed and weighted attribute dependency graph represents the dependencies among the decision system's conditional attributes (ADG) $\overline{G} = (\overline{V}, \overline{E}, \overline{w})$, each conditional attribute in the decision system is represented by a node in the node set $\overline{V}$, the set of edges $\overline{E}$ represents the dependencies between the attributes, and $\overline{w}: \overline{E} \to \mathbb{R}$ is a weighting function defined as $\overline{w}(\overline{i}, \overline{j}) = F(\overline{U}_{\overline{d}/\overline{j}}, \overline{U}_{\overline{d}/\overline{i}})$, $(\overline{i}, \overline{j}) \in \overline{E}$. The edge $\overline{i} \to \overline{j}$ and $\overline{j} \to \overline{i}$ represent how correct the classification is according to whether attribute $\overline{i}$ or $\overline{j}$ can be deduced from the classification according to $\overline{j}$ or $\overline{i}$, respectively.

Fig. 4.2(a) displays the ADG($\overline{G}$) for the sample decision system represented in Table 4.1, where the weights of the edges are calculated using Eq. (4.4) using the partitions that are provided by the relative indiscernibility relations in Table 4.2 (right column).

Creating a reduct from the attribute dependency graph
The ADG is nothing but a complete graph that shows how each attribute is dependent on the others. Following that, we keep only the most important edges. ADG's minimum spanning graph (MSG) is computed to keep only the most important edges [55]. Fig. 4.2(b) shows the MSG for the ADG in Fig. 4.2(a). Finally, a subset of the nodes (i.e., attributes) are chosen from the MSG using a greedy approach as described in Algorithm 4.1.

Assume an edge $\overline{i} \to \overline{j}$ in the MSG; the presence of this edge in the MSG indicates that the classification according to attribute $\overline{j}$ can be deduced quite precisely from knowledge of attribute $\overline{i}$ classification. Intuitively, if the goal is to reduce the number of attributes, it is assumed that including only $\overline{i}$ in

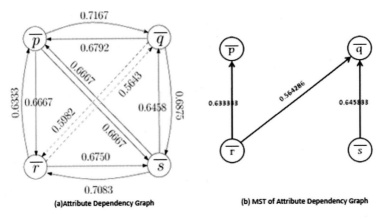

(a)Attribute Dependency Graph   (b) MST of Attribute Dependency Graph

Figure 4.2 (a) Table 4.1 represents ADG ($\overline{G}$) for the sample decision system. The dependency of attribute $\overline{j}$ on attribute $\overline{i}$ is indicated by the weight of the edge $\overline{i} \rightarrow \overline{j}$ (see text for details). (b) MST of ADG.

the reduced attribute set is sufficient (instead of both $\overline{j}$ and $\overline{i}$). The greedy approach in Algorithm 4.1 adheres to the preceding intuition.

The greedy algorithm begins by picking an essential MSG node (attribute). There are several graph centrality measures that can be used to determine the significance of nodes in a graph, for example, in-degree, weighted in-degree (where in-degree of a node is the sum of edges connected to that node), betweenness centrality, eigenvalue centrality, PageRank, and so on. The experiments were conducted using a variety of centrality measures, and it was discovered that the simple in-degree metric provides the best results for the suggested methodology [56].

As a result, the greedy method begins by identifying the node (attribute) $\overline{n}$ in the MSG with the highest in-degree. If there are any ties, they are resolved arbitrarily when selecting the node with the most in-degrees. The reduct is enhanced by including the highest in-degree node $\overline{n}$. The addition of attribute $\overline{n}$ in the reduct is likely to capture the classification according to any attribute (node) $\overline{j}$ in the MSG that is a neighbor of $\overline{n}$ to a significant extent in MSG [57].

As a result, the method removes all edges (dependencies) starting not only from $\overline{n}$, but also from any node that is $\overline{n}$'s neighbor. This technique is repeated until the MSG no longer has any edges.

If the algorithm described above is applied to the MSG in Fig. 4.2(b) (for the small decision system mentioned in Table 4.1), then the node which has the highest in-degree in that MSG is $\overline{q}$, whose adjacent nodes

---

Algorithm 4.1 Greedy algorithm for reduct generation from an attribute dependency graph

---

Require: Attribute set, $\overline{A}$.
Ensure: Reduced set of attributes RED

For each pair of attribute, $\bar{i}, \bar{j} \in \overline{A}$, compute $F(\overline{U}_{\bar{d}/\bar{i}}, \overline{U}_{\bar{d}/\bar{j}})$ according to Eq. (4.4).

Form a directed ADG $\overline{G} = (\overline{V}, \overline{E}, \overline{w})$, considering all attributes as nodes and $F(\overline{U}_{\bar{d}/\bar{i}}, \overline{U}_{\bar{d}/\bar{j}})$ as edge weights between each pair of nodes $\bar{i}, \bar{j} \in \overline{A}$.

Compute minimum spanning graph $\overline{MSG} = (\overline{V}, \overline{E_M})$ by selecting high-weight edges
$\{\overline{E_M}$ is the set of edges included in $\overline{MSG}\}$
$\{$Greedy computation of reduced attribute set$\}$
$RED \leftarrow \phi$
while $\overline{E_M} \neq \phi$ **do**
    $\{$loop until all edges are deleted$\}$
    $\bar{n} \leftarrow$ a node having the highest in-degree in $\overline{MSG}$
    $RED \leftarrow RED \cup \{\bar{n}\}$
    $S \leftarrow \{\bar{j} \mid (\bar{n}, \bar{j}) \in \overline{E_M}\}$ $\{$set of neighbors of n in $MSG\}$
    $\overline{E_M} \leftarrow \overline{E_M} - \{(i, j) \mid i = n \text{ or } \bar{i} \in \overline{S}\}$
end while
return RED

---

include $\bar{r}$ and $\bar{s}$. Thus $\bar{q}$ will be added in the reduct set and corresponding edges are excluded. The graph is subjected to the same procedure until all edges have been deleted. Hence the algorithm terminates with $RED = \{\bar{q}, \bar{p}\}$.

It is worth noting that the greedy approach described above may only select an approximate reduct. However, because the task of obtaining the exact reduct is NP-hard [40], to discover an approximate reduct, it is preferable to use a heuristic process. As an alternative to the greedy strategy described above, a graph community detection algorithm (specifically, Infomap) has been investigated as a method for selecting attributes [58] to group the ADG nodes into communities, and then, from each community, one representative node (attribute) is chosen. The greedy strategy outlined above, on the other hand, outperforms the methodology that uses a community detection method (see Section 5.5 for details).

Also note that the proposed algorithm can be executed such that it selects at most a specified (desired) number of features. As detailed above,

Table 4.3 Description of datasets from previous works used to illustrate effectiveness of the proposed attribute selection method.

Dataset ID	Instances	Attribute	Classes	Reference
Dataset 1	1065	63	spammers and non-spammers	[9]
Dataset 2	829	60	spammers, legitimates, and promoters	[10]
Dataset 3	2762	23	non-spam and spam	[12]
Dataset 4	7076	60	spam and non-spam	[13]

the proposed algorithm starts by identifying the node $\bar{n}$ which is having the maximum in-degree in the MSG and excluding all edges (dependencies) starting from $\bar{n}$ and any node which is an adjacent of $\bar{n}$. This process is then repeated, i.e., again the node having the highest in-degree in the remaining graph is chosen, and so on. Hence, the algorithm can be stopped when a desired number of nodes (attributes) have been selected by this process. However, the algorithm may stop selecting a lesser number of nodes than is specified (if all edges in the MSG are already deleted) [59].

It should also be emphasized that the proposed methodology is best suited to attributes with discrete or categorical values. In datasets with continuous features, discretization methods can be used to first discretize the attribute values, and then the feature selection procedure can be applied. For this, any discretization algorithm can be employed [60]. All of the tests in this chapter use Fayyad and Irani's well-known MDL discretization technique (implemented in the Weka tool) [61]. The proposed methodology's utility in enhancing spam classification in various types of online social media is discussed in the following sections [62].

4.4 Experimental dataset

To illustrate the effectiveness of the proposed attribute selection algorithm, it is applied over five different datasets, one of which has been prepared, and the other four are collected from previous research on spam classification on OSMs. The different datasets are described in this section [63].

4.4.1 Datasets from previous works

Here first the datasets are described which are collected from previous works on spam classification on OSMs. The experimental datasets have been made publicly available by the following four studies. The datasets are also outlined in Table 4.3.

1. **Dataset 1** – Benevenuto et al. [9] created a dataset of 1065 Twitter user profiles which they divided into two categories: non-spammers and spammers. Here classification is based on 62 criteria that capture a variety of user account features.
2. **Dataset 2** – This dataset was also created by Benevenuto et al. [10], to categorize people in online video networks into three categories: content boosters, legitimate users, and spammers. The dataset contains 60 features, including video attributes (which capture unique properties of each user's movies), social relationship attributes (derived from video response interactions), and individual user behavior attributes [64].
3. **Dataset 3** – This dataset is about "tip spam" in location-based social networks. Prepared by Costa et al. [12], the dataset consists of 2762 instances, 41 attributes, and two classes (spam and non-spam).
4. **Dataset 4** – This dataset, also prepared by Costa et al. [13], is similar to the above one (on spam in location-based social networks). However, it is larger, with 7076 instances and 60 attributes.

4.4.2 Collected dataset of spam tweets

A fifth dataset (Dataset 5) was prepared to differentiate legitimate tweets and spam posted on the Twitter OSM. Using the Twitter API [65], over a period of two days, a crawler was developed to collect a 1% random sample of tweets made publicly available by Twitter. Spam always contains URLs to spam websites, so tweets with URLs are highlighted out of all the tweets collected. A total of 343,791 tweets with URLs were collected. The next stage was to determine which tweets were spam and which were authentic (i.e., preparing the golden standard) [66].

Identification of spam tweets

Spam tweets are identified by checking whether any of the URLs in a tweet are banned, as shown below. Because tweets are limited to 140 characters, URLs are almost always abbreviated; as a result, all URLs in tweets are lengthened using HTTP redirects to arrive at the ultimate landing URL. Finally, a variety of spam blacklists were used to examine each URL (both the truncated version in the tweet and the final landing URL) – SURBL [67], Google Safe Browsing [68], Spamhaus [69], and Capture-HPC [70]. If any of the URLs present in a tweet (or the lengthened version of any of the URLs) is discovered to be on a blacklist, the tweet is considered spam; otherwise, the tweet is regarded legal. In total, 93,791 tweets have been identified as spam, with the other messages being deemed authentic [71].

It is worth noting that the dataset generated by the above methods has a potential flaw: some of the tweets that appear to be legal may actually contain spam URLs that the blacklists employed failed to detect [71]. However, considering the large number of URLs submitted every day on Twitter, manually verifying URLs is difficult; thus, blacklists are the only practical alternative, which has also been employed in earlier studies [11,44].

Attributes for spam vs. legitimate classification

For each of the tweets in the tagged collection, a set of 23 properties was identified. These characteristics, which are listed in Table 4.4, can be divided into three groups:

- *Text-based attributes* – These include unique character count, word count, hashtag count per tweet, digit count, other text-based properties of tweets, and number of spam words per tweet.
- *Attributes based on URLs* – These are the attributes of the URL(s) in the tweet. It is worth noting that the final landing URL is taken into account when extracting these properties (not the truncated version that appeared in the tweet). In addition, if a tweet has multiple URLs, these properties are averaged across all URLs [72].
- *Attributes based on the user's profile* – These attributes are features of the user account from which the tweet was sent. These qualities seek to capture concepts such as the user's popularity on the Twitter social network (no. of followers, no. of times listed), his/her activity (no. of followers, no. of tweets posted), and the account's age (in days).

It is worth noting that the 23 attributes discussed here are not a complete list of all attributes that can be used to distinguish between spam and authentic tweets. Only these properties are taken into account, as the majority of them may be derived directly from Twitter's live tweet stream. Only the URL-based attributes necessitate the enlargement of the tweet's abbreviated URL(s), which necessitates a minimal number of HTTP redirects. Only these features are highlighted because they are likely to be taken into account by systems aiming for real-time spam tweet classification, which necessitates real-time extraction of attributes from hundreds of millions of tweets. The performance of the suggested attribute selection technique on the datasets provided above is described in the next section.

4.5 Evaluating performance

The usefulness of the proposed technique in enhancing classification between non-spam and spam entities on OSMs is demonstrated in this

Table 4.4 Attributes for the spam tweets dataset (Dataset 5).

Sl.	Attribute name	A brief summary
	Attributes based on tweet text	
1	word_count	The number of words in a tweet
2	unique_char_count	The number of distinct characters present in the tweet
3	digit_count	The number of digits present in the tweet
4	hashtag_count	The number of hashtags used in a tweet
5	hashtags_per_word	The number of hashtags per word
6	position_of_hashtag	The location of a hashtag present in a tweet
7	swear_words_count	The total number of swear words present in the tweet
8	spam_words_in_tweet_count	The total number of spam words present in the tweet
	Attributes based on URL **(If a tweet has numerous URLs, average them out.)**	
9	url_count	The total number of URLs in a tweet
10	urls_per_word	The number of URLs in a tweet per word
11	expanded_url_length	URL length when expanded
12	dot_in_expanded_url	In an enlarged URL, the number of dots used
13	no_of_sub-domains	The total number of sub-domains
14	no_of_redirections	The total number of redirections
	Attributes based on user profile **(according to the user u who sent the tweet)**	
15	user_follower_count	The number of people who follow u
16	user_followee_count	Number of users whom u follows
17	followers_per_followee	Number of followers/number of followings
18	user_listed_count	Number of times u has been listed by other users
19	user_status_count	A user's total number of tweets
20	user_bio_exists	Boolean status of bio of a user account
21	spam_words_in_bio_count	The number of spam words in a Twitter account's bio
22	users_mentioned_count	The number of times other users have mentioned u
23	age_of_account	The number of days between when u's user account was created and when the tweet was published

section. The suggested algorithm's performance is compared to that of a number of alternative attribute selection methods, which are discussed in the following sections.

4.5.1 Baseline attribute selection strategies

The suggested attribute selection process is compared to a number of well-known baselines, which are described below.

(1) **Correlation feature selection (CFS):** This methodology [73] considers the predictive capacity of each individual trait, as well as the degree of redundancy between them, to assess the usefulness of a subset of attributes. It is preferable to use subsets of attributes that are substantially associated with the classification yet have low intercorrelation.

(2) **Consistency subset evaluation (CON):** When the training instances are projected onto the subset, the level of consistency in the class values is used to determine the effectiveness of a subset of attributes. The subset evaluator is typically used in conjunction with a search methodology that seeks out the smallest subset with consistency equal to the entire set of qualities, such as exhaustive search, random search, Best First, and rank search. The Best First search technology is used among all the search approaches [74].

(3) **Attribute ranking with respect to Information Gain (InfoGain):** The attributes are prioritized here depending on the amount of information gained by each attribute in relation to the class attribute [50]. The top-ranked $\bar{k}$ attributes are examined for comparison with the proposed attribute selection process, where $\bar{k}$ is the number of attributes identified by the proposed methodology.

(4) **Attribute ranking with respect to chi squared (χ^2):** The value of the chi squared statistic with regard to the class is used to measure the effectiveness of an individual attribute, and the attributes are sorted according to the chi squared statistic [50]. The top-ranked $\bar{k}$ attributes are picked in the same way as before, where $\bar{k}$ is the number of attributes chosen by the proposed approach.

(5) **Selection of attributes based on community detection (COMM):** This is a variation of the technique that was proposed. The ADG network is generated in the same manner as previously explained. After that, instead of using the greed attribute selection approach discussed previously, the significant nodes are chosen using a graph community detection mechanism over ADG.

To begin, the ADG is thresholded using a specific edge weight. Edges with higher edge weights than the average edge weight are honed. Because the initial ADG is a clique, community detection is useless; as a result, thresholding only recognizes the higher-weight edges. After that, Infomap [58], a popular community detection approach, is used. The popular community discovery method Infomap is then used to locate groupings of strongly linked nodes in the thresholded ADG. The benefit of Infomap is that it does not require any prior knowledge of the optimal amount of communities to include in the graph. Following that, one node from each recognized community is chosen, with the node with the greatest degree among all nodes in the community being chosen.[2] This approach is based on the following instinct. Because a community's attributes are likely to be extremely similar to one another, recognizing only one attribute from a group of similar qualities will aid in the selection of a smaller subset of attributes.

4.5.2 Classifiers used

For classification, the eight classifiers from the Weka toolkit are employed [75]: (i) RBF Network, (ii) naive Bayes, (iii) LWL, (iv), logistic regression, (v) Logit Boost, (vi) decision table, (vii), random tree, and (viii) OneR.

The classification is carried out for each dataset (described in Section 4.4) and each classifier using a conventional 10-fold cross-validation approach, in which the dataset is divided into 10 equal-sized partitions. The classification is repeated 10 times, with the classifier training on 9 of the 10 partitions each time and the remaining partition serving as a test set. The results of the 10 assessments are averaged to get the final evaluation outcome (for a certain classifier and dataset).

4.5.3 Evaluation measures

The efficiency and efficacy of classification are evaluated using the attribute sets chosen by the various methodologies to evaluate the performance of multiple attribute selection algorithms. The usual algorithm for encoding classification outcome in a confusion matrix (as described in Table 4.5) is employed to do this, considering standard measures such as recall, precision, accuracy, and the F-score.

The ratio of the number of items properly anticipated to be in that class to the total number of items predicted in that class is the precision with

2 Ties, if any, are resolved arbitrarily.

Table 4.5 A sample confusion matrix.

		Predicted	
		Spam	Legitimate
True	Spam	p	q
	Legitimate	r	s

Table 4.6 Different attribute selection algorithms select a different number of attributes.

Method	Number of attributes				
	Dataset 1	Dataset 2	Dataset 3	Dataset 4	Dataset 5
All attributes	63	60	23	60	23
CFS	8	14	5	7	10
CON	16	13	17	24	15
COMM	5	5	4	7	7
Proposed	15	36	3	5	6

regard to that class. Table 4.5 shows the confusion matrix; the precision (P) for the spam class is denoted as $P = p/(p + r)$. Recall (R) is defined as the ratio of the number of objects correctly predicted to belong to that class to the total number of items that really belong to that class. It is defined for the spam class as $R = p/(p+q)$. Next, accuracy (A) is the percentage of correctly classified items in the total number of objects, i.e., $A = (p+s)/(p+q+r+s)$. The F-score is the precision and recall's harmonic mean: $F = \frac{2PR}{P+R}$. The accuracy and F-score (which summarizes together precision and recall) are reported in detail.

4.5.4 Results

The proposed feature selection technique is compared to the baselines listed above in Table 4.6. The proposed attribute selection technique is utilized to pick subsets of attributes for each dataset. Each dataset is classified using all attributes, and each attribute selection algorithm evaluates the reduct attribute set, after which the performance of classification is compared using multiple attribute sets.

Number of attributes identified

The number of features identified by the various methodologies is shown in Table 4.6. The number of attributes detected by the proposed approach is smaller than that identified by all other techniques for three of the five datasets. The COMM baseline (community detection based on variation of the proposed approach) provides the greatest reduction of characteristics for Datasets 1 and 2. It is worth noting that the chi squared and InfoGain methods are not included in this study because they are both meant to pick the same amount of attributes as the suggested approach.

Common attributes selected by various methods

The number of similar attributes found by alternative attribute selection techniques, as well as the suggested algorithm, are shown in Table 4.7. For Dataset 1, for example, the set of 8 attributes chosen by CFS and the group of 15 attributes discovered by the proposed approach have 5 attributes in common. In each example, the common characteristics are also noted. In general, there is a lot of overlap between the qualities found by the proposed approach and those identified by other techniques for Dataset 2 and Dataset 1 (which has the most overlap), but it is considerably smaller for the remaining three datasets.

The findings of the various attribute selection approaches show that, for any given dataset, the majority of the algorithms identify a few key attributes. Table 4.8 displays examples of some of the most essential features found by at least three of the attribute selection approaches used in this study for each dataset.

For example, for Dataset 5, attributes such as "age_of_account," "followers_per_followee," and "user_follower_count" have been chosen by most of the feature selection strategies. In Dataset 1 as well (which focuses on identification and classification of spam accounts on Twitter), attributes based on reputation of the account (e.g., number of followers per followee) and "age_of_account" are prominent. These findings are to be expected, considering the importance of these characteristics in the detection of Twitter spam – as prior research has shown [9,6–8], user accounts that have recently been created sending out a lot of spam tweets have a low reputation (low user_follower_count and low age_of_account).

Similarly, most attribute selection approaches discover some specific attributes in Datasets 3 and 4 (both of these are concerned with the classification of spam suggestions in location-based social networks), i.e., the "Thumbs down" link (which are user-generated reputation scores), the number of words in the tip, the number of clicks on the location page, and similarly the number of followers on a particular Twitter account. Crowdsourced reputation assessments like the number of video ratings and comments, as well as the number of times videos are favorited, are effective for spam categorization in Dataset 2 (on spam in online video social networks).

Table 4.7 Number of common attributes identified by various attribute selection algorithms and the proposed algorithm.

Method	The number of selected attributes that are the same as for the proposed method				
	Dataset 1	Dataset 2	Dataset 3	Dataset 4	Dataset 5
CFS	5 (attr2, attr1, attr45, attr22, attr63)	11 (attr22, attr12, attr3, attr24, attr23, attr32, attr26, attr33, attr47, attr59, attr40)	1 (qLikes_tip)	2 (qLikes_tip, senticnet_tip)	2 (age_of_account, url_count)
CON	9 (attr53, attr2, attr15, ttr14, attr35, attr17, attr59, attr10, attr63)	8 (attr15, attr2, attr32, attr30, attr55, attr54, attr58, attr56)	3 (qClicks_plc, qWords_tip, qThumbs-down_plc)	5 (combined_tip, qWords_tip, qClicks_plc, senticnet_tip, qThumbs-down_plc)	6 (age_of_account, user_follower_count, user_status_count, user_followee_count, spam_words_in_tweet_count, followers_per_followee)
COMM	2 (attr22, attr16)	3 (attr55, attr51, attr59)	3 (qClicks_plc, qWords_tip, qClicks_tip, qThumbs-down_plc)	4 (combined_tip, qWords_tip, qClicks_plc, qThumbs-down_plc)	5 (followers_per_followee, age_of_account, spam_words_in_tweet_count, user_followee_count, user_follower_count)
InfoGain	14 (attr2, attr1, attr16, attr6, attr45, attr22, attr10, attr43, attr47, attr50, attr53, attr48, attr46, attr63)	36 (attr3, attr1, attr7, attr4, attr9, attr6, attr12, attr22, attr13, attr10, attr15, attr25, attr23, attr28, attr26, attr24, attr31, attr29, attr27, attr34, attr32, attr30, attr33, attr36, attr40, attr48, attr45, attr39, attr52, attr49, attr47, attr50, attr53, attr60, attr58, attr59)	1 (qClicks_plc)	3 (qClicks_plc, senticnet_tip, qThumbs-down_plc)	2 (age_of_account, user_follower_count)
ChiSqr	14 (attr2, attr1, attr16, attr6, attr22, attr10, attr45, attr43, attr48, attr46, attr50, attr47, attr63, attr53)	36 (attr1, attr4, attr3, attr7, attr9, attr6, attr10, attr13, attr23, attr15, attr12, attr26, attr24, attr22, attr29, attr27, attr25, attr32, attr30, attr28, attr36, attr33, attr31, attr45, attr39, attr34, attr49, attr47, attr40, attr53, attr50, attr48, attr60, attr59, attr58, attr52)	1 (rating_plc)	3 (qClicks_plc, senticnet_tip, qThumbs-down_plc)	3(user_follower_count, age_of_account, user_followee_count)

Classification performance

Following that, classification performance is compared using the reduct evaluated by the suggested approach and the subset of attributes chosen by the baseline attribute selection strategies. Table 4.9 and Table 4.10 show the mean accuracy and F-score of categorization using different attribute sets.

Table 4.8 Examples of significant attributes identified by at least three attribute selection algorithms for each dataset.

Dataset	Attributes identified by at least three algorithms
Dataset 1	attr1 (No. of followers per each follower), attr2 (% of tweets responded), attr22 (The average no. of mentions per tweet), attr45 (No. of followees of a user's followers), attr53 (The maximum amount of time elapsed between posts), attr63 (The user account's age)
Dataset 2	attr15 (The total no. of times that all of the videos that were responded to were marked as favorites), attr30 (The average no. of ratings for all videos that received responses), attr32 (The average no. of comments on all video responses), attr53 (Friendship count), attr55 (No. of uploaded videos), attr59 (The maximum no. of videos uploaded in a 24-hour period)
Dataset 3	qClicks_plc (No. of clicks on the location page), qWords_tip (The total no. of words in the tip), qThumbs-down_plc (Clicks on the link "Thumbs down")
Dataset 4	qWords_tip (No. of words present in the tip), qClicks_plc (No. of clicks on the place page), senticnet_tip (SenticNet value), qThumbs-down_plc (Clicks on the link "Thumbs down")
Dataset 5	age_of_account (The user account's age), user_follower_count (No. of followers), user_followee_count(No. of followees), followers_per_followee (No. of followees of a user's followers)

The provided values are the averages of the eight classifiers determined by the eight classification methods mentioned earlier in this section. The improvement in classification obtained using limited attribute sets compared to that obtained using all attributes demonstrates the efficiency of attribute selection approaches. Except for Dataset 2, for all datasets, in comparison to the other baseline techniques, the suggested algorithm's feature selection strategy enabled the best classification performance. Also, for Dataset 2, the proposed technique outperforms all other methods except CFS. It is also worth noting that the suggested approach outperforms the COMM baseline across all datasets – this discovery demonstrates the efficacy of the ADG's proposed greedy attribute selection technique.

Table 4.9 The performance of the classifiers for five datasets through eight classifiers: random tree, RBF network, naive Bayes, LWL, logistic regression, Logit Boost, OneR, and decision table. The performance evaluated across all eight classifiers is also presented for each dataset.

Method	All	CFS	CON	InfoGain	ChiSqr	COMM	Proposed
Dataset 1							
Naive Bayes	85.92	87.42	84.69	82.25	84.32	80.66	88.70
RBF network	86.29	88.08	84.98	83.57	83.19	80.94	86.67
Logistic regression	87.23	88.17	87.61	83.29	85.92	81.69	86.95
LWL	85.54	83.66	84.88	84.79	84.69	83.29	84.23
LogitBoost	86.85	87.04	87.23	87.42	86.01	83.66	87.04
Decision table	86.85	87.51	88.36	87.61	86.85	83.66	88.08
OneR	81.41	82.25	81.69	81.41	81.41	83.29	82.25
Random tree	82.25	80.94	81.6	82.16	81.31	78.87	85.80
Average	85.29	85.63	85.13	84.06	84.21	74.95	**86.21**
Dataset 2							
Naive Bayes	50.54	81.54	55.13	50.54	48.85	34.86	84.39
RBF network	81.18	83.47	80.46	81.18	82.99	77.20	81.42
Logistic regression	86.61	86.13	85.04	86.61	86.37	80.22	86.37
LWL	83.23	84.56	80.46	83.23	83.47	77.44	83.35
LogitBoost	88.66	88.66	87.69	88.66	87.94	79.98	87.21
Decision table	84.68	86.85	86.13	84.68	85.16	77.08	85.65
OneR	84.08	82.12	82.03	84.08	84.08	77.68	78.41
Random tree	82.75	84.07	81.91	82.75	82.63	73.82	83.72
Average	80.22	**84.68**	79.85	80.22	80.19	72.29	83.82
Dataset 3							
Naive Bayes	90.1	95.51	92.07	90.8	94.68	90.41	99.51
RBF network	89.18	98.05	91.23	89.21	95.44	95.22	96.56
Logistic regression	99.11	99.42	99.49	99.38	99.96	99.89	99.96
LWL	100	100	100	100	100	100	100
LogitBoost	100	100	100	100	100	100	100
Decision table	100	100	100	100	100	100	100
OneR	100	100	100	100	100	100	100
Random tree	98.12	100	99	98.88	100	100	99.96
Average	97.06	99.12	97.77	97.28	98.76	98.19	**99.50**
Dataset 4							
Naive Bayes	75.23	95.57	93.12	75.23	94.15	95.25	99.62
RBF network	89.7	96.11	91.3	89.7	94.09	95.66	97.44
Logistic regression	99.63	99.87	99.83	99.63	99.87	99.96	99.94
LWL	100	100	100	100	100	99.89	100
LogitBoost	100	100	100	100	100	100	100

continued on next page

Table 4.9 (continued)

Method	All	CFS	CON	InfoGain	ChiSqr	COMM	Proposed
Decision table	100	100	100	100	100	100	100
OneR	100	100	100	100	100	100	100
Random tree	98.00	100	98.10	97.71	99.99	99.96	99.87
Average	95.28	98.94	97.79	95.28	98.51	98.84	**99.61**
			Dataset 5				
Naive Bayes	84.4	79.40	45.67	70.82	76.77	74.55	83.67
RBF network	73.35	79.85	72.76	73.42	76.78	72.38	77.86
Logistic	74.34	82.69	79.72	73.58	79.98	73.58	79.72
LWL	82.48	78.48	78.13	72.34	77.94	72.15	76.52
LogitBoost	75.57	82.98	82.32	73.56	81.83	75.74	82.82
Decision table	75.56	78.56	72.65	72.63	76.47	74.66	77.85
OneR	78.48	78.48	78.48	73.58	78.88	71.06	78.48
Random tree	83.58	84.70	91.40	73.58	82.93	78.97	91.40
Average	78.47	80.64	75.14	72.94	78.95	74.14	**81.04**

Table 4.10 Classification performance as assessed by the F-score (F) with all characteristics and attributes identified using various attribute selection procedures. The performance of the classifiers is reported over five datasets and eight classifiers: RBF network, naive Bayes, LWL, logistic regression, Logit Boost, OneR, decision table, and random tree. For each dataset, the performance evaluated across all eight classifiers is also presented.

Methods	All	CFS	CON	InfoGain	ChiSqr	COMM	Proposed
			Dataset 1				
Naive Bayes	0.856	0.871	0.846	0.822	0.84	0.790	0.887
RBF network	0.858	0.877	0.847	0.828	0.827	0.791	0.863
Logistic regression	0.869	0.880	0.873	0.829	0.855	0.801	0.866
LWL	0.848	0.824	0.844	0.839	0.838	0.820	0.830
LogitBoost	0.866	0.867	0.870	0.872	0.857	0.829	0.868
Decision table	0.863	0.870	0.878	0.872	0.863	0.827	0.876
OneR	0.807	0.817	0.810	0.807	0.810	0.820	0.817
Random tree	0.822	0.809	0.815	0.822	0.812	0.790	0.862
Average	0.848	0.851	0.847	0.836	0.837	0.706	**0.858**
			Dataset 2				
Naive Bayes	0.536	0.826	0.590	0.536	0.516	0.338	0.862
RBF network	0.756	0.817	0.782	0.756	0.797	0.678	0.800
Logistic regression	0.864	0.855	0.840	0.864	0.858	0.724	0.832
LWL	0.831	0.841	0.763	0.831	0.831	0.677	0.817
LogitBoost	0.884	0.884	0.874	0.884	0.878	0.769	0.868
Decision table	0.844	0.863	0.858	0.844	0.849	0.714	0.853
OneR	0.834	0.834	0.814	0.822	0.822	0.694	0.778

continued on next page

Table 4.10 (*continued*)

Methods	All	CFS	CON	InfoGain	ChiSqr	COMM	Proposed
Random tree	0.830	0.849	0.819	0.830	0.825	0.743	0.837
Average	0.797	**0.846**	0.792	0.795	0.797	0.667	0.830
Dataset 3							
Naive Bayes	0.908	0.953	0.921	0.908	0.947	0.904	0.995
RBF network	0.892	0.966	0.921	0.892	0.954	0.952	0.966
Logistic regression	0.994	0.999	0.995	0.994	1.000	0.999	1.000
LWL	1.000	1.000	1.000	1.000	1.000	1.000	1.000
LogitBoost	1.000	1.000	1.000	1.000	1.000	1.000	1.000
Decision table	1.000	1.000	1.000	1.000	1.000	1.000	1.000
OneR	1.000	1.000	1.000	1.000	1.000	1.000	1.000
Random tree	0.989	1.000	0.994	0.989	1.000	1.000	1.000
Average	0.972	0.989	0.978	0.972	0.987	0.982	**0.995**
Dataset 4							
Naive Bayes	0.742	0.951	0.931	0.742	0.941	0.953	0.9960
RBF network	0.897	0.960	0.913	0.897	0.941	0.957	0.9740
Logistic regression	0.996	0.999	0.998	0.996	0.999	1.000	0.9990
LWL	1.000	1.000	1.000	1.000	1.000	0.999	1.000
LogitBoost	1.000	1.000	1.000	1.000	1.000	1.000	1.000
Decision table	1.000	1.000	1.000	1.000	1.000	1.000	1.000
OneR	1.000	1.000	1.000	1.000	1.000	1.000	1.000
Random tree	0.977	1.000	0.989	0.977	1.000	1.000	1.000
Average	0.951	0.988	0.978	0.951	0.985	0.989	**0.996**
Dataset 5							
Naive Bayes	0.843	0.793	0.436	0.701	0.761	0.745	0.836
RBF network	0.737	0.795	0.715	0.734	0.753	0.723	0.776
Logistic regression	0.744	0.821	0.791	0.736	0.787	0.736	0.791
LWL	0.831	0.782	0.711	0.724	0.765	0.722	0.766
LogitBoost	0.758	0.826	0.811	0.738	0.819	0.756	0.827
Decision table	0.757	0.785	0.724	0.727	0.758	0.746	0.779
OneR	0.783	0.784	0.774	0.735	0.784	0.710	0.784
Random tree	0.835	0.851	0.862	0.736	0.818	0.788	0.914
Average	0.786	0.805	0.728	0.729	0.781	0.741	**0.809**

As CFS is the most direct competitor to the proposed method, it was assessed whether the performance differences between the two methods are statistically significant. The performances of the proposed approach and CON are also measured. To that objective, the T-test (parameterized) and the Wilcoxon rank sum test (non-parameterized) were used [76] to see if there were any statistically significant differences.

Each dataset was subjected to statistical tests and tests were carried out using the set of 10 accuracy measures obtained by the 10-fold cross-

Table 4.11 Statistical significance testing of (*p*-values) for computing the F-score (F) and classification accuracy (A) using the proposed method's attributes and baselines CFS and CON.

Measure	Dataset 1		Dataset 2		Dataset 3		Dataset 4		Dataset 5	
	A	F	A	F	A	F	A	F	A	F
Comparison of the proposed technique with the CFS										
T-test	0.04519	0.03684	0.04163	0.01911	0.01041	0.00112	0.03217	0.01942	0.02193	0.03327
Wilcoxon	**0.11179**	0.03911	0.03622	0.03910	0.02341	0.00201	0.02119	0.04881	0.03911	0.04881
Comparison of the proposed technique with the CON										
T-test	0.03896	0.04458	**0.05522**	0.03246	0.02684	0.02914	0.04727	0.03481	**0.05239**	0.04914
Wilcoxon	0.01453	0.04521	**0.06752**	0.045291	0.03373	0.03166	0.04916	0.01153	**0.07193**	0.03722

validation procedure. A significance threshold of $p = 0.05$ in these tests means a 5% likelihood of determining that a difference exists when there is none. The null hypothesis is rejected if the value of p is less than or equal to the level of significance.

Table 4.11 shows the statistical test p-values, with values below 0.05 (indicating a significant difference) emphasized in boldface. In the majority of cases, the differences between the proposed method's performance and that of CFS are *not* statistically significant.

For Datasets 2 and 5, the proposed approach gives a significantly better classification accuracy than CON.

Note that in the experiments described above, for the chi squared and InfoGain attribute ranking algorithms, the same number of top-ranked attributes were chosen as selected by the proposed methodology. For each dataset, another set of experiments was conducted, where for the chi squared and InfoGain attribute ranking methods, the same number of top-ranked attributes were considered as selected by CFS and CON for the same dataset. For instance, Table 4.6 shows that for Dataset 1, CFS selected 8 attributes while CON selected 16 attributes. Hence, in one set of experiments, the top-ranked 8 attributes were selected for the chi squared and InfoGain methods. In another set of experiments, the top-ranked 16 attributes were selected for the chi squared and InfoGain methods for Dataset 1. It is observed in these experiments that even if the same number of top-ranked attributes were considered as selected by CFS and CON for the same dataset, the attribute set selected by the proposed approach still yields better classification performance than that selected by the chi squared and Info-Gain ranking methods. Detailed results are omitted for brevity.

Combining all of the preceding analyses, the following conclusion can be drawn.

(1) The suggested method not only provides a smaller subset of attributes for four of the five datasets (excluding Dataset 2), but it also provides better classification than existing attribute selection methods (despite the fact that not all improvements are statistically significant). In Dataset 2 also, the proposed algorithm results are better than all other baseline methods except CFS.

(2) CFS outperforms the proposed technique on Dataset 2; nonetheless, the differences in performance between the two strategies are *statistically insignificant*. It is difficult to pinpoint why the proposed technique performed worse than CFS on Dataset 2. It is worth noting that for Dataset 2, CFS selects 14 attributes, 11 of which are likewise selected by the suggested technique. CFS outperforms the proposed method because it chose three specific properties that were not detected by the proposed method – attr25 ("average duration of all videos uploaded"), attr39 ("average number of honors of all responded videos"), and attr60 ("average time between video uploads"). The proposed technique did not choose these three qualities since they were connected to other selected features in the ADG (so they were not taken into account for the reduction). For instance, if some features are known to be useful for specific domains such as online video networks, then special mechanisms can be incorporated so that these features get included in the reduct.

4.6 Conclusion

Because classification must be done in real-time over millions of data pieces, attribute selection is critical for improving classification of spam on OSMs. In this chapter, a rough set theory-based attribute selection method is explained, and the method is applied to spam categorization on OSMs. The importance of the proposed methodology is demonstrated through experiments on five different datasets: for the majority of the datasets, the proposed technique selects a smaller subset of attributes/features than other attribute selection methodologies, but results in better classification performance.

References

[1] H. Paul, K. Georgia, G.-M. Hector, Fighting spam on social web sites: a survey of approaches and future challenges, IEEE Internet Computing 11 (2007) 36–45.

[2] C. Godwin, L. Maozhen, A survey of emerging approaches to spam filtering, ACM Computing Surveys 44 (2) (2012) 9:1–9:27.

[3] G. Chris, T. Kurt, P. Vern, Z. Michael, @spam: the underground on 140 characters or less, in: Proceedings of ACM International Conference on Computer and Communications Security (CCS), 2010, pp. 27–37.

[4] S. Chhabra, A. Aggarwal, F. Benevenuto, P. Kumaraguru, Phi.sh/$oCiaL: the phishing landscape through short URLs, in: Proceedings of Collaboration, Electronic Messaging, Anti-Abuse and Spam Conference (CEAS), CEAS '11, ACM, New York, NY, USA, 2011, pp. 92–101, http://doi.acm.org/10.1145/2030376.2030387.

[5] S. Goswami, A.K. Das, Determining maximum cliques for community detection in weighted sparse networks, Knowledge and Information Systems 64 (2) (2022) 289–324, https://doi.org/10.1007/s10115-021-01631-y.

[6] Y. Sarita, R. Daniel, S. Grant, B.D. M, Detecting spam in a Twitter network, First Monday 15 (1) (2010) 1–13.

[7] L. Kyumin, C. James, W. Steve, Uncovering social spammers: social honeypots + machine learning, in: Proceedings of ACM International Conference on Research and Development in Information Retrieval (SIGIR), 2010, pp. 435–442.

[8] L. Kyumin, E.B. David, C. James, Seven months with the devils: a long-term study of content polluters on Twitter, in: L.A. Adamic, R.A. Baeza-Yates, S. Counts (Eds.), ICWSM, The AAAI Press, 2011, http://dblp.uni-trier.de/db/conf/icwsm/icwsm2011.html#LeeEC11.

[9] B. Fabrício, M. Gabriel, R. Tiago, A. Virgílio, Detecting spammers on Twitter, in: Proceedings of Collaboration, Electronic Messaging, Anti-Abuse and Spam Conference (CEAS), 2010.

[10] F. Benevenuto, T. Rodrigues, J. Almeida, M. Goncalves, V. Almeida, Detecting spammers and content promoters in online video social networks, in: IEEE INFOCOM Workshops 2009, 2009, pp. 1–2.

[11] M.-R. Juan, A. Lourdes, Detecting malicious tweets in trending topics using a statistical analysis of language, Expert Systems with Applications 40 (8) (2013) 2992–3000.

[12] H. Costa, F. Benevenuto, L.H. de Campos Merschmann, Detecting tip spam in location-based social networks, in: Proceedings of the 28th Annual ACM Symposium on Applied Computing (SAC), 2013.

[13] H. Costa, L.H. de Campos Merschmann, F. Barth, F. Benevenuto, Pollution, bad-mouthing, and local marketing: the underground of location-based social networks, Elsevier Information Sciences 279 (2014) 123–137.

[14] A. Mukherjee, S. Bhattacharyya, K. Ray, B. Gupta, A.K. Das, A study of public sentiment and influence of politics in COVID-19 related tweets, in: A.K. Das, J. Nayak, B. Naik, S. Dutta, D. Pelusi (Eds.), Computational Intelligence in Pattern Recognition, Springer, Singapore, 2022, pp. 655–665.

[15] M. Dash, H. Liu, Feature selection for classification, Intelligent Data Analysis 1 (1997) 131–156.

[16] P. Z, Rough sets: basic notion, International Journal of Computer & Information Sciences 11 (5) (1982) 344–356.

[17] Z. Pawlak, Rough set theory and its applications to data analysis, Cybernetics and Systems 29 (7) (1998) 661–688, https://doi.org/10.1080/019697298125470.

[18] P. Das, A.K. Das, Convolutional neural networks-based sentence level classification of crime documents, in: A.K. Das, J. Nayak, B. Naik, S. Dutta, D. Pelusi (Eds.), Computational Intelligence in Pattern Recognition, Springer, Singapore, 2022, pp. 65–73.

[19] S.R. W, S. Andrzej, Rough set methods in feature selection and recognition, Pattern Recognition Letters 24 (6) (2003) 833–849.

[20] C. Yaile, A. Delia, B. Rafael, Feature selection algorithms using rough set theory, in: Proceedings of IEEE International Conference on Intelligent Systems Design and Applications, 2007, pp. 407–411.

[21] A. Das, D. Pal, C. Mallick, A.K. Das, An unsupervised COVID-19 report summarizer for developing smart healthcare system, in: A.K. Das, J. Nayak, B. Naik, S. Dutta, D. Pelusi (Eds.), Computational Intelligence in Pattern Recognition, Springer, Singapore, 2022, pp. 157–168.

[22] C. Mallick, S. Das, A.K. Das, Evolutionary algorithm based summarization for analyzing COVID-19 medical reports, in: J. Nayak, B. Naik, A. Abraham (Eds.), Understanding COVID-19: The Role of Computational Intelligence, in: Studies in Computational Intelligence, Springer International Publishing, Cham, 2022, pp. 31–58.

[23] S. Chattopadhyay, T. Basu, A.K. Das, K. Ghosh, L.C.A. Murthy, Towards effective discovery of natural communities in complex networks and implications in e-commerce, Electronic Commerce Research 21 (4) (2021) 917–954, https://doi.org/10.1007/s10660-019-09395-y.

[24] A.H. Mark, Correlation-based feature selection for machine learning, Tech. Rep., The University of Waikato, Hamilton, New Zealand, 06 2000.

[25] W. Suge, L. Deyu, W. Yingjie, L. Hongxia, A feature selection method based on Fisher's discriminant ratio for text sentiment classification, in: L. Wenyin, L. Xiangfeng, W.F. Lee, L. Jingsheng (Eds.), Web Information Systems and Mining, Springer Berlin Heidelberg, Berlin, Heidelberg, 2009, pp. 88–97.

[26] Z. Xiangxin, L. Shengcai, L. Zhen, L. Rong, L.S. Z, Feature correlation filter for face recognition, in: L. Seong-Whan, L.S. Z (Eds.), Advances in Biometrics, Springer Berlin Heidelberg, Berlin, Heidelberg, 2007, pp. 77–86.

[27] M. Basu, S.D. Bit, S. Ghosh, Utilizing microblogs for optimized real-time resource allocation in post-disaster scenarios, Social Network Analysis and Mining 12 (1) (2021) 15, https://doi.org/10.1007/s13278-021-00841-0.

[28] S. Vanika, S. Preety, Correlation based feature selection for diagnosis of acute lymphoblastic leukemia, in: Proceedings of the Third International Symposium on Women in Computing and Informatics, WCI '15, ACM, New York, NY, USA, 2015, pp. 5–9, http://doi.acm.org/10.1145/2791405.2791423.

[29] K. Ron, Wrappers for performance enhancement and oblivious decision graphs, PhD thesis, Stanford University, Stanford, CA, USA, 1996, uMI Order No. GAX96-11989.

[30] R. Kohavi, G.H. John, Wrappers for feature subset selection, Artificial Intelligence 97 (1) (1997) 273–324, https://doi.org/10.1016/S0004-3702(97)00043-X, relevance, http://www.sciencedirect.com/science/article/pii/S000437029700043X.

[31] P. Bhattacharya, S. Paul, K. Ghosh, S. Ghosh, A. Wyner, DeepRhole: deep learning for rhetorical role labeling of sentences in legal case documents, Artificial Intelligence and Law (Nov. 2021), https://doi.org/10.1007/s10506-021-09304-5.

[32] H.M. Aghdam, G.-A. Nasser, B.M. Ehsan, Text feature selection using ant colony optimization, Expert Systems with Applications 36 (3, Part 2) (2009) 6843–6853.

[33] K. Hazra, T. Ghosh, A. Mukherjee, S. Saha, S. Nandi, S. Ghosh, S. Chakraborty, Sustainable text summarization over mobile devices: an energy-aware approach, Sustainable Computing: Informatics and Systems 32 (2021) 100607, https://doi.org/10.1016/j.suscom.2021.100607, https://www.sciencedirect.com/science/article/pii/S2210537921000950.

[34] M. Pabitra, M.C. A, P.S. K, Unsupervised feature selection using feature similarity, IEEE Transactions on Pattern Analysis and Machine Intelligence 24 (3) (2002) 301–312.

[35] B. Sanghamitra, B. Tapas, P. Mitra, M. Ujjwal, Integration of dense subgraph finding with feature clustering for unsupervised feature selection, Pattern Recognition Letters 40 (2014) 104–112.

[36] M. Zhang, J.T. Yao, A rough sets based approach to feature selection, in: Proceedings of IEEE Annual Meeting of the Fuzzy Information, 2004, pp. 1313–1317.

[37] L.-Y. Zhai, L.-P. Khoo, S.-C. Fok, Feature extraction using rough set theory and genetic algorithms – an application for the simplification of product quality evaluation, Computers & Industrial Engineering 43 (4) (2002) 661–676.

[38] C. Yumin, M. Duoqian, W. Ruizhi, A rough set approach to feature selection based on ant colony optimization, Pattern Recognition Letters 31 (3) (2010) 226–233.

[39] X. Guan, Q. Guo, J. Zhao, Z. chao Zhang, An attribute reduction algorithm based on rough set, information entropy and ant colony optimization, in: Proceedings of IEEE International Conference on Signal Processing, 2010, pp. 1313–1317.

[40] S. Andrzej, R. Cecylia, The discernibility matrices and functions in information systems, in: R. Słowinski (Ed.), Intelligent Decision Support. Handbook of Applications and Advances of the Rough Set Theory, in: Theory and Decision Library, vol. 11, Kluwer Academic Publishers, 1992, pp. 331–362.

[41] K. Jaber, N.A. A, A. Adeleh, The impact of feature selection on web spam detection, International Journal of Intelligent Systems and Applications 4 (9) (2012) 61–67.

[42] Z. Yudong, W. Shuihua, W. Lenan, Spam detection via feature selection and decision tree, Advanced Science Letters 5 (2) (2012) 726–730.

[43] T. Chi-Yao, S. Pin-Chieh, C. Ming-Syan, Cosdes: a collaborative spam detection system with a novel e-mail abstraction scheme, IEEE Transactions on Knowledge and Data Engineering 23 (5) (2011) 669–682.

[44] G. Hongyu, H. Jun, W. Christo, L. Zhichun, C. Yan, Y.Z. Ben, Detecting and characterizing social spam campaigns, in: Proceedings of the ACM SIGCOMM Internet Measurement Conference, IMC, Dec 2000.

[45] L. Sangho, K. Jong, WarningBird: a near real-time detection system for suspicious URLs in Twitter stream, IEEE Transactions on Dependable and Secure Computing 10 (3) (2013) 183–195.

[46] T. Kurt, G. Chris, M. Justin, P. Vern, S. Dawn, Design and evaluation of a real-time url spam filtering service, in: Proceedings of the 2011 IEEE Symposium on Security and Privacy, SP '11, IEEE Computer Society, Washington, DC, USA, 2011, pp. 447–462.

[47] A. Mandal, K. Ghosh, S. Ghosh, S. Mandal, A sequence labeling model for catchphrase identification from legal case documents, Artificial Intelligence and Law (Jul. 2021), https://doi.org/10.1007/s10506-021-09296-2.

[48] M. Basu, K. Ghosh, S. Ghosh, Information retrieval from microblogs during disasters: in the light of IRMiDis task, SN Computer Science 1 (1) (2020) 61, https://doi.org/10.1007/s42979-020-0065-1.

[49] A. Faraz, A. Muhammad, A generic statistical approach for spam detection in Online Social Networks, Computer Communications 36 (10–11) (2013) 1120–1129.

[50] Y. Yiming, P.J. O, A comparative study on feature selection in text categorization, in: Proceedings of the International Conference on Machine Learning (ICML), 1997, pp. 412–420.

[51] R. Mandal, S. Dutta, R. Banerjee, S. Bhattacharya, R. Ghosh, S. Samanta, T. Saha, City traffic speed characterization based on city road surface quality, in: J.M.R.S. Tavares, P. Dutta, S. Dutta, D. Samanta (Eds.), Cyber Intelligence and Information Retrieval, Springer, Singapore, 2022, pp. 515–524.

[52] D. Samanta, S. Dutta, M.G. Galety, S. Pramanik, A novel approach for web mining taxonomy for high-performance computing, in: J.M.R.S. Tavares, P. Dutta, S. Dutta, D. Samanta (Eds.), Cyber Intelligence and Information Retrieval, in: Lecture Notes in Networks and Systems, Springer, Singapore, 2022, pp. 425–432.

[53] A. Campan, T. Atnafu, T.M. Truta, J. Nolan, Is data collection through Twitter streaming api useful for academic research?, in: 2018 IEEE International Conference on Big Data (Big Data), 2018, pp. 3638–3643.

[54] W. Silke, W. Dorothea, Comparing Clusterings – an Overview, Tech. Rep. 4, Universität Karlsruhe (TH), 2007, http://digbib.ubka.uni-karlsruhe.de/volltexte/1000011477.

[55] S. Kumar, K.M. Carley, What to track on the Twitter streaming api? A knapsack bandits approach to dynamically update the search terms, in: 2019 IEEE/ACM International Conference on Advances in Social Networks Analysis and Mining (ASONAM), 2019, pp. 158–163.

[56] H. Efstathiades, D. Antoniades, G. Pallis, M.D. Dikaiakos, Distributed large-scale data collection in online social networks, in: 2016 IEEE 2nd International Conference on Collaboration and Internet Computing (CIC), 2016, pp. 373–380.

[57] A. Dwi Laksito, Kusrini, H. Sismoro, F. Rahmawati, M. Yusa, A comparison study of search strategy on collecting Twitter data for drug adverse reaction, in: 2018 International Seminar on Application for Technology of Information and Communication, 2018, pp. 356–360.

[58] Infomap - community detection, http://www.mapequation.org/code.html.

[59] P. Ray, A. Chakrabarti, Twitter sentiment analysis for product review using lexicon method, in: 2017 International Conference on Data Management, Analytics and Innovation (ICDMAI), 2017, pp. 211–216.

[60] G. Salvador, L. Julian, S.J. A, L. Victoria, H. Francisco, A survey of discretization techniques: taxonomy and empirical analysis in supervised learning, IEEE Transactions on Knowledge and Data Engineering 25 (4) (2013) 734–750.

[61] U.M. Fayyad, K.B. Irani, Multi-interval discretization of continuous valued attributes for classification learning, in: Proc. International Joint Conference on Artificial Intelligence, vol. 2, 1993, pp. 1022–1027.

[62] K. Jitkajornwanich, C. Kongthong, N. Khongsoontornjaroen, J. Kaiyasuan, S. Lawawirojwong, P. Srestasathiern, S. Srisonphan, P. Vateekul, Utilizing Twitter data for early flood warning in Thailand, in: 2018 IEEE International Conference on Big Data (Big Data), 2018, pp. 5165–5169.

[63] S.H. Archana, S.G. Winster, Drugs categorization based on sentence polarity analyzer for Twitter data, in: 2016 Second International Conference on Science Technology Engineering and Management (ICONSTEM), 2016, pp. 28–33.

[64] T. Jagić, L. Brkić, Hot topic detection using Twitter streaming data, in: 2020 43rd International Convention on Information, Communication and Electronic Technology (MIPRO), 2020, pp. 1730–1735.

[65] REST API Resources, Twitter Developers, https://dev.twitter.com/docs/api.

[66] R. Compton, C. Lee, T.-C. Lu, L. De Silva, M. Macy, Detecting future social unrest in unprocessed Twitter data: "emerging phenomena and big data", in: 2013 IEEE International Conference on Intelligence and Security Informatics, 2013, pp. 56–60.

[67] SURBL, http://www.surbl.org/.

[68] Google Safe Browsing API, https://developers.google.com/safe-browsing/.

[69] The Spamhaus Project, http://www.spamhaus.org/.

[70] Capture-HPC, https://projects.honeynet.org/capture-hpc/.

[71] R.D. Perera, S. Anand, K.P. Subbalakshmi, R. Chandramouli, Twitter analytics: architecture, tools and analysis, in: 2010 - MILCOM 2010 Military Communications Conference, 2010, pp. 2186–2191.

[72] C. Wang, L. Marini, C.-L. Chin, N. Vance, C. Donelson, P. Meunier, J.T. Yun, Social media intelligence and learning environment: an open source framework for social media data collection, analysis and curation, in: 2019 15th International Conference on eScience (eScience), 2019, pp. 252–261.

[73] M.A. Hall, Correlation-based feature subset selection for machine learning, PhD thesis, University of Waikato, Hamilton, New Zealand, 1998.

[74] H. Liu, R. Setiono, A probabilistic approach to feature selection - a filter solution, in: 13th International Conference on Machine Learning, 1996, pp. 319–327.

[75] H. Mark, F. Eibe, H. Geoffrey, P. Bernhard, R. Peter, W.I. H, The WEKA data mining software: an update, SIGKDD Explorations 11 (1) (2009) 10–18.

[76] W. Chris, S. George, The Wilcoxon rank-sum test, in: CHANCE ENCOUN-TERS: A First Course in Data Analysis and Inference, John Wiley & Sons, 2000, pp. 2354–2355.

CHAPTER 5

Ensemble summarization algorithms for microblog summarization

5.1 Introduction

Summarization of things in a cyber-physical society involves multidimensional summarization of a wide variety of data, including textual data from various online and offline sources, sensor data, and so on [1]. Especially, crowdsourced textual data from social media sites like Twitter are nowadays important sources of real-time information on ongoing events, including sociopolitical events, natural and man-made disasters, and so on. On such sites, microblogs are usually posted so rapidly and in such large volumes that it is not feasible for human users to go through all the posts. In such scenario, summarization of microblogs (tweets) is an important task [2,3].

A large number of extractive summarization algorithms have been proposed, both for general text summarization [4] and specifically for microblogs [5]. Few studies have also compared the performance of different summarization algorithms on microblogs [6,7]. In this work, rather than trying to come up with a new summarization algorithm, we investigate whether existing off-the-shelf summarization algorithms can be combined to produce better-quality summaries, compared to what is obtained from any of the individual algorithms [8].

Motivation

We selected nine well-known extractive summarization algorithms (stated in Section 5.2) and executed all of them on the same set of microblogs (our datasets are detailed in Section 5.5). All algorithms were made to generate summaries with a length of 30 tweets. Table 5.1 shows the overlap between the summaries generated by the different base algorithms for the same dataset (tweets posted during Typhoon Hagupit). The entry (i,j), $1 \leq i, j \leq 9$, in Table 5.1 shows the number of common tweets included in the summaries generated by the two algorithms A_i and A_j. It is evident that there is very low overlap between summaries generated

Data Analytics for Social Microblogging Platforms
https://doi.org/10.1016/B978-0-32-391785-8.00017-2

Table 5.1 Overlap of tweets in the summaries generated by different base algorithms, for the Typhoon Hagupit dataset.

Algorithm	CR	CW	FS	LR	LS	LH	MD	SB	SM
CR	–	0	0	0	0	0	0	0	0
CW	0	–	0	0	4	3	1	2	1
FS	0	0	–	0	3	2	0	0	0
LR	0	0	0	–	0	0	0	1	2
LS	0	4	3	0	–	6	0	1	0
LH	0	3	2	0	6	–	2	1	0
MD	0	1	0	0	0	2	–	1	0
SB	0	2	0	1	1	1	1	–	2
SM	0	1	0	2	0	0	0	2	–

by various base algorithms. Similar trends are observed for all our datasets. Thus, *different summarization algorithms usually select very different sets of tweets in the summaries for the same set of input tweets.* The different summarization algorithms are likely to estimate the relative importance of tweets based on different factors, and hence various summaries are likely to bring out different aspects of the input dataset. This large variation observed in the set of tweets selected by different summarization algorithms motivated us to devise ensemble techniques that can combine the views of multiple base algorithms to produce summaries better than what any of the base algorithms generates [9].

Present work

In this work, we propose two ensemble schemes – (i) EnGraphSumm, a graph-based *unsupervised* ensemble summarization algorithm, and (ii) Learn2Summ, a *supervised* ensemble summarization algorithm based on the learning-to-rank paradigm [10]. The intuition behind our proposed ensemble methods is as follows. Both the ensemble methods consider those tweets that have been selected by at least one base algorithm. The unsupervised method groups the tweets selected by the base algorithms based on some measure of tweet similarity and then selects one tweet from each group. In this way, the method attempts to select important tweets while reducing redundancy in the final summary [11]. The supervised ensemble algorithm attempts to learn a ranking of tweets according to importance, based on the rankings computed by different base algorithms and the performance of the base algorithms over a training set. The idea is to combine different rankings of tweets and learn how to rank tweets better (for inclusion in the final summary).

Motivated by the importance of microblog summarization during disaster events [5], we performed experiments over microblogs related to four recent disaster events. We show that the proposed ensemble algorithms can combine the outputs of multiple base algorithms to produce summaries that are of better quality than what is obtained from any of the base algorithms [12]. Specifically, our proposed ensemble algorithms achieve up to 8.4% higher Rouge-2 recall scores on average compared to the best-performing baseline. We demonstrate the summaries generated by the base algorithms and some of our ensemble algorithms over a small-sample dataset in the Supplementary Information accompanying this chapter (available at http://cse.iitkgp.ac.in/~saptarshi/docs/DuttaEtAl-IS-ensemble-summ-SuppleInfo.pdf).

To the best of our knowledge, this is one of the first attempts towards designing ensemble schemes for combining the outputs of multiple text summarization algorithms. Importantly, we do not assume any particular property of the base algorithms; hence, any extractive algorithm can be used in the proposed ensemble framework. Though the present work focuses on summarization of textual data (microblogs), the proposed ensemble approaches are applicable for different types of summarization problems that are important in today's cyber-physical society [1]. We envisage that this work will pave the way for several future works on ensemble summarization, similar to the successful use of ensemble techniques in data mining tasks such as classification and clustering [13].

5.2 Base summarization algorithms

In this section, we outline the base extractive summarization algorithms that we considered for the present work.

1. **Cluster-rank (CR):** Cluster-rank [14] segments a given document (the transcript) into clusters and then constructs a cluster-graph of the transcripts. Then the well-known PageRank algorithm is used to compute an "importance" score for each cluster. Also, a centroid-based approach is used to score each sentence within an important cluster. Finally, the algorithm starts from the highest-scoring sentence and includes sentences in the summary until the desired length is obtained.

2. **COWTS (CW):** COWTS [5] is specifically designed for summarizing microblogs posted during disaster situations. The algorithm identifies "content words" (nouns, verbs, numerals, etc.) from the microblogs and then uses an integer linear programming-based approach to select mi-

croblogs such that the presence of these content words in the summary is maximized.

3. **Frequency Summarizer (FS):** This algorithm is based on the simple idea that if a sentence contains the most recurrent words in the text, it is likely to cover most of the topics of the text. Based on this idea, the algorithm attempts to extract those sentences which cover the main topics of a given document.

4. **LexRank (LR):** LexRank [15] represents a given document as a graph based on intra-sentence cosine similarity. Then the importance of sentences in the document is computed based on the concept of eigenvector centrality in the graph. The sentences are then included in the summary in decreasing order of their importance.

5. **LSA (LS):** LSA [16] constructs a terms-by-sentences matrix A for a document and performs singular value decomposition on A to obtain the singular value matrix V^T, where each sentence is represented by the column vector. Then, it selects the k-th right singular vector from V^T. The sentence having the largest index value with the k-th right singular vector is included in the summary. This process is repeated until the desired summary length is obtained.

6. **LUHN (LH):** Luhn's algorithm [17] compiles a list of "content words" (after stopword removal and stemming) sorted by decreasing frequency, the index providing a significance measure of the word. On the sentence level, a "significance factor" is derived that reflects the number of occurrences of significant words within a sentence and the linear distance between them due to the intervention of non-significant words. All sentences are ranked in order of their significance factor, and the top-ranked sentences are selected for the summary.

7. **Mead (MD):** Mead [18] first detects topics by agglomerative clustering over the TF–IDF vector representation of the documents. Then, it uses the centroids to identify sentences in each cluster that are central to the topic of the entire cluster. The final score of each sentence is a combination of three scores – its *centroid value*, *positional value*, and *first-sentence overlap* – minus a *redundancy penalty* for each sentence that overlaps highly ranked sentences. Sentences are finally selected based on this score.

8. **SumBasic (SB):** SumBasic [19] uses a frequency-based sentence selection component, with a component to reweight the word probabilities in order to minimize redundancy. For each sentence, it assigns a weight equal to the average probability of occurrence of the words in the

sentence and picks the best-scoring sentence that contains the highest-probability word. It then updates the probabilities. The above steps are repeated until the desired summary length is attained.

9. **SumDSDR (SM):** Document Summarization based on Data Reconstruction [20] is an unsupervised framework for summarization. The relationship between sentences is measured using two objective functions – (i) linear reconstruction, which approximates the document by linear combinations of selected sentences, and (ii) non-negative linear reconstruction, which allows only additive, not subtractive, linear combinations. The summary is generated by minimizing the reconstruction error.

We selected the algorithms stated above, because either their implementations are readily available off-the-shelf or they are relatively easy to implement. The algorithms are available from the following websites: Frequency Summarizer (http://glowingpython.blogspot.in/2014/09/text-summarization-with-nltk.html), Mead (http://www.summarization.com/mead/), SumBasic (https://github.com/EthanMacdonald/SumBasic), SumDSDR (https://gist.github.com/satomacoto/4248449); LexRank, LSA, and LUHN are available as part of the Python Sumy package (https://pypi.python.org/pypi/sumy). Implementation of COWTS was obtained from our prior work [5], while ClusterRank was implemented by us. Note that apart from the ones described above, several other extractive summarization algorithms have also been developed, and they can also be utilized in our ensemble summarization frameworks (described in subsequent sections).

5.3 Unsupervised ensemble summarization

In this section, we describe unsupervised ensemble frameworks for summarization. We describe a baseline ensemble algorithm and our proposed graph-based algorithm EnGraphSumm.

Let $A_1, A_2, \ldots, A_N$ be the base summarization algorithms, where N is the number of algorithms considered. For a given set of microblogs, we first run each A_i and obtain summaries of a fixed length (K tweets). Then, we use the ensemble techniques on these summaries to obtain an ensemble summary of the same length (K tweets). Each base algorithm A_i selects a set of tweets to include in the summary; let S_i denote the set of tweets included in the summary output by A_i. The ensemble techniques consider the set of tweets $S = \bigcup_{N}^{i=1} S_i$, i.e., the set of tweets which have been selected by at least one base algorithm. Additionally, for a particular tweet t, let $A(t)$ denote the set of base algorithms which have selected t to include in their summary.

5.3.1 Baseline: voting approach

In this simple strategy, each tweet $t \in S$ is assigned a score $score(t) = |A(t)|$, i.e., the number of base algorithms that have selected this particular tweet to include in the summary. Basically, each base algorithm is considered to "vote" for the tweets that it includes in the summary. The tweets in S are ranked in decreasing order of this score, and the top K tweets are chosen to be included in the ensemble summary. If necessary, ties among tweets having the same score are broken by random selection.

5.3.2 EnGraphSumm: proposed ensemble algorithm

We now describe the algorithm EnGraphSumm, which consists of three steps. The pseudocode of the algorithm can be found in the Supplementary Information.

(1) Constructing a tweet similarity graph
EnGraphSumm first constructs an undirected graph G where the tweets in S are the nodes, and two nodes are connected by an edge if the two corresponding tweets are "similar." Several methods can be used to measure the similarity $sim(t_1, t_2)$ of two tweets t_1 and t_2. Specifically, we experiment with the following two methods:

1. Text similarity (TextSim): We consider two tweets to be similar if they contain similar words or terms. We represent a tweet as a bag (set) of words, after removing a standard set of English stopwords, punctuation symbols, URLs, @user mentions, etc. To measure the similarity $sim(t_1, t_2)$, we compute the Jaccard similarity between the bags (sets) of words in the two tweets. This similarity measure lies in the range [0, 1] where the maximum value 1 indicates two very similar tweets.

2. Vector similarity (VecSim): Here we consider two tweets to be similar if they have been selected by the same base algorithms to be included in the summaries. We represent a tweet as a binary vector of size N (the number of base summarization algorithms), where the i-th term of the vector is 1 if the tweet was included in the summary output by algorithm A_i and 0 otherwise. The similarity $sim(t_1, t_2)$ between two tweets is measured by the inner-product (termwise product) of the two corresponding vectors. Effectively, $sim(t_1, t_2) = |A(t_1) \cap A(t_2)|$ lies in the range [0, N], and a value of

$P \in [0, N]$ indicates that the two tweets were selected by P base algorithms in common.

3. Embedding similarity (EmbedSim): Here we construct embeddings of tweets using the popular text embedding tool Word2Vec [21] and measure the similarity between these embeddings. Specifically, we train Word2Vec on the given set of tweets (after stopword removal) using the Continuous Bag of Words (CBOW) model along with Hierarchical softmax and the following parameter values: vector size: 100, context size: 5, learning rate: 0.05, iterations: 500. Word2Vec gives a vector for each term (term-vector) which captures the semantic context of the term. The vector for a tweet (tweet-vector) is obtained by computing the average (mean) of the term-vectors in the tweet. The similarity between two tweets is measured as the cosine similarity of the tweet-vectors of the two tweets. This method can be considered as an improved version of TextSim, which can identify similarity between two tweets that are semantically similar but use different terms.

While constructing the graph G, we consider a similarity threshold sim_{th}, and an edge is added between two nodes (tweets) t_1 and t_2 if $sim(t_1, t_2) \geq sim_{th}$. The choice of sim_{th} is described later.

(2) Identifying groups of similar tweets (nodes in the graph)
Once the graph G is constructed, **EnGraphSumm** identifies groups of similar nodes (tweets). Several approaches can be taken to find groups of similar nodes, out of which we adopt the following:

1. Identifying connected components (ConComp): Since an edge between two nodes in G indicates that the two tweets are similar, identifying connected components in G is a straightforward way of detecting groups of similar tweets.

2. Identifying communities (Community): Various *community detection algorithms* for graphs can be used to identify sub-groups of nodes such that the nodes within the group are more densely connected to each other than to nodes outside this group. We use the popular Louvain algorithm [22] to find communities in G.

Note that text clustering algorithms can also be applied to identify groups of tweets (nodes) whose textual content is similar. We leave this direction for future work.

(3) Selecting a representative tweet from a group
Once a group of similar tweets (nodes) is identified, **EnGraphSumm** selects one tweet (node) from each group as a representative of the group and adds

it to the summary. This selection can be made in several ways, out of which we try the following:

1. Tweet with the maximum length (MaxLen): Here we select the tweet having the maximum string length, with the intuition that including a longer tweet would make the summary more informative.

2. Node with the maximum degree (MaxDeg): Out of an identified group of nodes, we select the node having the highest degree. This approach follows the intuition that a high-degree node in the similarity graph G is similar to more nodes in the group, and hence is a better representative of the group.

3. Tweet with maximum TF-IDF score (maxSumTFIDF): In this approach, we attempt to select more "informative" tweets. To this end, we use the popular information retrieval measures "term frequency" (TF) and "inverse document frequency" (IDF). A particular tweet t is considered as a bag (set) of words, as described in the TextSim approach. For each word $w \in t$, we compute (i) the term frequency of w in t and (ii) the IDF of w in the whole set of tweets. Both TF and IDF are log-normalized. Finally, the TF-IDF score of the tweet t is taken as the sum of TF-IDF scores of all words in t. Out of an identified group of similar tweets, we select the tweet with the highest TF-IDF score.

4. Tweet with maximum BM25 score (MaxSumBM25): Several prior works in information retrieval have observed that the BM25 ranking model [23] performs better than TF-IDF in case of short text like tweets. Hence in this version, the BM25 score [23] is computed for each distinct word, and then the score of each word in a tweet is summed up to get the BM25 score for the tweet. Out of an identified group of nodes, we select the node (tweet) having the highest BM25 score.

Algorithm 5.1 describes our proposed graph-based ensemble summarization algorithm. For a given similarity function $sim()$, we consider its range $[sim_{min}, sim_{max}]$. We initialize the threshold $sim_{th} = sim_{max}$ and construct the graph G accordingly – each node in the graph is a tweet, and there is an edge between two nodes if the similarity between the two corresponding tweets is higher than sim_{th}. Then we identify groups (connected components or communities) of similar tweets and select a representative tweet from each group of size larger than one, considering groups in decreasing order of their size.

Larger groups are given preference, since a larger number of similar tweets implies that the common topic of those tweets is more important.

Algorithm 5.1: EnGraphSumm: the proposed graph-based ensemble summarization algorithm

---

Input: S: Set of distinct tweets selected by base algorithms,
K: Desired length of the summary,
$sim()$: Method to measure similarity between two tweets,
sim_{max}: Maximum similarity,
sim_{min}: Minimum similarity,
sim_{dec}: Steps in the range $[sim_{min}, sim_{max}]$,
$Gnodes()$: Method to identify groups of similar nodes in a graph,
$Tselect()$: Method to select a tweet from a group of similar tweets

---

Output: A summary of tweets of length K

---

1 $sim_{th} = sim_{max}$ ▷ Initial threshold similarity
2 **while** *length of summary* $< K$ & $sim_{th} > sim_{min}$ **do**
3   Construct similarity graph G, where nodes are tweets in S, and nodes t_i and t_j are connected by an edge if $sim(t_i, t_j) \geq sim_{th}$
4   Identify groups of similar nodes using method $Gnodes()$
5   Rank groups in decreasing order of their size
6   **for** *each group g_i with size > 1 (considered in decreasing order of group size)* **do**
7   **if** *length of summary* $< K$ **then**
8   Select a representative node (tweet) t from g_i by method $Tselect()$
9   Add t to the summary
10   Remove all nodes in g_i from G
11     $sim_{th} = sim_{th} - sim_{dec}$ ▷ Reduce the threshold similarity
12   ▷ No more similar tweets and desired length is unreached
13 **if** *length of summary* $< K$ **then**
14   Rank remaining tweets in G in decreasing order of length
15   Include requisite number of top-ranked tweets to make the summary of length K
16 **return** Summary of length K tweets;

Note that once a representative tweet from a group is selected, the other tweets in the group are removed to prevent redundancy in the summary. In the next iteration, we reduce sim_{th} by a step sim_{dec} and construct G again. This process is repeated until sim_{th} becomes equal to the lowest possible similarity value sim_{min}. At this stage, if K tweets have not yet been included in the summary, then the remaining tweets are ranked in decreasing order of their string length, and the requisite number of top (longest) tweets are selected.

Selection of similarity threshold

Our experiments with various microblog datasets (described in Section 5.5) demonstrated that it is difficult to choose a suitable value for the threshold similarity sim_{th} that would work well for different datasets. Hence we took the following approach. For a given $sim()$, we consider its range $[sim_{min}, sim_{max}]$. We initialize the threshold $sim_{th} = sim_{max}$ and construct the graph G accordingly. Then we identify groups of similar tweets and select a representative tweet from each group of size larger than one, considering groups in decreasing order of their size. Larger groups are given preference, since a larger number of similar tweets implies that the common topic of those tweets is more important. Note that once a representative tweet from a group is selected, the other tweets in the group are removed to prevent redundancy in the summary. In the next iteration, we reduce sim_{th} by a step sim_{dec} and construct G again. This process is repeated until sim_{th} becomes equal to the lowest possible similarity value sim_{min}. At this stage, if K tweets have not yet been included in the summary, then the remaining tweets are ranked in decreasing order of their string length, and the requisite number of top (longest) tweets are selected.

For the TextSim function (Jaccard similarity), $sim_{min} = 0$, $sim_{max} = 1$, and we consider $sim_{dec} = 0.1$. For the VecSim similarity function, $sim_{min} = 0$, $sim_{max} = N$ (the number of base summarization algorithms), and we consider $sim_{dec} = 1$. The detailed pseudocode of the algorithm EnGraphSumm can be found in the accompanying Supplementary Information.

5.4 Supervised ensemble summarization

This section discusses supervised ensemble algorithms. Here we assume that the datasets are divided into two parts:

1. **Training set**: For these datasets, we assume we already know (i) the summaries generated by all base algorithms and (ii) some performance measure (e.g., Rouge scores) of the summaries generated by the base algorithms.

2. **Test set**: We utilize the training set to develop ensemble summarization algorithms for the test datasets.

As in Section 5.3, let the base summarization algorithms be $A_1, A_2, \ldots,$ A_N and let $A(t)$ denote the set of base algorithms which have selected the tweet t to include in their summary. Let $P(A_i)$ be some measure of the performance of A_i, $1 \leq i \leq N$, over the training set.

5.4.1 Baseline: weighted voting approach

Similar to the unsupervised voting approach, each base algorithm that selected a particular tweet t (while summarizing the test set) is considered to vote for t. Here, the vote of the base algorithm A_i is weighted by the performance of A_i over the training set. Thus, each tweet $t \in S$ (the union of sets of tweets selected by all the base algorithms) is assigned a "goodness score" $score(t) = \sum_{A_i \in A(t)} P(A_i)$, where $P(A_i)$ is the performance measure (e.g., Rouge score) of A_i. The tweets in S are ranked in decreasing order of this score, and the top K tweets are chosen to be included in the ensemble summary (ties, if any, broken by random selection).

5.4.2 Learn2Summ: proposed ensemble algorithm

We now describe **Learn2Summ** that is based on the popular Learning-to-Rank (L2R) paradigm [10]. For a particular training dataset, we compute $score(t)$ for each tweet t (as described above) and rank the tweets based on this score. Next we consider a *feature-vector* for each tweet; the features in the vector are detailed below. We learn a ranking model based on the feature-vectors and the ranked list of tweets according to $score(t)$, using standard L2R algorithms [10]. The learned ranking model is used to rank tweets for the test dataset, and the top-ranked K tweets are selected for inclusion in the ensemble summary.

Feature vectors: The features are meant to capture the type of tweets that get high scores, i.e., are selected by the base algorithms that perform well over the training datasets. We experiment with two types of vectors:

1. Base algorithms as features: We represent a tweet as a binary vector of size N (the number of base summarization algorithms), where the i-th term of the vector is 1 if the tweet was included in the summary output by algorithm A_i and 0 otherwise. These vectors are similar to those used for the VecSim unsupervised approach (in Section 5.3.2).

2. Text-based features: The text-based features essentially capture the informativeness of the tweets, so that the correlation of informativeness of the tweets with their ranking (if any) can be learned. For a tweet, we compute the following features (note that, apart from the first feature, all features

are computed after preprocessing the text by case-folding and removal of English stopwords):

(1) total number of words,

(2) number of words excluding English stopwords,

(3) sum of TF (term frequency) of all words,

(4) sum of IDF (inverse document frequency) of all words, where IDF of a word is computed based on all the tweets in a particular dataset,

(5) sum of TF-IDF of all words,

(6) number of hashtags,

(7) whether the tweet is a retweet (binary feature),

(8) number of user mentions,

(9) number of numerals,

(10) number of nouns,

(11) number of verbs,

(12) entropy, computed over all words w in the tweet t as $H(t) = -\sum_{w \in t}(p_w \cdot \log p_w)$, where p_w is the probability of occurrence of the word w in the particular dataset.

For the L2R algorithms, we used the RankLib library (https://sourceforge.net/p/lemur/wiki/RankLib/), which contains implementations of several popular L2R algorithms. Specifically, we experimented with the L2R algorithms RankBoost, RandomForest, and MART.

Note that if multiple training datasets are available, we obtain the ranked list and feature-vectors of tweets for each of the training datasets and learn a common ranking model from all the training datasets. The results are reported in the next section.

5.5 Experiments and results

We now describe our experiments and results. We start by describing the datasets and the evaluation measures used and then compare the performance of various summarization algorithms [24,25].

5.5.1 Experimental setup

Datasets

We reuse the datasets from our prior work [5], consisting of tweets posted during four recent disaster events:

(i) Bomb explosions in Hyderabad, India,

(ii) Typhoon Hagupit in the Philippines,

(iii) floods in Uttaranchal state of India, and

(iv) the Sandy Hook Elementary School shooting in the USA. The English tweets posted during each event were collected through the Twitter API using keyword search.

We initially considered the chronologically earliest 5000 tweets for each event. It is known that tweet streams often contain duplicates due to retweeting/reposting of tweets. We removed such duplicates which are not useful for the purpose of summarization [26]. After de-duplication the number of distinct tweets in the four datasets are respectively 1413, 1461, 2069, and 2080.

Evaluation of summarization algorithms

We follow the standard procedure of generating golden standard summaries by human annotators and then comparing the algorithm-generated summary with the golden standard ones [27,28]. Three human annotators were asked to independently summarize each of the datasets and prepare summaries of $K = 30$ tweets each. Each annotator is well versed in the English language and the use of social media, and none is an author of this paper.

We used the standard ROUGE recall scores of the (i) ROUGE-2 and (ii) ROUGE-L variants for evaluating the quality of the summaries [29]. These scores respectively measure what fraction of the (i) bigrams and (ii) longest matching sequence of words in the golden standard summaries are covered by the summaries produced by the algorithms [30].

Summarization is inherently a subjective process, and the same dataset can be summarized differently by different human annotators [31]. We actually observed signification variations in the summaries written by the three annotators for the same dataset. We quantify these variations in the Supplementary Information [32,33]. For computing the ROUGE scores reported in this chapter, all three summaries written by the annotators (for a given dataset) were collectively used as the golden standard.

Inter-annotator agreement over summaries

For evaluation of summarization algorithms, we followed the standard procedure of generating golden standard summaries by human annotators and then comparing the algorithm-generated summaries with the golden standard ones. Three human annotators were asked to independently summarize each of the datasets and prepare golden standard summaries for each dataset [34]. It is natural to observe how closely the golden standard summary written by one annotator resembles the summary written by another annotator [35–37]. To this end, we consider the summary written by one particular annotator (for a given set of tweets) as the golden standard and

Table 5.2 Performance of the base summarization algorithms, averaged over all datasets. The best performance (highlighted in boldface) is observed for the COWTS algorithm.

Base algorithm	Rouge-2 recall	Rouge-L recall
ClusterRank (CR)	0.08598	0.26838
COWTS (CW)	**0.17896**	**0.44539**
FreqSum (FS)	0.14732	0.36018
Lex-Rank (LR)	0.04890	0.15254
LSA (LS)	0.15994	0.42336
LUHN (LH)	0.16504	0.40145
Mead (MD)	0.11719	0.37086
SumBasic (SB)	0.10120	0.32899
SumDSDR (SM)	0.09848	0.26016

Table 5.3 Comparative ROUGE scores of summaries written by different human annotators. The summaries written by Annotator 1 are considered the golden standard, and the ROUGE scores of the summaries written by Annotator 2 and Annotator 3 are computed. Reported values are the averages over all four datasets.

Human annotator	Rouge-2 recall	Rouge-L recall
Annotator 2	0.16438	0.38233
Annotator 3	0.22082	0.47076

measure ROUGE scores for the summaries written by the other two annotators (for the same set of tweets).

The comparative ROUGE scores of the summaries written by the human annotators are reported in Table 5.3, averaged over the four datasets used in the work. Here the summaries written by Annotator 1 are considered as the golden standard and ROUGE scores of the summaries written by Annotator 2 and Annotator 3 are computed [38]. It is clear that the summaries written by Annotator 3 are more similar to the summaries written by Annotator 1 (higher ROUGE scores), as compared to the summaries written by Annotator 2. The results show that Annotator 2 performs better than all other algorithms, whereas Annotator 3 performs better than most of the base algorithms such as FreqSum, Lex-Rank, LSA, Mead, SumBasic, SumDSDR, and ClusterRank, but not COWTS and LUHN. Importantly, the ROUGE similarity between summaries written by two human annotators is in the same range as the ROUGE similarities between the summaries generated by the algorithms considered in the work and the golden standard summaries [39,40]. This observation implies that the variation in the summaries generated by the algorithms with respect to a human-generated golden standard is of a similar range as the variation in the summaries generated by two different annotators. As such, this observation brings out the subjectivity in the summarization process [41].

Considering that summarization is a subjective process, for evaluation of the algorithms, we computed ROUGE scores considering all three annotator-generated summaries as golden standards.

5.5.2 Performance of base algorithms

We first run all the base summarization algorithms (described in Section 5.2) on each dataset. Table 5.2 reports the performance of the base summarization algorithms, averaged over all the datasets. The COWTS algorithm performs the best for all the measures. This result is not surprising, since COWTS is especially developed for summarization of tweets posted during disaster events [42].

5.5.3 Performance of unsupervised ensemble algorithms

We apply the two unsupervised ensemble algorithms (described in Section 5.3) on the summaries produced by the base algorithms. Table 5.4 reports the performance of the ensemble algorithms, averaged over all the datasets. The voting method (baseline) performs worse than several of the base algorithms, which shows that ensemble summarization is not a trivial problem.

The proposed **EnGraphSumm** scheme performs better than all the base algorithms in several cases; the performances that are better than that of COWTS (the best base algorithm) are highlighted in boldface. In general, VecSim gives the best performance, followed by EmbedSim and then TextSim. Specifically, the best Rouge-2 recall score is obtained with the MaxLen function (8.4% higher than that of COWTS, the best-performing base algorithm), while the best Rouge-L recall score is obtained with the maxSumTFIDF function (3.3% higher than that of COWTS).

5.5.4 Performance of supervised ensemble algorithms

Now we describe the performance of the supervised ensemble algorithms described in Section 5.4. Since we have four datasets, we follow a training–

Table 5.4 Performance of the unsupervised ensemble algorithms in terms of Rouge-2 and Rouge-L recall scores, averaged over all datasets. The values better than COWTS (the best base algorithm) are highlighted in boldface [43].

Ensemble algorithm	Rouge-2	Rouge-L
Voting (baseline)	0.13976	0.36768
TextSim-ConComp-MaxDeg	0.15788	0.37436
TextSim-ConComp-MaxLen	0.16505	0.38597
TextSim-ConComp-maxSumTFIDF	0.15961	0.38040
TextSim-ConComp-MaxSumBM25	0.15867	0.37854
TextSim-Community-MaxDeg	0.14932	0.36934
TextSim-Community-MaxLen	0.14625	0.37206
TextSim-Community-maxSumTFIDF	0.14836	0.37281
TextSim-Community-MaxSumBM25	0.14193	0.36266
VecSim-ConComp-MaxDeg	**0.19196**	**0.44570**
VecSim-ConComp-MaxLen	**0.19397**	**0.45057**
VecSim-ConComp-maxSumTFIDF	**0.18863**	**0.45995**
VecSim-ConComp-MaxSumBM25	0.15601	0.37934
VecSim-Community-MaxDeg	0.14377	0.39565
VecSim-Community-MaxLen	0.14515	0.39102
VecSim-Community-maxSumTFIDF	**0.18984**	**0.45906**
VecSim-Community-MaxSumBM25	0.17147	0.39576
EmbedSim-ConComp MaxDeg	0.14615	0.36093
EmbedSim-ConComp-MaxLen	**0.17898**	0.40099
EmbedSim-ConComp-maxSumTFIDF	0.17283	0.39372
EmbedSim-ConComp-MaxSumBM25	0.16094	0.37756
EmbedSim-Community-MaxDeg	0.16573	0.37886
EmbedSim-Community-MaxLen	0.17800	0.39589
EmbedSim-Community-maxSumTFIDF	0.17356	0.39384
EmbedSim-Community-MaxSumBM25	0.17356	0.39384

testing approach analogous to *n-fold cross-validation* with $n = 4$, as follows. In each iteration, we use three of the datasets for training and the other as test dataset. We perform four iterations, where each dataset is considered as the test dataset in one iteration, and we report results averaged over the four iterations.

Table 5.5 shows the Rouge scores for the summaries generated by different ensemble algorithms. Similar to the unsupervised case, we find that the weighted voting scheme performs worse than some of the base algorithms [45]. Among the proposed ensemble algorithms, the RankBoost

Table 5.5 Performance of the supervised ensemble algorithms in terms of Rouge-2 and Rouge-L recall scores, averaged over all datasets [44]. The values better than those for COWTS (the best base algorithm) are highlighted in boldface.

Ensemble algorithm	Rouge-2	Rouge-L
Weighted voting (baseline)	0.13884	0.38941
RankBoost with base algos as features	0.16716	0.43417
RandomForest with base algos as features	0.16170	0.42942
RankBoost with text-based features	**0.18326**	0.43846
RandomForest with text-based features	**0.18940**	0.44172

L2R algorithm performs slightly better when the base algorithms are used as features, while the RandomForest L2R algorithm performs better with the text-based features [46]. The best performance is achieved using the RandomForest L2R algorithm with text-based features (Rouge-2 recall score: 0.189), which is a 5.8% improvement over the best base algorithm (COWTS). The Rouge-L score of this ensemble algorithm (0.442) is also very close to that of COWTS (0.445).

Overall, we see that among the proposed ensemble algorithms, the graph-based unsupervised algorithm performs better than the supervised algorithm, in terms of both Rouge-2 and Rouge-L recall scores. The Supplementary Information accompanying the chapter demonstrates the summaries generated by the base algorithms and some of the unsupervised algorithms developed in this work.

5.6 Demonstrating the input and output of summarization algorithms through an example

Several summarization algorithms have been used in this chapter, including base off-the-shelf summarization algorithms and ensemble ones. We demonstrate the input and output of these summarization algorithms through a small example. We consider a sample dataset of 50 tweets, randomly selected from the dataset of tweets related to the Sandy Hook Elementary School shooting incident. Table 5.6 shows the small dataset of 50 tweets.

We applied the base summarization algorithms on the small dataset of 50 tweets shown in Table 5.6 to obtain summaries of 20 tweets by each

Table 5.6 Sample dataset of 50 tweets related to the Sandy Hook Elementary School shooting incident (randomly selected subset of one of the datasets used in the paper).

RT @tommytomlinson:CBS reporting 27 dead in CT school shooting. I'm gonna pass on debating guns,or anything else, right now. Go hug yo.

Oh shit shooting in,a school in CT, hope girls steph and paul are fine.

Counselors shld b,avail 2 ALL ct school age kids Shooter reported dead at Connecticut,elementary school,http://t.co/w8OjtOhL.

Shooting at a Connecticut elementary school.Luckily, my son attends a different one.,Our hearts go out to all involved with this,tragedy.

RT@samaiahernandez: The scene walking towards school. #schoolshooting,http://t.co/OD9EM3oa.

RT @BuzzFeed: Photo,from the Newtown Bee of students evacuating elementary school where a,possible shooting is being reported http://t.c.

RT,@1010WINSNewYork: #Breaking: CBS News confirms 27 dead, 14 are children in,#Newtown, CT school #shooting.http://t.co/ejk8hBDF Listen.

For the previous,school shooters that are still alive in prison - you don't deserve to see,another day! #notolerance #noexcuses.

RT @piersmorgan:Any moment now, a gun nut will tweet me saying 'If all the kids in that,school had been armed, the shooters would have.

@WNEMTV5news:BREAKING: CBS News is reporting up to 27 are dead in an elementary school shooting in Connecticut>http://t.co/s5R5ivEC WHY?.

Newtown, Conn.you're all in my prayers today! Esp. all the children @ Sandy Hook school,Such a tragic and scary event! http://t.co/WxCBIRPI.

Horrified as I,watch the CT school shooting unfold. Is it time to talk about gun control,yet? #utpol.

Wow! I'm so,disgusted. Multiple people dead including children in a CT school shooting.Smh! RIP!!!.

A shooting in an elementary school? Really? There are truly some awful people in this world #senseless #justchildren.

RT @Autumn_Rose8: My heart goes out to the people of Newtown and all those involved in the,#SandyHook Shooting. Such a tragedy.

RT @JaCharLove_Xo: Wtf is wrong wit people!? Shooting up an elementary school tho? Like were does at make sense at

RT @derrickAaron:An elementary school shooting is one of the saddest things I've ever heard.

People are going to do a lot of crazy shit this week. First the shooting in Oregon and now a shooting at an elementary school in Connecticut.

RT @amanda_frankel:There was a shooting at an elementary school. I'm loosing all faith in humanity

#Breaking: CBS News,confirms 27 dead 14 are children in #Newtown CT school #shooting.http://t.co/ejk8hBDF Listen live http://t.co/MF3LU26R.

continued on next page

Table 5.6 (*continued*)

BREAKING: More on elementary school shooting: Apparent shooter is an adult 2 handguns recovered per state official @nbcnightlynews.
school in two weeks omg can someone pls shoot me im not ready yet omfg i wanna cry.
AP now reporting 27 dead, including 18 children at Connecticut school shooting. One gunman dead one still loose says ABC.
A shooting this morning at an elementary school in Connecticut. If we keep glorifying this shit w/ media coverage, it'll continue to happen.
State Police helicopter circling low in Newtown #schoolshooting http://t.co/wVxy8sBn.
what kind of sadistic mother fucker do you have to be to shoot up a fucking elementary school?? people sicken me.
RT @piersmorgan: Another day another horrific shooting - this time at an elementary school in Connecticut. America's gun culture has to.
RT @FoxNews:Multiple deaths reported in shooting at Connecticut elementary school,http://t.co/reswQing #SandyHookElementarySchool.
RT @GayanMW: Let's,take a moment to pay tribute to the innocent souls that were lost in the Connecticut elementary school shooting.
RT @FrankKnuckles:LORD HAVE MERCY: Pray 4 the families of this Connecticut elementary school shooting.
RT @CP24: A gunman was killed in the shooting at an elementary school in Newtown, Conn. local,official tells AP.
RT @KatyBaby02: Wtf a shooting in newtown elementary school 10 kids shot what has this world come to.
My Thoughts and,prayers are with the victims of the shooting at the elementary school. So sad. #Pray.
Another school shooting. People will say it's "unacceptable." A lie, of course when you consider nothing will be done about it.
RT @RHHIBent: "@slicKGilchrist:School shooting reported in Conn. this morning. SMH! http://t.co/ghEOEx5o" This has got to stop. Pray fo.
Another school shooting. Elementary school.Ugh .Another reason for Americans to feel like the country is coming apart.
I'm really over,this violence. It HAS got to stop. My thoughts & prayers go out right,now living through this fatal school shooting.
RT @AP: MORE: State,police respond to report of school shooting in Newtown, Conn.; lockdown in,place: http://t.co/NMcOYixP -BW.
BRUH RT,@eyewitnessnyc: Official confirms multiple fatalities in Newtown school shooting http://t.co/moc85BdS @breakingnews.
RT @kylebrennan1:Woah! Live interview with a parent in #Newtown just said the Sandy Hook Elementary School principal was shot and killed.
RT @CBS6: BREAKING:The principal and a school psychologist were killed in elementary school shooting http://t.co/tpfRXdZ2 #CT.

continued on next page

Table 5.6 (*continued*)

RT @eyewitnessnyc:LIVE: Continuing coverage of Sandy Hook Elementary School shooting in Connecticut http://t.co/EKNr1Xw4.
My heart goes out to all the kids, families and workers involved in the,elementary school shooting in Connecticut,this morning.
Who the hell goes to an elementary school and shoots kids? 27 dead already, what a shame.#prayers.
My prayers go out to all of the families affected in the Connecticut elementary school shooting.
Wtf a shooting in newtown elementary school 10 kids shot what has this world come to.
Who the hell shoots up an elementary school #sick.
My prayers go out to everyone affected by the school shooting in Connecticut.
Connecticut,elementary school evacuated after reported shooting http://t.co/yTLvl2fT.
My prayers and,condolences to all affected by the school shooting in CT. Hug your kids every,chance you get. Man is totally depraved.

algorithm. The summaries produced by the base algorithms are shown in the following tables:

ClusterRank: Table 5.7

COWTS: Table 5.8

Frequency Summarizer: Table 5.9

LexRank: Table 5.10

LSA: Table 5.11

LUHN: Table 5.12

Mead: Table 5.13

SumBasic: Table 5.14

SumDSDR: Table 5.15

We also applied some of the proposed ensemble algorithms on the small dataset of 50 tweets to obtain summaries of 20 tweets each. Specifically, we chose to demonstrate the outputs of some of the ensemble algorithms that achieved higher ROUGE scores than the best base algorithms. The summaries produced by the proposed ensemble algorithms are shown in the following tables:

VecSim-ConComp-maxSumTFIDF algorithm: Table 5.16

VecSim-ConComp-maxLen algorithm: Table 5.17

VecSim-Community-maxSumTFIDF algorithm: Table 5.18

Table 5.7 Summary generated by the Cluster-Rank (CR) algorithm.

People are going to do a lot of crazy shit this week. First the shooting in Oregon and now a shooting at an elementary school in Connecticut.

My prayers go out to all of the families affected in the Connecticut elementary school shooting.

My heart goes out to all the kids, families and workers involved in the,elementary school shooting in Connecticut this morning.

RT @CBS6: BREAKING: The principal and a school psychologist were killed in elementary school shooting http://t.co/tpfRXdZ2 #CT.

RT @CP24: A gunman was killed in the shooting at an elementary school in Newtown, Conn., local official tells AP.

"@WNEMTV5news: BREAKING: CBS News is reporting up to 27 are dead in an elementary school shooting in Connecticut>http://t.co/s5R5ivEC" WHY?.

RT @KatyBaby02: Wtf a shooting in newtown elementary school 10 kids shot what has this world come to.

RT @piersmorgan: Another day, another horrific shooting - this time at an elementary school in Connecticut. America's gun culture has to.

My prayers go out to everyone affected by the school shooting in Connecticut.

RT @amanda_frankel: There was a shooting at an elementary school. I'm loosing all faith in humanity.

RT @GayanMW: Let's take a moment to pay tribute to the innocent souls that were lost in the Connecticut elementary school shooting.

RT @FoxNews: Multiple deaths reported in shooting at Connecticut elementary school http://t.co/reswQing #SandyHookElementarySchool.

Wtf a shooting in newtown elementary school 10 kids shot what has this world come to.

RT @FrankKnuckles: LORD HAVE MERCY: Pray 4 the families of this Connecticut elementary school shooting.

RT @AP: MORE: State police respond to report of school shooting in Newtown, Conn.; lockdown in place: http://t.co/NMcOYixP -BW.

A shooting in an elementary school? Really?,There are truly some awful people in this world #senseless #justchildren.

Connecticut elementary school evacuated after reported shooting http://t.co/yTLvl2fT.

Oh shit shooting in a school in CT, hope girls steph and paul are fine.

RT @BuzzFeed: Photo from the Newtown Bee of students evacuating elementary school where a possible shooting is being reported http://t.c.

RT @1010WINSNewYork: #Breaking: CBS News confirms 27 dead, 14 are children in #Newtown, CT school #shooting.http://t.co/ejk8hBDF Listen.

Table 5.8 Summary generated by the COWTS (CW) algorithm.

My prayers go out to everyone affected by the school shooting in Connecticut.

#Breaking: CBS News confirms 27 dead, 14 are children in #Newtown, CT school #shooting.http://t.co/ejk8hBDF Listen live http://t.co/MF3LU26R.

I'm really over this violence. It HAS got to stop. My thoughts & prayers go out right now living through this fatal school shooting.

People are going to do a lot of crazy shit this week. First the shooting in Oregon and now a shooting at an elementary school in Connecticut.

My Thoughts and prayers are with the victims of the shooting at the elementary school. So sad. #Pray.

BREAKING: More on elementary school shooting: Apparent shooter is an adult, 2 handguns recovered per state official @nbcnightlynews.

BRUH RT @eyewitnessnyc: Official confirms multiple fatalities in Newtown school shooting http://t.co/moc85BdS @breakingnews.

A shooting this morning at an elementary school in Connecticut. If we keep glorifying this shit w/ media coverage, it'll continue to happen.

RT @GayanMW: Let's take a moment to pay tribute to the innocent souls that were lost in the Connecticut elementary school shooting.

Newtown, Conn. you're all in my prayers today! Esp. all the children @ Sandy Hook school Such a tragic and scary event! http://t.co/WxCBIRPI.

RT @AP: MORE: State police respond to report of school shooting in Newtown, Conn.; lockdown in place: http://t.co/NMcOYixP -BW.

State Police helicopter circling low in Newtown #schoolshooting http://t.co/wVxy8sBn.

RT @JaCharLove_Xo: Wtf is wrong wit people!? Shooting up an elementary school tho? Like were does at make sense at.

Another school shooting. Elementary school.,Ugh. Another reason for Americans to feel like the country is coming apart.

Horrified as I watch the CT school shooting unfold. Is it time to talk about gun control yet? #utpol.

RT @kylebrennan1: Woah! Live interview with a parent in #Newtown just said the Sandy Hook Elementary School principal was shot and killed.

what kind of sadistic mother fucker do you have to be to shoot up a fucking elementary school?? people sicken me.

RT @amanda_frankel: There was a shooting at an elementary school. I'm loosing all faith in humanity.

My prayers and condolences to all affected by the school shooting in CT. Hug your kids every chance you get. Man is totally depraved.

RT @tommytomlinson: CBS reporting 27 dead in CT school shooting. I'm gonna pass on debating guns, or anything else, right now. Go hug yo.

Table 5.9 Summary generated by the Frequency Summarizer (FS) algorithm.

Counselors shld b avail 2 ALL ct school age kids Shooter reported dead at Connecticut elementary school,http://t.co/w8OjtOhL.

"@WNEMTV5news: BREAKING: CBS News is reporting up to 27 are dead in an elementary school shooting in Connecticut>http://t.co/s5R5ivEC" WHY?.

RT @FoxNews: Multiple deaths reported in shooting at Connecticut elementary school http://t.co/reswQing #SandyHookElementarySchool.

RT @eyewitnessnyc: LIVE: Continuing coverage of Sandy Hook Elementary School shooting in Connecticut http://t.co/EKNr1Xw4.

Connecticut elementary school evacuated after reported shooting http://t.co/yTLvl2fT.

RT @BuzzFeed: Photo from the Newtown Bee of students evacuating elementary school where a possible shooting is being reported http://t.c.

Newtown, Conn. you're all in my prayers today! Esp. all the children @ Sandy Hook school Such a tragic and scary event! http://t.co/WxCBIRPI.

#Breaking: CBS News confirms 27 dead, 14 are children in #Newtown, CT school #shooting.http://t.co/ejk8hBDF Listen live http://t.co/MF3LU26R.

State Police helicopter circling low in Newtown #schoolshooting http://t.co/wVxy8sBn.

RT @AP: MORE: State police respond to report of school shooting in Newtown, Conn.; lockdown in place: http://t.co/NMcOYixP -BW.

BRUH RT @eyewitnessnyc: Official confirms multiple fatalities in Newtown school shooting http://t.co/moc85BdS @breakingnews.

Shooting at a Connecticut elementary school.,Luckily, my son attends a different one.,Our hearts go out to all involved with this tragedy.

People are going to do a lot of crazy shit this week. First the shooting in Oregon and now a shooting at an elementary school in Connecticut.

AP now reporting 27 dead, including 18 children at Connecticut school shooting. One gunman dead, one still loose, says ABC.

A shooting this morning at an elementary school in Connecticut. If we keep glorifying this shit w/ media coverage, it'll continue to happen.

RT @piersmorgan: Another day, another horrific shooting - this time at an elementary school in Connecticut. America's gun culture has to.

RT @GayanMW: Let's take a moment to pay tribute to the innocent souls that were lost in the Connecticut elementary school shooting.

RT @FrankKnuckles: LORD HAVE MERCY: Pray 4 the families of this Connecticut elementary school shooting.

My heart goes out to all the kids, families and workers involved in the,elementary school shooting in Connecticut this morning.

My prayers go out to all of the families affected in the Connecticut elementary school shooting.

Table 5.10 Summary generated by the LexRank(LR) algorithm.

RT @tommytomlinson: CBS reporting 27 dead in CT school shooting.

Counselors shld b avail 2 ALL ct school age kids Shooter reported dead at Connecticut elementary school,http://t.co/w8OjtOhL.

Shooting at a Connecticut elementary school.

RT @piersmorgan: Any moment now, a gun nut will tweet me saying 'If all the kids in that school had been armed, the shooters would have.

"@WNEMTV5news: BREAKING: CBS News is reporting up to 27 are dead in an elementary school shooting in Connecticut>http://t.co/s5R5ivEC" WHY?.

Multiple people dead including children in a CT school shooting.

A shooting in an elementary school?

RT @Autumn_Rose8: My heart goes out to the people of Newtown and all those involved in the #SandyHook Shooting.

People are going to do a lot of crazy shit this week.

RT @amanda_frankel: There was a shooting at an elementary school.

AP now reporting 27 dead, including 18 children at Connecticut school shooting.

RT @FoxNews: Multiple deaths reported in shooting at Connecticut elementary school http://t.co/reswQing #SandyHookElementarySchool.

RT @FrankKnuckles: LORD HAVE MERCY: Pray 4 the families of this Connecticut elementary school shooting.

RT @KatyBaby02: Wtf a shooting in newtown elementary school 10 kids shot what has this world come to.

Another school shooting.

Connecticut elementary school evacuated after reported shooting http://t.co/yTLvl2fT.

Elementary school.

RT @CBS6: BREAKING: The principal and a school psychologist were killed in elementary school shooting http://t.co/tpfRXdZ2 #CT. RT @eyewitnessnyc: LIVE:

Continuing coverage of Sandy Hook Elementary School shooting in Connecticut http://t.co/EKNr1Xw4.

My prayers go out to all of the families affected in the Connecticut elementary school shooting.

Table 5.11 Summary generated by the LSA (LS) algorithm.

Oh shit shooting in a school in CT, hope girls steph and paul are fine.

RT @BuzzFeed: Photo from the Newtown Bee of students evacuating elementary school where a possible shooting is being reported http://t.c.

RT @1010WINSNewYork: #Breaking: CBS News confirms 27 dead, 14 are children in #Newtown, CT school #shooting.http://t.co/ejk8hBDF Listen.

RT @piersmorgan: Any moment now, a gun nut will tweet me saying 'If all the kids in that school had been armed, the shooters would have.

"@WNEMTV5news: BREAKING: CBS News is reporting up to 27 are dead in an elementary school shooting in Connecticut>http://t.co/s5R5ivEC" WHY?.

RT @derrickAaron: An elementary school shooting is one of the saddest things I've ever heard.

#Breaking: CBS News confirms 27 dead, 14 are children in #Newtown, CT school #shooting.http://t.co/ejk8hBDF Listen live http://t.co/MF3LU26R.

BREAKING: More on elementary school shooting: Apparent shooter is an adult, 2 handguns recovered per state official @nbcnightlynews.

school in two weeks omg can someone pls shoot me im not ready yet omfg i wanna cry.

RT @piersmorgan: Another day, another horrific shooting - this time at an elementary school in Connecticut.

RT @FoxNews: Multiple deaths reported in shooting at Connecticut elementary school http://t.co/reswQing #SandyHookElementarySchool.

RT @GayanMW: Let's take a moment to pay tribute to the innocent souls that were lost in the Connecticut elementary school shooting.

RT @FrankKnuckles: LORD HAVE MERCY: Pray 4 the families of this Connecticut elementary school shooting.

RT @CP24: A gunman was killed in the shooting at an elementary school in Newtown, Conn., local official tells AP.

RT @KatyBaby02: Wtf a shooting in newtown elementary school 10 kids shot what has this world come to.

RT @AP: MORE: State police respond to report of school shooting in Newtown, Conn.; lockdown in place: http://t.co/NMcOYixP -BW.

BRUH RT @eyewitnessnyc: Official confirms multiple fatalities in Newtown school shooting http://t.co/moc85BdS @breakingnews.

Live interview with a parent in #Newtown just said the Sandy Hook Elementary School principal was shot and killed.

My heart goes out to all the kids, families and workers involved in the,elementary school shooting in Connecticut this morning.

Wtf a shooting in newtown elementary school 10 kids shot what has this world come to.

Table 5.12 Summary generated by the LUHN (LH) algorithm.

RT @tommytomlinson: CBS reporting 27 dead in CT school shooting.

Counselors shld b avail 2 ALL ct school age kids Shooter reported dead at Connecticut elementary school,http://t.co/w8OjtOhL.

RT @1010WINSNewYork: #Breaking: CBS News confirms 27 dead, 14 are children in #Newtown, CT school #shooting.http://t.co/ejk8hBDF Listen.

"@WNEMTV5news: BREAKING: CBS News is reporting up to 27 are dead in an elementary school shooting in Connecticut>http://t.co/s5R5ivEC" WHY?.

Newtown, Conn. you're all in my prayers today! Esp. all the children @ Sandy Hook school Such a tragic and scary event! http://t.co/WxCBIRPI.

Multiple people dead including children in a CT school shooting.

#Breaking: CBS News confirms 27 dead, 14 are children in #Newtown, CT school #shooting.http://t.co/ejk8hBDF Listen live http://t.co/MF3LU26R.

AP now reporting 27 dead, including 18 children at Connecticut school shooting.

RT @piersmorgan: Another day, another horrific shooting – this time at an elementary school in Connecticut.

RT @FoxNews: Multiple deaths reported in shooting at Connecticut elementary school http://t.co/reswQing #SandyHookElementarySchool.

RT @CP24: A gunman was killed in the shooting at an elementary school in Newtown, Conn., local official tells AP.

RT @KatyBaby02: Wtf a shooting in newtown elementary school 10 kids shot what has this world come to.

RT @AP: MORE: State police respond to report of school shooting in Newtown, Conn.; lockdown in place: http://t.co/NMcOYixP -BW.

BRUH RT @eyewitnessnyc: Official confirms multiple fatalities in Newtown school shooting http://t.co/moc85BdS @breakingnews.

Live interview with a parent in #Newtown just said the Sandy Hook Elementary School principal was shot and killed.

RT @CBS6: BREAKING: The principal and a school psychologist were killed in elementary school shooting http://t.co/tpfRXdZ2 #CT. RT @eyewitnessnyc: LIVE:

Continuing coverage of Sandy Hook Elementary School shooting in Connecticut http://t.co/EKNr1Xw4.

My heart goes out to all the kids, families and workers involved in the,elementary school shooting in Connecticut this morning.

My prayers go out to all of the families affected in the Connecticut elementary school shooting.

Wtf a shooting in newtown elementary school 10 kids shot what has this world come to.

Table 5.13 Summary generated by the Mead (MD) algorithm.

RT @tommytomlinson: CBS reporting 27 dead in CT school shooting.

I'm gonna pass on debating guns, or anything else, right now.

Oh shit shooting in a school in CT, hope girls steph and paul are fine.

Counselors shld b avail 2 ALL ct school age kids Shooter reported dead at Connecticut elementary school http://t.co/w8OjtOhL.

RT @BuzzFeed: Photo from the Newtown Bee of students evacuating elementary school where a possible shooting is being reported http://t.c.

"@WNEMTV5news: BREAKING: CBS News is reporting up to 27 are dead in an elementary school shooting in Connecticut>http://t.co/s5R5ivEC" WHY?.

Horrified as I watch the CT school shooting unfold.

Multiple people dead including children in a CT school shooting.

First the shooting in Oregon and now a shooting at an elementary school in Connecticut.

RT @piersmorgan: Another day, another horrific shooting - this time at an elementary school in Connecticut.

RT @FoxNews: Multiple deaths reported in shooting at Connecticut elementary school http://t.co/reswQing #SandyHookElementarySchool.

RT @GayanMW: Let's take a moment to pay tribute to the innocent souls that were lost in the Connecticut elementary school shooting.

RT @FrankKnuckles: LORD HAVE MERCY: Pray 4 the families of this Connecticut elementary school shooting.

RT @CP24: A gunman was killed in the shooting at an elementary school in Newtown, Conn., local official tells AP.

RT @KatyBaby02: Wtf a shooting in newtown elementary school 10 kids shot what has this world come to.

My Thoughts and prayers are with the victims of the shooting at the elementary school.

RT @CBS6: BREAKING: The principal and a school psychologist were killed in elementary school shooting http://t.co/tpfRXdZ2 #CT.

My heart goes out to all the kids, families and workers involved in the elementary school shooting in Connecticut this morning.

My prayers go out to all of the families affected in the Connecticut elementary school shooting.

My prayers and condolences to all affected by the school shooting in CT.

Table 5.14 Summary generated by the SumBasic (SB) algorithm.

Shooting at a Connecticut elementary school.,Luckily, my son attends a different one.,Our hearts go out to all involved with this tragedy.

A shooting this morning at an elementary school in Connecticut. If we keep glorifying this shit w/ media coverage, it'll continue to happen.

RT @1010WINSNewYork: #Breaking: CBS News confirms 27 dead, 14 are children in #Newtown, CT school #shooting.http://t.co/ejk8hBDF Listen.

Newtown, Conn. you're all in my prayers today!Esp. all the children @ Sandy Hook school Such a tragic and scary event! http://t.co/WxCBIRPI.

A shooting in an elementary school? Really?There are truly some awful people in this world #senseless #justchildren.

Horrified as I watch the CT school shooting unfold. Is it time to talk about gun control yet? #utpol.

Wow! I'm so disgusted. Multiple people dead including children in a CT school shooting. Smh! RIP!!!.

State Police helicopter circling low in Newtown #schoolshooting http://t.co/wVxy8sBn.

what kind of sadistic mother fucker do you have to be to shoot up a fucking elementary school?? people sicken me.

My Thoughts and prayers are with the victims of the shooting at the elementary school. So sad. #Pray.

RT @RHHIBent: @slicKGilchrist: School shooting reported in Conn. this morning.

I'm really over this violence. It HAS got to stop. My thoughts & prayers go out right now living through this fatal school shooting.

RT @kylebrennan1: Woah! Live interview with a parent in #Newtown just said the Sandy Hook Elementary School principal was shot and killed.

Live interview with a parent in #Newtown just said the Sandy Hook Elementary School principal was shot and killed.

Who the fuck goes to an elementary school and shoots kids? 27 dead already, what a shame. #prayers.

My prayers and condolences to all affected by the school shooting in CT. Hug your kids every chance you get. Man is totally depraved.

BREAKING: More on elementary school shooting: Apparent shooter is an adult, 2 handguns recovered per state official @nbcnightlynews.

RT @GayanMW: Let's take a moment to pay tribute to the innocent souls that were lost in the Connecticut elementary school shooting.

RT @1010WINSNewYork: #Breaking: CBS News confirms 27 dead, 14 are children in #Newtown, CT school #shooting.http://t.co/ejk8hBDF Listen.

Another school shooting. Elementary school.,Ugh. Another reason for Americans to feel like the country is coming apart.

Table 5.15 Summary generated by the SumDSDR (Document Summarization based on Data Reconstruction) algorithm.

A shooting in an elementary school? Really?,There are truly some awful people in this world #senseless #justchildren.
My prayers go out to all of the families affected in the Connecticut elementary school shooting.
#Breaking: CBS News confirms 27 dead, 14 are children in #Newtown, CT school #shooting.http://t.co/ejk8hBDF Listen live http://t.co/MF3LU26R.
Another school shooting. Elementary school.,Ugh. Another reason for Americans to feel like the country is coming apart.
RT @KatyBaby02: Wtf a shooting in newtown elementary school 10 kids shot what has this world come to.
RT @RHHIBent: "@slicKGilchrist: School shooting reported in Conn. this morning. SMH! http://t.co/ghEOEx5o" This has got to stop. Pray fo.
A shooting this morning at an elementary school in Connecticut. If we keep glorifying this shit w/ media coverage, it'll continue to happen.
Who the fuck goes to an elementary school and shoots kids? 27 dead already, what a shame. #prayers.
AP now reporting 27 dead, including 18 children at Connecticut school shooting. One gunman dead, one still loose, says ABC.
RT @CP24: A gunman was killed in the shooting at an elementary school in Newtown, Conn., local official tells AP.
I'm really over this violence. It HAS got to stop. My thoughts & prayers go out right now living through this fatal school shooting.
RT @FoxNews: Multiple deaths reported in shooting at Connecticut elementary school http://t.co/reswQing #SandyHookElementarySchool.
My Thoughts and prayers are with the victims of the shooting at the elementary school. So sad. #Pray.
Another school shooting. People will say it's "unacceptable." A lie, of course, when you consider nothing will be done about it.
Live interview with a parent in #Newtown just said the Sandy Hook Elementary School principal was shot and killed.
Who the fuck goes to an elementary school and shoots kids? 27 dead already, what a shame. #prayers.
Horrified as I watch the CT school shooting unfold. Is it time to talk about gun control yet? #utpol.
RT @Autumn_Rose8: My heart goes out to the people of Newtown and all those involved in the #SandyHook Shooting. Such a tragedy.
AP now reporting 27 dead, including 18 children at Connecticut school shooting. One gunman dead, one still loose, says ABC.
RT @KatyBaby02: Wtf a shooting in newtown elementary school 10 kids shot what has this world come to.

Table 5.16 Summary generated by the VecSim-ConComp-maxSumTFIDF ensemble algorithm.

"@WNEMTV5news: BREAKING: CBS News is reporting up to 27 are dead in an elementary school shooting in Connecticut>http://t.co/s5R5ivEC" WHY?.
RT @AP: MORE: State police respond to report of school shooting in Newtown, Conn.; lockdown in place: http://t.co/NMcOYixP -BW.
RT @BuzzFeed: Photo from the Newtown Bee of students evacuating elementary school where a possible shooting is being reported http://t.c.
RT @1010WINSNewYork: #Breaking: CBS News confirms 27 dead, 14 are children in #Newtown, CT school #shooting.http://t.co/ejk8hBDF Listen.
#Breaking: CBS News confirms 27 dead, 14 are children in #Newtown, CT school #shooting.http://t.co/ejk8hBDF Listen live http://t.co/MF3LU26R.
Counselors shld b avail 2 ALL ct school age kids Shooter reported dead at Connecticut elementary school,http://t.co/w8OjtOhL.
A shooting this morning at an elementary school in Connecticut. If we keep glorifying this shit w/ media coverage, it'll continue to happen.
RT @tommytomlinson: CBS reporting 27 dead in CT school shooting.
RT @kylebrennan1: Woah! Live interview with a parent in #Newtown just said the Sandy Hook Elementary School principal was shot and killed.
Newtown, Conn. you're all in my prayers today! Esp. all the children @ Sandy Hook school Such a tragic and scary event! http://t.co/WxCBIRPI.
RT @CBS6: BREAKING: The principal and a school psychologist were killed in elementary school shooting http://t.co/tpfRXdZ2 #CT. RT @eyewitnessnyc: LIVE:
Continuing coverage of Sandy Hook Elementary School shooting in Connecticut http://t.co/EKNr1Xw4.
Who the fuck goes to an elementary school and shoots kids?
RT @JaCharLove_Xo: Wtf is wrong wit people!? Shooting up an elementary school tho? Like were does at make sense at.
Counselors shld b avail 2 ALL ct school age kids Shooter reported dead at Connecticut elementary school http://t.co/w8OjtOhL.
RT @eyewitnessnyc: LIVE: Continuing coverage of Sandy Hook Elementary School shooting in Connecticut http://t.co/EKNr1Xw4.
RT @tommytomlinson: CBS reporting 27 dead in CT school shooting. I'm gonna pass on debating guns, or anything else, right now. Go hug yo .Counselors shld b avail 2 ALL ct school age kids Shooter reported dead at Connecticut elementary school,http://t.co/w8OjtOhL.
RT @CBS6: BREAKING: The principal and a school psychologist were killed in elementary school shooting http://t.co/tpfRXdZ2 #CT.
Wow! I'm so disgusted. Multiple people dead including children in a CT school shooting. Smh! RIP!!!.

Table 5.17 Summary generated by the VecSim-ConComp-maxLen ensemble algorithm.

RT @KatyBaby02: Wtf a shooting in newtown elementary school 10 kids shot what has this world come to.

RT @GayanMW: Let's take a moment to pay tribute to the innocent souls that were lost in the Connecticut elementary school shooting.

RT @BuzzFeed: Photo from the Newtown Bee of students evacuating elementary school where a possible shooting is being reported http://t.c.

RT @CP24: A gunman was killed in the shooting at an elementary school in Newtown, Conn., local official tells AP.

A shooting this morning at an elementary school in Connecticut. If we keep glorifying this shit w/ media coverage, it'll continue to happen.

Counselors shld b avail 2 ALL ct school age kids Shooter reported dead at Connecticut elementary school,http://t.co/w8OjtOhL.

RT @tommytomlinson: CBS reporting 27 dead in CT school shooting.

Live interview with a parent in #Newtown just said the Sandy Hook Elementary School principal was shot and killed.

RT @kylebrennan1: Woah! Live interview with a parent in #Newtown just said the Sandy Hook Elementary School principal was shot and killed.

AP now reporting 27 dead, including 18 children at Connecticut school shooting. One gunman dead, one still loose, says ABC.

RT @CBS6: BREAKING: The principal and a school psychologist were killed in elementary school shooting http://t.co/tpfRXdZ2 #CT. RT @eyewitnessnyc: LIVE:

Continuing coverage of Sandy Hook Elementary School shooting in Connecticut http://t.co/EKNr1Xw4.

BREAKING: More on elementary school shooting: Apparent shooter is an adult, 2 handguns recovered per state official @nbcnightlynews.

RT @piersmorgan: Any moment now, a gun nut will tweet me saying 'If all the kids in that school had been armed, the shooters would have.

Counselors shld b avail 2 ALL ct school age kids Shooter reported dead at Connecticut elementary school http://t.co/w8OjtOhL.

Shooting at a Connecticut elementary school.,Luckily, my son attends a different one.,Our hearts go out to all involved with this tragedy.

RT @tommytomlinson: CBS reporting 27 dead in CT school shooting. I'm gonna pass on debating guns, or anything else, right now. Go hug yo .Counselors shld b avail 2 ALL ct school age kids Shooter reported dead at Connecticut elementary school,http://t.co/w8OjtOhL.

RT @JaCharLove_Xo: Wtf is wrong wit people!? Shooting up an elementary school tho? Like were does at make sense at.

Wow! I'm so disgusted. Multiple people dead including children in a CT school shooting. Smh! RIP!!!.

Table 5.18 Summary generated by the VecSim-Community-maxSumTFIDF ensemble algorithm.

"@WNEMTV5news: BREAKING: CBS News is reporting up to 27 are dead in an elementary school shooting in Connecticut>http://t.co/s5R5ivEC" WHY?.

RT @AP: MORE: State police respond to report of school shooting in Newtown, Conn.; lockdown in place: http://t.co/NMcOYixP -BW.

RT @BuzzFeed: Photo from the Newtown Bee of students evacuating elementary school where a possible shooting is being reported http://t.c.

RT @1010WINSNewYork: #Breaking: CBS News confirms 27 dead, 14 are children in #Newtown, CT school #shooting.http://t.co/ejk8hBDF Listen.

#Breaking: CBS News confirms 27 dead, 14 are children in #Newtown, CT school #shooting.http://t.co/ejk8hBDF Listen live http://t.co/MF3LU26R.

A shooting this morning at an elementary school in Connecticut. If we keep glorifying this shit w/ media coverage, it'll continue to happen.

RT @tommytomlinson: CBS reporting 27 dead in CT school shooting.

Counselors shld b avail 2 ALL ct school age kids Shooter reported dead at Connecticut elementary school,http://t.co/w8OjtOhL.

RT @kylebrennan1: Woah! Live interview with a parent in #Newtown just said the Sandy Hook Elementary School principal was shot and killed.

Newtown, Conn. you're all in my prayers today! Esp. all the children @ Sandy Hook school Such a tragic and scary event! http://t.co/WxCBIRPI.

RT @CBS6: BREAKING: The principal and a school psychologist were killed in elementary school shooting http://t.co/tpfRXdZ2 #CT. RT @eyewitnessnyc: LIVE:

Continuing coverage of Sandy Hook Elementary School shooting in Connecticut http://t.co/EKNr1Xw4.

Who the fuck goes to an elementary school and shoots kids?

RT @JaCharLove_Xo: Wtf is wrong wit people!? Shooting up an elementary school tho? Like were does at make sense at.

Counselors shld b avail 2 ALL ct school age kids Shooter reported dead at Connecticut elementary school http://t.co/w8OjtOhL.

RT @eyewitnessnyc: LIVE: Continuing coverage of Sandy Hook Elementary School shooting in Connecticut http://t.co/EKNr1Xw4.

RT @tommytomlinson: CBS reporting 27 dead in CT school shooting. I'm gonna pass on debating guns, or anything else, right now. Go hug yo .Counselors shld b avail 2 ALL ct school age kids Shooter reported dead at Connecticut elementary school,http://t.co/w8OjtOhL.

RT @CBS6: BREAKING: The principal and a school psychologist were killed in elementary school shooting http://t.co/tpfRXdZ2 #CT.

Wow! I'm so disgusted. Multiple people dead including children in a CT school shooting. Smh! RIP!!!.

5.7 Conclusion

To our knowledge, this is the first attempt to develop ensemble summarization algorithms for text summarization. We summarize our contributions. (1) We show that different extractive summarization algorithms produce very different summaries for the same input data. (2) We propose two ensemble algorithms: (i) an unsupervised graph-based scheme and (ii) a supervised scheme based on L2R – for combining the outputs of multiple extractive summarization algorithms. (3) We demonstrate that it is possible to combine off-the-shelf summarization algorithms to achieve better summarization for microblogs. Specifically, the proposed unsupervised ensemble algorithm achieves up to 8.4% better Rouge-2 recall scores compared to the best base algorithm. In the future, we plan to extend the ensemble schemes to abstractive summarization algorithms, by considering different text fragments (instead of whole tweets) selected by abstractive algorithms for generating the ensemble summaries.

References

[1] H. Zhuge, Multi-Dimensional Summarization in Cyber-Physical Society, Morgan Kaufmann, 2016.

[2] S. Goswami, A.K. Das, Determining maximum cliques for community detection in weighted sparse networks, Knowledge and Information Systems 64 (2) (2022) 289–324, https://doi.org/10.1007/s10115-021-01631-y.

[3] A. Mukherjee, S. Bhattacharyya, K. Ray, B. Gupta, A.K. Das, A study of public sentiment and influence of politics in COVID-19 related tweets, in: A.K. Das, J. Nayak, B. Naik, S. Dutta, D. Pelusi (Eds.), Computational Intelligence in Pattern Recognition, Springer, Singapore, 2022, pp. 655–665.

[4] V. Gupta, G.S. Lehal, A survey of text summarization extractive techniques, IEEE Journal of Emerging Technologies in Web Intelligence 2 (3) (2010) 258–268.

[5] K. Rudra, S. Ghosh, P. Goyal, N. Ganguly, S. Ghosh, Extracting situational information from microblogs during disaster events: a classification-summarization approach, in: Proc. ACM CIKM, 2015.

[6] S. Mackie, R. McCreadie, C. Macdonald, I. Ounis, Comparing algorithms for microblog summarisation, in: Proc. CLEF, 2014.

[7] D.I. Inouye, J.K. Kalita, Comparing Twitter summarization algorithms for multiple post summaries, in: Proc. IEEE SocialCom / PASSAT, 2011.

[8] P. Das, A.K. Das, Convolutional neural networks-based sentence level classification of crime documents, in: A.K. Das, J. Nayak, B. Naik, S. Dutta, D. Pelusi (Eds.), Computational Intelligence in Pattern Recognition, Springer, Singapore, 2022, pp. 65–73.

[9] A. Das, D. Pal, C. Mallick, A.K. Das, An unsupervised COVID-19 report summarizer for developing smart healthcare system, in: A.K. Das, J. Nayak, B. Naik, S. Dutta, D. Pelusi (Eds.), Computational Intelligence in Pattern Recognition, Springer, Singapore, 2022, pp. 157–168.

[10] T.-Y. Liu, Learning to rank for information retrieval, Foundations and Trends in Information Retrieval 3 (3) (2009) 225–331.

[11] C. Mallick, S. Das, A.K. Das, Evolutionary algorithm based summarization for analyzing COVID-19 medical reports, in: J. Nayak, B. Naik, A. Abraham (Eds.), Understanding COVID-19: The Role of Computational Intelligence, in: Studies in Computational Intelligence, Springer International Publishing, Cham, 2022, pp. 31–58.

[12] S. Chattopadhyay, T. Basu, A.K. Das, K. Ghosh, L.C.A. Murthy, Towards effective discovery of natural communities in complex networks and implications in e-commerce, Electronic Commerce Research 21 (4) (2021) 917–954, https://doi.org/10.1007/s10660-019-09395-y.

[13] G. Seni, J. Elder, Ensemble Methods in Data Mining: Improving Accuracy Through Combining Predictions, Morgan and Claypool Publishers, 2010.

[14] N. Garg, B. Favre, K. Riedhammer, D. Hakkani-Tür, Clusterrank: a graph based method for meeting summarization, in: INTERSPEECH, ISCA, 2009, pp. 1499–1502.

[15] G. Erkan, D.R. Radev, Lexrank: graph-based lexical centrality as salience in text summarization, Journal of Artificial Intelligence Research 22 (1) (2004) 457–479.

[16] Y. Gong, X. Liu, Generic text summarization using relevance measure and latent semantic analysis, in: SIGIR, 2001, pp. 19–25.

[17] H.P. Luhn, The automatic creation of literature abstracts, IBM Journal of Research and Development 2 (2) (1958) 159–165.

[18] D.R. Radev, E. Hovy, K. McKeown, Introduction to the special issue on summarization, Computational Linguistics 28 (4) (2002) 399–408.

[19] A. Nenkova, L. Vanderwende, The impact of frequency on summarization, Tech. Rep., Microsoft Research, 2005.

[20] Z. He, C. Chen, J. Bu, C. Wang, L. Zhang, D. Cai, X. He, Document summarization based on data reconstruction, in: Proc. AAAI Conference on Artificial Intelligence, 2012, pp. 620–626.

[21] T. Mikolov, S.W.-t. Yih, G. Zweig, Linguistic regularities in continuous space word representations, in: Proceedings of the 2013 Conference of the North American Chapter of the Association for Computational Linguistics: Human Language Technologies (NAACL-HLT-2013), 2013.

[22] V.D. Blondel, J.-l. Guillaume, R. Lambiotte, E. Lefebvre, Fast unfolding of communities in large networks, Journal of Statistical Mechanics 2008 (2008) P10008.

[23] S.E. Robertson, H. Zaragoza, The probabilistic relevance framework: Bm25 and beyond, Foundations and Trends in Information Retrieval 3 (4) (2009) 333–389.

[24] R. Mandal, S. Dutta, R. Banerjee, S. Bhattacharya, R. Ghosh, S. Samanta, T. Saha, City traffic speed characterization based on city road surface quality, in: J.M.R.S. Tavares, P. Dutta, S. Dutta, D. Samanta (Eds.), Cyber Intelligence and Information Retrieval, Springer, Singapore, 2022, pp. 515–524.

[25] D. Samanta, S. Dutta, M.G. Galety, S. Pramanik, A novel approach for web mining taxonomy for high-performance computing, in: J.M.R.S. Tavares, P. Dutta, S. Dutta, D. Samanta (Eds.), Cyber Intelligence and Information Retrieval, in: Lecture Notes in Networks and Systems, Springer, Singapore, 2022, pp. 425–432.

[26] R.D. Perera, S. Anand, K.P. Subbalakshmi, R. Chandramouli, Twitter analytics: architecture, tools and analysis, in: 2010 - MILCOM 2010 Military Communications Conference, 2010, pp. 2186–2191.

[27] A. Mandal, K. Ghosh, S. Ghosh, S. Mandal, A sequence labeling model for catch-phrase identification from legal case documents, Artificial Intelligence and Law (2021), https://doi.org/10.1007/s10506-021-09296-2.

[28] M. Basu, K. Ghosh, S. Ghosh, Information retrieval from microblogs during disasters: in the light of IRMiDis task, SN Computer Science 1 (1) (2020) 61, https://doi.org/10.1007/s42979-020-0065-1.

[29] C.-Y. Lin, ROUGE: a package for automatic evaluation of summaries, in: Proc. Workshop on Text Summarization Branches Out, ACL, 2004.

[30] C.M. Yoshimura, H. Kitagawa, Tlv-bandit: bandit method for collecting topic-related local tweets, in: 2021 IEEE 4th International Conference on Multimedia Information Processing and Retrieval (MIPR), 2021, pp. 56–62.

[31] K. Hazra, T. Ghosh, A. Mukherjee, S. Saha, S. Nandi, S. Ghosh, S. Chakraborty, Sustainable text summarization over mobile devices: an energy-aware approach, Sustainable Computing: Informatics and Systems 32 (2021) 100607, https://doi.org/10.1016/j.suscom.2021.100607, https://www.sciencedirect.com/science/article/pii/S2210%537921000950.

[32] R. Compton, C. Lee, T.-C. Lu, L. De Silva, M. Macy, Detecting future social unrest in unprocessed Twitter data: "emerging phenomena and big data", in: 2013 IEEE International Conference on Intelligence and Security Informatics, 2013, pp. 56–60.

[33] G.A. Sandag, A.M. Manueke, M. Walean, Sentiment analysis of Covid-19 vaccine tweets in Indonesia using recurrent neural network (rnn) approach, in: 2021 3rd International Conference on Cybernetics and Intelligent System (ICORIS), 2021, pp. 1–7.

[34] P. Bhattacharya, S. Paul, K. Ghosh, S. Ghosh, A. Wyner, DeepRhole: deep learning for rhetorical role labeling of sentences in legal case documents, Artificial Intelligence and Law (2021), https://doi.org/10.1007/s10506-021-09304-5.

[35] R.D. Perera, S. Anand, K.P. Subbalakshmi, R. Chandramouli, Twitter analytics: architecture, tools and analysis, in: 2010 - MILCOM 2010 Military Communications Conference, 2010, pp. 2186–2191.

[36] P. Tatineni, B.S. Babu, B. Kanuri, G.R.K. Rao, P. Chitturi, C. Naresh, Post Covid-19 Twitter user's emotions classification using deep learning techniques in India, in: 2021 International Conference on Artificial Intelligence and Smart Systems (ICAIS), 2021, pp. 338–343.

[37] C. Wang, L. Marini, C.-L. Chin, N. Vance, C. Donelson, P. Meunier, J.T. Yun, Social media intelligence and learning environment: an open source framework for social media data collection, analysis and curation, in: 2019 15th International Conference on eScience (eScience), 2019, pp. 252–261.

[38] T. Jagić, L. Brkić, Hot topic detection using Twitter streaming data, in: 2020 43rd International Convention on Information, Communication and Electronic Technology (MIPRO), 2020, pp. 1730–1735.

[39] M. Basu, S.D. Bit, S. Ghosh, Utilizing microblogs for optimized real-time resource allocation in post-disaster scenarios, Social Network Analysis and Mining 12 (1) (2021) 15, https://doi.org/10.1007/s13278-021-00841-0.

[40] K. Jitkajornwanich, C. Kongthong, N. Khongsoontornjaroen, J. Kaiyasuan, S. Lawawirojwong, P. Srestasathiern, S. Srisonphan, P. Vateekul, Utilizing Twitter data for early flood warning in Thailand, in: 2018 IEEE International Conference on Big Data (Big Data), 2018, pp. 5165–5169.

[41] S.H. Archana, S.G. Winster, Drugs categorization based on sentence polarity analyzer for Twitter data, in: 2016 Second International Conference on Science Technology Engineering and Management (ICONSTEM), 2016, pp. 28–33.

[42] P. Ray, A. Chakrabarti, Twitter sentiment analysis for product review using lexicon method, in: 2017 International Conference on Data Management, Analytics and Innovation (ICDMAI), 2017, pp. 211–216.

[43] A. Dwi Laksito, Kusrini, H. Sismoro, F. Rahmawati, M. Yusa, A comparison study of search strategy on collecting Twitter data for drug adverse reaction, in: 2018 International Seminar on Application for Technology of Information and Communication, 2018, pp. 356–360.

[44] H. Efstathiades, D. Antoniades, G. Pallis, M.D. Dikaiakos, Distributed large-scale data collection in online social networks, in: 2016 IEEE 2nd International Conference on Collaboration and Internet Computing (CIC), 2016, pp. 373–380.

[45] A. Campan, T. Atnafu, T.M. Truta, J. Nolan, Is data collection through Twitter streaming api useful for academic research?, in: 2018 IEEE International Conference on Big Data (Big Data), 2018, pp. 3638–3643.

[46] S. Kumar, K.M. Carley, What to track on the Twitter streaming api? A knapsack bandits approach to dynamically update the search terms, in: 2019 IEEE/ACM International Conference on Advances in Social Networks Analysis and Mining (ASONAM), 2019, pp. 158–163.

CHAPTER 6

Graph-based clustering technique for microblog clustering

6.1 Introduction

The massive popularity of microblogging adds a dimension to the communication media and data generation, opening up a new domain for natural language processing (NLP) by discovering news stories, public opinion, or conversational topics [1–3]. Every day huge number of messages are posted on microblogging platforms such as Twitter, Facebook, etc. During any important event, the number of messages posted per second exceeds several thousand which causes information overload. It is a great challenge for the researchers to access that information efficiently for knowledge mining and to use it for further ongoing research work as trending topic analysis [4], user sentiment analysis [5], summarization [6], problem and spam detection [7], etc. In this chapter we are concentrating on summarization problem that is based on Twitter dataset.

Massive data flow motivates researchers to effectively mine for information by filtering and organization. The term information mining is related to the study of the computational process of discovering patterns in huge datasets to acquire knowledge involving the challenging techniques through data analysis. Data mining is an analytical phase in the knowledge discovery in databases process. Researchers in the field of data mining are focusing on extracting new fascinating facts from microblog data in order to expand the number of new interesting facts [8–10]. Data mining plays a vital role in filtering and organizing information to portray knowledge in a simpler manner, as microblogging sites have become important sources of real-time information, and all of the material is relatively unstructured by nature.

Twitter is a repository of a wide range of recent and popular useful information of trending and non-trending topics which are categorized by Twitter itself [11–13]. As Twitter is a microblogging website, much of the retrieved information is abbreviated or not completed; many posts contain irrelevant and redundant information, which leads to a demoralization of information. Any search result by the Twitter API generates a huge set of posts, so to fully comprehend a topic, it is required to receive a summary or a brief overview of these posts.

Data Analytics for Social Microblogging Platforms
https://doi.org/10.1016/B978-0-32-391785-8.00018-4

Tweet summarization is a process which generates a summary about a topic or product from a large number of tweets or dataset. This is a data mining process that involves building a system to collect and summarize information about the topic of Twitter posts. Tweet summarization can be very useful in many ways. For example, in marketing it can help in judging the success of a new launched product and analyzing reviews of a customer. It can also be useful at the time of a natural disaster to quickly obtain an overview of the whole situation [14–16].

We face several challenges in tweet summarization; people do not always express their opinion in the same way – several abbreviations, smileys, etc., are used in the comments. In many cases, a small difference between two pieces of text does not change the whole meaning that much. Some users may also use repeated words, slang, or different languages [17,18]. Some tweets are an exact copy of another tweet or tweets can contain similar URLs. Since huge datasets are available on social microblog sites like Facebook, YouTube, Twitter, etc., we have considered a Twitter dataset to obtain the summary of a trending topic, removing redundant, irrelevant tweets so that we can easily identify the important information distinctly which will be represented in the summarized dataset.

6.2 Related work

Text summarization is a prominent research topic these days. Several scholars are working on a solution to the challenge of summarizing one or multiple big text documents into useful text regions. The goal of the research work is to generate a summarized dataset from a large number of tweets by identifying clusters based on the network structure, i.e., communities, using a graph-based representation [19,20].

Authors [21] focused on the weighted graph clustering algorithm for community detection in large-scale networks, such as user relationships on social networks on the Internet. They presented a graph clustering technique based on the concept of density and attractiveness for weighted networks, including node weight and edge weight, because most networks in the actual world are weighted networks [22,23]. They also defined the user's core degree as node weight and users' attractiveness as edge weight after conducting deep analysis of the Sina microblog user network and the Renren social network. Ruifang et al. then conducted community detection experiments with the algorithm, with the results confirming the algorithm's effectiveness and reliability [24,25].

The goal of another study [26] was to examine and compare interaction patterns across various social networks. They did this by analyzing Renren, China's largest online social network, and Sina Weibo, China's most popular microblog service. Because of the asymmetry of user interactions, they characterized interaction networks as unidirectional weighted graphs. Following this concept, they looked at the fundamental interaction patterns first. Then authors looked at whether the weak ties hypothesis holds true in these interaction graphs and how it affected information dispersion [25]. Furthermore, authors simulated the temporal patterns of user interactions and used the temporal patterns to cluster people. Their findings showed that, while users on both sites had some similar interaction patterns, Sina Weibo users were more popular and diversified. Furthermore, the results of the study and simulations demonstrated that Sina Weibo was a more efficient medium for disseminating information. These findings provided the researchers with knowledge on how people engage on different social platforms and can be used to create more efficient information dissemination systems [27].

Another study [28] used density-based clustering to detect communities in social networks. The authors compared two well-known concepts for community detection, structural similarity of nodes and the number of interactions between nodes, which were implemented as distance functions in the algorithms SCAN [29] and DEN-GRAPH [30], respectively, in order to assess the advantages and limitations of these approaches. Furthermore, Subramani et al. proposed using a hierarchical technique for clustering to avoid the challenge of determining an acceptable density threshold for community detection, which was a major drawback of the SCAN and DENGRAPH algorithms in real-world applications. All of their tests were executed on datasets with varying features, such as Twitter and Enron data [31].

The goal of another study [32] was to offer a paradigm for node clustering in computerized social networks based on shared interests. In such networks, communities were primarily generated by user selection, which can be based on a variety of variables such as friendship, social position, and educational background. Such selection, however, may result in groupings with a low degree of resemblance. By building clusters of nodes with higher interest similarity, the suggested framework could improve the effectiveness of these social networks, maximizing the advantage that users derive from their involvement [33]. The framework was built on methods for finding communities in weighted networks, with graph edge weights determined by measurements of similarity between nodes' interests in specific subject areas. With actual benchmark situations over synthetic networks, the ability of these techniques to improve the sensitivity and resolution of community detection was examined. Authors also utilized the framework to determine the extent to which sample users of a popular online social application share common interests. Their findings showed that clusters produced via user selection had modest degrees of similarity, suggesting that their framework could be useful in establishing communities with greater interest coherence [34].

Clustering nodes in a graph is a common data mining technique for big network datasets. In this regard, Newman and Girvan [35] recently presented the Q function, an objective function for graph clustering that enables for automated cluster number selection. Higher Q function values have been demonstrated to correspond strongly with good network clustering empirically. Another study [36] illustrated how to rewrite optimizing the Q function as a spectrum relaxation problem in this study, and the authors presented two new spectral clustering methods that aim to maximize Q. The new methods were efficient and successful in finding both good clustering and the proper number of clusters across a variety of real-world network datasets, according to experimental results. Furthermore, spectral techniques were substantially faster for large sparse graphs, scaling generally linearly with the number of nodes n in the graph, unlike $O(n^2)$ for prior clustering algorithms based on the Q function. The adjacency matrix of a fully connected, weighted graph, where the nodes correspond to data points and the edge between two nodes is weighted by their similarity, can alternatively be considered as the similarity matrix of a dataset [37]. The challenge of data clustering can then be solved using graph-based methods for community detection or graph partitioning. Graph-based approaches search for balanced graph cuts, sometimes employing concepts from spectral graph theory, such as the spectral decomposition of the adjacency or the graph's Laplacian matrices [38]. In order to extract a similarity graph that preserves critical aspects of the dataset, methods for graph creation typically entail sparsification of the similarity (or distance) matrix using various heuristics (from simple thresholding to sophisticated regularizations). The ability to capture efficiently the local and global aspects of the data through graph-theoretical ideas that encapsulate naturally the notions of local neighborhoods, pathways, and global connections makes graph-based data representation appealing [39].

Statistical features of networked systems such as social networks and the World Wide Web have been the subject of a number of recent studies. The small-world property, power-law degree distributions, and network transitivity are among the properties that appear to be common to many networks, according to researchers. In this chapter, we will expore another characteristic of networks: community structure, in which network nodes are grouped together in tightly coupled groups with only loose connections between the groups [40]. The authors in [44] presented a method for discovering such communities based on the idea of finding community boundaries using centrality indices. They put their method to the test on computer-generated and real-world graphs with established community structures, and they found that it detected them with excellent sensitivity and reliability. They also used the approach to detect substantial and informative community divisions in two networks whose community structure is unknown: a cooperation network and a food web.

In many areas, including social sciences, engineering, and biology, automatic discovery of community structures in complicated networks is a critical challenge. To efficiently assess the quality of community structures, a quantitative metric called modularity (Q) has been developed. Since then, a number of communities finding methods have been created based on optimization of Q. This optimization problem, however, is NP-hard, and existing solutions are either inaccurate or computationally expensive. The authors of another work [41] presented an efficient spectral technique for Q optimization. When compared to existing algorithms and tested on a large number of synthetic or real-world networks, their solution was efficient and accurate. They also used that algorithm to find fascinating and important community structures in real-world networks in a variety of fields, including biology, medicine, and social sciences [42].

In many instances, dense subgraphs of sparse graphs (communities), which are present in most real-world complex networks, play a key role. However, computing them is often costly. Latapy et al. [43] proposed a measure of vertex similarity based on random walks that had several important advantages: it captures well the community structure in a network, it can be computed quickly, it works at different scales, and it can be used in an agglomerative algorithm to compute the community structure of a network efficiently.

The authors of another work [44] proposed a novel approach for analyzing a social network represented as a net of microblogging accounts. They detected not just the most popular topics on which users are providing their perspectives, but also the groups of people who chat about certain topic clusters, based on hashtags in user postings. They offered a novel hashtag filtration model and a community graph creation strategy to handle this problem, which was then employed by the community structures recognition algorithm. On three very large real-life (not synthetic) datasets, they validated the method. There were around 10^7 microblogging postings in each of them, with about 10^6 different hashtags. They also looked at the model's scalability, comparing how it performs when applied to a small number of randomly selected subsets versus the entire dataset. Their approach was a scalable filtering method that can generate graphs in which communities with shared interests can be identified. The crucial point to remember is that in their datasets, the minimum random sample size above which they might see a fairly comparable distribution of vertices and edge weights was 10% of the total followers [45].

Researchers have been interested in the community-based structure of communication on social networking platforms. However, the difficulty of discovering and describing hidden communities, as well as determining the appropriate level of user aggregation, remains unsolved. Online community research has evident social ramifications because it allows for the assessment of preference-based user grouping and the detection of socially dangerous groupings. The goal of this research is to compare and contrast techniques for analyzing huge user networks and extracting hidden user communities. The results demonstrate which algorithms are most appropriate for Twitter datasets of various sizes (dozens of thousands, hundreds of thousands, and millions of tweets). The authors of another work [46] showed that the Infomap and Leiden algorithms produce the best overall results, and we recommend combining them for discovering discursive communities based on user attributes or viewpoints. We also show that the generalized K-means algorithm is ineffective on large datasets, whereas a variety of other algorithms prioritize the discovery of a single large community over many that would better reflect reality.

Clauset, Newman, and Moore (CNM) introduced a community analysis algorithm to detect community structure in social networks. Unfortunately, the CNM algorithm does not scale well, and it can only be used in networks with up to 500,000 nodes. The authors of another work [47] showed that inefficient community structure analysis was caused by combining communities in an imbalanced manner and that a simple heuristic that aims to merge community structures in a balanced manner can greatly enhance community structure analysis. Datasets obtained from an existing social networking service with 5.5 million subscribers were used to test the proposed strategies. The heuristics were tested in three different ways. The fastest technique processed a 1-million-user SNS friendship network in 5 minutes (70 times faster than CNM) and a 4-million-user SNS friendship network in 35 minutes.

Modularity-based graph clustering techniques are being used in a variety of applications in the artificial intelligence and Web fields. Existing techniques, on the other hand, cannot be used on huge networks since they need iterative scanning of all vertices/edges. The purpose of another study [48] was to calculate high-modularity clusters from extremely large graphs with more than a few billion edges in a fast and efficient manner. Their technique was based on incrementally reducing unneeded vertices/edges and improving the order of vertex picks to compute clusters. In terms of calculation time, their approach surpassed all other modularity-based methods, and it found clusters with high modularity, according to their tests.

Microblogs such as Twitter have a large number of posts and hence can be a valuable source of information for a variety of domains. However, because tweets are so brief, the information density of each publication, or tweet, is too low. It is difficult to get relevant information from Twitter, such as the public opinion trend, due to the massive amount of data and low information density. Based on keyword graphs, the authors of [49] first detected the strongly linked groups of words. The vertices of the graphs were the frequent words, while the edges were the co-occurrences. To locate closely connected groups of words, they applied the maximum k-clique approach and summarized the tweets that include the terms in groups. With trials, they proved that the suggested method was effective for summarizing tweets and is superior to the existing method.

Traditional matching algorithms are insufficiently adept at matching users within social networks due to the rapid growth in the number of users utilizing social networks and the information that a social network demands about its users. Another work [50] introduced the use of clustering to create user communities, which were subsequently used to generate matches. Forming communities inside a social network helped to limit the number of users that the matching system must examine, as well as other issues that social networks face, such as the lack of knowledge about a new user's actions. A dataset taken from an online dating website was used to test the suggested approach. Empirical research suggested that using community data improves the accuracy of the matching process.

Luhn suggested a method in the 1950s for automatically extracting technical articles based on surface data such as word frequency [51]. The conceptual summarizing technique is proposed in the SCISOR system [52], which uses heuristics to choose bits of a concept graph produced from Down Jones newswire reports. Kupiec developed supervised learning and statistical methods to learn the probability that a document phrase will be chosen in the human summaries using a collection of 188 scientific documents as a training set and their associated human-authored summaries [53].

Automatic text summarization [54–62] is the method to mine relevant and useful information from a huge dataset. The mined information extracted from the automatic text summarization procedure can be used further for different NLP applications, such as information retrieval [63], text comprehension, and question answering.

In recent years, scholars have suggested a number of algorithms for various elements of document summarization. For content summarization, significant algorithms such as SumBasic [64] and Radev et al.'s centroid method [65] have been created. Vanderwende et al. [64] proposed the SumFocus algorithm, which implements a set of criteria or limits on topic changes during summary generation. For single-document summarization, the centroid technique calculates the centrality of a phrase with respect to the general topic of the document cluster. The TextRank method [66] is a graph-based approach that uses the PageRank algorithm [67] to construct an adjacency matrix and determine the most highly scoring sentences based on keywords in a document.

MEAD [65] is a flexible framework for multi-document and multilingual summarizing that is freely available. MEAD imposes a multiple summarizing method as well as measures for assessing multi-document summaries. In the proposed algorithm a graph-based network structure is deployed for community detection in tweet summarization. The proposed approach has been experimented with for a single-document Twitter dataset.

6.3 Background studies
6.3.1 Community detection
With the rise in popularity of social networking sites, we witness a growing number of people expressing their ideas online while also forming new social circles, making community detection a hot topic in network analysis research. Traditional techniques to detect and rate communities rely on

the network topology or some optimization metrics. However, when real-world networks get larger, the problem of community recognition grows more complicated, to the point where network structure qualities may not be enough to disclose specifics about user interactions, and semantic information from text may be useful as well. When examining various networks, it may be necessary to look for communities inside them. Social media algorithms can utilize community detection techniques to find people who share common interests and keep them connected. With the rise in popularity of social networking sites, we witness a growing number of people expressing their ideas online while also forming new social circles, making community detection a hot topic in network analysis research. Traditional techniques to community detection and rating rely on the network topology or some optimization metrics to find and rate communities. However, when real-world networks get larger, the problem of community recognition grows more complicated, to the point where network structure qualities may not be enough to disclose specifics about user interactions, and semantic information from text may be useful as well. In machine learning, community detection can be used to find groups with similar attributes and extract groups for a variety of reasons. This method can be used to find manipulative groups in a social network or a financial market, for example. Community detection methods are designed to locate communities based on network structure, such as strongly connected groupings of nodes; however, they often ignore node properties. A community is formed by nodes of similar types in a network. Intra-community edges are the edges that connect the nodes in a community. Inter-community edges are those that connect two or more communities. The intra-community and inter-community borders between distinct communities are depicted in Fig. 6.1. More intra-cluster edges and fewer inter-cluster edges are the two most critical variables for categorizing and evaluating this problem. The basic idea of edge betweenness, as established by Newman and Girvan, is based on the criteria listed above. They also created a metric called modularity to assess the quality of a specific cluster, and tackling the challenge of maximizing modularity is another viable strategy for community detection, which is an NP-hard problem. Modularity, while simple to compute, is difficult to optimize and is known to perform poorly when recognizing small groups [35]. It is possible to compare community detection to clustering. Clustering is a machine learning technique in which related data points are grouped together based on their qualities into a single cluster. Clustering is a larger subject in unsupervised machine learning that

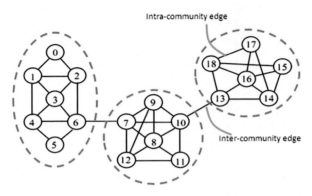

Figure 6.1 Community structure using graph showing intra-community edges and inter-community edges.

deals with many attribute types and can be used to networks. Community detection, on the other hand, is designed specifically for network analysis, which is based on a single attribute type called edges. Furthermore, clustering algorithms have a proclivity towards separating single peripheral nodes from the communities to which they should belong. Both clustering and community detection strategies, on the other hand, may be used to solve a wide range of network analysis problems, with varying benefits and drawbacks depending on the domain. Agglomerative methods and divisive methods are the two main types of community detection methods. Edges are added one by one to a network that only comprises nodes in agglomerative methods. From the stronger edge to the weaker edge, edges are added. Agglomerative procedures are followed by dividing methods. There, edges from a whole graph are eliminated one by one. We begin with an empty graph that has nodes from the original graph but no edges in agglomerative approaches. The edges are then added to the graph one by one, starting with the "stronger" edges and progressing to the "weaker" ones. This edge strength, also known as edge weight, can be measured using a variety of methods. In divisive approaches, we reverse the process. We start with the entire graph and remove the edges one by one. The highest-weighted edge is removed first. Because the weight of the remaining edges changes after an edge is removed, the edge weight computation is redone at each step. We receive clusters of densely connected nodes after a particular number of steps. Understanding and analyzing the structure of big and complex networks might benefit from community detection. This method is better ideal for network analysis than clustering since it takes advantage of the qualities of edges in graphs or networks. Clustering algorithms have a habit of separating isolated peripheral nodes from the communities to which they should belong. For network community detection, many alternative techniques have been suggested and implemented. Depending on the network's nature as well as the issue area to which it is applied, each of these has its own set of advantages and disadvantages.

Community representatives can be considered as an easy to visualize and understand summary of the whole network. Sometimes, a community can reveal the properties without releasing individual privacy information. There can be any number of communities in a given network and they can be of varying sizes. These characteristics make the detection procedure of communities very hard. However, many different techniques have been proposed in the domain of community detection. The Infomap tool [68] is used to detect communities by finding modules containing similar nodes.

Infomap method: Rosvall and Bergstrom's Infomap (2008) is another famous community discovery algorithm [68]. It improves the map equation, which achieves a balance between the difficulty of data compression and the problem of recognizing and retrieving essential patterns or structures within the data. The Louvain community finding approach is closely followed by this algorithm. Each node is assigned to its own module at first. The nodes are then transferred to neighboring modules in a random sequential manner, resulting in the greatest reduction of the map equation. If no move leads to a further reduction of the map equation, the node remains in its original place. The procedure is executed until the map equation can no longer be decreased in a different random sequential order each time. Finally, the network is rebuilt, with the lowest-level modules producing nodes at that level and nodes being joined into modules in the same way that previous-level nodes were. This hierarchical network rebuilding is continued until the map equation can no longer be lowered. Both undirected and directed graphs can be used with Infomap. Infomap returns a list of non-overlapping communities (node set partitions) as well as a decimal value that represents the total flow in that node.

Clustering is a common task in data mining, where input data is organized into groups (or clusters) so that data points within a group are more similar to each other than to data points outside the group. Such a task differs from supervised (or semi-supervised) classification, in which examples of the various classes are known in advance and used to train a computational model to assign other objects to the known groups. Clustering, on the other hand, seeks to discover natural, intrinsic sub-classes in data without assuming the number or type of clusters. Indeed, the principled determination of the number of clusters in an unsupervised manner, without the assumption of a generative model, is a key open issue in this field [69]. A dataset's similarity matrix can be viewed as the adjacency matrix of a fully connected, weighted graph, where the nodes correspond to data points and the edge between two nodes is weighted by their similarity. The problem of data clustering can then be solved using graph-based algorithms for community detection or graph partitioning. Graph-based methods typically search for balanced graph cuts, occasionally invoking notions from spectral graph theory, such as using the spectral decomposition of the graph's adjacency or Laplacian matrices. Graph construction methods typically involve sparsification of the similarity (or distance) matrix using various heuristics (from simple thresholding to sophisticated regularizations).

As is evident from the discussion above, there are a wide variety of clustering algorithms. It is a natural question which algorithm performs the best on a certain dataset. To answer this question, first some measures for cluster validation/evaluation need to be determined. The next section discusses some commonly used cluster validation measures.

6.3.2 WordNet

WordNet is an English-language lexical web dictionary. WordNet is widely used to find word synonyms. Nouns, verbs, adjectives, and adverbs are arranged into synsets in the WordNet [70] dictionary, each of which communicates a separate concept. The phrases "vehicle" and "automobile" are grouped together in a different synset; similarly, the words "close" and "shut" are synonyms and belong in the same synset. Different users can communicate the same sentiment using different words. WordNet is used to detect similarities between different tweet documents.

Words are connected together in the WordNet database by their semantic ties. It is like a graph-structured supercharged dictionary like Thesaurus. Synsets build relationships with other synsets to form a hierarchy of concepts ranging from the very broad ("entity," "state") through the moderately abstract ("animal") to the highly precise ("entity," "state") ("plankton"). Some terminologies include hypernyms, which are more general synsets, and hyponyms, which are more particular synsets. Hypernyms and hyponyms have an "is-a" relationship. Synonymy is the most common relationship between terms in WordNet, such as between the words shut and close or car and automobile. Synonyms – words that mean the same thing and can be used interchangeably in a variety of situations – are grouped into unorganized groupings (synsets). A modest number of "conceptual relations" connect each of WordNet's 117,000 synsets to other synsets. A synset also includes a brief definition ("gloss") and, in most cases, one or more short lines demonstrating how the synset elements are used. There are as many synsets as there are word forms with different meanings. As a result, every form–meaning pair in WordNet is distinct. The super-subordinate relationship is the most frequently encoded among synsets (also called hyperonymy, hyponymy, or ISA relation). It connects more generic synsets such as furniture and piece of furniture to more particular ones such as bed and bunkbed. As a result, according to WordNet, the category furniture includes bed, which includes bunkbed; conversely, the category furniture includes concepts such as bed and bunkbed. All noun hierarchies eventually lead back to the root node object. The hyponymy relationship is transitive, meaning that if an armchair is a kind of chair and a chair is a type of furniture, then an armchair is a type of furniture. WordNet distinguishes between types (common nouns) and instances (non-common nouns) (specific persons, countries, and geographic entities). As a result, an armchair is a type of chair, and Barack Obama is a president. In their hierarchies, instances are always leaf (terminal) nodes. Between synsets like chair and back, backrest, seat, and leg, there is a part-whole relationship known as meronymy. Parts are inherited from their superiors: if a chair has legs, then so does an armchair. Parts are not passed down "upward" since they may be unique to specific types of items rather than the class as a whole: chairs and types of chairs have legs, but not all types of furniture do. Verb synsets are also organized into hierarchies; verbs at the bottom of the tree (troponyms) indicate progressively particular ways of describing an occurrence, as in communicate–talk–whisper. Volume (as in the example above) is merely one dimension along which verbs can be expanded; the specific method expressed depends on the semantic field. Others include speed (move–jog–run) and emotional intensity (like–love–idolize). Buy–pay, succeed–try, show–see, and other verbs that describe occurrences that must and unidirectionally necessitate one another are related. Antonymy is used to order adjectives. The strong semantic contract of their members is reflected in pairs of "direct" antonyms such as wet–dry and young–old. Each of these polar adjectives is linked to a number of "semantically similar" ones: parched, arid, dessicated, and bone-dry are all associated to dry, whereas wet is linked to soggy, flooded, and so on. Semantically comparable adjectives are "indirect antonyms" of the opposite pole's component. Relational adjectives (also known as "pertainyms") refer to the nouns from which they are derived (criminal–crime). The majority of the WordNet's

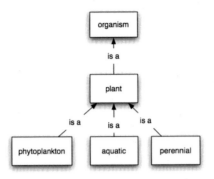

Figure 6.2 Illustration of semantic relationships between words.

relations connect words from the same part of speech (POS). Thus, Word-Net really consists of four sub-nets, one each for nouns, verbs, adjectives, and adverbs, with few cross-POS pointers. Cross-POS relations include the "morphosemantic" links that hold among semantically similar words sharing a stem with the same meaning: observe (verb), observant (adjective), and observation/observatory (nouns).

As illustrated in Fig. 6.2, WordNet also provides a hierarchical structure of related words. Synsets of words can be organized as a graph, and the similarity of synsets can be assessed based on the shortest path between them. The proposed method's performance was boosted by crucial semantic properties like WordNet path similarity.

6.3.2.1 SumBasic

SumBasic [71] is a multi-document summarizer based on frequency. Sum-basic computes the probability distribution across the words of a sentence using a multinomial distribution function. Each sentence is given a score based on the average chance of the words in the sentence occurring. The sentences with the highest ratings are then chosen. The word probabilities and sentence scores are updated in a sequential manner until the appropriate summary length is reached. Word probabilities are updated in a natural method to deal with repetition in multi-document input. SumBasic, a summarizer that uses a frequency-based sentence selection component with a component to reweight the word probabilities in order to avoid redundancy, is defined through the following algorithm:

Step 1. Calculate the probability distribution for the words w_i in the input, $p(w_i)$, for each i:

$$p(w_i) = \frac{n}{N},$$

where N is the total number of content word tokens in the input and n is the number of times the word appears in the input.

Step 2. Assign a weight to each sentence S_j in the input equal to the average likelihood of the terms in the sentence:

$$weight(S_j) = \sum_{w_i \in S_j} \frac{p(w_i)}{\{|w_i|w_i \in S_j|\}}.$$

Step 3. Choose the highest-scoring sentence with the highest-probability word.

Step 4. Update the probability of each word w_i in the sentence chosen in Step 3:

$$p_{new}(w_i) = p_{old}(w_i).p_{old}(w_i).$$

Step 5. Return to Step 2 if the desired summary length has not been obtained.
   The following are some of the benefits of SumBasic:
   (i)   It is used to make the goal of a document clear.
   (ii) The reader has more convenience and versatility.
   (iii) From various texts, it creates a shorter and more concise form.

6.4 Proposed methodology

The input dataset for automatic tweet summarization is gathered by downloading streams of tweets posted on the website, profile details of certain people, and so on. The goal of the proposed methodology is to identify a set of important tweets which will summarize and represent the entire tweet dataset. For the dataset syntactically or semantically identical features are identified and similarity factors are measured, and using a directed graph-based network modularity approach different types of summaries are generated using the Infomap community detection technique.

Table 6.1 A sample dataset of "Uttarakhand flood".

Tweet ID	Tweets
1	15,000 tourists stranded due to landslide in Uttarakhand
2	Its raining heavily luvly weather in UTTARAKHAND.
3	8 perish as rains lash Uttarakhand Char Dhamyatra suspended http://t.co/cH6pcRrD41
4	cc: @MrsGandhi look at this Anti-hindu rains "@timesofindia: Rains bring ChardhamYatra to a halt in Uttarakhand http://t.co/JU7dXy6eHS."
5	8 perish as rains lash Uttarakhand, Char Dhamyatra suspended.

6.4.1 Dataset

The Twitter API was used to obtain an experimental dataset of 2921 tweets. They were specifically collected by keyword matching from a 1% random sample of tweets made publicly available by Twitter. Keywords like "Uttarakhand" and "flood" were used to find tweets related to the disaster. Each tweet has a distinct tweet ID. Table 6.1 shows some sample tweets from the dataset.

6.4.2 Similarity identification

Similarity identification is the finding of common words between any pair of tweets. It can be based on URL, hashtag, user name, word count, and cosine distance.

Similar URL count

If a common URL exists between two tweets, the number of common URLs is used to calculate the URL tweet similarity count. If the first tweet has the URL "www.bing.com" and the second tweet also includes "www.bing.com," the frequency will be 1, otherwise it will stay 0.

Similar hashtag count

We can presume that people who use those popular tags on Twitter are interested in the issues. If they wish to have an impact on global opinion regarding a certain topic (or promote their own), they must tag their posts without any misspellings. As a result, hashtags connected to prominent issues in a specific society (for example, followers of a celebrity) must be used more frequently than other hashtags [44]. The term "frequency" refers to the number of times a hashtag appears in a single user's post as well as the number of times a hashtag appears in many users' posts. The number of comparable common hashtags between any two tweets is known as the hashtag tweet similarity count. If both tweets contain the hashtag "#movie," the hashtag tweet similarity count is 1.

Similar user name count

Similarly, the tweet similarity counts are examined if any user name is common for any pair of tweets. Because the user name "@abhi" may appear in two different tweets, the user name tweet similarity count will be used.

6.4.3 Dataset preprocessing

Microblogging datasets consist of several symbols, repeating letters, abbreviations, etc., so document preprocessing or filtering of unprocessed Twitter datasets is needed which will be further used for summarization of Twitter data. Stopwords like am, is, are, to, at, etc., are not very important to find the similar meaning between any of the tweet pair. So firstly the stopwords are removed from the dataset. As the similarity counts based on URLs, hashtags, and user names are already considered, URLs, hashtags, and user names are also removed from the dataset. Also in this step punctuation, whitespaces, special characters (for example, $, @, !,), etc., are removed. So, the data filtering approaches include the following processes: removal of stopwords, removal of URLs, removal of hashtags, removal of user names, removal of punctuation, removal of repetitive letters, and removal of whitespace.

6.4.4 Similarity measure

After dataset filtration it is mandatory to find out the similarity measure among the tweets in the dataset and categorize similar types of tweets. To evaluate the similarity measure along with similarity count based on URLs, hashtags, and user names, a few another important measures are considered such as cosine similarity and Levenshtein distance.

In this research work it is assumed that any pair of tweets having more than two similar or semantically similar (as per WordNet synset) words are considered as similar. Combining all these factors, finally a tweet similarity score is computed for every pair of tweets. The following examples briefly show the cosine and Levenshtein distance.

Cosine similarity

The cosine distance evaluates the similarity between every pair of tweets. The cosine distance is directly proportional to the similar words in any pair of tweet. For example, for $s1 =$ "This is a foo bar sentence," $s2 =$ "This sentence is similar to a foo bar sentence," and $s3 =$ "Hello world," $c1 =$

Table 6.2 Extracted categorized feature set.

Feature category	Feature set
Syntactical features	Levenshtein distance
	Cosine distance
	Frequency of common words
	Frequency of common hashtags
	Frequency of common URLs
	Frequency of common user names
Semantics features	WordNet synset similarity
	WordNet path similarity

cosinesimilarity(s1, s2) = 0.861640436855 and c2 = cosinesimilarity(s2,s3) = 0.174077655956. As words in strings s1 and s2 are more similar, they yield a higher cosine similarity value, and because string s2 and s3 are less similar, they yield a lower cosine similarity value.

Levenshtein distance

The Levenshtein distance between two strings is the number of modifications required to transform one string (s1) into the other string (s2). It allows for single-character edits such as deletion, insertion, and substitution.

For example, for s1="helloIndia" and s2="halloindia," the Levenshtein distance is 2.

Thus the sweet similarity score is evaluated by considering simple summation of syntactical and semantic features listed in Table 6.2, which include Levenshtein distance, cosine distance, similarity count of words (syntactical and semantic), hashtags, URLs, and user name. Table 6.2 shows the categorized feature set based on which the similarity measure is evaluated.

6.4.5 Graph generation

Based on the similarity measurement among the tweets, a weighted directed graph is produced. A graph is an ordered pair G = (V, E) that consists of a set of V vertices or nodes and a set of E edges. Every tweet is treated as a node, with two directed edges connecting each pair of nodes. As the cosine distance can vary for the same pair of tweets based on the sequence of tweets passed in the function, between every pair of tweets two separate tweet similarity scores have been generated. Considering five tweets, given in Table 6.1, a directed weighted graph is constructed as shown in Fig. 6.3.

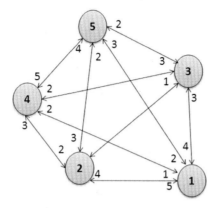

Figure 6.3 Total graph: Considering all edges.

Taking all tweets as nodes and the graph as a whole, G has been generated, which is named here as Total graph. If N nodes or tweet documents are considered, the total number of edges will be $\frac{N(N-1)}{2}$. Three distinct types of summaries have been prepared based on this graph. The following are some of them:

6.4.6 Summarization

Text summarization is the creation of a short, accurate, and fluent summary of a longer text document. Automatic text summarization methods are greatly needed to address the ever-growing amount of text data available online. This could help to discover relevant information and to consume relevant information faster. Consider the internet, which is made up of web pages, news stories, status updates, blogs, and many other things. Because the data is unstructured, the best we can do is perform search and glance over the results. Much of this text material has to be reduced to shorter, focused summaries that capture the important elements, so we can explore it more easily and to ensure that the summaries include the information we need. We need automatic text summarization tools for the below mentioned reasons:

1. Summaries help you save time by reducing the amount of time you spend reading.
2. Summaries aid in the selection of documents when conducting research.
3. The efficacy of indexing is improved by automatic summarization.

4. Human summarizers are more prejudiced than automatic summarizing techniques.
5. Because they give individualized information, personalized summaries are important in question-answering systems.
6. Commercial abstract services can enhance the volume of texts they can handle by using automatic or semi-automatic summarizing systems.

There are two main approaches to summarizing text documents:

1. extractive methods,
2. abstractive methods.

To create the new summary, extractive text summarization selects phrases and sentences from the original document. Techniques include rating the importance of phrases in order to select just those that are most essential to the source's meaning. To capture the meaning of the source content, abstractive text summarization entails creating whole new words and sentences. This is a more difficult strategy, but it is also the one that humans will employ in the end. The content of the original document is selected and compressed using traditional methods. Most effective text summarizing methods are extractive because they are easier to implement, whereas abstractive alternatives offer the promise of more universal solutions.

The act of constructing a concise and coherent version of a lengthier document is known as automatic text summarizing, or simply text summarization. We (humans) are often good at this sort of assignment since it necessitates first comprehending the content of the original material and then distilling the meaning and capturing key features in the new description. The goal of automatic summarizing studies is to create approaches that allow a computer to generate summaries that closely resemble those produced by humans. Generating words and phrases that convey the meaning of the source content is not enough. The summary should be factual and read as if it were a separate paper.

Total summary

After generation of the directed total graph, G, a community detection algorithm has been executed on the graph using the Infomap tool. Infomap [68] optimizes the map equation, which takes advantage of the information theoretic duality between compressing data and recognizing and retrieving relevant patterns or structures within the data. Using a network-based clustering technique [68], communities are identified which represent sets of distinct tweet IDs. Finally distinct tweets are identified mapping the tweet ID into tweets and summaries are generated considering one representative tweet from each community, which is named total summary.

Total degree summary

Based on the out-degree of the directed total graph, G, a summary has been generated. In the graph, a higher out-degree of a node implies more information going out from the node. From the Infomap output for each module, a representative set of nodes or tweets can be identified which are similar in nature. Instead of considering module representatives, as a summary entry the highest-degree node has been chosen from each set corresponding to modules and a summary file has been generated which is named total degree summary.

Total length summary

As in the experimental dataset, microblogging datasets such as the Twitter dataset are considered. The maximum length of a tweet is 140 characters, so it can be considered that tweets having maximum or near-maximum length are more informative. So, instead of considering a module representative as a summary entry, the highest-length node has been chosen from each set corresponding to modules and a summary file has been generated which is named total length summary.

Threshold graph

For another summary generation approach, the total graph, G', is thresholded. A threshold weight is evaluated by taking the mean weight of all the weights associated to all edges in the directed graph. From the graph, selected edges are removed whose weights are less than the threshold weight. So, in the thresholded graph, numbers of edges are lower than the number of edges in the total graph G. Here, in the sample dataset, the thresholded value is 2.5 and edges generated are 10. The thresholded graph, G, is given in Fig. 6.4.

Using the above-mentioned approach taken for the total graph, three different types of summary have been generated for the thresholded graph: thresholded summary, thresholded degree summary, and thresholded length summary.

6.5 Results and discussion

Six different types of summaries have been generated using the proposed method. To compare performance, a number of summaries have been com-

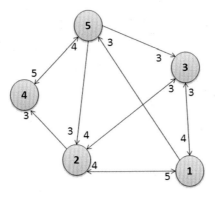

Figure 6.4 Threshold graph: Considering edges above the threshold value.

piled as an expert summary, which has been evaluated by a number of experts. A common strategy, Sumbasic, is considered as an alternative approach. As a result, the performance of the proposed strategy is compared to the above-mentioned approaches in this evaluation. Sumbasic [2] is a noteworthy algorithm that selects words that appear more frequently across the entire manuscript with a higher probability than words that occur less frequently. It is intended to support the finding that terms that appear frequently in the document have a higher probability of appearing in human summaries than words that appear less frequently.

Using standard metrics such as recall (R), precision (P), F-measure (F), and accuracy (A), the proposed methodology's performance is evaluated. The sentences extracted by both the proposed system and the experts are labeled as correct, whereas the sentences extracted by the proposed system but not by the experts are labeled as wrong and the sentences extracted by the experts but not by the proposed system are labeled as missed. The ratio of the number of items accurately predicted to be in that class to the total number of items (right and incorrect) predicted in that class is the precision with respect to that class. The correct class' precision (P) is $P = \text{correct}/(\text{correct} + \text{wrong})$. The ratio of the number of sentences properly predicted to be in that class to the total number of items (correct and missed) actually belonging to that class is the recall (R) for that class. The positive class' recall is $R = \text{correct}/(\text{correct} + \text{missed})$. The accuracy (A) is the percentage of correctly categorized items in the total number of items. Finally, the F-measure ($F = \frac{2PR}{P+R}$) represents the harmonic mean of accuracy and recall. The F-measure is particularly significant because it combines precision and recall.

Table 6.3 Prediction performance, averaged over all six labeled datasets.

Method	Precision (P)	Recall (R)	F-measure (F)	Accuracy (A)
Sumbasic	0.770	0.625	0.690	69.03%
Total summary	0.651	0.763	0.702	70.24%
Total degree summary	0.591	0.893	0.712	71.16%
Total length summary	0.611	0.841	0.708	70.78%
Threshold summary	0.558	1.036	0.725	72.53%
Threshold degree summary	0.567	0.991	0.722	72.15%
Threshold length	0.553	1.063	0.728	72.77%

The experimental results show that the proposed approaches give better results than Sumbasic (Table 6.3).

6.6 Conclusion

Based on syntactic and semantic aspects of a text-based microblog dataset, this chapter provides a simple and successful methodology for tweet summarization. The success of finding text similarity was increased by using a lexical method such as WordNet. The proposed method outperforms various previous methods. Summarizing datasets is extremely difficult due to the lack of structure. As a result of the optimization methodology, the proposed method's performance can be improved. We show that clustering can be done in a completely unsupervised manner (without assuming knowledge of the number of clusters), whereas other standard methods require the number of clusters to be given as an input.

References

[1] S. Goswami, A.K. Das, Determining maximum cliques for community detection in weighted sparse networks, Knowledge and Information Systems 64 (2) (2022) 289–324, https://doi.org/10.1007/s10115-021-01631-y.

[2] A. Mukherjee, S. Bhattacharyya, K. Ray, B. Gupta, A.K. Das, A study of public sentiment and influence of politics in COVID-19 related tweets, in: A.K. Das, J. Nayak, B. Naik, S. Dutta, D. Pelusi (Eds.), Computational Intelligence in Pattern Recognition, Springer, Singapore, 2022, pp. 655–665.

[3] P. Das, A.K. Das, Convolutional neural networks-based sentence level classification of crime documents, in: A.K. Das, J. Nayak, B. Naik, S. Dutta, D. Pelusi (Eds.), Computational Intelligence in Pattern Recognition, Springer, Singapore, 2022, pp. 65–73.

[4] S. Asur, B.A. Huberman, Predicting the future with social media, in: Proceedings of the 2010 IEEE/WIC/ACM International Conference on Web Intelligence and Intelligent Agent Technology - Volume 01, WI-IAT '10, IEEE Computer Society, Washington, DC, USA, 2010, pp. 492–499.

[5] A. Bermingham, M. Conway, L. McInerney, N. O'Hare, A.F. Smeaton, Combining social network analysis and sentiment analysis to explore the potential for online radicalisation, in: Proceedings of the 2009 International Conference on Advances in Social Network Analysis and Mining, ASONAM '09, IEEE Computer Society, Washington, DC, USA, 2009, pp. 231–236.

[6] W. Xu, R. Grishman, A. Meyers, A. Ritter, A preliminary study of tweet summarization using information extraction, in: Proceedings of the Workshop on Language Analysis in Social Media, ASONAM '09, Association for Computational Linguistics, Atlanta, Georgia, 2013, pp. 20–29.

[7] F. Ahmed, J. Erman, Z. Ge, A.X. Liu, J. Wang, H. Yan, Detecting and localizing end-to-end performance degradation for cellular data services, in: Proceedings of the 2015 ACM SIGMETRICS International Conference on Measurement and Modeling of Computer Systems, Portland, OR, USA, June 15-19, 2015, 2015, pp. 459–460.

[8] A. Campan, T. Atnafu, T.M. Truta, J. Nolan, Is data collection through Twitter streaming api useful for academic research?, in: 2018 IEEE International Conference on Big Data (Big Data), 2018, pp. 3638–3643.

[9] S. Kumar, K.M. Carley, What to track on the Twitter streaming api? A knapsack bandits approach to dynamically update the search terms, in: 2019 IEEE/ACM International Conference on Advances in Social Networks Analysis and Mining (ASONAM), 2019, pp. 158–163.

[10] H. Efstathiades, D. Antoniades, G. Pallis, M.D. Dikaiakos, Distributed large-scale data collection in online social networks, in: 2016 IEEE 2nd International Conference on Collaboration and Internet Computing (CIC), 2016, pp. 373–380.

[11] A. Das, D. Pal, C. Mallick, A.K. Das, An unsupervised COVID-19 report summarizer for developing smart healthcare system, in: A.K. Das, J. Nayak, B. Naik, S. Dutta, D. Pelusi (Eds.), Computational Intelligence in Pattern Recognition, Springer, Singapore, 2022, pp. 157–168.

[12] C. Mallick, S. Das, A.K. Das, Evolutionary algorithm based summarization for analyzing COVID-19 medical reports, in: J. Nayak, B. Naik, A. Abraham (Eds.), Understanding COVID-19: The Role of Computational Intelligence, in: Studies in Computational Intelligence, Springer International Publishing, Cham, 2022, pp. 31–58.

[13] S. Chattopadhyay, T. Basu, A.K. Das, K. Ghosh, L.C.A. Murthy, Towards effective discovery of natural communities in complex networks and implications in e-commerce, Electronic Commerce Research 21 (4) (2021) 917–954, https://doi.org/10.1007/s10660-019-09395-y.

[14] A. Dwi Laksito, Kusrini, H. Sismoro, F. Rahmawati, M. Yusa, A comparison study of search strategy on collecting Twitter data for drug adverse reaction, in: 2018 International Seminar on Application for Technology of Information and Communication, 2018, pp. 356–360.

[15] P. Ray, A. Chakrabarti, Twitter sentiment analysis for product review using lexicon method, in: 2017 International Conference on Data Management, Analytics and Innovation (ICDMAI), 2017, pp. 211–216.

[16] K. Jitkajornwanich, C. Kongthong, N. Khongsoontornjaroen, J. Kaiyasuan, S. Lawawirojwong, P. Srestasathiern, S. Srisonphan, P. Vateekul, Utilizing Twitter data for early flood warning in Thailand, in: 2018 IEEE International Conference on Big Data (Big Data), 2018, pp. 5165–5169.

[17] M. Basu, S.D. Bit, S. Ghosh, Utilizing microblogs for optimized real-time resource allocation in post-disaster scenarios, Social Network Analysis and Mining 12 (1) (2021) 15, https://doi.org/10.1007/s13278-021-00841-0.

[18] P. Bhattacharya, S. Paul, K. Ghosh, S. Ghosh, A. Wyner, DeepRhole: deep learning for rhetorical role labeling of sentences in legal case documents, Artificial Intelligence and Law (Nov. 2021), https://doi.org/10.1007/s10506-021-09304-5.

[19] S.H. Archana, S.G. Winster, Drugs categorization based on sentence polarity analyzer for Twitter data, in: 2016 Second International Conference on Science Technology Engineering and Management (ICONSTEM), 2016, pp. 28–33.

[20] T. Jagić, L. Brkić, Hot topic detection using Twitter streaming data, in: 2020 43rd International Convention on Information, Communication and Electronic Technology (MIPRO), 2020, pp. 1730–1735.

[21] R. Liu, S. Feng, R. Shi, W. Guo, Weighted graph clustering for community detection of large social networks, in: 2nd International Conference on Information Technology and Quantitative Management, ITQM 2014, Procedia Computer Science 31 (2014) 85–94, https://doi.org/10.1016/j.procs.2014.05.248, https://www.sciencedirect.com/science/article/pii/S1877050914004256.

[22] K. Hazra, T. Ghosh, A. Mukherjee, S. Saha, S. Nandi, S. Ghosh, S. Chakraborty, Sustainable text summarization over mobile devices: an energy-aware approach, Sustainable Computing: Informatics and Systems 32 (2021) 100607, https://doi.org/10.1016/j.suscom.2021.100607, https://www.sciencedirect.com/science/article/pii/S2210537921000950.

[23] A. Mandal, K. Ghosh, S. Ghosh, S. Mandal, A sequence labeling model for catchphrase identification from legal case documents, Artificial Intelligence and Law (Jul. 2021), https://doi.org/10.1007/s10506-021-09296-2.

[24] R. Compton, C. Lee, T.-C. Lu, L. De Silva, M. Macy, Detecting future social unrest in unprocessed Twitter data: "emerging phenomena and big data", in: 2013 IEEE International Conference on Intelligence and Security Informatics, 2013, pp. 56–60.

[25] R.D. Perera, S. Anand, K.P. Subbalakshmi, R. Chandramouli, Twitter analytics: architecture, tools and analysis, in: 2010 - MILCOM 2010 Military Communications Conference, 2010, pp. 2186–2191.

[26] J. Lin, Z. Li, D. Wang, K. Salamatian, G. Xie, Analysis and comparison of interaction patterns in online social network and social media, in: 2012 21st International Conference on Computer Communications and Networks (ICCCN), 2012, pp. 1–7.

[27] M. Basu, K. Ghosh, S. Ghosh, Information retrieval from microblogs during disasters: in the light of IRMiDis task, SN Computer Science 1 (1) (2020) 61, https://doi.org/10.1007/s42979-020-0065-1.

[28] K. Subramani, A. Velkov, I. Ntoutsi, P. Kroger, H.-P. Kriegel, Density-based community detection in social networks, in: 2011 IEEE 5th International Conference on Internet Multimedia Systems Architecture and Application, 2011, pp. 1–8.

[29] X. Xu, N. Yuruk, Z. Feng, T.A.J. Schweiger, Scan: a structural clustering algorithm for networks, in: Proceedings of the 13th ACM SIGKDD International Conference on Knowledge Discovery and Data Mining, KDD '07, Association for Computing Machinery, New York, NY, USA, 2007, pp. 824–833.

[30] T. Falkowski, A. Barth, M. Spiliopoulou, Dengraph: a density-based community detection algorithm, in: IEEE/WIC/ACM International Conference on Web Intelligence (WI'07), 2007, pp. 112–115.

[31] P. Tatineni, B.S. Babu, B. Kanuri, G.R.K. Rao, P. Chitturi, C. Naresh, Post Covid-19 Twitter user's emotions classification using deep learning techniques in India, in: 2021 International Conference on Artificial Intelligence and Smart Systems (ICAIS), 2021, pp. 338–343.

[32] E. Jaho, M. Karaliopoulos, I. Stavrakakis, Iscode: a framework for interest similarity-based community detection in social networks, in: 2011 IEEE Conference on Computer Communications Workshops (INFOCOM WKSHPS), 2011, pp. 912–917.

[33] R. Mandal, S. Dutta, R. Banerjee, S. Bhattacharya, R. Ghosh, S. Samanta, T. Saha, City traffic speed characterization based on city road surface quality, in: J.M.R.S. Tavares, P. Dutta, S. Dutta, D. Samanta (Eds.), Cyber Intelligence and Information Retrieval, Springer, Singapore, 2022, pp. 515–524.

[34] D. Samanta, S. Dutta, M.G. Galety, S. Pramanik, A novel approach for web mining taxonomy for high-performance computing, in: J.M.R.S. Tavares, P. Dutta, S. Dutta, D. Samanta (Eds.), Cyber Intelligence and Information Retrieval, in: Lecture Notes in Networks and Systems, Springer, Singapore, 2022, pp. 425–432.

[35] M.E.J. Newman, M. Girvan, Finding and evaluating community structure in networks, Physical Review E 69 (2) (Feb 2004), https://doi.org/10.1103/physreve.69.026113.

[36] S. White, P. Smyth, A spectral clustering approach to finding communities in graph, in: SDM, 2005.

[37] C. Wang, L. Marini, C.-L. Chin, N. Vance, C. Donelson, P. Meunier, J.T. Yun, Social media intelligence and learning environment: an open source framework for social media data collection, analysis and curation, in: 2019 15th International Conference on eScience (eScience), 2019, pp. 252–261.

[38] L.W. Hagen, A.B. Kahng, New spectral methods for ratio cut partitioning and clustering, IEEE Transactions on Computer-Aided Design of Integrated Circuits and Systems 11 (1992) 1074–1085.

[39] B. Cheng, J. Yang, S. Yan, Y. Fu, T.S. Huang, Learning with ℓ^1-graph for image analysis, IEEE Transactions on Image Processing 19 (4) (2010) 858–866, https://doi.org/10.1109/TIP.2009.2038764.

[40] G.A. Sandag, A.M. Manueke, M. Walean, Sentiment analysis of Covid-19 vaccine tweets in Indonesia using recurrent neural network (rnn) approach, in: 2021 3rd International Conference on Cybernetics and Intelligent System (ICORIS), 2021, pp. 1–7.

[41] J. Ruan, W. Zhang, An efficient spectral algorithm for network community discovery and its applications to biological and social networks, in: Seventh IEEE International Conference on Data Mining (ICDM 2007), 2007, pp. 643–648.

[42] C.M. Yoshimura, H. Kitagawa, Tlv-bandit: bandit method for collecting topic-related local tweets, in: 2021 IEEE 4th International Conference on Multimedia Information Processing and Retrieval (MIPR), 2021, pp. 56–62.

[43] P. Pons, M. Latapy, Computing communities in large networks using random walks, in: P. Yolum, T. Güngör, F. Gürgen, C. Özturan (Eds.), Computer and Information Sciences - ISCIS 2005, Springer Berlin Heidelberg, Berlin, Heidelberg, 2005, pp. 284–293.

[44] T. Hachaj, M.R. Ogiela, Clustering of trending topics in microblogging posts: a graph-based approach, Future Generations Computer Systems 67 (2017) 297–304, https://doi.org/10.1016/j.future.2016.04.009, https://www.sciencedirect.com/science/article/pii/S0167739X16300863.

[45] A. Nsouli, A. Mourad, D. Azar, Towards proactive social learning approach for traffic event detection based on Arabic tweets, in: 2018 14th International Wireless Communications Mobile Computing Conference (IWCMC), 2018, pp. 1501–1506.

[46] I. Blekanov, S.S. Bodrunova, A. Akhmetov, Detection of hidden communities in Twitter discussions of varying volumes, Future Internet 13 (11) (2021), https://doi.org/10.3390/fi13110295, https://www.mdpi.com/1999-5903/13/11/295.

[47] K. Wakita, T. Tsurumi, Finding community structure in mega-scale social networks: [extended abstract], in: Proceedings of the 16th International Conference on World Wide Web, WWW '07, Association for Computing Machinery, New York, NY, USA, 2007, pp. 1275–1276.

[48] H. Shiokawa, Y. Fujiwara, M. Onizuka, Fast algorithm for modularity-based graph clustering, in: Proceedings of the Twenty-Seventh AAAI Conference on Artificial Intelligence, AAAI'13, AAAI Press, 2013, pp. 1170–1176.

[49] T.-Y. Kim, J. Kim, J. Lee, J.-H. Lee, A tweet summarization method based on a keyword graph, in: Proceedings of the 8th International Conference on Ubiquitous Information Management and Communication, ICUIMC '14, Association for Computing Machinery, New York, NY, USA, 2014.

[50] S. Alsaleh, R. Nayak, Y. Xu, Finding and matching communities in social networks using data mining, in: 2011 International Conference on Advances in Social Networks Analysis and Mining, 2011, pp. 389–393.

[51] H.P. Luhn, The automatic creation of literature abstracts, IBM Journal of Research and Development 2 (2) (1958) 159–165, https://doi.org/10.1147/rd.22.0159.

[52] L.F. Rau, P.S. Jacobs, U. Zernik, Information extraction and text summarization using linguistic knowledge acquisition, Information Processing & Management 25 (4) (1989) 419–428, https://doi.org/10.1016/0306-4573(89)90069-1, http://www.sciencedirect.com/science/article/pii/0306457389900691.

[53] J. Kupiec, J. Pedersen, F. Chen, A trainable document summarizer, in: Proceedings of the 18th Annual International ACM SIGIR Conference on Research and Development in Information Retrieval, SIGIR '95, ACM, New York, NY, USA, 1995, pp. 68–73.

[54] M. Hassel, Resource lean and portable automatic text summarization, PhD thesis, KTH, Numerical Analysis and Computer Science, NADA, 2007, qC 20100712.

[55] K. Spärck Jones, Automatic summarising: the state of the art, Information Processing & Management 43 (6) (2007) 1449–1481, https://doi.org/10.1016/j.ipm.2007.03.009.

[56] R. Barzilay, M. Elhadad, Using lexical chains for text summarization, in: Proceedings of the ACL/EACL 1997 Workshop on Intelligent Scalable Text Summarization, 1997, pp. 10–17, http://research.microsoft.com/en-us/um/people/cyl/download/papers/lexical-chains.pdf.

[57] I. Mani, Advances in Automatic Text Summarization, MIT Press, Cambridge, MA, USA, 1999.

[58] M. Hassel, Exploitation of named entities in automatic text summarization for Swedish, in: Proceedings of NODALIDA 03 - 14 th Nordic Conference on Computational Linguistics, May 30-31 2003, 2003.

[59] M. Hassel, Evaluation of Automatic Text Summarization - a practical implementation, Licentiate thesis, Department of Numerical Analysis and Computer Science, Royal Institute of Technology, Stockholm, Sweden, May 2004, http://nlp.lacasahassel.net/publications/hasselthesis04lic.pdf.

[60] I. Mani, M.T. Maybury, Automatic summarization, in: Association for Computational Linguistic, 39th Annual Meeting and 10th Conference of the European Chapter, Companion Volume to the Proceedings of the Conference: Proceedings of the Student Research Workshop and Tutorial Abstracts, July 9-11, 2001, Toulouse, France, 2001, p. 5.

[61] C. Nobata, S. Sekine, H. Isahara, R. Grishman, Summarization system integrated with named entity tagging and (ie) pattern discovery, in: Proceedings of the Third International Conference on Language Resources and Evaluation, LREC 2002, May 29-31, 2002, Las Palmas, Canary Islands, Spain, 2002, http://www.lrec-conf.org/proceedings/lrec2002/pdf/119.pdf.

[62] H. Dalianis, E. Astrom, E. Åström, Swenam-a Swedish named entity recognizer its construction, training and evaluation, 2001.

[63] G. Salton, Automatic Text Processing: The Transformation, Analysis, and Retrieval of Information by Computer, Addison-Wesley Longman Publishing Co., Inc., Boston, MA, USA, 1989.

[64] L. Vanderwende, H. Suzuki, C. Brockett, A. Nenkova, Beyond sumbasic: task-focused summarization with sentence simplification and lexical expansion, Information Processing & Management 43 (6) (2007) 1606–1618, https://doi.org/10.1016/j.ipm.2007.01.023.

[65] D.R. Radev, T. Allison, S. Blair-Goldensohn, J. Blitzer, A. Çelebi, S. Dimitrov, E. Drábek, A. Hakim, W. Lam, D. Liu, J. Otterbacher, H. Qi, H. Saggion, S. Teufel, M. Topper, A. Winkel, Z. Zhang, MEAD - a platform for multidocument multilingual

text summarization, in: Proceedings of the Fourth International Conference on Language Resources and Evaluation, LREC 2004, May 26-28, 2004, Lisbon, Portugal, 2004, http://www.lrec-conf.org/proceedings/lrec2004/pdf/757.pdf.

[66] S. Brin, L. Page, The anatomy of a large-scale hypertextual web search engine, Computer Networks and ISDN Systems 30 (1–7) (1998) 107–117, https://doi.org/10.1016/S0169-7552(98)00110-X.

[67] L. Page, S. Brin, R. Motwani, T. Winograd, The pagerank citation ranking: Bringing order to the web, 1999.

[68] Infomap - community detection, http://www.mapequation.org/code.html.

[69] Z. Liu, M. Barahona, Graph-based data clustering via multiscale community detection, Applied Network Science 5 (1) (Jan 2020), https://doi.org/10.1007/s41109-019-0248-7.

[70] Wordnet – a lexical database for English, http://wordnet.princeton.edu/.

[71] A. Nenkova, L. Vanderwende, The impact of frequency on summarization, Tech. Rep., Microsoft Research, 2005.

CHAPTER 7

Genetic algorithm-based microblog clustering technique

7.1 Introduction

The Twitter microblogging platform (https://twitter.com/) is one of the most popular sites on the Internet today, with millions of users posting brief messages (known as "tweets") about a variety of topics and events on a daily basis. Twitter's core strength is real-time updates on current events, which are utilized in a variety of applications such as evaluating public opinion on various subjects, real-time incident detection, and so on [1]. Every day, lots of tweets are published, and the quantity of tweets is significantly higher after major events such as floods or earthquakes. It would be impossible for someone to scroll through the tweet stream to follow the event because there are too many tweets. In this case, clustering of comparable tweets such that the user only sees a few tweets in each cluster is an efficient technique to reduce the user's information load [2].

Despite the fact that document clustering is a well-established field of research [3], grouping tweets is challenging due to their tiny size (at most 140 characters) and their noisy nature – due to the size constraint, tweets frequently contain acronyms, colloquial language, and so on. As a result, traditional data mining and natural language processing approaches rarely work well with tweets [4].

In this chapter we suggest a new tweet clustering technique that combines a classic clustering algorithm (K-means) with an evolutionary approach (genetic algorithms [GAs]). Despite the fact that both of these methods have been utilized for clustering in many previous works (as explained in the next section), no previous work has attempted to combine the two strategies to our knowledge.

We do tests on a sample of tweets from a recent tragedy, the Uttarakhand floods of 2013. The suggested methodology is compared to a number of standard clustering techniques, including K-means, hierarchical clustering, density-based clustering, and graph clustering algorithms. According to various established measures for evaluating clustering, the suggested methodology outperforms the baseline methodologies [3].

Data Analytics for Social Microblogging Platforms
https://doi.org/10.1016/B978-0-32-391785-8.00019-6

The chapter is organized as follows. Section 7.2 discusses related work, while Section 7.3 discusses the suggested methodology in depth. Section 7.4 discusses the dataset that was obtained, as well as the evaluation of the proposed methodology and baseline methods. Section 7.5 brings the chapter to a close.

7.2 Related work

7.2.1 Clustering of tweets

There have been some previous studies on tweet clustering. Kang et al. recommended a clustering algorithm based on affinity propagation for related tweets [5]. Cheong [6] used an unsupervised self-organizing feature map as a machine learning-based clustering approach to find intra-topic user and message clusters on Twitter. As a complementary step to text classification, Thomas et al. [7] presented an efficient text classification system based on semi-supervised clustering. The method was more accurate than the similarity measure for text processing, which was used to calculate distance.

Yang and Leskovec [8] devised a clustering method based on temporal propagation patterns. Karypis et al. [9] presented a hierarchical clustering algorithm based on dynamic modeling that considered the dynamic nature of cluster modes and adaptive merging decisions. Natural clusters of various forms and sizes can be discovered using this method, depending on the difference in clustering model. It sports a two-phase framework that has been built effectively using various graph representations suitable for various application domains [10]. For clustering tweets, Dueck et al. [11] suggested an affinity propagation approach. Rangrej et al. [12] recently compared the performance of three clustering algorithms in clustering short text documents: K-means, affinity propagation, and singular value decomposition.

For clustering microblog data, some researchers have used graph-based techniques [13]. Dutta et al. [14] suggested a clustering technique for tweets that also conducts summarization, based on a graph-based community discovery approach. A graph-based approach known as the TextRank algorithm [15] was used to discover the most highly ranked sentences based on keywords in a document, where ranks are determined by the PageRank algorithm. In the SCISOR system [16], a concept graph was given for a Down Jones newswire stories dataset to construct conceptual summarization. Many previous works [17,18], including clustering data obtained from online social networks, have used GAs for clustering. Adel et al. [19] developed a Twitter data clustering approach based on a cellular evolutionary algorithm. Hajeer et al. [20] proposed a technique involving GAs to perform graph-based clustering. As previously noted, several procedures for clustering texts have been tested, including traditional methods like K-means and evolutionary approaches like GAs [21]. Ramage et al. [22] employed labeled latent Dirichlet allocation to topically cluster tweets in a different way.

Aside from clustering, Genc et al. [23] employed a Wikipedia-based classification strategy to categorize tweets using semantic distance as a classification metric to compare distances between Wikipedia sites [24]. Using GA, Soumi et al. [25] proposed a method to categorize microblogging data. In another work, Soumi et al. [26] proposed a feature selection-based clustering algorithm which can increase the effectiveness of clustering. Many existing clustering approaches, such as K-means, rely on the number of clusters being specified by the user. A user's ability to precisely estimate the number of clusters for data collection is frequently problematic. The number of clusters is usually determined automatically by GAs [27]. They, on the other hand, usually choose the genes and the amount of genes at random. If we can find the proper genes in the original population, GAs have a better chance of producing a high-quality clustering result than if we chose the genes at random. Through a novel initial population selection strategy, Rahman et al. [28] offered a novel GA-based clustering technique capable of automatically determining the proper number of clusters and identifying the right genes. It generated high-quality cluster centers with the help of our innovative fitness function and gene rearrangement operation. The centers were then put into K-means as initial seeds, allowing the initial seeds to adapt as needed, resulting in an even higher-quality clustering solution. On 20 natural datasets used in their work, experimental results showed a statistically significant superiority (according to the sign test analysis) of their technique over five recent techniques based on six evaluation criteria.

7.2.2 Genetic algorithms

GA is a computational search tool that finds exact or approximate answers to optimization and search issues. GAs are a type of evolutionary algorithm that employs evolutionary biological processes like mutation, inheritance, crossover, and selection (also called recombination). In most cases, evolution begins with a population of randomly created individuals and proceeds in generations [29,30]. Every generation, the fitness of every member in the population is assessed, and several individuals from the current population are picked (depending on their fitness) and modified to generate a new population. The new population is employed in the algorithm's following iteration [30]. The algorithm ends when the population has attained a suitable fitness level or a maximum number of generations has been produced. The following are the steps of a basic GA:

Step 1: Initialization
The primary or initial solutions of candidates for population are mostly generated in a random manner across the search space.

Step 2: Evaluation
The fitness values of the candidate solutions are evaluated only when a new population is formed or when the population is initialized.

Step 3: Selection
More instances of solutions are given through selection with a high level of fitness, and the idea of survival possibilities based on being the fittest is imposed on the candidates' answers. The primary concept of choice is to pick the best solutions and prioritize them. As a result, a variety of selection strategies have been proposed to achieve this goal [31]. Roulette wheel selection, stochastic universal selection, ranking selection, and tournament selection are among these processes.

Step 4: Recombination
Parts of two or more of the main solutions are combined to create new and improved solutions (i.e., offspring). There are various ways to accomplish this, and efficient performance is dependent on a well-designed recombination process.

Step 5: Mutation
When two or more parental chromosomes are recombined, it results in mutation modification, which is a local and random technique to solve a problem [32]. There are many different forms of mutations; however, most mutations involve one or more changes in the particular feature(s). To put it another way, mutation takes a random trip across the candidate solution area.

Step 6: Replacement
The initial parental population is replaced by the offspring population, which is caused through selection, recombination, and mutation. In GA, a variety of replacement mechanisms are used, including steady state replacement, elitist replacement, and generationwise replacement.

Step 7: Repeat

Repeat Steps 2 through 6 until the termination condition is reached.

Unlike traditional search methods, GA is based on a population of candidate solutions [33]. The population size, which is a user-specified parameter, is one of the key factors influencing GA performance and scalability. For example, a small population size may result in immature convergence and solutions that are subpar. However, a large population may result in the waste of valuable computing time. Many previous works [34,35], including clustering data obtained from online social networks, have used GA for clustering [36]. In addition, numerous procedures for clustering documents have been tested, including traditional methods like K-means and evolutionary approaches like GA [37]. To the best of our knowledge, no previous research has attempted to integrate these two methodologies. For example, Hajeer et al. [11] proposed employing evolutionary algorithms to cluster online social network communities based on graphs. Adel et al. [12] suggested a Twitter dataset clustering approach based on a cellular evolutionary algorithm.

As previously noted, several procedures for clustering documents [1] have been tested, including traditional methods such as K-means and evolutionary approaches such as GA. To the best of our knowledge, no previous research has attempted to integrate these two methodologies [38]. The suggested clustering framework integrates GA with regular K-means clustering, and it is demonstrated that it outperforms numerous standard clustering methods such as hierarchical clustering algorithms, K-means, and graph-based clustering algorithms [39].

K-means clustering

One of the most often used unsupervised learning algorithms is the K-means clustering technique [40,41]. It follows a simple iterative method to divide the data into k clusters, where k is set a priori. The first step is to define k centers, one for each cluster. These centers should be positioned intelligently, because different locations may lead to different results. As a result, it is preferable to place them at the maximum possible distance apart from each other [42]. The next step is to analyze each object in a dataset and associate it with the center that is closest to it. When no object is pending, the first step is finished and early clustering is done. At this point, k new centers are computed by calculating means of the k clusters obtained in the earlier step, and these new centers are set as centers of the clusters [43]. It is a strategy or procedure that has been utilized a lot in the past to imitate k robotically separated groups of datasets. It advances by selecting cluster centers with k initials. K-means is a clustering algorithm that is almost universally used. It creates a divide between an engage about objects among k groups that reduces the size of certain objective functions, most notably the squared error function, which reveals round-form clusters. The parameter k is fixed, thus it should stay among the increases that limit its use after streaming and data evolution [44]. As a result, K-means clustering is a partition clustering technique that organizes a collection of items into k clusters by maximizing a standard function. After these k new centers are obtained, a new binding between the identical items and the nearest new centroid is required. During execution of the loop, k centers modify their position step by step until the algorithm converges [45].

Unfortunately, for any particular dataset, there is no general theoretical method for determining the necessary number of clusters. Comparing the results of numerous executions with varying k values and selecting the best one based on a set of criteria is a straightforward approach [46]. However, one must exercise caution because, by definition, raising k results in reduced error function values, but larger k values also raise the risk of overfitting [47].

7.3 Clustering using genetic algorithms and K-means

The use of GA with K-means is a more purposeful approach. Various clustering algorithms based on GA have been proposed in recent years. There is a wide range of approaches that combine the ability of K-means in partitioning data with algorithms that perform adaptive search processes to seek out nearest optimal solutions for the optimization problem. This chapter proposes a clustering framework that incorporates evolutionary algorithms as well as classic K-means clustering [48]. In this chapter an algorithm for clustering using a combination of GA and the popular K-means greedy algorithm is proposed. The main idea of this algorithm is to use the genetic search approach to generate new clusters using the famous two-point crossover and then apply the K-means technique to further improve the quality of the formed clusters in order to speed up the search process [49]. In Algorithm 7.1, the process is given briefly, and each step is described in depth below.

A toy dataset of five tweets is used to demonstrate different parts of the process, as illustrated in Table 7.1. The tweets are based on a dataset of tweets posted during the 2013 floods in Uttaranchal, India, which is de-

---

Algorithm 7.1 Tweet clustering algorithm

Require: $\overline{N}$ tweets, desired number of clusters, $\overline{K}$.
Ensure: Tweets are grouped together into $\overline{K}$ clusters.

Remove special characters, URLs, and stopwords from tweets before posting;

Recognize all separate terms in the tweets and define $\overline{M}$ as the number of distinct terms;

Generate an $\overline{N} \times \overline{M}$ document-term matrix DT where each row represents a tweet and each column represents a separate word;

Create a basic GA population with 100 chromosomes $\overline{c}_i$, $i = 1, 2, 3, .., 100$;

Create a P population matrix having one row for each $\overline{c}_i$ and $\overline{M}$ columns, where each cell is randomly filled with 0 or 1;

while GA has not converged OR a set number of iterations has not been completed **do**

    for all $\overline{c}_i$, $i = 1, 2, 3, .., 100$, **do**

        Make a matrix having $\overline{N}$ rows (each corresponding to a tweet) and those columns j of DT for which $P[i; j] = 1$;

        K-means is used to cluster the rows of the matrix. Assess your fitness of $\overline{c}_i$, by evaluating the quality of the clustering;

    end for

    Crossover using the GA selection steps (roulette wheel technique)

    The best-fit solutions are integrated from the newly created child chromosomes to choose chromosomes for the new population.

end while

As the final clustering of the tweets, output the clustering corresponding to the fittest chromosome of the final population.

---

tailed in Section 7.5. As stated in Section 7.5, opinion of several human volunteers suggested that the dataset contains five dissimilar types of information, thus suggesting the number of clusters in the dataset to be five. The algorithm is also evaluated considering the number of clusters to be four and six, as the optimal number of clusters may vary from what the human volunteers identified.

Preprocessing: Non-textual elements such as @usernames, smileys, question marks, exclamation marks, and other symbols in tweets act as noise and worsen clustering/classification jobs. As a result, the tweets are preprocessed

Table 7.1   A sample dataset of five tweets to demonstrate the genetic algorithm-based clustering algorithm.

Tweet ID	Text
T1	Uttarakhand: Nature's fury June 2013: [url] via @youtube
T2	Uttarakhand monsoon rains 'kill 10': At least 10 people are killed in landslides and flooding [url]
T3	Thousands of pilgrims reported stuck in the hilly regions of Uttarakhand. They were on their way to various Hindu shrines. #Monsoon #India
T4	Avg rainfall in uttarakhand was 61mm. This year it already received 154mm. That's 190% of avg rainfall @abpnewstv
T5	praying for my family nd muluk ppl in #Uttarak- hand.. hope everything will be fine soon:) GOD SAVE ALL

Table 7.2   Document term matrix for the toy dataset shown in Table 7.1.

ID	Uttarakhand	nature	fury	monsoon	rains	landslide	pilgrims	stuck	regions	hindu	shrines	family	hope
T1	1	1	1	0	0	0	0	0	0	0	0	0	0
T2	1	0	0	1	1	1	0	0	0	0	0	0	0
T3	1	0	0	1	0	0	1	1	1	1	1	0	0
T4	1	0	0	0	0	0	0	0	0	0	0	0	0
T5	1	0	0	0	0	0	0	0	0	0	0	1	1

to remove certain characters. The tweets are also lower cased and a standard set of English stopwords are deleted. Also, for hashtags like "#uttarakhand," the "#" symbol is ignored; in other words, the two terms "#uttarakhand" and "uttarakhand" are considered to be identical.

Forming document–term matrix: Each tweet is effectively a group of separate phrases after the preprocessing stage. In the whole set of tweets, the set of all distinct phrases is computed. Let $\overline{N}$ be the number of tweets and let $\overline{M}$ be the number of distinct phrases in the full set of tweets. Distinct terms are denoted as $t_1, t_2, \ldots\ldots, t_{\overline{M}}$. Then a two-dimensional $\overline{N} \times \overline{M}$ matrix is created, with rows representing individual tweets and columns representing distinct terms. The entries in the matrix represent the presence or absence of specific terms in the tweets; for example, the (i, j)-th entry in the matrix is 1 if the i-th tweet contains t_j, otherwise it is 0. The sample document-term matrix for the toy tweet dataset in Table 7.1 is displayed in Table 7.2, where $\overline{N} = 5$ and $\overline{M} = 13$.

It should be noted that the above matrix could have been weighted, with the (i, j)-th entry representing the frequency of t_j in the i-th tweet.

However, because tweets are so short (at most 140 characters), words are rarely repeated within the same tweet. As a result, only the presence or absence of words is taken into account.

GA-based clustering: GA is an adaptive heuristic search algorithm that simulates natural selection and survival of the fittest in the evolutionary process. GA starts by producing a collection of probable solutions (chromosomes) at random, which is referred to as an initial population. The parameter values that make up a solution are stored on the chromosomes. GA iterates through numerous generations by performing genetic operations to the population, and after each generation, it seeks out the best answer [50]. The first step in each generation is to use an optimization function to calculate the fitness value of chromosomes. Three basic genetic operators are applied to chromosomes once the fitness value is calculated. The first genetic operator is a selection operator, in which two parent chromosomes are chosen from a pool of randomly generated chromosomes based on their high-quality fitness value in order to undertake the following operations. The second operator is crossover, which generates two child chromosomes from two parent chromosomes utilizing crossover operators such as single-point, uniform, and heuristics-based operators [51]. A mutation is the next operator, and it is used to avoid getting caught in local minima. The mutation has a very minimal chance of changing the gene value. Children's chromosomes, as well as select elite chromosomes, are passed down to the following generation. When one of the halting criteria is met or the maximum number of generations is achieved, the algorithm comes to a halt [52]. As previously stated, this methodology combines an evolutionary (GA) approach with a traditional clustering approach (K-means). The methodology is described further below. For the GA, an initial population set of 100 chromosomes $\bar{c}_i$ is formed at random with $i = 1, 2, 3, ..., 100$. As a result, an initial population matrix with 100 rows (each row representing a chromosome) and $\overline{M}$ columns is generated (each column corresponds to a distinct term in the vocabulary, as described above). The population matrix is initially filled at random, i.e., each entry is assigned a random value of 1 or 0. If the (i, j)-th entry in the matrix is 1, it means that the term t_j is a feature of the chromosome $\bar{c}_i$. A sample initial population matrix is shown in Table 7.3, where each tuple represents a chromosome and each column represents a distinct term.

The following procedure is used to estimate the fitness of each chromosome. A separate two-dimensional matrix is created for each chromosome $\bar{c}_i$, $i \in \{1, 2, ..., 100\}$. This matrix contains $\overline{N}$ rows corresponding to $\overline{N}$

Table 7.3 Sample initial population matrix.

Chromosome	G_1	G_2	G_3	G_4	G_5	..	..	G_M
$Chrom_1$	1	0	1	1	0	0	0	1
$Chrom_2$	0	0	0	1	0	1	1	0
..	1	0	0	1	0	0	1	1
..	1	0	0	1	0	1	1	0
$Chrom_{100}$	0	1	0	1	0	1	1	1

tweets, as well as only those columns from the document–term matrix for which the corresponding columns in the row for $\bar{c}_i$ in the initial population matrix are 1. In other words, the chromosome $\bar{c}_i$ matrix is a projection of the document–term matrix that contains only the terms (columns) t_j for which the (i, j)-th entry in the initial population matrix is 1. As an example, 100 such matrices are computed, one for each of the 100 chromosomes. To cluster the rows, the K–means algorithm is applied to each of these matrices. The value of K (number of clusters) is chosen based on an estimate of how many clusters may exist in the original dataset; this choice is discussed in the following section. $U_I = \{X_1, X_2, X_3, X_4, \ldots\ldots, X_K\}$ are assumed as the K clusters corresponding to the chromosome $\bar{c}_i$. The Davies–Bouldin index (DBIndex) is used to assess the quality of the clustering U_i (discussed in Chapter 8). Smaller DBIndex values indicate higher-quality clusters that are compact and well separated.

The K–means clustering algorithm is then applied on the dataset, considering the value of K as 4, 5, and 6; as mentioned earlier in the chapter, five sorts of information were detected by the human annotators, hence the number of clusters is considered to be around 5. After applying the K–means clustering method for each chromosome, the validity index measure *DB index* is evaluated to identify the fittest chromosome from the population matrix. To design the GA according to this problem, DBIndex(U) is considered to frame the objective function and the resultant value of the objective function $F(\bar{C}_i)$ is considered as fitness value for the population set. The DBIndex finds the set of clusters that are compact and well separated. Small DBIndex(U) values indicate high-quality clusters. The objective function $F(\bar{C}_i)$ is defined as follows:

$$F(C_i) = w * DBIndex(U) + (1 - w) * \frac{\text{number of features in a chromosome}}{\text{total number of features}},$$

(7.1)

where w is the chromosomal length weighting factor that determines the relative relevance of DBIndex. This value will vary between 0 and 1. A

Table 7.4 Matrix that corresponds to a specific chromosome $\bar{c}_1$ in Table 7.3. The document-term matrix is projected into this matrix shown in Table 7.2, comprising all rows and only those columns in the initial population matrix that contain 1 in the row corresponding to $\bar{c}_1$ in Table 7.3.

Tweets	Uttarakhand	fury	monsoon	hope
T_1	1	1	0	0
T_2	1	0	1	0
T_3	1	0	1	0
T_4	1	0	0	0
T_5	1	0	0	1

lower value of the weighting factor means less importance to DBIndex and more value to the length of the chromosome. A higher value of the weighting factor means more importance to DBIndex and less value to the length of the chromosome [53]. The method is tested for various values of w, and the best results are observed for $w = 0.1, 0.2, 0.3$. In general, it is preferred to have chromosomes having a lower number of features, so that the clustering can be quicker. See Table 7.4.

Following the basic procedures of selection and crossover, GA is applied to the population matrix. The 20% fittest chromosomes are chosen from the population for each selection (using the fitness function described above). The remaining chromosomes (80%) are chosen using one of the selection procedures. Roulette wheel selection is used to pick the chromosomes in this study. The following population is created using crossover in the next phase. Crossover produces two new child chromosomes or solutions for each two-parent chromosome. Two chromosomes (two parents and two children) are chosen as the best chromosomes with the lowest fitness value out of the four [54]. The freshly formed child chromosomes produce a new population of solutions combining the best picked chromosomes, which will be employed in GA's next stage. In the following iteration of GA, the K-means clustering technique is performed to the new population matrix (as in the previous iteration), and the fitness value for each chromosome in the newly produced population is evaluated using the objective function [55].

GA is iterated until it converges or reaches a predetermined number of iterations. The fittest chromosome in the present population is considered after GA, and the K-means clustering corresponding to this chromosome is output as the tweet clustering.

7.4 Evaluating performance

This section compares the performance of different clustering methods. The comparison of performance is conducted using a collection of standard metrics for evaluation of cluster quality [56]. The Calinski–Harabasz index (CH), Silhouette index (S), Davies–Bouldin index (DB), I-index (I), Dunn index (D), and Xie–Beni index (XB) are some of the typical metrics used to assess clustering quality. For the Silhouette index (S), Dunn index (D), Calinski–Harabasz index (CH), and I-index (I), higher values indicate good performance, while for the Davies–Bouldin index (DB) and the Xie–Beni index (XB), lower values indicate better performance. All experiments are carried out on the four Twitter datasets mentioned in Section 7.5.

7.5 Experimental dataset

Similar to the previous chapter, we decided to experiment on microblogs posted during emergency events. Millions of messages are posted everyday on microblogs during any emergency event, such as natural calamity, election, sports events like IPL, the world cup, the Hyderabad bomb explosion, the Uttarakhand flood, and the Sandy Hook Elementary School shooting. During emergency events, thousands of tweets are posted in short durations of time, and since time is critical during such events, it is necessary to get a quick overview of the situation. In such a case, clustering similar messages so that the user only sees a few messages from each cluster is an effective way to reduce the user's information load. So, one of the primary applications of clustering is to reduce information overload during emergency events. Hence we focus on clustering of tweets posted during some specific emergency events.

Twitter is one of the most popular websites on the Internet today, with millions of users posting real-time messages (tweets) on various topics of interest. The content that becomes popular on Twitter (i.e., is discussed by a large number of users) on a specific day can be used for a variety of purposes, including content recommendation and marketing and advertisement campaigns. One of the most intriguing aspects of Twitter is its real-time nature; at any given time, millions of Twitter users are exchanging opinions on various topics or incidents/events that are currently taking place in any part of the world. As a result, the content posted on Twitter is extremely useful for gathering real-time news on a wide range of topics.

This section describes the dataset used in the various experiments. Twitter's online social network offers an API5 for collecting various types of data, such as streams of tweets posted on the website, profile details of specific users, and so on. Twitter, in particular, provides a 1% random sample of all tweets posted on the Twitter website worldwide.

Tweets posted during the following emergency events are considered for clustering experiments.

1. **HDBlast** – In the Indian city of Hyderabad, there were two bomb incidents [57].
2. **SHShoot** – At Sandy Hook Elementary School in Connecticut, an assailant killed 20 children and 6 adults [58].
3. **UFlood** – Floods and landslides have wreaked havoc in India's Uttaranchal state [59].
4. **THagupit** – Typhoon Hagupit, a powerful typhoon, hit the Philippines [60].

Table 7.4 gives examples of tweets of Hagupit Typhoon. Keyword-based matching is used to collect relevant tweets using the Twitter API [61]. For example, for the HDBlast event, the terms "bomb," "Hyderabad," and "blast" were utilized, while for the SHShoot event, the phrases "Sandyhook" and "shooting" were considered. For the Uttaranchal flood, the keywords considered are "Uttaranchal," "flood," and "landslide," and for the Typhoon Hagupit in the Philippines, keywords used to collect relevant tweets of the events are "Typhoon" and "Hagupit." For each occurrence, the first 5000 tweets are taken into account. Because the same information is regularly retweeted/reposted by several people, it is well known that tweets commonly contain duplicates and near-duplicates [62].

It should be noted that the events chosen include both man–made and natural disasters that occurred in diverse parts of the world. As a result, the tweets' vocabulary and linguistic style are likely to be diverse. Table 7.5 shows an example dataset of five tweets. The tweets were extracted from a dataset of tweets sent during the 2013 floods in India's Uttaranchal state.

Creating golden standard clusters

To evaluate clustering algorithms, a golden standard must be created against which the clustering obtained by various methods can be evaluated. Human feedback is commonly used to obtain the golden standard clustering. Three human volunteers were tasked with identifying the various types of information contained in the tweets and clustering/grouping the tweets by type of information. Each of the human volunteers made identical discoveries, identifying five main forms of information in the tweet datasets:

(1) tweets informing of casualties or property damage,

Table 7.5   A sample dataset of "Uttarakhand flood".

Tweet ID	Tweets
1	58 dead, over 58,000 trapped as rain batters Uttarakhand, UP.may god save d rest.NO RAIN is a problem.RAIN is a bigger problem.
2	Heavy rains wreak havoc in Uttarakhand, flood warning in UP, Delhi http://t.co/WOrNLlbmOp.
3	Harbhajan Singh stuck in Uttarakhand rains, tweets he's fine http://t.co/q0tTeZCpiZ.
4	RT @BJPRajnathSingh: I appeal to all BJP workers in Uttarakhand to provide every possible help and relief to flood affected people.
5	RT @amitvkaushik: Uttarakhand flood. Helpline numbers are: 0135-2710335, 2710233.

(2) tweets including climate-related information,

(3) tweets containing information on the helpline,

(4) general population conclusions, sympathy, and petitions for the influenced population, and

(5) news about government/political responses to the disaster.

Table 7.6 displays examples of each type of tweet related to the UFlood event. As a result, the golden standard (created by human volunteers) categorizes tweets into five groups. In the next sections, different clustering techniques for microblogs are discussed in detail.

7.5.1 Parameter selection for the algorithms

The study considers a set of distinct tweets in the GA-based tweet clustering technique. Because many users on Twitter post very similar or duplicate tweets, such duplicate tweets are ignored and only distinct tweets are considered. Three parameters must be determined before using the GA-based tweet clustering method:

(1) the weight factor (w)'s value,

(2) the total number of clusters to be computed, and

(3) the GA's stopping criterion – whether to stop after a specified number of iterations or keep going until the algorithm converges.

It is worth noting that the third component (stopping condition) is crucial for clustering tweets during a live event. Although the evolutionary algorithm should be run until convergence, because tweets must be clustered fast during an ongoing event, stopping after a specified number of iterations may be more practical. To determine appropriate values for the three elements mentioned above, different instances of the proposed method were

Table 7.6 Examples of tweets about the Uttaranchal floods. Human volunteers identified tweets containing five different types of information.

Information type	Sample tweet text
Casualties info	8 dead, 3700 pilgrims stranded as incessant rains batter Uttarakhand: Eight persons were killed on Sunday. 100 houses collapse; 25 dead, over 50 missing as rain batters Uttarakhand http://t.co/m8zrc3PQub.
Climate info	RT-ANI_news: In Uttarkashi *Uttarakhand*, flash floods triggered by heavy rains wash away houses along the river. RT-kirankhurana: 02/05 Destruction in Uttarakhand due to Heavy Rains:-joinAAP
Helpline info	RT-PIB_India: IAF launches operation 'Rahat' to help stranded pilgrims & tourists in Uttarakhand & HP. RT-rahulmanthattil: #Uttarakhand flood helpline numbers: 0135-2710334, 0135-2710335, 0135-2710233. Please share ! –annavetticad.
Public opinion	Prayers for Uttarakhand. Just shows you should never take life for granted. Irony: the relatives of the Kedarnath flood victims praying to the same gods that the victims had so devotedly gone to visit.
Political news	RT-IndiaSpeaksPR: Rahul Gandhi promises to reach out to the victims in Kedarnath once Congress confirms that it would be secular to do so. Seems CM Vijay Bahuguna has no time to utter a few words of comfort to the people of #Uttarakhand, who are dealing with life & death.#shame.

run with different selections for the factors, and the clustering performance was compared using the metrics mentioned before. The following options are specifically considered.

(1) **Weight factor:** The best results were obtained for low values of w ($w = 0.1, 0.2, 0.3, ..., 0.9$). As a result, only the values $w = 0.1, 0.2, 0.3$ are reported in the findings.

(2) **Number of clusters:** Since the golden standard (provided by human volunteers) indicated five clusters, three variations of the suggested methodology are tested, with four, five, and six clusters, respectively.

(3) **Stopping criterion:** Two examples of the proposed approach are considered: one in which the process is run until convergence and the other in which the process is performed until the GA has completed 100 iterations.

7.5.2 Baseline clustering algorithms

The clustering approaches developed in this chapter (as stated in the earlier sections of this chapter) are compared with three classical clustering methods – density-based clustering, K-means, and hierarchical clustering. The reader can refer to [63] for detailed descriptions of these clustering methods. There are different broad approaches for clustering, such as partition-based, hierarchical-based, density-based, and graph–based approaches.

7.5.2.1 Partition-based clustering

A partitioning method [64] creates k ($k \leq n$) clusters distinct from each other given a dataset of n items. The algorithm divides the data into k groups that must all meet the following criteria: (1) there must be at least one object in each group and (2) each object must belong to only one group (hard clustering). In general, the algorithms employ an iterative relocation strategy based on an objective function that aims to increase partitioning by transferring objects from one cluster to another. The general criterion for good partitioning is that objects belonging to the same group are close to each other, whilst objects belonging to other clusters are far apart. There are a variety of other factors for measuring the quality of clusters [65]. Some common partition-based clustering methods are described below.

(A) K-means clustering

The K-means clustering technique is one of the most widely used unsupervised learning algorithms [40,41]. It uses a straightforward iterative algorithm to divide a dataset into k clusters, with k predetermined. The first step is to determine the number of centers (k) that will be used for each cluster. These centers should be strategically placed, as different sites may yield varied outcomes. As a result, it is preferable to space them as far apart as feasible. The next step is to consider each object belonging to a given dataset and associate it to the nearest center. When no object is pending, the first step is finished and an early clustering is done. At this point, k new centers are computed by calculating means of the k clusters obtained in the earlier step, and these new centers are set as centers of the clusters. After these k new centers are obtained, a new binding has to be done between the same objects and the nearest new centroid. During execution of the loop, k centers modify their position step by step until the algorithm converges. A flowchart of K-means clustering which consists of six essential stages is depicted in Fig. 7.2.

Unfortunately, for any particular dataset, there is no general theoretical method for determining the necessary number of clusters. Comparing the results of numerous executions with varying k values and selecting the best one based on a set of criteria is a straightforward approach. However, one must exercise caution, since, while increasing k results in reduced error function values by definition, it also raises the risk of overfitting [47].

(B) K-medoids clustering

Because an object with an unusually large value can significantly alter the distribution of objects in the discovered clusters, the K-means clustering algorithm is sensitive to outliers. Instead of using the mean value of the items in a cluster, the most centrally situated object in the cluster is utilized as a point of reference in the K-medoids approach. As a result, object partitioning can still be done using the principle of minimizing the sum of dissimilarities between each item and its associated point of reference.

In the presence of noise and outliers, the K-medoids approach has been found to be more robust than the K-means method, because a medoid is less influenced by outliers or other extreme values than a mean [66]. However, K-medoid processing is more expensive than the K-means technique. The user must supply the value of k, the number of clusters, in both approaches. PAM [67], a common K-medoids partitioning technique, works well for low-volume datasets but fails to scale well for high-volume datasets.

(C) Partitioning methods in large databases

To deal with huge datasets, a sampling-based method called Clustering LARge Applications (CLARA) [68] can be utilized. CLARA's concept is that instead of considering the entire collection of items, a tiny subset of the original objects is chosen as the dataset's representations. PAM [67] is then used to pick medoids from the representatives. If the sample is chosen at random, it should be fairly representative of the original dataset. The representative items (medoids) chosen are likely to be similar to those chosen from the entire dataset. CLARA extracts several samples from the dataset, applies PAM to each sample, and outputs the best clustering result. As a result, CLARA is capable of handling larger datasets than PAM. Each iteration is $O(ks^2 + k(n - k))$ in complexity, where s, k, and n are the sample size, number of clusters, and total number of objects, respectively.

A K-medoids approach called Clustering Large Applications based upon RANdomized Search (CLARANS) [68] has also been proposed to increase the quality and scalability of CLARA. This method combines the sampling technique with PAM; however, it is not limited to a single sample at a specific time. CLARANS represents a sample with some randomness in each phase of the search, whereas CLARA has a fixed sample at every step of the search. The clustering approach can be described as a network search in which each node represents a potential solution, such as a set of K-medoids.

7.5.2.2 Hierarchical clustering

According to the proximity matrix, hierarchical clustering algorithms group the objects of a given dataset into a hierarchical structure [69]. A dendrogram is commonly used to illustrate the outcomes of hierarchical clustering. The dendrogram's root node represents the entire dataset, whereas each leaf node is treated as an item. The height of the dendrogram usually reflects the distance between each pair of clusters or objects or a cluster and an object, and the intermediate nodes describe the degree to which the objects are proximate to each other. By slicing the dendrogram at various levels, clustering can be produced.

Agglomerative methods and divisive methods are two types of hierarchical clustering algorithms [70,69]. Agglomerative clustering begins with a set of N clusters, each of which contains exactly one item. Then, a series of merge procedures are performed, culminating in all items being placed in the same group. Divisive clustering, on the other hand, works in the other direction. The entire dataset is assigned to a cluster in the first stage, and then the items are divided one by one until all clusters are singletons.

With the need to handle large-scale datasets in data mining and other fields, several novel hierarchical clustering approaches have emerged in recent years, such as ROCK [71], CURE [72], BIRCH [73], and Chameleon [9], which have substantially enhanced clustering performance. Despite the fact that divided clustering is not often employed in reality, some examples may be found in [74], where two divisive clustering methods, MONA and DIANA, are discussed.

7.5.2.3 Density-based clustering

Clusters of arbitrary forms have been discovered using density-based clustering methods [75]. Typically, these clusters are dense groups of objects in a dataset's space divided by low-density regions (representing noise). DENCLUE and DBSCAN [76] are two common density-based spatial clustering algorithms.

DBSCAN: In geographical datasets with noise, the DBSCAN algorithm creates areas with suitable high density into clusters and identifies clusters of arbitrary shape. It defines a cluster as a maximum set of density-connected

objects and looks for clusters by inspecting every object in the dataset's
ϵ-neighborhood. If the ϵ-neighborhood of an item p contains more objects than a threshold, a new cluster is created with p as the core object.
Then DBSCAN iteratively gathers directly density-reachable items from
the core objects, perhaps merging a few density-reachable clusters. When
no additional points can be added to any of the clusters, the operation
ends. DBSCAN's computational complexity is $O(nlogn)$ if a spatial index
is employed, where n is the number of items; otherwise, it is $O(n^2)$. The
user-defined parameters have an impact on the algorithm.

DENCLUE: DENCLUE is a clustering algorithm based on a collection
of density distribution functions:

   (i)   The control of each data object can be formally modeled with the
help of a mathematical function, called an "influence function," that
describes the impact of a data point within its neighborhood.

 (ii)   The total of the effect functions of all data items can be used to
model the overall density of a data space logically.

(iii)   The density attractors, which are surrounding maxima of the overall
density function, can then be identified mathematically to determine
clusters.

There are several advantages of the DENCLUE method in comparison
with other clustering algorithms:

   (i)   It is scientifically justified and it generalizes previous clustering techniques such as partition-based, hierarchical, and locality-based clustering.

 (ii)   For datasets with a lot of noise, it offers good clustering properties.

(iii)   In high-dimensional datasets, it allows for a succinct mathematical
description of arbitrarily formed clusters.

(iv)   Grid cells are used to store information about grid cells that include
data points. It organizes these cells into a tree-based access structure, making it much faster than some popular techniques, such as
DBSCAN. The approach, on the other hand, necessitates careful selection of the density parameter and the noise threshold, as these
factors can have a substantial impact on the quality of the clustering
solutions.

7.5.2.4 Graph clustering algorithms

Clustering (also known as community detection in the context of graphs)
methods for graphs/networks are designed to locate communities based on

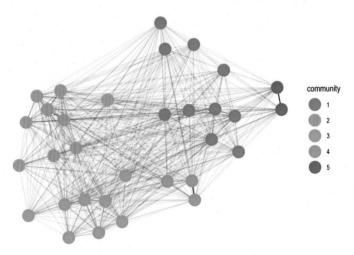

Figure 7.1 Community structure in a graph showing intra-community edges and inter-community edges.

the network topology, such as tightly connected groups of nodes. In graph-based clustering, data are represented as graphs before applying community detection algorithms. The edge weight in the graph can be calculated using a variety of similarity measures. A community is formed when nodes in a network are of the same type. Intra-community edges are the edges that connect the nodes within a community. Inter-community edges are nodes that connect nodes from different communities. Fig. 7.1 depicts intra-community and inter-community edges between distinct communities in a tiny graph. A popular graph clustering algorithm is described below.

Infomap method

Rosvall and Bergstrom (2008) [77] developed another popular community discovery technique, Infomap. It improves the map equation, which achieves a balance between the difficulty of data compression and the problem of recognizing and retrieving essential patterns or structures within the data. The Louvain community finding approach is closely followed by this algorithm. Each node is initially given to its own module. Then, in a random sequential order, each node is transferred to the nearby modules, resulting in the greatest reduction of the map equation. The node remains in its original position if no move leads to a further reduction of the map equation. Every time, the operation is repeated in a different random sequential order, until the map equation can no longer be reduced. Finally,

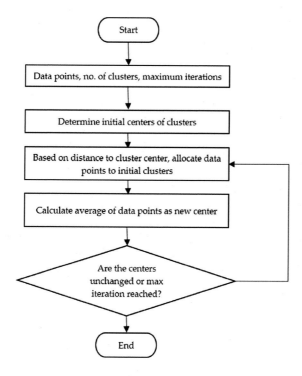

Figure 7.2 A flowchart of K-means clustering.

the network is recreated, with the lowest-level modules producing nodes at that level, and nodes are connected into modules in the same way as the previous-level nodes. This hierarchical network rebuilding is continued until the map equation can no longer be lowered. Both undirected and directed graphs can be used with Infomap. Infomap returns a list of non-overlapping communities (node set partitions) as well as a decimal value that represents the total flow in that node.

As is evident from the discussion above, there are a wide variety of clustering algorithms. It is a natural question which algorithm performs the best on a certain dataset. To answer this question, first some measures for cluster validation/evaluation need to be determined. The next section discusses some commonly used cluster validation measures.

For implementing these clustering algorithms, the Weka machine learning toolkit [78] has been used, which is a renowned tool for data mining, clustering, classification, and feature selection. The default parameters of the Weka toolkit have been used in all cases. For those algorithms that need the number of clusters as an input parameter, the number of clusters has been specified to be five, since the human annotators observed five different types of information in the datasets being considered.

7.5.3 Cluster validation indices

There are many approaches to quantify the quality of clusters. Jain and Dubes called the difficulty of determining the number of clusters "the fundamental problem of cluster validity" [79]. Clustering methods divide the dataset's items into a specific number of subsets. Although the number of clusters k is known for some applications, in most cases, k is unknown and must be calculated only from the item itself. Many clustering techniques use k as an input parameter, and it is self-evident that the quality of the resulting clusters is heavily influenced by the estimation of k.

Cluster validation, an important issue in cluster analysis, is the measurement of goodness of a cluster [56] relative to others created by clustering algorithms using different parameter values. Several cluster validation metrics, such as connectedness, separation, compactness, and combinations, use a clustering method and the underlying dataset as inputs and use data intrinsic to the dataset to assess cluster quality. The next sections discuss some of these cluster validation methods.

(A) Compactness
Compactness is an indicator of the scattering of the objects within a particular cluster. It measures cluster compactness or homogeneity, with intra-cluster variance as their most popular representative. Numerous variants of measuring intra-cluster homogeneity are possible such as the evaluation of maximum or average pairwise intra-cluster distances, maximum or average center-based similarities, or the use of graph-based methods.

(B) Connectedness
Connectedness is used to determine how well a given partitioning agrees with the concept of connectedness, that is, to what extent a partitioning considers local density and groups items in the data space with their nearest neighbors.

(C) Separation
Separation is a measure of how isolated clusters are from one another. It determines how far particular clusters are separated. For example, the average weighted inter-cluster distance, where the distance between two distinct clusters is estimated as the distance between cluster centroids or as the min-

imal distance between objects belonging to different clusters, is a generic rating for partitioning.

(D) Combinations of the above measures

The above measures can be combined to measure cluster quality considering multiple aspects. Combinations of compactness and separation are particularly popular, as the two classes of measures show an opposite tendency. Thus, a number of measures assess both inter-cluster separation and intra-cluster homogeneity and calculate a final score as the linear or nonlinear combination of the two measures. Some of these cluster validation measures are discussed below.

Davies–Bouldin validity index: The Davies–Bouldin index (DBIndex) [80] is a function that equals the sum of intra-cluster scatter divided by inter-cluster separation. Let $U = \{X_1, X_2, X_3, X_4, ..., X_k\}$ be the k-cluster obtained by a clustering algorithm. To measure the goodness of the cluster U, the DBIndex is calculated as follows:

$$DBIndex(U) = \frac{1}{K} \sum_{i=1}^{k} \max_{i=j} \left\{ \frac{\Delta(X_i) + \Delta(X_j)}{\delta(X_i, X_j)} \right\}. \tag{7.2}$$

Here, $\Delta(X_i)$ is the intra-cluster distance in X_i, i.e., the distance between the farthest objects in cluster X_i, and $\delta(S, T)$ is the inter-cluster distance of X_i and X_j, i.e., the distance between X_i and X_j.

Dunn's validity index: The Dunn index (D) [81] estimates intra-cluster compactness using the smallest pairwise distance between objects in distinct clusters as the inter-cluster separation and the maximum diameter among all clusters. The Dunn validation index (DN) is determined using Eq. (7.3) for every partition of clusters, where X_i denotes the i-th cluster. Here, $d(X_i, X_j)$ is the distance between clusters X_i and X_j, $d'(X_1)$ is the intra-cluster distance of cluster X_1, and k is the number of clusters. The aim of this measure is to minimize the intra-cluster distances and maximize the inter-cluster distances. As a result, the number of clusters that maximizes D_N is considered the optimal number, where

$$D = \min_{1 \leq i \leq k} \left\{ \min_{1 \leq j \leq k; i \neq j} \left\{ \frac{d(X_i, X_j)}{\max_{1 \leq l \leq k} (d'(X_l))} \right\} \right\}. \tag{7.3}$$

I-index: As illustrated in Eq. (7.4), the I-index (I) [82] evaluates separation based on the maximum distance between cluster centers and compactness based on the sum of distances between objects and their cluster center:

$$I(k) = \left(\frac{1}{k} \cdot \frac{\sum_j \| x_j - \bar{c} \|_2}{\sum_{k=1}^{K} \sum_{j \in c_k} \| x_j - \bar{c} \|_2} \cdot \max_{i,j} \| (c_i - c_j) \| \right)^p.$$ (7.4)

Here the power p is a constant, which normally is set to be 2.

CH-index: The Calinski–Harabasz index (CH) [83] assesses cluster validity using the average sum of squares between and within clusters:

$$CH = \frac{traceB/(K-1)}{traceW/(N-K)},$$ (7.5)

$$traceB = \sum_{k=1}^{K} | C_k | \| \overline{C_k} - \bar{x} \|^2,$$ (7.6)

$$traceW = \sum_{k=1}^{K} \sum_{i=1}^{K} w_{k,i} \| \overline{x_i} - \overline{C_k} \|^2,$$ (7.7)

where N is the number of objects in the dataset, K is number of clusters ($K \in N$), W is the squared differences of all objects in a cluster from their respective cluster center, and B is the error sum of squares between distinct clusters (inter-cluster). The index's most notable feature is that, on the one hand, trace W will begin with a rather big value. As the number of clusters K approaches the ideal clustering solution in K∗ groups, the value should fall dramatically due to increasing cluster compactness. When the optimal solution is reached, an increase in compactness and, as a result, a drop in value may occur; however, this decrease should be noticeably reduced. Trace T, on the other hand, should act in the opposite way, increasing in value as the number of clusters K grows, but relaxing in its rise if K is greater than K∗. The optimal number of clusters is determined by the CH-index's maximum value.

Silhouette index: The Silhouette index (S) [84] assesses clustering performance using the pairwise difference between inter- and intra-cluster distances. Eq. (7.8) shows how the Silhouette index (S) is calculated for k clusters:

$$S = \frac{1}{k} \sum_{i=1}^{k} \frac{b_i - a_i}{max(a_i, b_i)},$$ (7.8)

where a_i is the average dissimilarity of the i-th item to all other objects in the same cluster and b_i is the average dissimilarity of the i-th object to all objects in the nearest cluster. From Eq. (7.8), we can deduce that $-1 \leq SC \leq 1$. If the Silhouette value is close to 1, the sample is considered "well clustered" and assigned to the correct cluster. If the Silhouette value is close to 0, the sample may be assigned to the cluster closest to it, and the sample will be equally far from both. If the Silhouette value is close to -1, the sample is "misclassified" and placed in the middle of the clusters. As a result, the number of clusters with the highest SC-index value is considered the optimal number.

XB-index: The Xie–Beni index (XB) [85] is a fuzzy clustering index that takes advantage of compactness and separation. The compactness-to-separation ratio is taken into account by XB. Eq. (7.9) is a mathematical expression for the XB index for a given dataset X and a partition with K clusters:

$$XB(K) = \frac{V_c(K)/N}{V_s(K)} = \frac{\sum_{n=1}^{N} \sum_{k=1}^{K} u_{k,n}^m \parallel x_n - c_k \parallel^2}{NX \min_{i,j} \parallel c_i - c_j \parallel}, \qquad (7.9)$$

where $V_c(K)$ represents the compactness measure when the dataset is grouped into K clusters, which is given by $\sum_{n=1}^{N} \sum_{k=1}^{K} u_{k,n}^m \parallel x_n - c_k \parallel^2$, where $c_k = \sum_{n=1}^{N} u_{k,n}^m x_n / \sum_{n=1}^{N} u_{k,n}^m$ is the centroid of the k-th cluster. The degree of separation between clusters is represented by $Vs(K)$. In general, the best clustering performance for the dataset X is obtained by solving $\min k \in [2, N-1] XB(K)$.

7.5.4 Comparison of proposed methodology with baselines

Finally, we compare the suggested methodology's performance to that of the baseline approaches discussed earlier. As previously stated, we employ the recommended methodology with the parameters that yield the best results ($w = 0.1$, five or six clusters calculated, GA run for 100 iterations). The number of clusters must be selected a priori for the baseline methods K-means, density-based clustering, and hierarchical clustering, thus we run each baseline algorithm with four, five, and six clusters independently (as we did for the proposed methodology). The Infomap graph clustering algorithm, unlike previous algorithms, does not require the number of clusters as an input.

According to the numerous indicators discussed earlier, Table 7.7 compares the performance of the proposed methodology to that of the baseline approaches. The best performance is displayed in boldface for each metric.

Table 7.7 Comparing the performance of the proposed methodology with that of several baseline clustering methods.

Clustering method	Silhouette	Calinski–Harabasz	DB	I-index	Xie–Beni	Dunn
Proposed method (six clusters, w = 0.1)	**0.989**	35.692	**0.050**	1.245	**0.045**	**10.102**
Proposed method (five clusters, w = 0.1)	0.942	**70.001**	0.312	2.698	0.07114	2.125
K-means (four clusters)	0.633	4.809	0.665	4.414	2.997	1.602
K-means (five clusters)	0.498	3.988	0.688	3.675	52.415	0.981
K-means (six clusters)	0.512	3.810	0.788	3.403	5.36	1.102
Density-based (four clusters)	0.612	4.228	0.789	4.014	5.198	2.148
Density-based (five clusters)	0.799	5.875	0.787	3.989	1.212	1.933
Density-based (six clusters)	0.401	3.405	0.89	3.271	9.136	0.998
Hierarchical (four clusters)	0.801	4.569	0.516	**4.697**	0.454	1.495
Hierarchical (five clusters)	0.812	5.017	0.517	4.590	0.345	1.312
Hierarchical (six clusters)	0.874	4.998	0.478	3.789	0.305	1.301
Infomap (16 communities identified)	0.515	0.847	0.912	0.968	101.8	0.498

All measures except the I–index show that the suggested methodology outperforms all baseline approaches (for which hierarchical clustering achieves the best performance). These findings show that the proposed GA-based strategy for clustering tweets outperforms the competition.

7.6 Conclusion

This method, which is detailed above, is a Twitter clustering methodology that blends an evolutionary approach (GA) with a traditional strategy (K-means). For many years, GA has been widely employed for clustering. To the best of our knowledge, this is the first time GA has been used to cluster Twitter hashtags. This is also the first time hashtags have been clustered without any preprocessing or domain expertise. On a live dataset acquired from Twitter, we tested our proposed new model. This dataset's benchmark results are not available; therefore, we cannot compare our model's outcomes to theirs. The proposed approach outperforms numerous standard clustering approaches, according to the results of the experiments. It has been discovered that GA has the ability to divide a dataset into an unknown number of groups. The use of label-based representation and the use of K-means techniques and strategies improves and enhances the offspring produced by the group-based crossover, and there is no need to fix the cluster numbers. Cluster processing was used to obtain the center point in order to reduce the problem's complexity. We would like to improve the clustering method in the future so that the appropriate number of clusters can be discovered automatically. We also wish to look into different clustering applications, such as summarizing a tweet stream. Clustering microblog data is one of the difficult jobs that might lead to pattern detection and the identification of user potentials and interests, according to the findings of this study. Another difficulty in categorizing microblog data is the dataset's incremental nature. Future study, on the other hand, must demonstrate the effectiveness of dynamic clustering for incremental datasets in order to discover information in an upgraded system.

References

[1] S. Goswami, A.K. Das, Determining maximum cliques for community detection in weighted sparse networks, Knowledge and Information Systems 64 (2) (2022) 289–324, https://doi.org/10.1007/s10115-021-01631-y.

[2] A. Mukherjee, S. Bhattacharyya, K. Ray, B. Gupta, A.K. Das, A study of public sentiment and influence of politics in COVID-19 related tweets, in: A.K. Das, J. Nayak, B. Naik, S. Dutta, D. Pelusi (Eds.), Computational Intelligence in Pattern Recognition, Springer, Singapore, 2022, pp. 655–665.

[3] A. Das, D. Pal, C. Mallick, A.K. Das, An unsupervised COVID-19 report summarizer for developing smart healthcare system, in: A.K. Das, J. Nayak, B. Naik, S. Dutta, D. Pelusi (Eds.), Computational Intelligence in Pattern Recognition, Springer, Singapore, 2022, pp. 157–168.

[4] P. Das, A.K. Das, Convolutional neural networks-based sentence level classification of crime documents, in: A.K. Das, J. Nayak, B. Naik, S. Dutta, D. Pelusi (Eds.), Computational Intelligence in Pattern Recognition, Springer, Singapore, 2022, pp. 65–73.

[5] B.J. Frey, D. Dueck, Clustering by passing messages between data points, Science 315 (2007) 2007.

[6] C. Marc, L.V.C. S, A study on detecting patterns in Twitter intra-topic user and message clustering, in: ICPR, IEEE Computer Society, 2010, pp. 3125–3128, http://dblp.uni-trier.de/db/conf/icpr/icpr2010.html#CheongL10.

[7] T.A. Mariam, R. MG, An efficient text classification scheme using clustering, Procedia Technology 24 (2016) 1220–1225.

[8] Y. Jaewon, L. Jure, Patterns of temporal variation in online media, in: Proceedings of the Fourth ACM International Conference on Web Search and Data Mining, ACM, 2011, pp. 177–186.

[9] K. George, H.E.-H. Sam, V. Kumar, Chameleon: hierarchical clustering using dynamic modeling, Computer 32 (8) (1999) 68–75, https://doi.org/10.1109/2.781637.

[10] C. Mallick, S. Das, A.K. Das, Evolutionary algorithm based summarization for analyzing COVID-19 medical reports, in: J. Nayak, B. Naik, A. Abraham (Eds.), Understanding COVID-19: The Role of Computational Intelligence, in: Studies in Computational Intelligence, Springer International Publishing, Cham, 2022, pp. 31–58.

[11] D. Delbert, Affinity propagation: clustering data by passing messages, PhD thesis, Citeseer, 2009.

[12] R. Aniket, K. Sayali, A.V. Tendulkar, Comparative study of clustering techniques for short text documents, in: Proceedings of the 20th International Conference Companion on World Wide Web, ACM, 2011, pp. 111–112.

[13] C. Zhang, D. Lei, Q. Yuan, H. Zhuang, L.M. Kaplan, S. Wang, J. Han, Geoburst+: effective and real-time local event detection in geo-tagged tweet streams, ACM TIST 9 (3) (2018) 34:1–34:24.

[14] S. Dutta, S. Ghatak, M. Roy, S. Ghosh, A.K. Das, A graph based clustering technique for tweet summarization, in: Reliability, Infocom Technologies and Optimization (ICRITO) (Trends and Future Directions), 2015, pp. 1–6.

[15] B. Sergey, P. Lawrence, The anatomy of a large-scale hypertextual web search engine, Computer Networks and ISDN Systems 30 (1–7) (1998) 107–117, https://doi.org/10.1016/S0169-7552(98)00110-X.

[16] L.F. Rau, P.S. Jacobs, U. Zernik, Information extraction and text summarization using linguistic knowledge acquisition, Information Processing & Management 25 (4) (1989) 419–428, https://doi.org/10.1016/0306-4573(89)90069-1, http://www.sciencedirect.com/science/article/pii/0306457389900691.

[17] R.H. Sheikh, M.M. Raghuwanshi, A.N. Jaiswal, Genetic algorithm based clustering: a survey, in: 2008 First International Conference on Emerging Trends in Engineering and Technology, 2008, pp. 314–319.

[18] U. Maulik, S. Bandyopadhyay, Genetic algorithm-based clustering technique, Pattern Recognition 33 (9) (2000) 1455–1465, https://doi.org/10.1016/S0031-3203(99)00137-5, http://www.sciencedirect.com/science/article/pii/S0031320399001375.

[19] A. Amr, E.F. E, B. Amr, Clustering tweets using cellular genetic algorithm, Journal of Computer Science 10 (2014) 1269–1280.

[20] M.H. Hajeer, A. Singh, D. Dasgupta, S. Sanyal, Clustering online social network communities using genetic algorithms, CoRR, arXiv:1312.2237 [abs], 2013, pp. 90–91, arXiv:1312.2237, http://arxiv.org/abs/1312.2237.

[21] A.C. C, Z. ChengXiang, A survey of text clustering algorithms, in: C.C. Aggarwal, C. Zhai (Eds.), Mining Text Data, Springer, 2012, pp. 77–128, http://dblp.uni-trier.de/db/books/collections/Mining2012.html#AggarwalZ12a.

[22] R. Daniel, D.S. T, D.J. Liebling, Characterizing microblogs with topic models, in: ICWSM, The AAAI Press, 2010, http://dblp.uni-trier.de/db/conf/icwsm/icwsm2010.html#RamageDL10.

[23] G. Yegin, S. Yasuaki, N.J. V, Discovering context: classifying tweets through a semantic transform based on Wikipedia, in: Proceedings of the 6th International Conference on Foundations of Augmented Cognition: Directing the Future of Adaptive Systems, FAC'11, Springer-Verlag, 2011, pp. 484–492.

[24] S. Chattopadhyay, T. Basu, A.K. Das, K. Ghosh, L.C.A. Murthy, Towards effective discovery of natural communities in complex networks and implications in e-commerce, Electronic Commerce Research 21 (4) (2021) 917–954, https://doi.org/10.1007/s10660-019-09395-y.

[25] S. Dutta, S. Ghatak, S. Ghosh, A.K. Das, A genetic algorithm based tweet clustering technique, in: Computer Communication and Informatics (ICCCI), 2017, pp. 1–6.

[26] D. Soumi, G. Sujata, D. Asit, M. Gupta, D. Sayantika, Feature selection based clustering on micro-blogging data, in: International Conference on Computational Intelligence in Data Mining (ICCIDM-2017), 2017, pp. 885–895.

[27] M. Basu, S.D. Bit, S. Ghosh, Utilizing microblogs for optimized real-time resource allocation in post-disaster scenarios, Social Network Analysis and Mining 12 (1) (2021) 15, https://doi.org/10.1007/s13278-021-00841-0.

[28] M.A. Rahman, M.Z. Islam, A hybrid clustering technique combining a novel genetic algorithm with k-means, Knowledge-Based Systems 71 (2014) 345–365, https://doi.org/10.1016/j.knosys.2014.08.011, https://www.sciencedirect.com/science/article/pii/S0950705114002937.

[29] P. Bhattacharya, S. Paul, K. Ghosh, S. Ghosh, A. Wyner, DeepRhole: deep learning for rhetorical role labeling of sentences in legal case documents, Artificial Intelligence and Law (Nov. 2021), https://doi.org/10.1007/s10506-021-09304-5.

[30] K. Hazra, T. Ghosh, A. Mukherjee, S. Saha, S. Nandi, S. Ghosh, S. Chakraborty, Sustainable text summarization over mobile devices: an energy-aware approach, Sustainable Computing: Informatics and Systems 32 (2021) 100607, https://doi.org/10.1016/j.suscom.2021.100607, https://www.sciencedirect.com/science/article/pii/S2210537921000950.

[31] A. Mandal, K. Ghosh, S. Ghosh, S. Mandal, A sequence labeling model for catchphrase identification from legal case documents, Artificial Intelligence and Law (Jul. 2021), https://doi.org/10.1007/s10506-021-09296-2.

[32] M. Basu, K. Ghosh, S. Ghosh, Information retrieval from microblogs during disasters: in the light of IRMiDis task, SN Computer Science 1 (1) (2020) 61, https://doi.org/10.1007/s42979-020-0065-1.

[33] R. Mandal, S. Dutta, R. Banerjee, S. Bhattacharya, R. Ghosh, S. Samanta, T. Saha, City traffic speed characterization based on city road surface quality, in: J.M.R.S. Tavares, P. Dutta, S. Dutta, D. Samanta (Eds.), Cyber Intelligence and Information Retrieval, Springer, Singapore, 2022, pp. 515–524.

[34] G. Satish, T. Durga, P. Nagamma, G. Kumkum, Optimal clustering method based on genetic algorithm, in: D. Kusum, N. Atulya, P. Millie, B.J. Chand (Eds.), Proceedings of the International Conference on Soft Computing for Problem Solving (SocProS 2011), December 20-22, 2011, Springer India, India, 2012, pp. 295–303.

[35] W. Song, S.C. Park, Genetic algorithm-based text clustering technique, in: J. Licheng, W. Lipo, G. Xin-bo, L. Jing, W. Feng (Eds.), Advances in Natural Computation, Springer Berlin Heidelberg, Berlin, Heidelberg, 2006, pp. 779–782.

[36] D. Samanta, S. Dutta, M.G. Galety, S. Pramanik, A novel approach for web mining taxonomy for high-performance computing, in: J.M.R.S. Tavares, P. Dutta, S. Dutta, D. Samanta (Eds.), Cyber Intelligence and Information Retrieval, in: Lecture Notes in Networks and Systems, Springer, Singapore, 2022, pp. 425–432.

[37] A.C. C, Z. ChengXiang, A Survey of Text Clustering Algorithms, Springer US, Boston, MA, 2012, pp. 77–128.

[38] A. Campan, T. Atnafu, T.M. Truta, J. Nolan, Is data collection through Twitter streaming api useful for academic research?, in: 2018 IEEE International Conference on Big Data (Big Data), 2018, pp. 3638–3643.

[39] S. Kumar, K.M. Carley, What to track on the Twitter streaming api? A knapsack bandits approach to dynamically update the search terms, in: 2019 IEEE/ACM International Conference on Advances in Social Networks Analysis and Mining (ASONAM), 2019, pp. 158–163.

[40] K. Tapas, M.D. M, N.N. S, P.C. D, S. Ruth, W.A. Y, An efficient k-means clustering algorithm: analysis and implementation, IEEE Transactions on Pattern Analysis and Machine Intelligence 24 (7) (2002) 881–892, https://doi.org/10.1109/TPAMI.2002.1017616.

[41] M.P. D, M.T. Brendan, Model-based clustering of microarray expression data via latent Gaussian mixture models, Bioinformatics 26 (21) (2010) 2705–2712, https://doi.org/10.1093/bioinformatics/btq498, arXiv:/oup/backfile/content_public/journal/bioinformatics/26/21/10.1093/bioinformatics/btq498/2/btq498.pdf.

[42] H. Efstathiades, D. Antoniades, G. Pallis, M.D. Dikaiakos, Distributed large-scale data collection in online social networks, in: 2016 IEEE 2nd International Conference on Collaboration and Internet Computing (CIC), 2016, pp. 373–380.

[43] A. Dwi Laksito, Kusrini, H. Sismoro, F. Rahmawati, M. Yusa, A comparison study of search strategy on collecting Twitter data for drug adverse reaction, in: 2018 International Seminar on Application for Technology of Information and Communication, 2018, pp. 356–360.

[44] P. Ray, A. Chakrabarti, Twitter sentiment analysis for product review using lexicon method, in: 2017 International Conference on Data Management, Analytics and Innovation (ICDMAI), 2017, pp. 211–216.

[45] K. Jitkajornwanich, C. Kongthong, N. Khongsoontornjaroen, J. Kaiyasuan, S. Lawawirojwong, P. Srestasathiern, S. Srisonphan, P. Vateekul, Utilizing Twitter data for early flood warning in Thailand, in: 2018 IEEE International Conference on Big Data (Big Data), 2018, pp. 5165–5169.

[46] S.H. Archana, S.G. Winster, Drugs categorization based on sentence polarity analyzer for Twitter data, in: 2016 Second International Conference on Science Technology Engineering and Management (ICONSTEM), 2016, pp. 28–33.

[47] T.I. V, L.D. J, L.A. I, Neural network studies. 1. Comparison of overfitting and overtraining, Journal of Chemical Information and Computer Sciences 35 (5) (1995) 826–833, https://doi.org/10.1021/ci00027a006, https://pubs.acs.org/doi/abs/10.1021/ci00027a006.

[48] T. Jagić, L. Brkić, Hot topic detection using Twitter streaming data, in: 2020 43rd International Convention on Information, Communication and Electronic Technology (MIPRO), 2020, pp. 1730–1735.

[49] R. Compton, C. Lee, T.-C. Lu, L. De Silva, M. Macy, Detecting future social unrest in unprocessed Twitter data: "emerging phenomena and big data", in: 2013 IEEE International Conference on Intelligence and Security Informatics, 2013, pp. 56–60.

[50] P. Tatineni, B.S. Babu, B. Kanuri, G.R.K. Rao, P. Chitturi, C. Naresh, Post Covid-19 Twitter user's emotions classification using deep learning techniques in India, in: 2021 International Conference on Artificial Intelligence and Smart Systems (ICAIS), 2021, pp. 338–343.

[51] C. Wang, L. Marini, C.-L. Chin, N. Vance, C. Donelson, P. Meunier, J.T. Yun, Social media intelligence and learning environment: an open source framework for social media data collection, analysis and curation, in: 2019 15th International Conference on eScience (eScience), 2019, pp. 252–261.

[52] N. Gambhava, K. Kotecha, Social media hashtag clustering using genetic algorithm, International Journal of Advanced Research in Engineering and Technology 9 (1) (2018) 12–25.

[53] G.A. Sandag, A.M. Manueke, M. Walean, Sentiment analysis of Covid-19 vaccine tweets in Indonesia using recurrent neural network (rnn) approach, in: 2021 3rd International Conference on Cybernetics and Intelligent System (ICORIS), 2021, pp. 1–7.

[54] C.M. Yoshimura, H. Kitagawa, Tlv-bandit: bandit method for collecting topic-related local tweets, in: 2021 IEEE 4th International Conference on Multimedia Information Processing and Retrieval (MIPR), 2021, pp. 56–62.

[55] A. Nsouli, A. Mourad, D. Azar, Towards proactive social learning approach for traffic event detection based on Arabic tweets, in: 2018 14th International Wireless Communications Mobile Computing Conference (IWCMC), 2018, pp. 1501–1506.

[56] L. Yanchi, L. Zhongmou, X. Hui, G. Xuedong, J. Wu, Understanding of internal clustering validation measures, in: Proceedings of the 2010 IEEE International Conference on Data Mining, ICDM '10, IEEE Computer Society, Washington, DC, USA, 2010, pp. 911–916.

[57] Hyderabad blasts – Wikipedia, http://en.wikipedia.org/wiki/2013_Hyderabad_blasts, February 2013.

[58] Sandy Hook Elementary School shooting – Wikipedia, http://en.wikipedia.org/wiki/Sandy_Hook_Elementary_School_shooting, December 2012.

[59] North India floods – Wikipedia, http://en.wikipedia.org/wiki/2013_North_India_floods, June 2013.

[60] Typhoon Hagupit – Wikipedia, http://en.wikipedia.org/wiki/Typhoon_Hagupit, December 2014.

[61] REST API Resources, Twitter Developers, https://dev.twitter.com/docs/api.

[62] T. Ke, A. Fabian, H. Claudia, G.-J. Houben, G. Ujwal, Groundhog day: near-duplicate detection on Twitter, in: Proc. Conference on World Wide Web (WWW), 2013.

[63] J.A. K, M.M. N, F.P. J, Data clustering: a review, ACM Computing Surveys 31 (3) (1999) 264–323, https://doi.org/10.1145/331499.331504, http://doi.acm.org/10.1145/331499.331504.

[64] C.H. Lee, C.H. Hung, S.J. Lee, A comparative study on clustering algorithms, in: 2013 14th ACIS International Conference on Software Engineering, Artificial Intelligence, Networking and Parallel/Distributed Computing, 2013, pp. 557–562.

[65] S.-R. Sandra, V. Ana, D.R. Rebeca, P.-A. Jose, Comparing tag clustering algorithms for mining Twitter users' interests, in: 2013 International Conference on Social Computing, 2013, pp. 679–684.

[66] P.M. I, Outlier detection algorithms in data mining systems, Programming and Computer Software 29 (4) (2003) 228–237, https://doi.org/10.1023/A:1024974810270.

[67] E. Zhou, S. Mao, M. Li, Z. Sun, Pam spatial clustering algorithm research based on cuda, in: 2016 24th International Conference on Geoinformatics, 2016, pp. 1–7.

[68] K. Ari, M. Nicholas, K. Akshay, M. Andrew, A hierarchical algorithm for extreme clustering, in: Proceedings of the 23rd ACM SIGKDD International Conference on Knowledge Discovery and Data Mining, KDD '17, ACM, New York, NY, USA, 2017, pp. 255–264, http://doi.acm.org/10.1145/3097983.3098079.

[69] S. Das, A. Abraham, A. Konar, Automatic clustering using an improved differential evolution algorithm, IEEE Transactions on Systems, Man and Cybernetics. Part A. Systems and Humans 38 (1) (2008) 218–237, https://doi.org/10.1109/TSMCA.2007. 909595.

[70] D. Manoranjan, P. Simona, S. Peter, Efficient parallel hierarchical clustering, in: D. Marco, V. Marco, L. Domenico (Eds.), Euro-Par 2004 Parallel Processing, Springer Berlin Heidelberg, Berlin, Heidelberg, 2004, pp. 363–371.

[71] S. Guha, K. Shim, R. Rastogi, Rock: a robust clustering algorithm for categorical attributes, in: Proceedings 15th International Conference on Data Engineering (Cat. No. 99CB36337), 1999, pp. 512–521.

[72] S. Guha, R. Rastogi, K. Shim, Cure: an efficient clustering algorithm for large databases, Information Systems 26 (1) (2001) 35–58, https://doi.org/10.1016/S0306-4379(01)00008-4, http://www.sciencedirect.com/science/article/pii/S0306437901000084.

[73] Z. Tian, R. Raghu, L. Miron, Birch: an efficient data clustering method for very large databases, SIGMOD Record 25 (2) (1996) 103–114, https://doi.org/10.1145/235968.233324, http://doi.acm.org/10.1145/235968.233324.

[74] K. L, R.P. J, Finding Groups in Data: an Introduction to Cluster Analysis, Wiley, 1990.

[75] S. Vivek, H.N. Bharathi, Study of density based algorithms, International Journal of Computer Applications 69 (2013) 1–4.

[76] R. Prabahari, D.V. Thiagarasu, Density based clustering using Gaussian estimation technique, in: Density Based Clustering Using Gaussian Estimation Technique, vol. 2, 2015, pp. 4078–4081.

[77] Infomap - community detection, http://www.mapequation.org/code.html.

[78] H. Mark, F. Eibe, H. Geoffrey, P. Bernhard, R. Peter, W.I. H, The WEKA data mining software: an update, SIGKDD Explorations 11 (1) (2009) 10–18.

[79] J.A. K, D.R. C, Algorithms for Clustering Data, Prentice-Hall, Inc., Upper Saddle River, NJ, USA, 1988.

[80] D.D. L, B.D. W, A cluster separation measure, IEEE Transactions on Pattern Analysis and Machine Intelligence 1 (2) (1979) 224–227, https://doi.org/10.1109/TPAMI. 1979.4766909.

[81] U. Maulik, S. Bandyopadhyay, Performance evaluation of some clustering algorithms and validity indices, IEEE Transactions on Pattern Analysis and Machine Intelligence 24 (12) (2002) 1650–1654, https://doi.org/10.1109/TPAMI.2002.1114856.

[82] H. Cui, K. Zhang, Y. Fang, S. Sobolevsky, C. Ratti, B.K.P. Horn, A clustering validity index based on pairing frequency, IEEE Access 5 (2017) 24884–24894, https://doi.org/10.1109/ACCESS.2017.2743985.

[83] R. Xu, J. Xu, D.C. Wunsch, A comparison study of validity indices on swarm-intelligence-based clustering, IEEE Transactions on Systems, Man and Cybernetics. Part B. Cybernetics 42 (4) (2012) 1243–1256, https://doi.org/10.1109/TSMCB.2012.2188509.

[84] R. Peter, Silhouettes: a graphical aid to the interpretation and validation of cluster analysis, Journal of Computational and Applied Mathematics 20 (1) (1987) 53–65, https://doi.org/10.1016/0377-0427(87)90125-7.

[85] M. Mai, H. Katsuhiro, N. Akira, Xie-beni-type fuzzy cluster validation in fuzzy co-clustering of documents and keywords, in: Y.I. Cho, E.T. Matson (Eds.), Soft Computing in Artificial Intelligence, Springer International Publishing, Cham, 2014, pp. 29–38.

PART 3

Attribute selection to improve spam classification

CHAPTER 8

Feature selection-based microblog clustering technique

8.1 Introduction

In recent times, microblogging has become a huge source of real-time information. During any important event such as a natural calamity, elections, and sports event like IPL and the world cup, thousands of messages are posted on microblogging sites. The fast information exchange of microblogging sites can cause information overload. Microblogging posts contain at most 140 characters [1]. They also contain noisy and redundant data. In recent years, online social networks have grown in popularity. Microblog platforms like Sina and Twitter have grown in importance as real-time information sources for breaking news, information sharing, and event participation [2]. This service allows users to communicate their thoughts and objectives in tiny textual snippets on a daily or even hourly basis. When it comes to use, users frequently have to sift through a vast amount of data in order to get what they are looking for. Creating a logical cluster hierarchy for a microblog corpus can thus be a crucial step in organizing these brief, ambiguous, and even non-specific microblogs [3]. In recent years, much effort has been put into clustering microblog corpora using machine learning approaches. Semi-supervised clustering, which uses minimal previous knowledge to help with unsupervised clustering, has recently attracted attention of the data mining and machine learning community. Researchers have proposed a number of methods for the clustering of microblogs. Some researchers experiment with semi-supervised priors to see how they affect clustering accuracy. Microblogs are notorious for lacking label information, and labeling the massive volumes of messages takes time and effort [4]. Given the high cost of obtaining supervised data, it is critical to design a system for automatically obtaining informative information in order to increase clustering performance. Microblog research has been increasingly popular in recent years in the field of text mining. To cluster microblog messages, several typical studies simply use certain traditional unsupervised learning approaches [5]. These methods are unable to address the flaws of microblog data, such as its high dimension and sparseness. Microblog research has been increasingly popular in recent years in the field

Data Analytics for Social Microblogging Platforms
https://doi.org/10.1016/B978-0-32-391785-8.00021-4

of text mining. To cluster microblog messages, several typical studies simply use certain traditional unsupervised learning approaches. These methods are unable to address the flaws of microblog data, such as its high dimension and sparseness [6–8].

For our experiment, we considered a Twitter streaming dataset which was obtained using the Twitter API [9]. Twitter facilitates searching by keywords or topics to identify related tweets. It is not possible for any user to go through all the posts/tweets related to a topic. Using common feature engineering techniques, a significant number of features to represent tweets are regularly generated. Many of these characteristics have the potential to diminish classifier performance while also increasing computing costs. Feature selection strategies can be used to pick an appropriate subset of features, potentially lowering the computing cost of training a classifier and boosting classification performance [5]. Despite its advantages, feature selection in the context of tweet sentiment has received little attention. Because of the variety of tweets, feature engineering approaches for Twitter data might potentially yield tens of thousands of features, although each instance will only have a handful of the total feature set (the remaining features will be blank) because tweets are limited to 140 characters. Feature selection algorithms choose a subset of features, reducing the amount of time it takes to classify tweets. Furthermore, by removing duplicate or unnecessary features and avoiding overfitting, feature selection can improve classifier performance [10]. In such a scenario, an effective way to reduce the information load on the user is to group similar posts, so that the user might see only a few messages in each cluster. Another challenge of microblogging data is the large volumes, which increase the time necessary to cluster the data into sub-groups. Selected features which represent the characteristics of the cluster can be identified from each cluster. Feature selection focuses on reduction of overfitting. Feature selection employs dimensionality reduction for a given dataset where selected features are the important features which are sufficient to represent the dataset independently. This reduced dimension of the dataset can also reduce the clustering time effectively. Clustering also makes the data summarization task easier, which is another well-established problem in information retrieval [11].

In the proposed clustering approach, a dataset is preprocessed first. Latent Dirichlet allocation (LDA) [12] is a generative process that can be used to identify the features capable of identifying a topic in the dataset, and the returned list of features can be used to represent each topic in the entire dataset. The Hamming distance is used to identify clusters. A minimal distance-valued cluster is determined as the target cluster for that data tuple after Hamming distance is measured between each topic-feature vector and a data tuple. Using this approach the entire dataset can be clustered into multiple groups [13].

The proposed clustering approach was applied over a microblogs dataset related to four disaster events. Classical clustering methods such as K-means and hierarchical clustering are also applied on the same dataset. The performance of the different algorithms is evaluated using the standard clustering index measure. As a whole, the proposed approach achieves better performance than the classical methods for the microblogging dataset [14].

The rest of the chapter is organized as follows. A short literature survey on clustering of microblogging datasets is presented in Section 8.2. Section 8.3 describes the proposed clustering approach. The microblog datasets used for the algorithm are described in Section 8.4, while Section 8.5 discusses the results of the comparison among the various clustering algorithms. The paper is concluded in Section 8.6 with some potential future research directions.

8.2 Related work

Many prior works have been conducted on microblogging data clustering. Hill et al. [15] discuss how social network-based clusters can capture homophily along with the possibility that a network-based attribute approach might not only capture homophily but can also be used instead of demographic attributes to determine the similarity in user behavior, thus preserving privacy of the user-base.

Cheong [16] attempts to detect intra-topic user and message clusters in Twitter by incorporating an unsupervised self-organizing feature map as a machine learning-based clustering tool. Thomas et al. [17] propose an efficient text classification scheme using clustering based on semi-supervised clustering as a complementary step to text classification. The method provides better accuracy than the similarity measure for text processing used for distance calculation.

Yang and Leskovec [18] have proposed a clustering method using temporal patterns of propagation. Karypis et al. [19] propose a hierarchical clustering algorithm using dynamic modeling which takes into account the dynamic modes of clusters and the adaptive merging decision, that is, depending upon the difference in clustering model it can discover natural clusters of various shapes and sizes. It sports a two-phase framework that has been built effectively using various graph representations suitable for various application domains.

Dueck et al. [20] propose an affinity propagation algorithm for clustering tweets. Dutta et al. [21] use a graph-based community detection algorithm for clustering tweets and then use the clustering output for summarization. Recently, Rangrej et al. [22] conducted a comparative study on three clustering algorithms – K-means, affinity propagation, and singular value decomposition – and compared their performance in clustering short text documents. Apart from clustering, Gencet et al. [23] used a Wikipedia-based classification technique to categorize tweets considering semantic distance as classification metric to evaluate distance between their closest Wikipedia pages. Using a genetic algorithm-based approach, Soumi et al. [24] proposed a method to categorize microblogging data. In another work, Soumi et al. [25] proposed a feature selection-based clustering algorithm which can increase the effectiveness of clustering.

The authors of [26] focused on the weighted graph clustering algorithm for community detection in large-scale networks, such as user relationships on online social networks. They presented a graph clustering technique based on the concept of density and attractiveness for weighted networks, including node weight and edge weight, because most networks in the actual world are weighted networks. They also defined the user's core degree as node weight and users' attractiveness as edge weight after conducting deep analysis on the Sina microblog user network and the Renren social network. Ruifang et al. then conducted community detection experiments with the algorithm, with the results confirming the algorithm's effectiveness and reliability.

The goal of another study [27] was to examine and compare interaction patterns across various social networks. Authors did this by analyzing Renren, China's largest online social network, and Sina Weibo, China's most popular microblog service. Because of the asymmetry of user interactions, they characterized interaction networks as unidirectional weighted graphs. Following this concept, they looked at the fundamental interaction patterns first. Then the authors looked at whether the weak ties hypothesis holds true in these interaction graphs and how it affected information dispersion. Furthermore, the authors simulated the temporal patterns of user interactions and used the temporal patterns to cluster people. Their findings showed that, while users on both sites had some similar interaction patterns, Sina Weibo users were more popular and diversified. Furthermore, the results of the study and simulations demonstrated that Sina Weibo was a more efficient medium for disseminating information. These findings provided the researchers with knowledge on how people engage on different social platforms and can be used to create more efficient information dissemination systems.

Another study [28] used density-based clustering to detect communities in social networks. The authors compared two well-known concepts for community detection, structural similarity of nodes, and the number of interactions between nodes, which were implemented as distance functions in the algorithms SCAN [29] and DEN-GRAPH [30], respectively, in order to assess the advantages and limitations of these approaches. Furthermore, Subramani et al. proposed using a hierarchical technique for clustering to avoid the challenge of determining an acceptable density threshold for community detection, which was a major drawback of the SCAN and DENGRAPH algorithms in real-world applications. All of their tests were executed on datasets with varying features, such as Twitter and Enron data.

Traditional matching algorithms are insufficiently adept at matching users within social networks due to the rapid growth in the number of users utilizing social networks and the information that a social network demands about its users. Another study [31] introduced the use of clustering to create user communities, which were subsequently used to generate matches. Forming communities inside a social network helped to limit the number of users that the matching system must examine, as well as other issues that social networks face, such as the lack of knowledge about a new user's actions. A dataset taken from an online dating website was used to test the suggested approach. Empirical research suggested that using community data improves the accuracy of the matching process.

The goal of another study [32] was to offer a paradigm for node clustering in computerized social networks based on shared interests. In such networks, communities were primarily generated by user selection, which can be based on a variety of variables such as friendship, social position, and educational background. Such selection, however, may result in groupings with a low degree of resemblance. By building clusters of nodes with high interest similarity, the suggested framework could improve the effectiveness of these social networks, maximizing the advantage that users derive from their involvement. The framework was built on methods for finding communities in weighted networks, with graph edge weights determined by measurements of similarity between nodes' interests in specific subject areas. With actual benchmark situations over synthetic networks, the ability of these techniques to improve the sensitivity and resolution of community detection was examined. Authors also utilized the framework to determine the extent to which sample users of a popular online social application share common interests. Their findings showed that clusters produced via user selection had modest degrees of similarity, suggesting that their framework could be useful in establishing communities with greater interest coherence.

Clustering nodes in a graph is a common data mining technique for big network datasets. In this regard, Newman and Girvan [33] recently presented the Q function, an objective function for graph clustering that allows for automated cluster number selection. High Q function values have been empirically demonstrated to correspond strongly with good network clustering. The authors of [34] illustrated how to rewrite optimizing the Q function as a spectrum relaxation problem in this study, and they presented two new spectral clustering methods that aim to maximize Q. The new methods were efficient and successful in finding both good clustering and the proper number of clusters across a variety of real-world network datasets, according to experimental results. Furthermore, spectral techniques were substantially faster for large sparse graphs, scaling generally linearly with the number of nodes n in the graph, unlike $O(n^2)$ for prior clustering algorithms based on the Q function.

Statistical features of networked systems such as social networks and the World Wide Web have been the subject of a number of recent studies. The small-world property, power-law degree distributions, and network transitivity are among the properties that appear to be common to many networks, according to researchers. In this article, we will look at another characteristic of many networks: community structure, in which network nodes are grouped together in tightly knit groups with only loose connections between them. The authors of [35] presented a method for discovering such communities based on the idea of finding community boundaries using centrality indices. They put their method to the test on computer-generated and real-world graphs with established community structures, and they found that it detected them with excellent sensitivity and reliability. They also used the approach to detect substantial and informative community divisions in two networks whose community structure is unknown: a cooperation network and a food web.

In many areas, including as social sciences, engineering, and biology, automatic discovery of community structures in complicated networks is a critical challenge. To efficiently assess the quality of community structures, a quantitative metric called modularity (Q) has been developed. Since then, a number of communities finding methods have been created based on optimization of Q. This optimization problem, however, is NP-hard, and existing solutions are either inaccurate or computationally expensive. The authors of [36] presented an efficient spectral technique for modularity optimization in their study. When compared to existing algorithms and tested on a large number of synthetic or real-world networks, their solution was efficient and accurate. They also used that algorithm to find fascinating and important community structures in real-world networks in a variety of fields, including biology, medicine, and social sciences.

In many instances, dense subgraphs of sparse graphs (communities), which are present in most real-world complex networks, play a key role. However, computing them is often costly. Latapy et al. [37] proposed a measure of vertex similarity based on random walks that had several important advantages: it captures well the community structure in a network, it can be computed quickly, it works at different scales, and it can be used in an agglomerative algorithm to compute the community structure of a network efficiently.

The authors of [38] proposed a novel approach for analyzing a social network represented as a net of microblogging accounts in this research. They detected not just the most popular topics on which users are providing their perspectives, but also the groups of people who chat about certain topic clusters, based on hashtags in user postings. They offered a novel hashtags filtration model and a community graph creation strategy to handle this problem, which was then employed by the community structures recognition algorithm. On three very large real-life (not synthetic) datasets, they validated their method. There were around 10^7 microblogging postings in each of them, with about 10^6 different hashtags. They also looked at the model's scalability, comparing how it performs when applied to a small number of randomly selected subsets versus the entire dataset. Their approach was a scalable filtering method that can generate graphs in which communities with shared interests can be identified. The crucial point to remember is that in their datasets, the minimum random sample size above which they might see a fairly comparable distribution of vertices and edge weights was 10% of the total followers.

Researchers have been interested in the community-based structure of communication on social networking platforms. However, the difficulty of discovering and describing hidden communities, as well as determining the appropriate level of user aggregation, remains unsolved. Online community research has evident social ramifications because it allows for the assessment of preference-based user grouping and the detection of socially dangerous groupings. The goal of this research is to compare and contrast techniques for analyzing huge user networks and extracting hidden user communities. The results demonstrate which algorithms are most appropriate for Twitter datasets of various sizes (dozens of thousands, hundreds of thousands, and millions of tweets). The authors of [39] show that the Infomap and Leiden algorithms produce the best overall results, and we recommend combining them for discovering discursive communities based on user attributes or viewpoints. We also show that the generalized K-means algorithm is ineffective on large datasets, whereas a variety of other algorithms prioritize the discovery of a single large community over many that would better reflect reality.

Data mining and intelligent processing are becoming increasingly crucial as the big data era progresses, and modeling based on unique intelligent processing is required. Because of the brief nature of microblog posts, as well as their linguistic unreliability and lexical incompleteness, it is important to analyze and cluster comparable posts together for further data mining and recommendation. One study [40] used the K-means clustering algorithm to partition the huge data into the corresponding k groups and then proposed a novel modeling approach to partition the big data into the corresponding k groups.

With the rapid advancement of computer science and technology, it has become a big issue for users to obtain relevant or required information rapidly. People can use text categorization to answer this question. In the subject of automatic text categorization, feature selection has become one of the most important strategies. One study [41] proposed a new technique of text feature selection based on information gain and a genetic algorithm. This method selected a feature based on the amount of information gained in conjunction with the frequency of items. Meanwhile, for information filtering systems, this method's fitness function was modified to completely incorporate weight, text, and vector similarity dimension, among other factors. The experiments showed that the strategy can reduce the size of the text vector and enhance the text classification precision.

Feature selection is a procedure that extracts a number of feature subsets from the original feature set that are the most indicative of the original meaning. Because some data outliers are removed, it considerably decreases text processing time and improves accuracy. With the rapid development of Web 2.0 and the continued expansion of the Internet, brief texts such as microblogs have become increasingly significant in people's daily lives. Existing feature selection approaches, on the other hand, are unable to extract these short text features efficiently, resulting in a significant reduction in short text classification and clustering performance. The authors of [42] proposed a new feature selection method based on part of speech and HowNet in this regard. They identified words with more information via different parts of speech depending on the composition of the text property, and then enhanced the semantic properties of these words using HowNet, giving brief text more valuable qualities. To examine the effects of brief text classification, they employed a test dataset gathered from a Sina microblog and applied F1-Measure's micro- and macroaverages. The results suggested that the short text feature chosen by our method contains a significant amount of information and produces accurate classification results.

Seyednaser et al. [43] proposed a term labeling-based technique for interactive text documents. The user was asked to cluster the top keyterms linked with document clusters iteratively by the algorithm. The clustering approach was guided by the keyterm clusters. They presented a new text clusterer that used word clusters instead of typical clustering techniques. The terms in a document corpus were grouped together. The term clusters were distilled using a greedy technique to remove non-discriminative broad terms. Then, for each distilled term cluster, they described a heuristic strategy for extracting seed documents. Finally, these seeds were utilized to group all papers. On some real-world text datasets, they compared interactive term labeling to a baseline interactive term selection system. Their term labeling was more effective than the baseline term selection approach with an equal amount of user effort, according to the trials.

Identifying a subset of the most valuable features that gives the same results as the whole collection of features is what feature selection entails. A feature selection algorithm can be assessed in terms of both efficiency and efficacy. While efficiency refers to the amount of time it takes to locate a subset of features, effectiveness refers to the subset's quality. Another work [44] proposed and experimentally evaluated a fast clustering-based feature selection method (FAST) based on these criteria. The FAST algorithm was split into two parts. Graph theoretic clustering methods were used to partition characteristics into clusters in the initial stage. The most representative feature from each cluster that was strongly related to target classes was chosen in the second stage to construct a subset of features. Because the properties in various clusters are relatively independent, FAST's clustering-based technique was likely to produce a subset of valuable and independent features. Authors used the efficient minimum-spanning tree clustering method to ensure FAST's efficiency. An empirical study was used to assess the FAST algorithm's efficiency and efficacy.

The development of current scientific data collection techniques has resulted in a massive accumulation of data from various sectors. Cluster analysis is a popular data analysis technique. It is the technique of recognizing groupings of similar things in massive datasets without using explicit features to group them. When the clusters are of varied sizes, densities, and shapes, spotting them can be difficult. This research presents a novel technique for density-based clustering. Another work [45] took a new approach to discovering clusters that exist within a cluster, based on DBSCAN, which was regarded a pioneer of density-based clustering techniques. The technique was evaluated based on several criteria such as the number of clusters produced, noise ratio on distance change, time elapsed to build a cluster, unclustered instances, and wrongly clustered instances.

Data mining and intelligent processing are becoming increasingly crucial as the big data era unfolds, and modeling on novel processed big data is required. Because of the short text qualities of microblog posts and the linguistic unreliability of their features, it is important to analyze and cluster these comparable posts together for data mining and recommendation. The K-means clustering algorithm was used in a study [46], and then a novel modeling approach was used to partition the microblog entries into the appropriate k comparable groups. In addition, a two-phase iteration feature selection approach was developed. A clustering algorithm was proposed based on this paradigm. The suggested approach made advantage of the partition concept to avoid outliers and noise in the data. Finally, to summarize each individual cluster, a proposed cluster abstractive summarization approach was provided. Users can quickly learn the most important information about a cluster based on this. The experiment demonstrated the practicality of the approach, and some existing issues and future work were also discussed.

Yan et al. [47] employed AGNES to create a subject hierarchy and successfully organize the texts. They showed that hierarchical clustering of tweets paired with a text length- and structure-based filtering procedure yields good results. In AGNES, the number of clusters is automatically decided by the features of the data, which is a significant benefit in the face of a microblog with a wide range of topics. However, it encounters two issues: (1) processing the large-scale microblog takes too long and (2) some faults that occur easily at the start of the algorithm are difficult to remedy due to the method's irreversible process.

Table 8.1 Document-term matrix for the toy dataset shown in Table 8.4.

Tweet ID	attr$_1$	attr$_2$	attr$_3$	...	...	attr$_Z$
T_1	1	1	1	0	0	0
T_2	1	0	0	1	1	1
T_3	1	0	0	1	0	0
T_4	1	0	0	0	0	0
T_5	1	0	0	0	0	1
..	0	0	1	0	0	1
T_M	0	0	0	1	1	0

8.3 Microblog clustering algorithms

8.3.1 Data preprocessing

Microblogging data often contains non-textual characters like smileys, @usernames, exclamation/question marks, etc., which act as noise and reduce clustering performance. So datasets need to be preprocessed. Initially, stopwords, URLs, numerals, addresses, user mentions, emails, and special characters are removed from the dataset.

This section describes the proposed methodology in detail. Each tuple in the dataset represents a single message or post or tweet (document) on Twitter. The whole dataset is tokenized first and a list of unique tokens are identified. Then a document-term matrix is generated where rows (M) represent individual tweets and the columns represent distinct terms/tokens (Z). The entries in the matrix represent the presence (1) or absence (0) of a particular term/token in the post/tweet. Table 8.4 shows the corresponding matrix for the set of tweets in Table 8.1.

Next, the dimension of the document-term matrix is reduced using an information theoretic approach. So, for each term/token, conditional probability (p-values) is evaluated using Bayes' rule. The standard formula for Bayes' rule is

$$P(H \mid E) = \frac{[P(E \mid H) * P(H)]}{P(E)}. \tag{8.1}$$

Here H indicates the occurrence of a token in the entire dataset and E indicates the occurrence of a token in all tweets.

Then, the mean p-value is computed and compared with the p-value of each individual term/token. Terms/tokens are discarded from the document-term matrix whose p-value is higher than the mean p-value.

Table 8.2 Reduced document-term matrix.

Tweet ID	$attr_1$	$attr_2$	$attr_5$	...	$attr_G$
T_1	1	1	0	0	0
T_2	1	0	1	1	1
T_3	1	0	1	0	0
T_4	1	0	0	0	0
T_5	1	0	0	0	1
..	0	0	1	0	1
T_M	0	0	1	1	0

According to Shannon's theory of communication, the mean p-value represents the average information yield [48]. The method derived by Shannon clearly states that the token with a lower p-value yields a higher self-information content, as shown in Eq. (8.2). Now a new subset of terms/tokens and a new document-term matrix(M x G) are regenerated, as shown in Table 8.2. We have

$$I(W_n) = f(P(W_n)). \qquad (8.2)$$

The proposed algorithm aims to cluster the dataset. The methodology is briefly outlined in Algorithm 8.1. Before clustering we are considering a topic modeler approach to identify the probable number of clusters. So, the LDA topic modeler is used here which is a generative process that can be used to identify the features capable of identifying a topic in the dataset [49]. LDA is a statistical generative process that takes three inputs, n (the number of topics), α, and θ (α and θ are hyperparameters, i.e., parameters of prior distribution), and returns n-tuples, where each tuple represents a topic and its corresponding features are used to identify the topic. The overall run-time complexity [50] of LDA is $O((NT)^t(N+t)^3)$.

The expression is a polynomial in nature when the total number of topics is constant. The inference function belongs to the NP-hard class of problems when the number of topics is large. The number of topics is relatively small in our experimental datasets and thus LDA performs well [51]. If the number of topics is large for any dataset, the performance of the LDA algorithm may decline. The inference function, thus, has to be augmented in such a way that the LDA algorithm performs better even if the number of topics becomes significantly large for a dataset.

Algorithm 8.1 Microblogging data clustering algorithm based on feature selection

---

Require: L tweets
Ensure: Tweets partitioned into T clusters.
    Preprocess all tweets in the dataset by removing stopwords, special characters, user mentions, URLs, Emails;
    Stem all the tokens;
    Create the corpus C as the list of unique tokens that forms the entire dataset;
    Let N = distinct number of tokens in corpus;
    Compute DM = document-term matrix of order L x N;
    for each token in C **do**
        Compute p-value using conditional probability of occurrence of each term by Bayes rule;
    end for
    Calculate the mean p-value(mp);
    for all $C_i, i \in [1, L]$ **do**
        Remove token if p > mp
    end for
    Reform the document-term matrix (DM) based on the new reduced corpus;
    Use Bayesian inference to compute the parameters alpha and theta from DM;
    z= Number of zero elements in DM;
    N= Total number of elements in DM;
    P(z) = z/N;
    P(Nz) = 1-P(z) where Nz;
    Calculate number of topics T = ceiling [length (C) / P(Nz)];
    Run LDA(T, alpha, theta) and store feature/topic in list FL;
    Prepare document-feature matrix (D);
    Prepare F, a feature matrix that maps each feature per topic with respect to the total features returned by LDA;
    i,j=0
    while data in D **do**
        for all $vector_i, i \in [1, F]$ **do**
            Calculate Hamming distance between data and vector as d = Hamming (data, $vector_i$);
            Update the Distances[i][j++] vector with the Hamming distance, d;
        end for
        for all $row_i, i \in [1, Distances]$ **do**
            Calculate and store the mean value of the present row in list row–mean
        end for
    end while
    while data in D **do**
        for all $x, x \in [0, distance]$ **do**
            for all $v, v \in [0, x]$ **do**
                if v <= row-mean [index(x)] **then**
                    Mark and store corresponding tweet to cluster c = index(row-mean)
                else
                    Continue
                end if
            end for
        end for
    end while

Table 8.3   Topic feature matrix.

Tweet ID	$attr_1$	$attr_2$	$attr_5$	...	$attr_K$
$Topic_1$	0	1	1	0	0
$Topic_2$	1	0	1	0	1
$Topic_3$	0	1	1	0	1
$Topic_K$	1	1	0	0	0

To apply LDA on the experimental dataset, we need to measure α and θ using the Bayesian inference function:

$$p(\widetilde{x} \mid X, \alpha) = \int_{\theta} p(\widetilde{x} \mid \theta) p(\theta \mid X, \alpha) d\theta. \qquad (8.3)$$

With the help of the information theoretic approach (Shannon's approach), the optimal number of groups into which a text dataset can be divided is determined. Using Shannon's formula for calculating the information yield of a particular message, we have reduced the total number of features that are initially generated by extracting the corpus from the dataset, i.e., the number of unique features that can be used to represent the entire dataset. This number can be used as the optimal number of topics to be detected from the dataset [52].

We compute this value as an inverse probability of zero elements. That is, if in the document-term matrix the total number of elements is N and the total number of zeros is K, then the probability of occurrence of zeros can be calculated as I=K/N as the event is an independent one. Thus the probability of occurrence of non-zero elements would be T=1-I. The optimal number of topics is then derived as ceiling = [length (corpus) / T].

The LDA method not only identifies the topics but also returns a list of reduced features (term/token) that can be used to represent the entire dataset and also to reduce the size of data that can later be processed by the clustering algorithm. LDA returns the list of reduced features K. Then a topic-feature matrix (F) is generated considering T x K dimensions, where T is the total number of topics and K is the total number of features. If a feature f is present in a topic, the attribute is marked as 1; otherwise, it is marked as 0. Table 8.3 shows the corresponding matrix.

Considering LDA-computed features, another smaller document-feature matrix (D) is generated to represent the tweets as binary vectors. The document-feature matrix is an L x K matrix where L is the total number of tweets and K is the total number of features. The matrix is formed using the same principle as the document-feature matrix is prepared [53].

In the topic-feature matrix F, each row of the matrix represents a feature vector to describe a particular topic. To identify the tweet topic, the correlation mean Hamming distance is measured for each topic considering the mean distance between all tweet vectors in the document-feature matrix (D) and each topic vector in the topic-feature matrix (F). Each tweet is assigned to that topic/cluster whose tweet–topic Hamming distance is less than or equal to the mean distance value. The proposed clustering algorithm is based on a greedy approach [54]. All the tweets are assigned to distinct clusters; the overlapping clustering concept is not considered in the proposed approach.

8.4 Dataset for clustering algorithms

We have collected data from Twitter using the API [9] with keyword-based matching. Keywords like "Uttarakhand" and "flood" were used to select tweets relevant to the Uttarakhand flood. Similarly, keywords "Hyderabad," "bomb," and "blast" were used to extract tweets related to the HDBlast event, and the keywords "Sandyhook" and "shooting" were used to identify tweets related to the SHShoot event. We have chosen tweets related to a specific event during natural disasters and social emergencies. In this section the datasets are described briefly which were used for clustering algorithms [55].

We considered tweets posted during the following emergency events.
1. **HDBlast** – Two bomb explosions occurred in the city of Hyderabad, India [56].
2. **SHShoot** – An assailant killed 20 children and 6 adults at Sandy Hook Elementary School in Connecticut, USA [57].
3. **THagupit** – A strong cyclone code-named Typhoon Hagupit hit the Philippines [58].
4. **UFlood** – Devastating floods and landslides occurred in the Uttaranchal state of India [59].

Table 8.4 gives examples of tweets on Hagupit Typhoon.

8.5 Experimental results

We describe the experimental results in this section. The proposed approach is compared here with several classical clustering methods such as K-means and hierarchical clustering algorithms. To compare the performance of the proposed clustering algorithm, we have used a few clustering

Table 8.4 Examples of tweets related to the Hagupit Typhoon event.

Tweet ID	Example tweets (extract from tweet text)
T_1	JTWC forecasts 22W (#Hagupit) to be near Yap by Thursday as 70-knot typhoon. Who'll bet it is more like 140-knots? http://t.co/lkGOJBcwOG
T_2	The maximum storm surge height is 0.1 m in #Colonia, Micronesia. This height is estimated for 04 Dec 2014 03 HOURS UTC #HAGUPIT #22W
T_3	CURRENT INFRARED IMAGE OF TROPICAL DEPRESSION #22W (#HAGUPIT) http://t.co/tJLPGlC3wR
T_4	#CHINA (CMA) SAYS, #HAGUPIT TO HIT #PHILLIPPINES WITH MAXIMUM WIND SPEED OF 245 KM/H (CAT-4 HURRICANE) ON 06 DEC 2014 http://t.co/Q9AVnae896
T_5	#Hagupit Predicted Path/Track of #TyphoonHagupit http://t.co/ms4VpDwyTQ http://t.co/DMBJgdGIAO

methods like (1) K-means clustering and (2) hierarchical clustering on the tweet dataset. K-means is an unsupervised learning algorithm which follows a simple and easy method to classify a given dataset through a number of clusters. Hierarchical clustering involves creation of clusters that have ordering from top to bottom. The widely used toolkit Weka was used for the above-mentioned methodologies.

Two common clustering algorithms for document clustering are agglomerative hierarchical clustering and K-means. Although slower, agglomerative hierarchical clustering is frequently presented as "better" than K-means. Scatter/Gather, a document browsing system based on clustering, uses a hybrid technique that includes both K-means and agglomerative hierarchical clustering in the document domain [60]. Because of its efficiency, K-means is used, while agglomerative hierarchical clustering is used for its quality [61]. The clustering approaches developed in this chapter (as stated in the earlier sections of this chapter) are compared with a few classical clustering methods – K-means and hierarchical clustering. The details of the clustering approaches are given below.

Partition-based clustering

Given a dataset of n objects, a partitioning method [62] constructs k ($k \leq n$) clusters disjoint to each other. The algorithm classifies the data into k groups, which together satisfy the following: (1) each group must contain at least one object and (2) each object must belong to exactly one group (hard clustering). The algorithms generally use some iterative relocation technique based on some objective function that attempts to improve the partitioning by moving objects from one cluster to another. The general criterion of a good partitioning is that objects in the same group are closed to each other, whereas objects of different clusters are distant from each other [63]. There are several kinds of other criteria [64] for judging the quality of clusters. Some common partition-based clustering is described below.

K-means clustering

The K-means clustering algorithm is one of the most commonly used unsupervised learning algorithms [65,66]. It follows a simple iterative method to cluster a dataset into k clusters, where k is set a priori. The first step is to define k centers, one for each cluster. These centers should be positioned intelligently, because different locations may lead to different results. So the best choice is to place them at the maximum possible distance apart from each other. The next step is to consider each object belonging to a given dataset and associate it to the nearest center. When no object is pending, the first step is finished and an early clustering is done. At this point, k new centers are computed by calculating means of the k clusters obtained in the earlier step, and these new centers are set as centers of the clusters [67]. After these k new centers are obtained, a new binding has to be done between the same objects and the nearest new centroid. During execution of the loop, k centers modify their position step by step until the algorithm converges.

Unfortunately, there is no universal theoretical method to find the desired number of clusters for any given dataset. A simple approach is to compare the results of several executions with different k values and choose the best one according to a given criterion. However, one needs to be careful because, by definition, increasing k results in reduced error function values, but higher k values simultaneously increase the risk of overfitting [68].

Hierarchical clustering

Hierarchical clustering algorithms [69,70] organize the objects of the given dataset into a hierarchical structure according to the proximity matrix. The hierarchical clustering results are usually depicted by a *dendrogram*. The root node of the dendrogram represents the whole dataset and every leaf node is considered as an object [71]. The intermediate nodes, thus, describe the extent to which the objects are proximal to each other, and the height of the dendrogram usually expresses the distance between each pair of clusters or objects or a cluster and an object. The clustering can be obtained by cutting the dendrogram at different levels.

The hierarchical clustering algorithms are generally classified as agglomerative methods and divisive methods [69,70]. Agglomerative clustering starts with N clusters and each of them includes exactly one object. A series of merge operations then follow that finally leads to all objects being included in the same group. On the other hand, divisive clustering proceeds in a reverse direction. At the primary step, the whole dataset belongs to one cluster and then the items are successively divided until all clusters are singleton clusters.

In recent years, with the requirement for handling large-scale datasets in data mining and other fields, many new hierarchical clustering techniques such as CURE [72], ROCK [73], Chameleon [19], and BIRCH [74] have appeared and greatly improved the clustering performance. Though divisive clustering is not commonly used in practice, some of its applications can be found in [75]. Two divisive clustering algorithms, namely MONA and DIANA, are described in [75].

8.5.1 Cluster validation indices

There are a set of standard metrics [76] to evaluate the quality of clustering produced by the different methodologies. Jain and Dubes called the difficulty of determining the number of clusters "the fundamental problem of cluster validity" [77]. The clustering algorithms partition objects of the dataset into a particular number of subsets. Although for several applications the number of clusters k is known, in most of the cases, k is unknown and needs to be estimated exclusively from the object itself. Many clustering algorithms take k as an input parameter, and it is obvious that the quality of resulting clusters is largely dependent on the estimation of k.

Two measurements of cluster "goodness" or quality are employed for clustering. Internal quality measures are a form of metric that allows us to compare different sets of clusters without relying on external knowledge. We will employ an "overall similarity" measure based on the pairwise similarity of documents in a cluster, as indicated in the previous section. The other form of measure compares the groups produced by clustering techniques to recognized classes, allowing us to assess how well the clustering is working [78]. An external quality measure is the name for this type of metric. Entropy is an external measure that determines the "goodness" of unnested clusters or clusters at one level of a hierarchical clustering. There are numerous alternative quality criteria, and depending on which one is chosen, the performance and relative ranking of different clustering algorithms might differ significantly. However, if one clustering algorithm outperforms another on a number of these criteria, we can be quite confident that it is the optimal clustering algorithm for the circumstance under consideration [79]. Cluster validation, an important issue in cluster analysis, is the measurement of goodness of a cluster relative to others created by clustering algorithms using different parameter values. Several cluster validation measures, like compactness, connectedness, separation, and combinations of these, take a clustering method and the underlying dataset as the input and employ information intrinsic to the dataset to review the quality of the clusters. Some of these cluster validation measures are discussed below.

(A) Compactness

Compactness is an indicator of the scattering of the objects within a particular cluster. It measures clusters compactness or homogeneity, with intra-cluster variance as their most popular representative. Numerous variants of measuring intra-cluster homogeneity are possible such as the evaluation of maximum or average pairwise intra-cluster distances, maximum or average center-based similarities, or the use of graph-based methods [80].

(B) Connectedness

Connectedness can be used to assess how well a given partitioning agrees with the conception of connectedness, i.e., to what degree a partitioning examines local densities and groups objects together with their nearest neighbors in the data space.

(C) Separation

Separation is an indicator of the isolation of clusters from one another. It measures the degree of separation between individual clusters. For example, a general rating for a partitioning can be stated as the average weighted inter-cluster distance, where the distance between two individual clusters is computed as the distance between cluster centroids or as the minimum distance between objects belonging to different clusters [80].

(D) Combinations of the above measures

The above measures can be combined to measure cluster quality considering multiple aspects. Combinations of compactness and separation are particularly popular, as the two classes of measures show an opposite tendency. Thus, a number of measures assess both inter-cluster separation and intra-cluster homogeneity and calculate a final score as the linear or nonlinear combination of the two measures. Some of these cluster validation measures are discussed below.

Davies–Bouldin validity index: The Davies–Bouldin index (DBIndex) [81] is a function defined as the ratio of the sum of intra-cluster scatter to inter-cluster separation. Let $U = \{X_1, X_2, X_3, X_4, \ldots, X_k\}$ be the k-cluster obtained by a clustering algorithm. To measure the goodness of the cluster U, the DBIndex is calculated as follows:

$$DBIndex(U) = \frac{1}{K} \sum_{i=1}^{k} \max_{i=j} \left\{ \frac{\Delta(X_i) + \Delta(X_j)}{\delta(X_i, X_j)} \right\}. \tag{8.4}$$

Here, $\Delta(X_i)$ is the intra-cluster distance in X_i, i.e., the distance between the most remote objects in cluster X_i, and $\delta(S, T)$ is the inter-cluster distance of X_i and X_j, i.e., the distance between X_i and X_j.

Dunn's validity index: The Dunn index (D) [82] uses the minimum pairwise distance between objects in different clusters as the inter-cluster separation and the maximum diameter among all clusters to estimate the intra-cluster compactness. For any partition of clusters, where X_i signifies the i-th cluster, Dunn's validation index (DN) is calculated with Eq. (8.5). Here, $d(X_i, X_j)$ is the distance between clusters X_i and X_j, $d'(X_1)$ is the intra-cluster distance of cluster X_1, and k is the number of clusters. The aim of this measure is to minimize the intra-cluster distances and maximize the inter-cluster distances [83]. Therefore, the number of cluster that maximizes D_N is taken as the optimal number of clusters. We have

$$D = \min_{1 \le i \le k} \left\{ \min_{1 \le j \le k; i \ne j} \left\{ \frac{d(X_i, X_j)}{\max_{1 \le l \le k}(d'(X_l))} \right\} \right\}. \tag{8.5}$$

I-index: The I-index (I) [84] measures separation based on the maximum distance between cluster centers and measures compactness based on the sum of distances between objects and their cluster center:

$$I(k) = \left(\frac{1}{k} \cdot \frac{\sum_j \| x_j - \bar{c} \|_2}{\sum_{k=1}^{K} \sum_{j \in c_k} \| x_j - \bar{c} \|_2} \cdot \max_{i,j} \| (c_i - c_j) \| \right)^p. \tag{8.6}$$

Here the power p is a constant, which normally is set to be 2.

CH-index: The Calinski–Harabasz index (CH) [85] evaluates cluster validity based on the average inter- and intra-cluster sum of squares:

$$CH = \frac{traceB/(K-1)}{traceW/(N-K)}, \tag{8.7}$$

$$traceB = \sum_{k=1}^{K} \mid C_k \mid \| \, \overline{C_k} - \overline{x} \, \|^2, \tag{8.8}$$

$$traceW = \sum_{k=1}^{K} \sum_{i=1}^{K} w_{k,i} \| \, \overline{x_i} - \overline{C_k} \, \|^2, \tag{8.9}$$

where N is the number of objects in the dataset, K is the number of clusters ($K \in N$), B denotes the error sum of squares between different clusters (inter-cluster), and W is the squared differences of all objects in a cluster from their respective cluster center (intra-cluster). An important characteristic of the index is the fact that on the one hand trace W will start at a comparably large value. With an increasing number of clusters K, approaching the optimal clustering solution in K* groups, the value should significantly decrease due to an increasing compactness of each cluster [86]. As soon as the optimal solution is exceeded an increase in compactness and thereby a decrease in value might still occur; this decrease, however, should be large. On the other hand, trace T should behave in the opposite direction, getting higher as the number of clusters K increases, but should also reveal a kind of softening in its rise if K gets larger than K*. The maximum value of the CH-index is the optimal number of clusters.

Silhouette index: The Silhouette index (S) [87] validates the clustering performance based on the pairwise difference of inter- and intra-cluster distances. The Silhouette index (S) for k clusters is calculated as follows:

$$S = \frac{1}{k} \sum_{i=1}^{k} \frac{b_i - a_i}{max(a_i, b_i)}, \tag{8.10}$$

where a_i is the mean dissimilarity of the i-th object to all other objects in the same cluster and b_i is the minimum average dissimilarity of the i-th object with all objects in the closest cluster. It follows from Eq. (8.10) that $-1 \le SC \le 1$. If the Silhouette value is close to 1, then the sample is "well clustered" and assigned to an appropriate cluster [88]. If the Silhouette value is close to 0, the sample could be assigned to another cluster closest to it, and the sample lies equally far away from both clusters. If the Silhouette value is close to -1, the sample is "misclassified" and is merely placed somewhere in between the clusters. So a greater value of the SC-index indicates a better number of clusters.

XB-index: The Xie–Beni index (XB) [89] is an index of fuzzy clustering which considers the ratio between the compactness and separation metrics.

Table 8.5 Selection of parameters for the proposed methodology. The best performance according to each metric is marked in bold in each case.

Method	S	CH	DB	I	XB	D
Uttarakhand dataset						
Proposed method	**0.1925**	3.1057	**0.759**	0.0548	**2.0994**	**1.172**
K-means method	0.17	3.2381	1.5100	**2.7545**	67.5705	0.871
Hierarchical method	0.164	**5.8153**	0.898	1.0472	2.4204	0.858
HYDB dataset						
Proposed method	**0.2643**	3.336	**0.887**	0.111	**1.5077**	**1.201**
K-means method	0.037	3.6289	1.513	0.3264	70.1213	0.964
Hierarchical method	0.044	**5.3888**	0.967	**3.5806**	1.6293	0.797
Hagupit dataset						
Proposed method	**0.2708**	43.4864	**0.795**	0.1425	**0.1319**	**1.52**
K-means method	0.2065	0.2567	1.682	**0.8984**	508.5419	0.976
Hierarchical method	0.025	15.1149	1.026	0.001	1.439	0.766
Sandy Hook Dataset						
Proposed method	**0.2643**	11.1302	**0.651**	0.1119	**0.558**	1.057
K-means method	0.152	12.2388	1.566	**1.6661**	1616.9	0.731
Hierarchical method	0.102	**16.036**	0.936	0.0749	100.3326	**0.833**

The XB-index for a given dataset X with a partition with K clusters is mathematically written as

$$XB(K) = \frac{V_c(K)/N}{V_s(K)} = \frac{\sum_{n=1}^{N} \sum_{k=1}^{K} u_{k,n}^m \parallel x_n - c_k \parallel^2}{NX \min_{i,j} \parallel c_i - c_j \parallel}, \qquad (8.11)$$

where $V_c(K)$ represents the compactness measure when the dataset is grouped into K clusters, which is given by $\sum_{n=1}^{N} \sum_{k=1}^{K} u_{k,n}^m \parallel x_n - c_k \parallel^2$, where $c_k = \sum_{n=1}^{N} u_{k,n}^m x_n / \sum_{n=1}^{N} u_{k,n}^m$ is the centroid of the k-th cluster, and $V_s(K)$ is the degree of separation between clusters. In general, an optimal K is found by solving $\min_{k \in [2,N-1]} XB(K)$ to produce the best clustering performance for the dataset X.

Of these indices, some are maximization indices and some are minimization indices. For the DB-index and the XB-index, smaller values indicate better clustering performance, while for the Dunn index, the Silhouette index, the CH-index, and the I-index, higher values indicate better clustering performance. The reader is referred to [76] for a detailed description of all these metrics.

8.5.2 Metrics for evaluating clustering

Table 8.5 compares the performance of the proposed methodology with that of the classical approaches, according to the various metrics. The best performance according to each metric is highlighted in boldface.

The proposed methodology performs better than all the baseline approaches according to all the metrics except the I-index and the CH-index (for which hierarchical clustering achieves the best performance). These results indicate the superior performance of the proposed feature selection-based tweet clustering approach. We emphasize that we are not claiming that K-means or its variants are the "ideal" document clustering approach [86]. K-means has a number of flaws, including initialization, and in reality, it sometimes fails to locate clusters that correspond to the intended document classifications. The broad technique of K-means, on the other hand, appears to be better suited to documents than the agglomerative hierarchical clustering approach [88].

8.6 Conclusion

For tweet sentiment categorization, feature engineering methods generally yield a huge number of features. When a large number of instances are combined, the resulting dataset can have a high dimensionality. Furthermore, it is computationally difficult to train classifiers on a huge dataset. Feature selection, which has gotten minimal attention in tweet sentiment classification research, selects an ideal collection of features, reducing the dataset's dimensionality, lowering computational costs, and maybe improving classification accuracy. In the proposed work, we have presented a method to cluster a set of microblogging data or tweets by generating the topic model and then reducing the features from the generated topic model. This work introduces a simple and effective methodology for tweet clustering combining feature selection. The experimental results show that the proposed algorithm performs better than some standard clustering approaches. As future work, we would like to improve the clustering algorithm, so that it can be applied for large datasets of microblogging websites. We can extend the work to generate a topic-oriented summary of tweets by using automated summarization techniques. Primarily the clustering technique follows a greedy selection method, which could be substituted by a suitable backtracking selection method to produce more coherent clusters and thus improve the overall performance. This study could also be expanded to include other datasets, in order to determine if the trends discovered in this work are also present in other datasets.

References

[1] S. Goswami, A.K. Das, Determining maximum cliques for community detection in weighted sparse networks, Knowledge and Information Systems 64 (2) (2022) 289–324, https://doi.org/10.1007/s10115-021-01631-y.

[2] A. Mukherjee, S. Bhattacharyya, K. Ray, B. Gupta, A.K. Das, A study of public sentiment and influence of politics in COVID-19 related tweets, in: A.K. Das, J. Nayak, B. Naik, S. Dutta, D. Pelusi (Eds.), Computational Intelligence in Pattern Recognition, Springer, Singapore, 2022, pp. 655–665.

[3] P. Das, A.K. Das, Convolutional neural networks-based sentence level classification of crime documents, in: A.K. Das, J. Nayak, B. Naik, S. Dutta, D. Pelusi (Eds.), Computational Intelligence in Pattern Recognition, Springer, Singapore, 2022, pp. 65–73.

[4] A. Das, D. Pal, C. Mallick, A.K. Das, An unsupervised COVID-19 report summarizer for developing smart healthcare system, in: A.K. Das, J. Nayak, B. Naik, S. Dutta, D. Pelusi (Eds.), Computational Intelligence in Pattern Recognition, Springer, Singapore, 2022, pp. 157–168.

[5] C. Mallick, S. Das, A.K. Das, Evolutionary algorithm based summarization for analyzing COVID-19 medical reports, in: J. Nayak, B. Naik, A. Abraham (Eds.), Understanding COVID-19: The Role of Computational Intelligence, in: Studies in Computational Intelligence, Springer International Publishing, Cham, 2022, pp. 31–58.

[6] K. Lee, D. Palsetia, R. Narayanan, M.M.A. Patwary, A. Agrawal, A. Choudhary, Twitter trending topic classification, in: 2011 IEEE 11th International Conference on Data Mining Workshops, 2011, pp. 251–258.

[7] A. Zubiaga, D. Spina, V. Fresno, R. Martínez, Classifying trending topics: a typology of conversation triggers on Twitter, in: Proceedings of the 20th ACM International Conference on Information and Knowledge Management, CIKM '11, Association for Computing Machinery, New York, NY, USA, 2011, pp. 2461–2464.

[8] B. Sriram, D. Fuhry, E. Demir, H. Ferhatosmanoglu, M. Demirbas, Short text classification in Twitter to improve information filtering, in: Proceedings of the 33rd International ACM SIGIR Conference on Research and Development in Information Retrieval, SIGIR '10, Association for Computing Machinery, New York, NY, USA, 2010, pp. 841–842.

[9] REST API Resources, Twitter Developers, https://dev.twitter.com/docs/api.

[10] J.D. Prusa, T.M. Khoshgoftaar, D.J. Dittman, Impact of feature selection techniques for tweet sentiment classification, in: FLAIRS Conference, 2015.

[11] S. Chattopadhyay, T. Basu, A.K. Das, K. Ghosh, L.C.A. Murthy, Towards effective discovery of natural communities in complex networks and implications in e-commerce, Electronic Commerce Research 21 (4) (2021) 917–954, https://doi.org/10.1007/s10660-019-09395-y.

[12] D.M. Blei, A.Y. Ng, M.I. Jordan, Latent Dirichlet allocation, Journal of Machine Learning Research 3 (2003) 993–1022, http://dl.acm.org/citation.cfm?id=944919.944937.

[13] M. Basu, S.D. Bit, S. Ghosh, Utilizing microblogs for optimized real-time resource allocation in post-disaster scenarios, Social Network Analysis and Mining 12 (1) (2021) 15, https://doi.org/10.1007/s13278-021-00841-0.

[14] P. Bhattacharya, S. Paul, K. Ghosh, S. Ghosh, A. Wyner, DeepRhole: deep learning for rhetorical role labeling of sentences in legal case documents, Artificial Intelligence and Law (2021), https://doi.org/10.1007/s10506-021-09304-5.

[15] S. Hill, A. Benton, L. Ungar, S. Macskassy, A. Chung, J.H. Holmes, A cluster-based method for isolating influence on Twitter, 2016.

[16] M. Cheong, V.C.S. Lee, A study on detecting patterns in Twitter intra-topic user and message clustering, in: ICPR, IEEE Computer Society, 2010, pp. 3125–3128, http://dblp.uni-trier.de/db/conf/icpr/icpr2010.html#CheongL10.

[17] A.M. Thomas, M. Resmipriya, An efficient text classification scheme using clustering, Procedia Technology 24 (2016) 1220–1225.

[18] J. Yang, J. Leskovec, Patterns of temporal variation in online media, in: Proceedings of the Fourth ACM International Conference on Web Search and Data Mining, ACM, 2011, pp. 177–186.

[19] G. Karypis, E.-H.S. Han, V. Kumar, Chameleon: hierarchical clustering using dynamic modeling, Computer 32 (8) (1999) 68–75, https://doi.org/10.1109/2.781637.

[20] D. Dueck, Affinity propagation: clustering data by passing messages, PhD thesis, Citeseer, 2009.

[21] S. Dutta, S. Ghatak, M. Roy, S. Ghosh, A.K. Das, A graph based clustering technique for tweet summarization, in: 2015 4th International Conference on Reliability, Infocom Technologies and Optimization (ICRITO) (Trends and Future Directions), 2015, pp. 1–6.

[22] A. Rangrej, S. Kulkarni, A.V. Tendulkar, Comparative study of clustering techniques for short text documents, in: Proceedings of the 20th International Conference Companion on World Wide Web, ACM, 2011, pp. 111–112.

[23] G. Yegin, S. Yasuaki, N.J. V, Discovering context: classifying tweets through a semantic transform based on Wikipedia, in: Proceedings of the 6th International Conference on Foundations of Augmented Cognition: Directing the Future of Adaptive Systems, FAC'11, Springer-Verlag, 2011, pp. 484–492.

[24] S. Dutta, S. Ghatak, S. Ghosh, A.K. Das, A genetic algorithm based tweet clustering technique, in: Computer Communication and Informatics (ICCCI), 2017, pp. 1–6.

[25] D. Soumi, G. Sujata, D. Asit, M. Gupta, D. Sayantika, Feature selection based clustering on micro-blogging data, in: International Conference on Computational Intelligence in Data Mining (ICCIDM-2017), 2017, pp. 885–895.

[26] R. Liu, S. Feng, R. Shi, W. Guo, Weighted graph clustering for community detection of large social networks, in: 2nd International Conference on Information Technology and Quantitative Management, ITQM 2014, Procedia Computer Science 31 (2014) 85–94, https://doi.org/10.1016/j.procs.2014.05.248, https://www.sciencedirect.com/science/article/pii/S1877050914004256.

[27] J. Lin, Z. Li, D. Wang, K. Salamatian, G. Xie, Analysis and comparison of interaction patterns in online social network and social media, in: 2012 21st International Conference on Computer Communications and Networks (ICCCN), 2012, pp. 1–7.

[28] K. Subramani, A. Velkov, I. Ntoutsi, P. Kroger, H.-P. Kriegel, Density-based community detection in social networks, in: 2011 IEEE 5th International Conference on Internet Multimedia Systems Architecture and Application, 2011, pp. 1–8.

[29] X. Xu, N. Yuruk, Z. Feng, T.A.J. Schweiger, Scan: a structural clustering algorithm for networks, in: Proceedings of the 13th ACM SIGKDD International Conference on Knowledge Discovery and Data Mining, KDD '07, Association for Computing Machinery, New York, NY, USA, 2007, pp. 824–833.

[30] T. Falkowski, A. Barth, M. Spiliopoulou, Dengraph: a density-based community detection algorithm, in: IEEE/WIC/ACM International Conference on Web Intelligence (WI'07), 2007, pp. 112–115.

[31] S. Alsaleh, R. Nayak, Y. Xu, Finding and matching communities in social networks using data mining, in: 2011 International Conference on Advances in Social Networks Analysis and Mining, 2011, pp. 389–393.

[32] E. Jaho, M. Karaliopoulos, I. Stavrakakis, Iscode: a framework for interest similarity-based community detection in social networks, in: 2011 IEEE Conference on Computer Communications Workshops (INFOCOM WKSHPS), 2011, pp. 912–917.

[33] M.E.J. Newman, M. Girvan, Finding and evaluating community structure in networks, Physical Review E 69 (2) (2004), https://doi.org/10.1103/physreve.69.026113.

[34] S. White, P. Smyth, A spectral clustering approach to finding communities in graphs: Proceedings of the 2005 SIAM International Conference on Data Mining (SDM), pp. 274–285.

[35] M. Girvan, M.E.J. Newman, Community structure in social and biological networks, Proceedings of the National Academy of Sciences 99 (12) (2002) 7821–7826, https://doi.org/10.1073/pnas.122653799, arXiv:https://www.pnas.org/content/99/12/7821.full.pdf, https://www.pnas.org/content/99/12/7821.

[36] J. Ruan, W. Zhang, An efficient spectral algorithm for network community discovery and its applications to biological and social networks, in: Seventh IEEE International Conference on Data Mining (ICDM 2007), 2007, pp. 643–648.

[37] P. Pons, M. Latapy, Computing communities in large networks using random walks, in: P. Yolum, T. Güngör, F. Gürgen, C. Özturan (Eds.), Computer and Information Sciences - ISCIS 2005, Springer Berlin Heidelberg, Berlin, Heidelberg, 2005, pp. 284–293.

[38] T. Hachaj, M.R. Ogiela, Clustering of trending topics in microblogging posts: a graph-based approach, Future Generations Computer Systems 67 (2017) 297–304, https://doi.org/10.1016/j.future.2016.04.009, https://www.sciencedirect.com/science/article/pii/S0167739X16300863.

[39] I. Blekanov, S.S. Bodrunova, A. Akhmetov, Detection of hidden communities in Twitter discussions of varying volumes, Future Internet 13 (11) (2021), https://doi.org/10.3390/fi13110295, https://www.mdpi.com/1999-5903/13/11/295.

[40] K. Gao, B.-q. Zhang, Modelling on clustering algorithm based on iteration feature selection for micro-blog posts, in: Proceedings of 2014 International Conference on Modelling, Identification Control, 2014, pp. 295–299.

[41] S. Lei, A feature selection method based on information gain and genetic algorithm, in: 2012 International Conference on Computer Science and Electronics Engineering, vol. 2, 2012, pp. 355–358.

[42] Z. Liu, W. Yu, W. Chen, S. Wang, F. Wu, Short text feature selection for microblog mining, in: 2010 International Conference on Computational Intelligence and Software Engineering, 2010, pp. 1–4.

[43] S. Nourashrafeddin, E. Milios, D. Arnold, Interactive text document clustering using feature labeling, in: Proceedings of the 2013 ACM Symposium on Document Engineering, DocEng '13, Association for Computing Machinery, New York, NY, USA, 2013, pp. 61–70.

[44] Q. Song, J. Ni, G. Wang, A fast clustering-based feature subset selection algorithm for high-dimensional data, IEEE Transactions on Knowledge and Data Engineering 25 (1) (2013) 1–14, https://doi.org/10.1109/TKDE.2011.181.

[45] G.H. Shah, An improved dbscan, a density based clustering algorithm with parameter selection for high dimensional data sets, in: 2012 Nirma University International Conference on Engineering (NUiCONE), 2012, pp. 1–6.

[46] K. Gao, B.-q. Zhang, Modelling on microblog posts clustering based on iteration feature selection and abstractive summarisation, International Journal of Modelling, Identification and Control 24 (2) (2015) 110–119, https://doi.org/10.1504/IJMIC.2015.071886.

[47] X. Yan, H. Zhao, Chinese microblog topic detection based on the latent semantic analysis and structural property, Journal of Networks 8 (2013) 917–923.

[48] K. Hazra, T. Ghosh, A. Mukherjee, S. Saha, S. Nandi, S. Ghosh, S. Chakraborty, Sustainable text summarization over mobile devices: an energy-aware approach, Sustainable Computing: Informatics and Systems 32 (2021) 100607, https://doi.org/ 10.1016/j.suscom.2021.100607, https://www.sciencedirect.com/science/article/pii/ S2210537921000950.

[49] A. Mandal, K. Ghosh, S. Ghosh, S. Mandal, A sequence labeling model for catch-phrase identification from legal case documents, Artificial Intelligence and Law (2021), https://doi.org/10.1007/s10506-021-09296-2.

[50] D. Sontag, D. Roy, Complexity of inference in latent Dirichlet allocation, in: J. Shawe-Taylor, R.S. Zemel, P.L. Bartlett, F. Pereira, K.Q. Weinberger (Eds.), Advances in Neural Information Processing Systems, vol. 24, Curran Associates, Inc., 2011, pp. 1008–1016, http://papers.nips.cc/paper/4232-complexity-of-inference-in-latent-dirichlet-allocation.pdf.

[51] M. Basu, K. Ghosh, S. Ghosh, Information retrieval from microblogs during disasters: in the light of IRMiDis task, SN Computer Science 1 (1) (2020) 61, https://doi.org/ 10.1007/s42979-020-0065-1.

[52] R. Mandal, S. Dutta, R. Banerjee, S. Bhattacharya, R. Ghosh, S. Samanta, T. Saha, City traffic speed characterization based on city road surface quality, in: J.M.R.S. Tavares, P. Dutta, S. Dutta, D. Samanta (Eds.), Cyber Intelligence and Information Retrieval, Springer, Singapore, 2022, pp. 515–524.

[53] D. Samanta, S. Dutta, M.G. Galety, S. Pramanik, A novel approach for web mining taxonomy for high-performance computing, in: J.M.R.S. Tavares, P. Dutta, S. Dutta, D. Samanta (Eds.), Cyber Intelligence and Information Retrieval, in: Lecture Notes in Networks and Systems, Springer, Singapore, 2022, pp. 425–432.

[54] A. Campan, T. Atnafu, T.M. Truta, J. Nolan, Is data collection through Twitter streaming api useful for academic research?, in: 2018 IEEE International Conference on Big Data (Big Data), 2018, pp. 3638–3643.

[55] S. Kumar, K.M. Carley, What to track on the Twitter streaming api? A knapsack bandits approach to dynamically update the search terms, in: 2019 IEEE/ACM International Conference on Advances in Social Networks Analysis and Mining (ASONAM), 2019, pp. 158–163.

[56] Hyderabad blasts – Wikipedia, http://en.wikipedia.org/wiki/2013_Hyderabad_blasts, February 2013.

[57] Sandy Hook Elementary School shooting – Wikipedia, http://en.wikipedia.org/wiki/ Sandy_Hook_Elementary_School_shooting, December 2012.

[58] Typhoon Hagupit – Wikipedia, http://en.wikipedia.org/wiki/Typhoon_Hagupit, December 2014.

[59] North India floods – Wikipedia, http://en.wikipedia.org/wiki/2013_North_India_ floods, June 2013.

[60] H. Efstathiades, D. Antoniades, G. Pallis, M.D. Dikaiakos, Distributed large-scale data collection in online social networks, in: 2016 IEEE 2nd International Conference on Collaboration and Internet Computing (CIC), 2016, pp. 373–380.

[61] M. Steinbach, G. Karypis, V. Kumar, A comparison of document clustering techniques, in: KDD Workshop on Text Mining, 2000.

[62] C.H. Lee, C.H. Hung, S.J. Lee, A comparative study on clustering algorithms, in: 2013 14th ACIS International Conference on Software Engineering, Artificial Intelligence, Networking and Parallel/Distributed Computing, 2013, pp. 557–562.

[63] A. Dwi Laksito, Kusrini, H. Sismoro, F. Rahmawati, M. Yusa, A comparison study of search strategy on collecting Twitter data for drug adverse reaction, in: 2018 International Seminar on Application for Technology of Information and Communication, 2018, pp. 356–360.

[64] S.-R. Sandra, V. Ana, D.R. Rebeca, P.-A. Jose, Comparing tag clustering algorithms for mining Twitter users' interests, in: 2013 International Conference on Social Computing, 2013, pp. 679–684.

[65] Kanungo Tapas, Mount David M, Netanyahu Nathan S, Piatko Christine D, Silverman Ruth, Wu Angela Y, An efficient k-means clustering algorithm: analysis and implementation, IEEE Transactions on Pattern Analysis and Machine Intelligence 24 (7) (2002) 881–892, https://doi.org/10.1109/TPAMI.2002.1017616.

[66] McNicholas Paul D, Murphy Thomas Brendan, Model-based clustering of microarray expression data via latent Gaussian mixture models, Bioinformatics 26 (21) (2010) 2705–2712, https://doi.org/10.1093/bioinformatics/btq498, arXiv:/oup/backfile/content_public/journal/bioinformatics/26/21/10.1093/bioinformatics/btq498/2/btq498.pdf.

[67] P. Ray, A. Chakrabarti, Twitter sentiment analysis for product review using lexicon method, in: 2017 International Conference on Data Management, Analytics and Innovation (ICDMAI), 2017, pp. 211–216.

[68] Tetko Igor V, Livingstone David J, Luik Alexander I, Neural network studies. 1. Comparison of overfitting and overtraining, Journal of Chemical Information and Computer Sciences 35 (5) (1995) 826–833, https://doi.org/10.1021/ci00027a006, arXiv:https://pubs.acs.org/doi/pdf/10.1021/ci00027a006.

[69] D. Manoranjan, P. Simona, S. Peter, Efficient parallel hierarchical clustering, in: D. Marco, V. Marco, L. Domenico (Eds.), Euro-Par 2004 Parallel Processing, Springer Berlin Heidelberg, Berlin, Heidelberg, 2004, pp. 363–371.

[70] S. Das, A. Abraham, A. Konar, Automatic clustering using an improved differential evolution algorithm, IEEE Transactions on Systems, Man and Cybernetics. Part A. Systems and Humans 38 (1) (2008) 218–237, https://doi.org/10.1109/TSMCA.2007.909595.

[71] K. Jitkajornwanich, C. Kongthong, N. Khongsoontornjaroen, J. Kaiyasuan, S. Lawawirojwong, P. Srestasathiern, S. Srisonphan, P. Vateekul, Utilizing Twitter data for early flood warning in Thailand, in: 2018 IEEE International Conference on Big Data (Big Data), 2018, pp. 5165–5169.

[72] S. Guha, R. Rastogi, K. Shim, Cure: an efficient clustering algorithm for large databases, Information Systems 26 (1) (2001) 35–58, https://doi.org/10.1016/S0306-4379(01)00008-4, http://www.sciencedirect.com/science/article/pii/S0306437901000084.

[73] S. Guha, K. Shim, R. Rastogi, Rock: a robust clustering algorithm for categorical attributes, in: Proceedings 15th International Conference on Data Engineering (Cat. No. 99CB36337), 1999, pp. 512–521.

[74] Z. Tian, R. Raghu, L. Miron, Birch: an efficient data clustering method for very large databases, SIGMOD Record 25 (2) (1996) 103–114, https://doi.org/10.1145/235968.233324, http://doi.acm.org/10.1145/235968.233324.

[75] K. L, R.P. J, Finding Groups in Data: an Introduction to Cluster Analysis, Wiley, 1990.

[76] Y. Liu, Z. Li, H. Xiong, X. Gao, J. Wu, Understanding of internal clustering validation measures, in: Proceedings of the 2010 IEEE International Conference on Data Mining, ICDM '10, IEEE Computer Society, Washington, DC, USA, 2010, pp. 911–916.

[77] J.A. K, D.R. C, Algorithms for Clustering Data, Prentice-Hall, Inc., Upper Saddle River, NJ, USA, 1988.

[78] S.H. Archana, S.G. Winster, Drugs categorization based on sentence polarity analyzer for Twitter data, in: 2016 Second International Conference on Science Technology Engineering and Management (ICONSTEM), 2016, pp. 28–33.

[79] T. Jagić, L. Brkić, Hot topic detection using Twitter streaming data, in: 2020 43rd International Convention on Information, Communication and Electronic Technology (MIPRO), 2020, pp. 1730–1735.

[80] R. Compton, C. Lee, T.-C. Lu, L. De Silva, M. Macy, Detecting future social unrest in unprocessed Twitter data: "emerging phenomena and big data", in: 2013 IEEE International Conference on Intelligence and Security Informatics, 2013, pp. 56–60.

[81] D.D. L, B.D. W, A cluster separation measure, IEEE Transactions on Pattern Analysis and Machine Intelligence 1 (2) (1979) 224–227, https://doi.org/10.1109/TPAMI.1979.4766909.

[82] U. Maulik, S. Bandyopadhyay, Performance evaluation of some clustering algorithms and validity indices, IEEE Transactions on Pattern Analysis and Machine Intelligence 24 (12) (2002) 1650–1654, https://doi.org/10.1109/TPAMI.2002.1114856.

[83] R.D. Perera, S. Anand, K.P. Subbalakshmi, R. Chandramouli, Twitter analytics: architecture, tools and analysis, in: 2010 - MILCOM 2010 Military Communications Conference, 2010, pp. 2186–2191.

[84] H. Cui, K. Zhang, Y. Fang, S. Sobolevsky, C. Ratti, B.K.P. Horn, A clustering validity index based on pairing frequency, IEEE Access 5 (2017) 24884–24894, https://doi.org/10.1109/ACCESS.2017.2743985.

[85] R. Xu, J. Xu, D.C. Wunsch, A comparison study of validity indices on swarm-intelligence-based clustering, IEEE Transactions on Systems, Man and Cybernetics. Part B. Cybernetics 42 (4) (2012) 1243–1256, https://doi.org/10.1109/TSMCB.2012.2188509.

[86] P. Tatineni, B.S. Babu, B. Kanuri, G.R.K. Rao, P. Chitturi, C. Naresh, Post Covid-19 Twitter user's emotions classification using deep learning techniques in India, in: 2021 International Conference on Artificial Intelligence and Smart Systems (ICAIS), 2021, pp. 338–343.

[87] R. Peter, Silhouettes: a graphical aid to the interpretation and validation of cluster analysis, Journal of Computational and Applied Mathematics 20 (1) (1987) 53–65, https://doi.org/10.1016/0377-0427(87)90125-7.

[88] C. Wang, L. Marini, C.-L. Chin, N. Vance, C. Donelson, P. Meunier, J.T. Yun, Social media intelligence and learning environment: an open source framework for social media data collection, analysis and curation, in: 2019 15th International Conference on eScience (eScience), 2019, pp. 252–261.

[89] M. Mai, H. Katsuhiro, N. Akira, Xie-beni-type fuzzy cluster validation in fuzzy co-clustering of documents and keywords, in: Y.I. Cho, E.T. Matson (Eds.), Soft Computing in Artificial Intelligence, Springer International Publishing, Cham, 2014, pp. 29–38.

CHAPTER 9

Dimensionality reduction techniques in microblog clustering models

9.1 Introduction

The rapidly growing popularity of online social media provides flexible and attractive platforms to the users for information exchange, which results in a massive repository of dissimilar data which opens up several research challenges to the researchers. In recent times, Twitter has become one of the most popular microblogging web applications for communication, accessed by an exponentially growing number of online social network users [1]. On a daily basis, more than 640 million active users post more than 550 million messages (microblogs or tweets) on Twitter from all over the world. Twitter plays a major role in several activities such as prediction of match results, spreading awareness of natural calamities, sociopolitical activity, and so on. Thus, this huge source of easily accessible information opens up potential cross-domain opportunities for researchers, businesses, and decision makers. Even an individual user can get hundreds of tweets in his/her timeline every day, which can cause information overload for users. It is a hectic task for anyone to go through all the tweets to acquire information on a particular topic [2,3].

As stated earlier, microblogging sites such as Twitter have hundreds of millions of posts per day, and even an individual user can get hundreds of posts in his/her timeline every day, which can cause information overload for users [4]. An effective way to reduce the information load on the users is to cluster similar tweets, so that the user might see only a few tweets in each cluster. Though document clustering is a well-established area of research, clustering of microblog data is difficult due to the very small size of messages giving very little context and their noisy nature – due to the size restriction, microblog data often contain abbreviations, colloquial language, and so on. Hence, traditional data mining/natural language processing techniques do not usually perform well for tweets [5].

An effective approach to reduce the information overload is to group or "cluster" similar tweets so that a user may see only a few messages in that

Data Analytics for Social Microblogging Platforms
https://doi.org/10.1016/B978-0-32-391785-8.00022-6

group. The standard text clustering algorithms are not suitable for tweets because of the unstructured, sparse, and incremental nature of tweets. Unlike structured and formal English texts, tweets are filled with colloquial language, emoticons, slang, URLs, and misspelled or abbreviated words. The short and informal nature of tweets makes it difficult for traditional clustering techniques to extract valuable insights from them. Hence, a novel clustering procedure is proposed in this paper which can discover significant groupings even among the inadequate, unstructured, and dynamic information on Twitter [6]. In the proposed clustering approach, apart from concentrating on dimensionality reduction, document vectorization models are also adopted along with graph-based clustering. Experimental results on several microblog datasets show that the proposed methodology performs better than standard and classical text clustering algorithms.

An effective approach to reduce the information overload is to group or "cluster" similar tweets so that a user may see only a few messages in that group and get an idea. The standard text clustering algorithms are not suitable for tweets because of the unstructured, sparse, and incremental nature of tweets. Unlike structured and formal English texts, tweets are filled with colloquial language, emoticons, slang, URLs, and misspelled or abbreviated words. The short and informal nature of tweets makes it difficult for traditional clustering techniques to extract valuable insights from them. Hence, a novel clustering procedure is proposed which can discover significant groupings even among the inadequate, unstructured, and dynamic information on Twitter. Experimental results on several microblog datasets show that the proposed methodology performs better than standard and classical text clustering algorithms [7].

In this section, a clustering methodology is proposed to identify similar groups (clusters) of tweets based on a dimensionality reduction mechanism. Microblog data contains a huge number and high diversity of terms (dimensions) since a particular term can be spelled or abbreviated arbitrarily and used differently by different users. Hence, to address the clustering problem, it is necessary to address the dimensionality reduction problem in order to identify similar groups of elements efficiently [8].

9.2 Literature survey

Clustering of microblogs is a very significant challenge in the social media analysis domain, which has resulted in some high-quality research works over the years. Miyamoto et al. [9] used a fuzzy neighborhood model for analyzing the tweets and then used two kernel-based methods along with pairwise constraints for clustering the tweets. Streamcube is a hierarchical spatiotemporal hashtag clustering system which has been proposed by Feng [10]. In their research, a spatiotemporal hierarchy inspired by quad-tree and datacube is used to perform hashtag and clustering according to a divide and conquer strategy at the last steps [11]. Then an event ranking algorithm is used that helps users to identify local and burst events (which is one of the main problems that clustering solves). Perez–Tellez et al. [12] proposed a method of clustering the microblog texts associated to any organization for online reputation management. They introduced the unsupervised TEM-Full and TEM-FULL+F methods to enrich term representation of tweets that are later used for clustering which has enabled clustering algorithms such as K-means to obtain superior performance in clustering.

In Modi et al. [13], a combination of textual similarity, co–occurrence frequency, and graph clustering has been used to cluster hashtags of tweets into meaningful topic groups. Another combination of Principal Component Analysis(PCA) and a variety of classification algorithms has been used to classify the tweets into those respective topic groups which were retrieved from the hashtag clustering. Chung [14] has used a clustering approach to detect emerging events with near-real-time analysis capability. They have made this possible by using a new kind of density-based clustering method called Incremental DBSCAN. The shape of the clusters continuously changes over time when a tweet is inserted or when a tweet is removed from the sliding window [15].

Kevin et al. [16] claimed that unsupervised learning approaches like latent Dirichlet allocation (LDA) and K-means-based clustering algorithms do not perform well for tweet clustering and give results which are quite different from the semantic topics that one generally wishes to differentiate. On the other hand, supervised algorithms like the Rocchio classifier with a simple bag-of-words (as features) using different vocabularies is quite efficient for identifying tweets according to their broad genres. Hashtags have been used as the target label to classify the tweets. In our prior work [17] also, LDA [82] was used to extract the topics from tweets that can be used as features in the document feature matrix to map each feature to a topic.

Another method for clustering is given in Yıldırım [18], where useful features are extracted and evaluated to determine how they can imply the topical relationship between different microblog posts. Then by combining the features, distances between the posts are calculated by taking the help of Wikipedia articles to understand the semantic meaning of terms. Finally, clustering is performed [19].

Karypis et al. [20] proposed a hierarchical clustering-based algorithm to identify natural clusters of various shapes and sizes, using dynamic modeling to portray dynamic modes of clusters and the adaptive merging decision. Another method was proposed where the concept graph from the dataset Dow Jones newswire stories to generate a conceptual summarization method in the SCISOR system Rau [21].

Mathioudakis et al. [22] proposed a clustering algorithm to find the most trending topics with the help of bursty keywords and their co-occurrences. For clustering of Twitter data, Ramage et al. [23] proposed an algorithm using LDA for labeling. Cataldi et al. [24] proposed a topic-graph to cluster emerging topics on Twitter based on term frequency and user authority. An innovative approach [25] was proposed to find user's topical interests leveraging Wikipedia as a knowledge base. Hila et al. [26] proposed a novel clustering approach to group real-world incidents on Twitter. We previously proposed a microblogging clustering method using an optimization technique such as a genetic algorithm [17].

As stated earlier, it is common for an individual user to receive hundreds of tweets per day from his/her followees, and it is not possible for most users to go through all the tweets. Social microblogging sites are increasingly being used as information media, to get up-to-date information on various topics of interest, including various ongoing events such as sociopolitical events, sports events, natural disasters, etc. Moreover, many of the tweets contain very similar information due to retweeting and reposting. Hence, this redundant information may cause information overload for the users [27]. In this scenario, mechanisms to deal with the information overload need to be developed. One effective way of dealing with the information overload on Twitter is organizing the information by clustering similar tweets into related sub-groups, so that the user might see only a few tweets in each cluster. Hence methodologies need to be developed for helping users to utilize such information systems. This chapter focuses primarily on organizing the information, which is one of the important research challenges [28].

9.3 Proposed methodology

The proposed algorithm consists of three steps (apart from preprocessing the data):

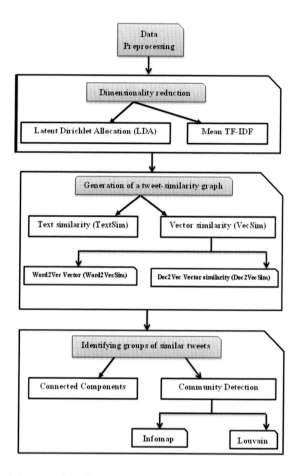

Figure 9.1 Block diagram of the dimensionality reduction-based clustering model.

(1) dimensionality reduction,

(2) constructing a tweet similarity graph, where the nodes are individual tweets and the edges indicate similarity between two terminal nodes (tweets), and

(3) identifying groups of similar nodes (tweets) in the graph.

Each of the steps can be done in various ways, as described below. Fig. 9.1 shows the block diagram of the said dimensionality reduction-based clustering model.

Data preprocessing

Microblog data is unstructured by nature and often contains non-textual characters such as special characters, shortened URLs, emojis, punctuation, abbreviations, abusive words, emoticons, @usernames, and many more. These can degrade clustering performance; hence, initially the dataset is preprocessed to reduce the noise. As in the previously described methods, the microblog dataset is preprocessed, including the following processes: removal of URLs, numerals, user mentions, emails, special characters, and stemming using standard a Porter stemmer for English. To achieve the data preprocessing, the following steps are followed.

Removal of user names and URLs

Words that start with "@" refer to user annotation which does not contribute significant meaning in a dataset. Similarly many users (mostly spammers) post various URLs in shorten format while posting in microblogs, so this unnecessary information can be removed to identify significant data for further analysis [29].

Removal of stopwords

Stopwords are words which do not include vital significance to be used in a text for data analysis. So these words can be filtered out from the dataset to ignore vast amounts of unnecessary information [30].

Stemming

Stemming generally refers to a basic heuristic procedure that chops off the ends of words to accomplish this goal correctly most of the time and comprises the removal of derivational affixes. Porter's algorithm is one of the most popular and effective algorithm for stemming English.

Removal of punctuation and non–textual characters

In this method all the non-textual characters and punctuation are removed.

Removal of repeating letters and additional white spaces

In this method all whitespace characters, including spaces and tabs with a blank space, and repeating letters are removed.

(1) Dimensionality reduction

Before performing the clustering, the dimension of the dataset is reduced to consider only important terms so that the performance of the clustering can be enhanced. Dimensionality reduction is one of the most significant steps of this methodology, and it enables the clustering algorithms to better cluster the data. This dimensionality reduction step sets the ground for extracting features that are actually important and enables the subsequent similarity and community detection algorithms to perform better, resulting in a superior clustering of the dataset as compared to traditional methods [31,32]. Specifically, the following two methods are performed for the dimensionality reduction.

(a) Latent Dirichlet allocation (LDA), a topic modeler

This method selects a set of important terms for each topic in the dataset. LDA [33] accepts the number of topics to be identified as a parameter, so for each dataset human volunteers were asked to discover the different types of information contained in the tweets and then cluster/group the tweets according to the type of information. Thus from the opinion of the volunteers, an estimation of the number of probable topics can be made, which can be considered as input parameter for LDA. To apply LDA initially the dataset is tokenized into a term dictionary. Then the tokenized dataset is converted into a document-term matrix, whose entries denote which terms are contained in which document. Finally LDA is executed on the document-term matrix, specifying the number of topics and the number of passes as parameters [34]. LDA [33] returns the list of topics, along with all related words for each topic. A weight is associated to each word for a particular topic that signifies the importance/relevance of the word in that specific topic. A reduced list of words related to each topic is identified considering the words having non-zero weights for the said topic. Then, a list of important terms is generated considering the union of all the terms selected by LDA for each topic and all the hashtags in the dataset. Note that hashtags are used on Twitter to mark a specific topic being discussed; hence hashtags play an important role in indicating the topic of tweets. Hence, hashtags are considered in the list of important terms [35].

(b) Thresholding with average TF-IDF score

In this approach, the important words are identified using the popular information retrieval measures "term frequency" (TF) and "inverse document frequency" (IDF). In a dataset, each tweet is represented as a bag (set) of words. The term frequency of a word in a tweet (document) refers to the number of occurrences of the word in the document [36]. The IDF of a word is computed based on the total number of occurrences of the word in the whole corpus. Finally, for each term, the TF-IDF score is generated computing the product of TF and IDF scores. A high TF-IDF score for a term implies more importance of the term in the document corpus. Hence, the terms having a lower TF-IDF score than a threshold (which is considered as the mean TF-IDF score across all terms) are dropped. For the subsequent steps, only the more important terms having TF-IDF scores higher than the threshold are considered [37].

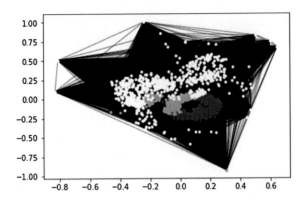

Figure 9.2 Sample tweet similarity graph for the Uttarakhand flood (UFlood) dataset.

(2) Constructing a tweet similarity graph

In this step, an undirected graph G is constructed where each tweet is represented as a node and an edge between two nodes is drawn if the corresponding two tweets are "similar." For each pair of tweets, a similarity score is computed which is further represented as edge weight in the tweet similarity graph G [38]. Fig. 9.2 shows a sample tweet similarity graph for the Uttarakhand flood (UFlood) dataset where the tweets are represented as nodes and edges represent similarity between the tweets. As the dataset consists of 2069 tweets, this graph has 2069 nodes and 2,139,346 edges. The similarity among tweets is calculated using different methodologies. Specifically, the following two methods are used in this work:

(a) Text similarity (TextSim)

In this approach, two tweets are said to be similar if they contain common words or terms. Already each tweet is represented using a reduced term list (after the dimensionality reduction step), so to measure similarity, Jaccard similarity is computed between every pair of tweets that are represented by the reduced bags (sets) of words. The similarity score lies in the range [0, 1]. These scores are considered as edge weights in the tweet similarity graph, G.

(b) Vector similarity (VecSim)

In this approach, each tweet is represented as a vector and then tweet similarity is measured between each pair of tweet vectors. The following vectorization approaches are used to construct the vector from a tweet.

(i) Word2Vec vector similarity (Word2VecSim)

The popular text embedding method Word2Vec [39] is used to obtain for each term a vector (embedding) which captures the semantic context of the term. Word2Vec is a shallow, two-layer neural network that processes text input, reconstructs the linguistic and semantic context of words, and automatically builds word embeddings. The output is basically a feature vector space that can be extended up to several hundreds of dimensions with each unique word in the training corpus being assigned a corresponding vector [40]. Word vectors are located in the vector space in such a way that semantically similar words fall together. Specifically, the continuous bag of words (CBOW) model of Word2Vec is used, and the following parameters are set to train Word2Vec: vector size: 100, context size: 5, learning rate: 0.05, number of iterations: 500. The Gensim library has been used for implementation.[1]

For each term, Word2Vec gives a vector (term-vector) which represents the semantic context of the term. The vector for a tweet (tweet-vector) is represented by computing the mean of the term-vectors of the terms in the tweet. To find the semantic similarity between two tweets, vector cosine similarity is computed between the pair of tweet-vectors. This Word2Vec vector similarity method can be considered as an enhanced version of TextSim, which can estimate similarity between two tweets that are semantically analogous but use dissimilar terms.

(ii) Doc2Vec vector similarity (Doc2VecSim)

Similar to the Word2Vec approach, in this approach as well each tweet is represented as a vector using the Doc2Vec model. Doc2 is an unsupervised algorithm which is very similar to Word2Vec. Doc2Vec [41] uses a numeric representation of a document irrespective of its length. Doc2Vec is essentially an extension to Word2Vec, but while Word2Vec calculates a feature vector for every word in the document, Doc2Vec calculates a feature vector for every document in the set of documents. Doc2Vec considers the Word2Vec model and paragraph vectors to predict the next word [42]. The distributed bag of words (PV-DBOW) model has been used for training the Doc2Vec algorithm. The parameters used in the model are: vector size: 300, window: 7, minimum count: 3, negative: 5, seed: 1, sample: 1e−3. The Gensim implementation was used.[2]

---

[1] https://radimrehurek.com/gensim/models/word2vec.html.
[2] https://radimrehurek.com/gensim/models/doc2vec.html.

Doc2Vec helps to capture the semantic relationship between different documents (in this case, tweets) that goes beyond the traditional linking using the same words. Doc2Vec is trained on the given set of tweets after the reduction of dimension. Similar to the previous approach, tweet similarity is represented evaluating cosine similarity between two tweet-vectors.

(3) Identifying groups of similar tweets (nodes in the graph)

Once the tweet similarity graph G is constructed, the groups of similar nodes (tweets) are identified to address the clustering problem. Based on a graphical approach and the tweet similarity score, groups of similar tweets are identified. Several approaches can be considered to identify groups of similar nodes, out of which the following are adopted:

(a) Identifying connected components (ConCom)

In this approach, connected components are identified from the undirected graph, G, to detect similar groups of nodes (tweets). As per graph theory, a connected component of an undirected graph is a sub-graph in which any two nodes are connected with each other by paths and which is associated with no extra nodes in the super-graph. Each connected component in the tweet similarity graph represents individual clusters of similar tweets, since two nodes (tweets) are connected only if they are similar [43].

(b) Identifying communities

To identify similar groups of nodes (tweets) in the tweet similarity graph G, several community detection algorithms [44] are applied. In this approach, densely connected nodes form a community. Popular community detection algorithms are considered for experiments:

(i) Infomap: In this approach, the community detection algorithm Infomap [45] is applied. For the undirected tweet similarity graph, Infomap identifies a set of communities that are non–overlapping by nature.

(ii) Louvain: Using the Louvain method [46], communities are identified within a tweet similarity graph based on densely connected nodes in the graph.

Thus, each community identified by a community detection algorithm from the tweet similarity graph is identified as a cluster of tweets.

9.4 Dataset

For the experiments, four different datasets were collected from Twitter using the Twitter API (2006) [47] with keyword-based matching. Given the critical need of information organization (including clustering) during disaster/emergency situations, the experiment focuses on sets of tweets posted during various disaster/emergency events:

1. HDBlast – Hyderabad bomb explosions (2013) [48] – Two bomb explosions occurred in the city of Hyderabad, India.
2. SHShoot – USA Sandy Hook (2012) [49] – An assailant killed 6 adults and 20 children at Sandy Hook Elementary School in Connecticut, USA.
3. THagupit – Typhoon Hagupit (2014) [50] – A strong cyclone code-named Typhoon Hagupit hit the Philippines.
4. UFlood – North India floods (2013) [51] – Devastating floods and landslides in the Uttaranchal state of India.

In Chapter 3, a detailed description of the datasets is given.

9.4.1 Generating golden standard clusters

To evaluate the performance of clustering algorithms [13], it is required to develop a golden standard with which the clustering obtained by various algorithms will be compared. It is customary to obtain the golden standard clustering through human feedback [52]. Three human volunteers were asked to find the different types of information contained in the tweets and to cluster/group the tweets according to the type of information. The observations of each of the human volunteers were similar – they recognized five distinct types of information in the tweet datasets:

(1) tweets informing about casualties or damage to assets,
(2) tweets giving climate-related updates,
(3) tweets giving helpline-related information,
(4) conclusions of the general population, sympathy, and petitions for the influenced population, and
(5) news about government/political advances with respect to the disaster circumstance.

Table 9.1 shows examples of tweets of each type. Consequently, the golden standard (created by human volunteers) clusters the tweets in five groups.

9.5 Results and discussion

9.5.1 Baseline clustering algorithms

The clustering approaches developed in this chapter (as stated in the earlier sections of this chapter) are compared with three classical clustering meth-

Table 9.1 Examples of tweets related to the North India floods (2013). Five different types of information were identified by human volunteers/experts.

Information type	Sample tweets of UFlood dataset
Casualties info	8 dead, 37050 pilgrims stranded as incessant rains batter Uttarakhand: Eight persons were slaughtered on Sunday. 100 households collapse; 25 dead, over 50 missing as rain batters Uttarakhand http://t.co/m8zrc3PQub.
Climate info	RT @ANI_news: In Uttarkashi (Uttarakhand), flash floods triggered by heavy rains wash away houses along the river. http://t.co/MvrOwGwca6. RT @kirankhurana: 02/05 Destruction in Uttarakhand due to Heavy Rains: @joinAAP
Helpline info	RT @LDAPIB_India: IAF launches operation 'Rahat' to help stranded pilgrims &tourists in Uttarakhand & HP. http://t.co/8J8n4OLG1u. RT @rahulmanthattil:#Uttarakhand flood helpline numbers : 0135-2710334, 0135-2710335, 0135-2710233. Please share ! @annavetticad.
Public opinion	Prayers for Uttarakhand. Just shows you should never take life for granted. Irony: the families of the Kedarnath flood victims praying to the same gods that the victims had so devotedly gone to visit.
News Info	RT @IndiaSpeaksPR: Rahul Gandhi promises to reach out to the victims in Kedarnath once Congress confirms that it would be secular to do so. Seems CM Vijay Bahuguna has no time to utter a few words of comfort to the people of #Uttarakhand, who are dealing with life & death. #shame.

ods – density-based clustering, K-means, and hierarchical clustering [53]. The reader can refer to [54] for detailed descriptions of these clustering methods. There are different broad approaches for clustering, such as partition-based, hierarchical-based, density-based, and graph-based clustering.

9.5.1.1 Partition-based clustering

A partitioning method [55] creates k ($k \leq n$) clusters distinct from each other given a dataset of n items. The algorithm divides the data into k groups that must all meet the following criteria: (1) there must be at least one object in each group and (2) each object must belong to only one group (hard clustering). In general, the algorithms employ an iterative relocation strategy based on an objective function that aims to increase partitioning by transferring objects from one cluster to another [56]. The general criterion for good partitioning is that objects belonging to the same group are close to each other, whilst objects belonging to other clusters are far apart. There are a variety of other factors for measuring the quality of clusters [57]. Some common partition-based clustering methods are described below.

(A) K-means clustering

The K-means clustering technique is one of the most widely used un-supervised learning algorithms [58,59]. It uses a straightforward iterative algorithm to divide a dataset into k clusters, with k predetermined. The first step is to determine the number of centers (k) that will be used for each cluster. These centers should be strategically placed, as different sites may yield varied outcomes. As a result, it is preferable to space them as far apart as feasible. The next step is to consider each object belonging to a given dataset and associate it to the nearest center. When no object is pending, the first step is finished and an early clustering is done. At this point, k new centers are computed by calculating means of the k clusters obtained in the earlier step, and these new centers are set as centers of the clusters. After these k new centers are obtained, a new binding has to be done between the same objects and the nearest new centroid. During execution of the loop, k centers modify their position step by step until the algorithm converges. A flowchart of K-means clustering which consists of six essential stages is depicted in Fig. 9.3.

Unfortunately, for any particular dataset, there is no general theoretical method for determining the necessary number of clusters. Comparing the results of numerous executions with varying k values and selecting the best one based on a set of criteria is a straightforward approach. However, one must exercise caution, since, while increasing k results in reduced error function values by definition, it also increases the risk of overfitting [60].

(B) K-medoids clustering

Because an object with an unusually large value can significantly alter the distribution of objects in the discovered clusters, the K-means clustering algorithm is sensitive to outliers. Instead of using the mean value of the items in a cluster, the most centrally situated object in the cluster is utilized as a point of reference in the K-medoids approach. As a result, object partitioning can still be done using the principle of minimizing the sum of dissimilarities between each item and its associated point of reference.

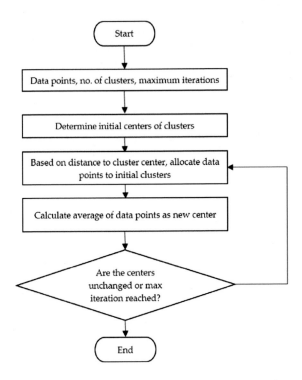

Figure 9.3 A flowchart of K-means clustering.

In the presence of noise and outliers, the K-medoids approach has been found to be more robust than the K-means method, because a medoid is less influenced by outliers or other extreme values than a mean [61]. However, K-medoid processing is more expensive than the K-means technique. The user must supply the value of k, the number of clusters, in both approaches. Partitioning around medoids (PAM) [62], a common K-medoids partitioning technique, works well for low-volume datasets but fails to scale well for high-volume datasets.

(C) Partitioning methods in large databases

To deal with huge datasets, a sampling-based method called Clustering LARge Applications (CLARA) [63] can be utilized. CLARA's concept is that instead of considering the entire collection of items, a tiny subset of the original objects is chosen as the dataset's representations. PAM [62] is then used to pick medoids from the representatives. If the sample is chosen at random, it should be fairly representative of the original dataset. The representative items (medoids) chosen are likely to be similar to those chosen from the entire dataset. CLARA extracts several samples from the dataset, applies PAM to each sample, and outputs the best clustering result. As a result, CLARA is capable of handling larger datasets than PAM. Each iteration is $O(ks^2 + k(n - k))$ in complexity, where s, k, and n are the sample size, number of clusters, and total number of objects, respectively.

A K-medoids approach called Clustering Large Applications based upon RANdomized Search (CLARANS) [63] has also been proposed to increase the quality and scalability of CLARA. This method combines the sampling technique with PAM; however, it is not limited to a single sample at a specific time. CLARANS represents a sample with some randomness in each phase of the search, whereas CLARA has a fixed sample at every step of the search. The clustering approach can be described as a network search in which each node represents a potential solution, such as a set of K-medoids.

9.5.1.2 Hierarchical clustering

According to the proximity matrix, hierarchical clustering algorithms group the objects of a given dataset into a hierarchical structure [65]. A dendrogram is commonly used to illustrate the hierarchical clustering results. The dendrogram's root node represents the entire dataset, whereas each leaf node is treated as an item. The height of the dendrogram usually reflects the distance between each pair of clusters or objects or a cluster and an object, and the intermediate nodes describe the degree to which the objects are proximate to each other. By slicing the dendrogram at various levels, clustering can be produced.

Agglomerative methods and divisive methods are two types of hierarchical clustering algorithms [64,65]. Agglomerative clustering begins with a set of N clusters, each of which contains exactly one item. After then, a series of merge procedures are performed, culminating in all items being placed in the same group. Divisive clustering, on the other hand, works in the other direction. The entire dataset is assigned to a cluster in the first stage, and then the items are divided one by one until all clusters are singletons.

With the need to handle large-scale datasets in data mining and other fields, several novel hierarchical clustering approaches have emerged in recent years, such as ROCK [66], CURE [67], BIRCH [68], and Chameleon [20], which have substantially enhanced clustering performance. Despite the fact that divided clustering is not often employed in reality, some examples may be found in [69], where two divisive clustering methods, MONA and DIANA, are discussed [69].

9.5.1.3 Density-based clustering

Clusters of arbitrary forms have been discovered using density-based clustering methods [70]. Typically, these clusters are dense groups of objects in a dataset's space divided by low-density regions (representing noise). DENCLUE and DBSCAN [71] are two commonly used density–based spatial clustering algorithms.

DBSCAN: In geographical datasets with noise, the DBSCAN algorithm creates areas with suitable high density into clusters and identifies clusters of arbitrary shape. It defines a cluster as a maximum set of density-connected objects and looks for clusters by inspecting every object in the dataset's ϵ-neighborhood. If the ϵ-neighborhood of an item p contains more objects than a threshold, a new cluster is created with p as the core object. Then DBSCAN iteratively gathers directly density-reachable items from the core objects, perhaps merging a few density-reachable clusters. When no additional points can be added to any of the clusters, the operation ends. DBSCAN's computational complexity is $O(n\log n)$ if a spatial index is employed, where n is the number of items; otherwise, it is $O(n^2)$. The user-defined parameters have an impact on the algorithm.

DENCLUE: DENCLUE is a clustering algorithm based on the following collection of density distribution functions:

(i)   The control of each data object can be formally modeled with the help of a mathematical function, called an "influence function," that describes the impact of a data point within its neighborhood.

(ii) The total of the effect functions of all data items can be used to model the overall density of a data space logically.

(iii) The density attractors, which are surrounding maxima of the overall density function, can then be identified mathematically to determine clusters.

There are several advantages of the DENCLUE method in comparison with other clustering algorithms:

(i)   It is scientifically justified and it generalizes previous clustering techniques such as partition-based, hierarchical, and locality-based clustering.

(ii) For datasets with a lot of noise, it offers good clustering properties.

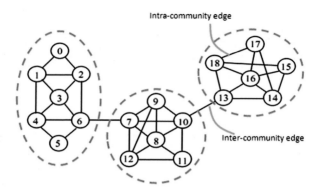

Figure 9.4 Community structure in a graph showing intra-community edges and inter-community edges.

(iii) In high-dimensional datasets, it allows for a succinct mathematical description of arbitrarily formed clusters.

(iv) Grid cells are used to store information about grid cells that include data points. It organizes these cells into a tree-based access structure, making it much faster than some popular techniques, such as DBSCAN. The approach, on the other hand, necessitates careful selection of the density parameter and the noise threshold, as these factors can have a substantial impact on the quality of the clustering solutions.

9.5.1.4 Graph clustering algorithms

Clustering (also known as community detection in the context of graphs) methods for graphs/networks are designed to locate communities based on the network topology, such as tightly connected groups of nodes. In graph-based clustering, data are represented as a graph before applying a community detection algorithm. The edge weight in the graph can be calculated using a variety of similarity measures. A community is formed when nodes in a network are of the same type. Intra-community edges are the edges that connect the nodes within a community. Inter-community edges are nodes that connect nodes from different communities. Fig. 9.4 depicts intra-community and inter-community edges between distinct communities in a tiny graph. A popular graph clustering algorithm is described below.

Infomap method

Rosvall and Bergstrom (2008) [45] developed a popular community discovery technique, Infomap. It improves the map equation, which achieves a balance between the difficulty of data compression and the problem of recognizing and retrieving essential patterns or structures within the data. The Louvain community finding approach is closely followed by this algorithm. Each node is initially given to its own module. Then, in a random sequential order, each node is transferred to the nearby modules, resulting in the greatest reduction of the map equation. The node remains in its original position if no move leads to a further reduction of the map equation. Every time, the operation is repeated in a different random sequential order, until the map equation can no longer be reduced. Finally, the network is recreated, with the lowest-level modules producing nodes at that level, and nodes are connected into modules in the same way as the previous-level nodes. This hierarchical network rebuilding is continued until the map equation can no longer be reduced. Both undirected and directed graphs can be used with Infomap. Infomap returns a list of non-overlapping communities (node set partitions) as well as a decimal value that represents the total flow in that node.

As is evident from the discussion above, there are a wide variety of clustering algorithms. It is a natural question which algorithm performs the best on a certain dataset. To answer this question, first some measures for cluster validation/evaluation need to be determined. The next section discusses some commonly used cluster validation measures.

For implementing these clustering algorithms, the Weka machine learning toolkit [72] has been used, which is a renowned tool for data mining, clustering, classification, and feature selection. The default parameters of the Weka toolkit have been used in all cases. For those algorithms that need the number of clusters as an input parameter, the number of clusters has been specified to be five, since the human annotators observed five different types of information in the datasets being considered.

9.5.2 Cluster validation indices

There are a set of standard metrics [73] to evaluate the quality of clustering produced by the different methodologies. Jain and Dubes called the difficulty of determining the number of clusters "the fundamental problem of cluster validity" [74]. The clustering algorithms partition objects of the dataset into a particular number of subsets. Although for several applications the number of clusters k is known, in most cases, k is unknown and needs to be estimated exclusively from the object itself. Many clustering algorithms take k as an input parameter, and it is obvious that the quality of resulting clusters is largely dependent on the estimation of k.

Two measurements of cluster "goodness" or quality are employed for clustering. Internal quality measures are metrics that allow us to compare different sets of clusters without relying on external knowledge. We will employ an "overall similarity" measure based on the pairwise similarity of documents in a cluster, as indicated in the previous section. Other measures compare the groups produced by clustering techniques to recognized classes, allowing us to assess how well the clustering is working. This type of metric is called external quality measure. Entropy is an external measure that determines the "goodness" of unnested clusters or clusters at one level of a hierarchical clustering. There are numerous alternative quality criteria, and depending on which one is chosen, the performance and relative ranking of different clustering algorithms might differ significantly. However, if one clustering algorithm outperforms another on a number of these criteria, we can be quite confident that it is the optimal clustering algorithm for the circumstance under consideration. Cluster validation, an important issue in cluster analysis, is the measurement of goodness of a cluster relative to others created by clustering algorithms using different parameter values. Several cluster validation measures, like compactness, connectedness, separation, and combinations of these, take a clustering method and the underlying dataset as the input and employ information intrinsic to the dataset to review the quality of the clusters. Some of these cluster validation measures are discussed below.

(A) Compactness

Compactness is an indicator of the scattering of the objects within a particular cluster. It measures clusters' compactness or homogeneity, with intra-cluster variance as their most popular representative. Numerous variants of measuring intra-cluster homogeneity are possible such as the evaluation of maximum or average pairwise intra-cluster distances, maximum or average center-based similarities, or the use of graph-based methods.

(B) Connectedness

Connectedness can be used to assess how well a given partitioning agrees with the conception of connectedness, i.e., to what degree a partitioning examines local densities and groups objects together with their nearest neighbors in the data space.

(C) Separation

Separation is an indicator of the isolation of clusters from one another. It measures the degree of separation between individual clusters. For example, a general rating for a partitioning can be stated as the average weighted inter-cluster distance, where the distance between two individual clusters is computed as the distance between cluster centroids or as the minimum distance between objects belonging to different clusters.

(D) Combinations of the above measures

The above measures can be combined to measure cluster quality considering multiple aspects. Combinations of compactness and separation are particularly popular, as the two classes of measures show an opposite tendency. Thus, a number of measures assess both inter-cluster separation and intra-cluster homogeneity and a final score can be calculates as the linear or non-linear combination of the two measures. Some of these cluster validation measures are discussed below.

Davies–Bouldin validity index: The Davies–Bouldin index (DBIndex) [75] is defined as the ratio of the sum of intra-cluster scatter to inter-cluster separation. Let $U = \{X_1, X_2, X_3, X_4, \ldots\ldots, X_k\}$ be the k-cluster obtained by a clustering algorithm. To measure the goodness of the cluster U, the DBIndex is calculated as follows:

$$DBIndex(U) = \frac{1}{K} \sum_{i=1}^{k} \max_{i=j} \left\{ \frac{\Delta(X_i) + \Delta(X_j)}{\delta(X_i, X_j)} \right\}. \tag{9.1}$$

Here, $\Delta(X_i)$ is the intra-cluster distance in X_i i.e., the distance between the most remote objects in cluster X_i, and $\delta(S, T)$ is the inter-cluster distance of X_i and X_j, i.e., the distance between X_i and X_j.

Dunn's validity index: The Dunn index (D) [76] uses the minimum pairwise distance between objects in different clusters as the inter-cluster separation and the maximum diameter among all clusters to estimate the intra-cluster compactness. For any partition of clusters, where X_i signifies the i-th cluster, Dunn's validation index (DN) is calculated with Eq. (9.2). Here, $d(X_i, X_j)$ is the distance between clusters X_i and X_j, $d'(X_1)$ is the intra-cluster distance of cluster X_1, and k is the number of clusters. The aim of this measure is to minimize the intra-cluster distances and maximize the inter-cluster distances. Therefore, the number of clusters that maximizes

D_N is taken as the optimal number of clusters:

$$D = \min_{1 \le i \le k} \left\{ \min_{1 \le j \le k; i \ne j} \left\{ \frac{d(X_i, X_j)}{\max_{1 \le l \le k} (d'(X_l))} \right\} \right\}. \tag{9.2}$$

I–index: The I-index (I) [77] measures separation based on the maximum distance between cluster centers and measures compactness based on the sum of distances between objects and their cluster center:

$$I(k) = \left(\frac{1}{k} \cdot \frac{\sum_j \| x_j - \bar{c} \|_2}{\sum_{k=1}^{K} \sum_{j \in c_k} \| x_j - \bar{c} \|_2} \cdot \max_{i,j} \| (c_i - c_j) \| \right)^p. \tag{9.3}$$

Here the power p is a constant, which normally is set to be 2.

CH–index: The Calinski–Harabasz index (CH) [78], which evaluates the cluster validity measure based on the average inter- and intra-cluster sum of squares:

$$CH = \frac{traceB/(K-1)}{traceW/(N-K)}, \tag{9.4}$$

$$traceB = \sum_{k=1}^{K} |C_k| \| \overline{C_k} - \bar{x} \|^2, \tag{9.5}$$

$$traceW = \sum_{k=1}^{K} \sum_{i=1}^{K} w_{k,i} \| \bar{x}_i - \overline{C_k} \|^2, \tag{9.6}$$

where N is the number of objects in the dataset, K is the number of clusters ($K \in N$), B denotes the error sum of squares between different clusters (inter-cluster), and W is the squared differences of all objects in a cluster from their respective cluster center (intra-cluster). An important characteristic of the index is the fact that on the one hand trace W will start at a comparably large value. With an increasing number of clusters K, approaching the optimal clustering solution in K* groups, the value should significantly decrease due to an increasing compactness of each cluster. As soon as the optimal solution is exceeded an increase in compactness and thereby a decrease in value might still occur; this decrease, however, should be notably smaller. On the other hand, trace T should behave in the opposite direction, getting higher as the number of clusters K increases, but should also reveal a kind of softening in its rise if K gets larger than K*. The maximum value of the CH-index is the optimal number of clusters.

278 Data Analytics for Social Microblogging Platforms

Silhouette index: The Silhouette index (S) [79] validates the clustering performance based on the pairwise difference of inter- and intra-cluster distances. To construct the Silhouette index (S) for k clusters, Eq. (9.7) is used:

$$S = \frac{1}{k} \sum_{i=1}^{k} \frac{b_i - a_i}{max(a_i, b_i)}, \tag{9.7}$$

where a_i is the mean dissimilarity of the i-th object to all other objects in the same cluster and b_i is the minimum average dissimilarity of the i-th object with all objects in the closest cluster. It follows from Eq. (9.7) that $-1 \leq SC \leq 1$. If the Silhouette value is close to 1, then the sample is "well clustered" and assigned to an appropriate cluster. If the Silhouette value is close to 0, the sample could be assigned to another cluster closest to it, and the sample lies equally far away from both clusters. If the Silhouette value is close to -1, the sample is "misclassified" and is merely placed somewhere in between the clusters. So a greater value of the SC-index indicates a better number of clusters.

XB-index: The Xie–Beni index (XB) [80] is an index of fuzzy clustering which considers the ratio between compactness and separation. The XB for a given dataset X with a partition with K clusters is mathematically written as

$$XB(K) = \frac{V_c(K)/N}{V_s(K)} = \frac{\sum_{n=1}^{N} \sum_{k=1}^{K} u_{k,n}^m \parallel x_n - c_k \parallel^2}{NX \min_{i,j} \parallel c_i - c_j \parallel}, \tag{9.8}$$

where $V_c(K)$ represents the compactness measure when the dataset is grouped into K clusters, which is given by $\sum_{n=1}^{N} \sum_{k=1}^{K} u_{k,n}^m \parallel x_n - c_k \parallel^2$, where $c_k = \sum_{n=1}^{N} u_{k,n}^m x_n / \sum_{n=1}^{N} u_{k,n}^m$ is the centroid of the k-th cluster, and $V_s(K)$ is the degree of separation between clusters. In general, an optimal K is found by solving $\min_{k \in [2, N-1]} XB(K)$ to produce the best clustering performance for the dataset X.

(1) Comparing the variations of dimensionality reduction-based clustering methods

Several variations of the dimensionality reduction-based clustering method were proposed for clustering. Table 9.2, Table 9.3, Table 9.4, and Table 9.5 show the performance of different variations on the UFlood, HDBlast, SHShoot, and THagupit datasets, respectively. Table 9.6 gives the average performance of both the baselines and the proposed algorithms across all the datasets. For each dataset, the experiments are done with various combinations of the steps used for dimensionality reduction (LDA or TF-IDF),

Table 9.2 Performance of the proposed and baseline algorithms for the UFlood dataset.

Clustering method	S	CH	DB	I	XB	D
LDA-TextSim-ConCom	0.233	0.662	0.807	2.121	2.986	0.808
LDA-TextSim-Infomap	0.163	5.119	0.785	1.896	2.310	0.811
LDA-TextSim-Louvain	0.239	0.673	0.810	2.121	2.812	0.813
LDA-Word2VecSim-ConCom	0.258	7.021	0.652	0.111	2.239	1.011
LDA-Word2VecSim-Infomap	0.179	4.820	0.763	2.091	3.011	0.810
LDA-Word2VecSim-Louvain	0.261	7.121	0.649	0.121	2.296	1.095
LDA-Doc2VecSim-ConCom	0.266	7.019	0.647	0.139	2.241	1.027
LDA-Doc2VecSim-Infomap	0.189	4.710	0.780	2.128	3.230	0.809
LDA-Doc2VecSim-Louvain	0.260	7.017	0.649	0.142	2.238	1.078
TF-IDF-TextSim-ConCom	0.246	6.070	0.717	2.250	3.790	0.815
TF-IDF-TextSim-Infomap	0.175	7.920	0.765	1.430	2.390	0.778
TF-IDF-TextSim-Louvain	0.245	6.120	0.722	2.290	3.800	0.825
TF-IDF-Word2VecSim-ConCom	**0.468**	**12.050**	**0.550**	2.753	**0.422**	**1.142**
TF-IDF-Word2VecSim-Infomap	0.227	8.110	0.871	1.620	2.560	0.887
TF-IDF-Word2VecSim-Louvain	0.394	10.970	0.642	2.112	0.657	1.067
TF-IDF-Doc2VecSim-ConCom	0.346	11.050	0.640	2.601	0.512	1.132
TF-IDF-Doc2VecSim-Infomap	0.214	7.020	0.855	1.091	2.410	0.843
TF-IDF-Doc2VecSim-Louvain	0.340	10.870	0.641	2.102	0.568	1.088
Baseline techniques						
K-means method	0.170	3.238	1.510	**2.755**	67.571	0.871
Hierarchical method	0.164	5.815	0.898	1.047	2.420	0.858
Density-based	0.158	3.405	0.877	2.271	9.136	0.998

measuring the textual similarity between tweets (TextSim, Word2vecSim, or Doc2vecSim), and identifying similar groups of nodes (connected components or communities). The best values obtained for each measure are highlighted in boldface.

Table 9.2 shows the comparative results for the dataset UFlood. For this dataset, the TF-IDF-Word2VecSim-ConCom approach performs better than other proposed approaches and the baseline algorithms. Only the I-index value of the K-means algorithm is slightly better than that of the proposed approach; however, the difference is not statistically significant (the I-index value for the K-means algorithm is 2.755, whereas for TF-IDF-Word2VecSim-ConCom the value is 2.753).

Table 9.3 shows the comparative results for the dataset HDBlast. For this dataset, the TF-IDF-Doc2VecSim-ConCom proposed approach performs

Table 9.3 Performance of the proposed and baseline algorithms for the HDBlast dataset.

Clustering method	S	CH	DB	I	XB	D
LDA-TextSim-ConCom	0.125	5.005	1.127	2.104	1.371	0.770
LDA-TextSim-Infomap	0.117	4.782	1.209	1.332	1.160	1.0970
LDA-TextSim-Louvain	0.128	5.101	1.130	2.210	1.390	0.810
LDA-Word2VecSim-ConCom	0.250	5.690	0.810	3.210	1.170	1.360
LDA-Word2VecSim-Infomap	0.123	4.902	1.367	1.461	1.190	1.110
LDA-Word2VecSim-Louvain	0.270	5.230	0.801	3.420	1.180	1.290
LDA-Doc2VecSim-ConCom	0.243	5.570	0.793	3.321	1.189	1.397
LDA-Doc2VecSim-Infomap	0.126	4.863	1.326	1.459	1.170	1.102
LDA-Doc2VecSim-Louvain	0.269	5.150	0.813	3.460	1.169	1.278
TF-IDF-TextSim-ConCom	0.354	7.452	0.402	3.390	0.135	1.690
TF-IDF-TextSim-Infomap	0.134	4.820	1.339	1.398	1.240	1.160
TF-IDF-TextSim-Louvain	0.393	7.598	0.413	3.310	0.140	1.710
TF-IDF-Word2VecSim-ConCom	0.467	10.110	0.330	3.402	0.140	1.141
TF-IDF-Word2VecSim-Infomap	0.202	3.572	1.112	1.102	0.987	1.012
TF-IDF-Word2VecSim-Louvain	0.403	10.065	0.321	3.487	0.151	1.180
TF-IDF-Doc2VecSim-ConCom	**0.502**	**10.946**	**0.236**	**4.581**	**0.125**	**1.760**
TF-IDF-Doc2VecSim-Infomap	0.218	3.403	1.125	1.117	0.887	1.134
TF-IDF-Doc2VecSim-Louvain	0.498	10.776	0.374	3.505	0.163	1.683
Baseline techniques						
K-means method	0.037	3.629	1.513	0.326	70.121	0.964
Hierarchical method	0.044	5.389	0.967	3.581	1.629	0.797
Density-based	0.034	4.887	1.368	1.443	2.371	0.811

better than other proposed approaches and all the baseline algorithms, for all the cluster quality measures.

Table 9.4 shows the comparative results for the dataset SHShoot. For this dataset, the TF-IDF-Word2VecSim-Louvain proposed approach performs better than the other proposed approaches and the baseline algorithms (K-means, hierarchical, and density-based clustering).

Table 9.5 shows the comparative results for the dataset THagupit. For this dataset, the TF-IDF-Word2VecSim-Louvain proposed approach performs better than other proposed approaches and the baseline algorithms.

Table 9.6 shows the average results, averaged over all the four datasets. The outcome shows that on average, the TF-IDF-Word2VecSim-ConCom approach is more effective in clustering tweets in terms of indices such as Calinski–Harabasz (CH) [78], Davies–Bouldin (DB) [75], and Xie–Beni (XB) [80]. The TF-IDF-Doc2VecSim-ConCom approach achieves the

Table 9.4 Performance of the proposed and baseline algorithms for the SHShoot dataset.

Clustering method	S	CH	DB	I	XB	D
LDA-TextSim-ConCom	0.160	17.078	1.560	1.587	1.561	0.791
LDA-TextSim-Infomap	0.141	14.770	0.792	1.404	1.362	0.695
LDA-TextSim-Louvain	0.152	16.001	0.650	1.580	1.467	0.789
LDA-Word2VecSim-ConCom	0.159	14.980	0.610	1.610	1.448	0.748
LDA-Word2VecSim-Infomap	0.149	14.240	0.766	1.484	1.411	0.706
LDA-Word2VecSim-Louvain	0.157	15.120	0.670	1.680	1.459	0.772
LDA-Doc2VecSim-ConCom	0.148	15.010	0.640	1.623	1.532	0.740
LDA-Doc2VecSim-Infomap	0.141	14.630	0.799	1.429	1.345	0.715
LDA-Doc2VecSim-Louvain	0.153	15.220	0.690	1.690	1.580	0.736
TF-IDF-TextSim-ConCom	0.167	16.240	0.660	1.622	1.171	0.737
TF-IDF-TextSim-Infomap	0.151	15.150	0.802	1.530	1.498	0.713
TF-IDF-TextSim-Louvain	0.169	15.530	1.740	1.580	1.103	0.769
TF-IDF-Word2VecSim-ConCom	0.172	17.123	0.565	1.64199	0.880	0.891
TF-IDF-Word2VecSim-Infomap	0.143	14.980	0.891	1.459	1.393	0.715
TF-IDF-Word2VecSim-Louvain	**0.178**	**17.178**	**0.541**	**1.735**	**0.764**	**0.914**
TF-IDF-Doc2VecSim-ConCom	0.160	17.078	1.560	1.587	0.873	0.861
TF-IDF-Doc2VecSim-Infomap	0.145	14.760	0.880	1.423	1.411	0.728
TF-IDF-Doc2VecSim-Louvain	0.159	16.110	1.610	1.710	0.984	0.837
Baseline techniques						
K-means method	0.152	12.239	1.566	1.666	1616.9	0.731
Hierarchical method	0.102	16.036	0.936	0.075	100.333	0.833
Density-based	0.128	14.856	1.376	1.457	1.394	0.774

best values for the I–index (I) [77] and the Dunn index (D) [76]. According to the Silhouette (S) index [79], TF-IDF-Word2VecSim-Louvain performs better. Fig. 9.5 represents the average comparative chart for four datasets.

By analyzing all the results of the dimensionality reduction-based clustering, it is evident that:

(i) For dimensionality reduction, TF-IDF gives better performance compared to LDA.

(ii) Detection of connected components from the tweet similarity graph leads to better performance in most cases compared to the Louvain and Infomap community detection algorithms.

(iii) Word2Vec similarity and Doc2Vec similarity perform quite similar to each other, mainly because the underlying technology in both of them is very similar. Note that when using the Word2Vec similarity algorithm, the word vectors were generated for every word in a

Table 9.5 Performance of the proposed and baseline algorithms for the THagupit dataset.

Clustering method	S	CH	DB	I	XB	D
LDA–TextSim–ConCom	0.230	0.732	0.683	1.680	0.870	1.111
LDA–TextSim–Infomap	0.115	6.824	0.916	1.010	0.950	1.020
LDA–TextSim–Louvain	0.340	0.719	0.669	1.960	0.820	1.139
LDA–Word2VecSim–ConCom	0.590	0.707	0.583	2.182	0.780	1.270
LDA–Word2VecSim–Infomap	0.120	6.789	0.923	1.129	0.934	1.018
LDA–Word2VecSim–Louvain	0.650	0.712	0.542	2.008	0.743	1.264
LDA–Doc2VecSim–ConCom	0.640	0.723	0.501	2.258	0.620	1.290
LDA–Doc2VecSim–Infomap	0.160	7.992	0.845	1.117	0.873	1.111
LDA–Doc2VecSim–Louvain	0.598	0.765	0.512	2.380	0.581	1.300
TF–IDF–TextSim–ConCom	0.276	10.340	0.389	2.048	0.216	1.230
TF–IDF–TextSim–Infomap	0.198	7.346	0.866	2.314	0.841	1.180
TF–IDF–TextSim–Louvain	0.248	11.060	0.372	2.168	0.214	1.270
TF–IDF–Word2VecSim–ConCom	0.511	16.230	0.248	4.217	0.223	1.650
TF–IDF–Word2VecSim–Infomap	0.235	8.443	0.744	2.246	0.793	1.310
TF–IDF–Word2VecSim–Louvain	**0.701**	**16.677**	**0.204**	**4.331**	**0.180**	**1.890**
TF–IDF–Doc2VecSim–ConCom	0.493	16.110	0.262	4.168	0.193	1.550
TF–IDF–Doc2VecSim–Infomap	0.227	8.632	0.783	2.578	0.725	1.370
TF–IDF–Doc2VecSim–Louvain	0.467	15.890	0.259	3.345	0.245	1.450
Baseline techniques						
K–means method	0.207	0.257	1.682	0.898	508.542	0.976
Hierarchical method	0.025	15.115	1.026	0.001	1.439	0.766
Density-based	0.134	3.960	0.792	0.972	1.230	1.010

tweet and then the average over all the word vectors was considered to get the tweet vector. When using the Doc2Vec algorithm, the model was trained to give vectors for the tweets directly.

The results indicate the superior performance of the proposed dimensionality reduction-based clustering approach. This method performs the best in terms of most of the measures across all the datasets. For all the datasets, dimensionality reduction-based clustering achieves the best values for the measures CH-index, XB-index, and Dunn index (D). For the I-index (I), in the Hagupit dataset this approach gives best performance, whereas feature selection-based clustering approach gives the best performance for the remaining two datasets (HDBlast and UFlood). For the S-index (S), apart from the SHShoot dataset, dimensionality reduction-based clustering gives the best performance for all datasets.

Table 9.6 Average performance of the proposed and baseline algorithms averaged over all four datasets.

Clustering method	S	CH	DB	I	XB	D
LDA–TextSim–ConCom	0.187	5.869	1.044	1.873	1.697	0.870
LDA–TextSim–Infomap	0.134	7.874	0.926	1.411	1.446	0.906
LDA–TextSim–Louvain	0.215	5.624	0.814	1.968	1.621	0.888
LDA–Word2VecSim–ConCom	0.314	7.100	0.663	1.778	1.409	1.097
LDA–Word2VecSim–Infomap	0.143	7.688	0.955	1.542	1.637	0.911
LDA–Word2VecSim–Louvain	0.335	7.046	0.666	1.808	1.420	1.106
LDA–Doc2VecSim–ConCom	0.325	7.081	0.645	1.836	1.395	1.114
LDA–Doc2VecSim–Infomap	0.154	8.048	0.938	1.532	1.655	0.934
LDA–Doc2VecSim–Louvain	0.320	7.038	0.666	1.917	1.391	1.098
TF–IDF–TextSim–ConCom	0.261	10.026	0.542	2.328	1.328	1.118
TF–IDF–TextSim–Infomap	0.165	8.808	0.942	1.667	1.492	0.958
TF–IDF–TextSim–Louvain	0.264	10.077	0.813	2.337	1.314	1.143
TF–IDF–Word2VecSim–ConCom	0.405	**13.878**	**0.424**	1.905	**0.416**	1.206
TF–IDF–Word2VecSim–Infomap	0.202	8.778	0.905	1.607	1.433	0.981
TF–IDF–Word2VecSim–Louvain	**0.419**	13.723	0.427	2.915	0.438	1.262
TF–IDF–Doc2VecSim–ConCom	0.375	13.795	0.674	**3.234**	0.426	**1.326**
TF–IDF–Doc2VecSim–Infomap	0.201	8.455	0.911	1.552	1.358	1.018
TF–IDF–Doc2VecSim–Louvain	0.366	13.412	0.720	2.665	0.490	1.264
Baselines techniques						
K-means method	0.141	4.841	1.568	1.411	565.783	0.886
Hierarchical method	0.084	10.589	0.957	1.175	26.455	0.813
Density-based	0.114	6.777	1.103	1.536	3.532	0.898

Finally, among the different variations of the dimensionality reduction-based approach, it has been observed that TF–IDF used for dimensionality reduction along with Word2Vec similarity and connected components detection performs the best, followed by TF–IDF along with Doc2Vec and connected components detection. For unstructured data, TF–IDF is one of the most effective ways to reduce the dimension when identifying important features. It measures the relative importance of each term in the dataset. From another perspective, Doc2Vec and Word2Vec are effective tools for representing words as vectors that capture the semantics of the words.

These vectorization approaches provide a better representation of terms considering the semantic relation of each term with other terms found in the vicinity, and this approach is especially effective for social media content where the semantics of a term often depends on the particular

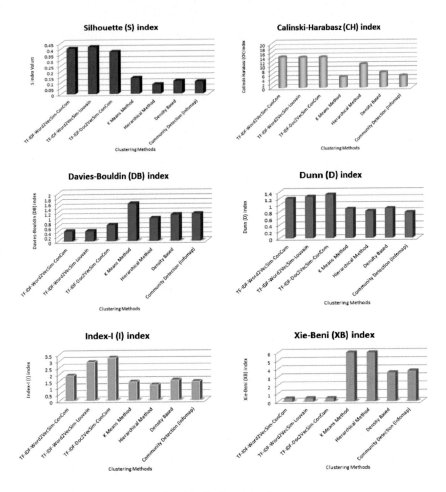

Figure 9.5 The average comparative chart for four datasets.

context in which it is used. Overall, it is evident from the results that traditional clustering algorithms such as K-means [58,59], hierarchical [64,65], density-based [70], and graph-based community detection [81] perform poorly compared to the proposed approaches. This poor performance of traditional approaches is due to the informally written information in microblogs. The proposed clustering methods perform well because of the use of dimensionality reduction and semantic methods for estimating similarity between tweets.

9.6 Conclusion

In this chapter a novel approach has been proposed for clustering microblogs or tweets by utilizing dimensionality reduction, followed by a graph-based approach. The results of the experiments show that the proposed algorithms perform better than various standard clustering approaches, such as hierarchical, density-based, K-means, and graph-based community detection techniques (Louvain, Infomap). According to the results of the experiments, TF-IDF used for dimensionality reduction along with Word2Vec similarity and connected components detection performs the best, followed by TF-IDF along with Doc2Vec and connected components detection.

The clustering algorithms developed in this chapter consider a static set of tweets. In reality, tweets come in a continuous stream, and clustering and summarization need to be performed periodically in a dynamic setting. It is a challenging future research direction to extend the summarization and clustering methods to dynamic data streams. The clustering methods developed in this chapter have considered only tweets in English. They can be extended so that they can process tweets in both English and non-English languages and even code-mixed tweets (where multiple languages are used in the same post).

References

[1] S. Goswami, A.K. Das, Determining maximum cliques for community detection in weighted sparse networks, Knowledge and Information Systems 64 (2) (2022) 289–324, https://doi.org/10.1007/s10115-021-01631-y.

[2] A. Mukherjee, S. Bhattacharyya, K. Ray, B. Gupta, A.K. Das, A study of public sentiment and influence of politics in COVID-19 related tweets, in: A.K. Das, J. Nayak, B. Naik, S. Dutta, D. Pelusi (Eds.), Computational Intelligence in Pattern Recognition, Springer, Singapore, 2022, pp. 655–665.

[3] P. Das, A.K. Das, Convolutional neural networks-based sentence level classification of crime documents, in: A.K. Das, J. Nayak, B. Naik, S. Dutta, D. Pelusi (Eds.), Computational Intelligence in Pattern Recognition, Springer, Singapore, 2022, pp. 65–73.

[4] A. Das, D. Pal, C. Mallick, A.K. Das, An unsupervised COVID-19 report summarizer for developing smart healthcare system, in: A.K. Das, J. Nayak, B. Naik, S. Dutta, D. Pelusi (Eds.), Computational Intelligence in Pattern Recognition, Springer, Singapore, 2022, pp. 157–168.

[5] C. Mallick, S. Das, A.K. Das, Evolutionary algorithm based summarization for analyzing COVID-19 medical reports, in: J. Nayak, B. Naik, A. Abraham (Eds.), Understanding COVID-19: The Role of Computational Intelligence, in: Studies in Computational Intelligence, Springer International Publishing, Cham, 2022, pp. 31–58.

[6] S. Chattopadhyay, T. Basu, A.K. Das, K. Ghosh, L.C.A. Murthy, Towards effective discovery of natural communities in complex networks and implications in e-commerce, Electronic Commerce Research 21 (4) (2021) 917–954, https://doi.org/10.1007/s10660-019-09395-y.

[7] M. Basu, S.D. Bit, S. Ghosh, Utilizing microblogs for optimized real-time resource allocation in post-disaster scenarios, Social Network Analysis and Mining 12 (1) (2021) 15, https://doi.org/10.1007/s13278-021-00841-0.

[8] P. Bhattacharya, S. Paul, K. Ghosh, S. Ghosh, A. Wyner, DeepRhole: deep learning for rhetorical role labeling of sentences in legal case documents, Artificial Intelligence and Law (2021), https://doi.org/10.1007/s10506-021-09304-5.

[9] S. Miyamoto, S. Suzuki, S. Takumi, Clustering in tweets using a fuzzy neighborhood model, in: 2012 IEEE International Conference on Fuzzy Systems, 2012, pp. 1–6.

[10] W. Song, S.C. Park, Genetic algorithm-based text clustering technique, in: J. Licheng, W. Lipo, G. Xin-bo, L. Jing, W. Feng (Eds.), Advances in Natural Computation, Springer Berlin Heidelberg, Berlin, Heidelberg, 2006, pp. 779–782.

[11] K. Hazra, T. Ghosh, A. Mukherjee, S. Saha, S. Nandi, S. Ghosh, S. Chakraborty, Sustainable text summarization over mobile devices: an energy-aware approach, Sustainable Computing: Informatics and Systems 32 (2021) 100607, https://doi.org/10.1016/j.suscom.2021.100607, https://www.sciencedirect.com/science/article/pii/S2210537921000950.

[12] F. Perez-Tellez, D. Pinto, J. Cardiff, P. Rosso, On the difficulty of clustering microblog texts for online reputation management, in: Proceedings of the 2nd Workshop on Computational Approaches to Subjectivity and Sentiment Analysis (WASSA 2.011), Association for Computational Linguistics, Portland, Oregon, 2011, pp. 146–152, https://aclanthology.org/W11-1719.

[13] A. Modi, Classification of tweets via clustering of hashtags, 2011.

[14] C.-H. Lee, Mining spatio-temporal information on microblogging streams using a density-based online clustering method, Expert Systems with Applications 39 (10) (2012) 9623–9641, https://doi.org/10.1016/j.eswa.2012.02.136.

[15] A. Mandal, K. Ghosh, S. Ghosh, S. Mandal, A sequence labeling model for catch-phrase identification from legal case documents, Artificial Intelligence and Law (2021), https://doi.org/10.1007/s10506-021-09296-2.

[16] K.D. Rosa, R. Shah, B. Lin, A. Gershman, R. Frederking, Topical clustering of tweets, in: 3rd Workshop on Social Web Search and Mining, 2011.

[17] S. Dutta, S. Ghatak, S. Ghosh, A.K. Das, A genetic algorithm based tweet clustering technique, in: Computer Communication and Informatics (ICCCI), 2017, pp. 1–6.

[18] A. Yıldırım, S. Üsküdarlı, A. Özgür, Identifying topics in microblogs using Wikipedia, PLoS ONE 11 (3) (2016) e0151885.

[19] M. Basu, K. Ghosh, S. Ghosh, Information retrieval from microblogs during disasters: in the light of IRMiDis task, SN Computer Science 1 (1) (2020) 61, https://doi.org/10.1007/s42979-020-0065-1.

[20] G. Karypis, E.-H. Han, V. Kumar, Chameleon: hierarchical clustering using dynamic modeling, Computer 32 (8) (1999) 68–75, https://doi.org/10.1109/2.781637.

[21] L.F. Rau, P.S. Jacobs, U. Zernik, Information extraction and text summarization using linguistic knowledge acquisition, Information Processing & Management 25 (4) (1989) 419–428, https://doi.org/10.1016/0306-4573(89)90069-1, http://www.sciencedirect.com/science/article/pii/0306457389900691.

[22] M. Michael, K. Nick, Twittermonitor: trend detection over the Twitter stream, in: Proceedings of the 2010 ACM SIGMOD International Conference on Management of Data, SIGMOD '10, ACM, 2010, pp. 1155–1158.

[23] Ramage Daniel, Dumais Susan, Dan Liebling, Characterizing microblogs with topic models, in: ICWSM, The AAAI Press, 2010, http://dblp.uni-trier.de/db/conf/icwsm/icwsm2010.html#RamageDL10.

[24] C. Mario, D.C. Luigi, C. Schifanella, Emerging topic detection on Twitter based on temporal and social terms evaluation, in: Proceedings of the Tenth International Workshop on Multimedia Data Mining, MDMKDD '10, ACM, 2010, pp. 4:1–4:10.

[25] Michelson Matthew, Macskassy Sofus A, Discovering users' topics of interest on Twitter: a first look, in: Proceedings of the Fourth Workshop on Analytics for Noisy Unstructured Text Data, AND '10, ACM, 2010, pp. 73–80.

[26] N. Mor, B. Hila, G. Luis, Hip and trendy: characterizing emerging trends on Twitter, Journal of the American Society for Information Science and Technology 62 (5) (2011) 902–918.

[27] R. Mandal, S. Dutta, R. Banerjee, S. Bhattacharya, R. Ghosh, S. Samanta, T. Saha, City traffic speed characterization based on city road surface quality, in: J.M.R.S. Tavares, P. Dutta, S. Dutta, D. Samanta (Eds.), Cyber Intelligence and Information Retrieval, Springer, Singapore, 2022, pp. 515–524.

[28] D. Samanta, S. Dutta, M.G. Galety, S. Pramanik, A novel approach for web mining taxonomy for high-performance computing, in: J.M.R.S. Tavares, P. Dutta, S. Dutta, D. Samanta (Eds.), Cyber Intelligence and Information Retrieval, in: Lecture Notes in Networks and Systems, Springer, Singapore, 2022, pp. 425–432.

[29] A. Campan, T. Atnafu, T.M. Truta, J. Nolan, Is data collection through Twitter streaming api useful for academic research?, in: 2018 IEEE International Conference on Big Data (Big Data), 2018, pp. 3638–3643.

[30] S. Kumar, K.M. Carley, What to track on the Twitter streaming api? A knapsack bandits approach to dynamically update the search terms, in: 2019 IEEE/ACM International Conference on Advances in Social Networks Analysis and Mining (ASONAM), 2019, pp. 158–163.

[31] H. Efstathiades, D. Antoniades, G. Pallis, M.D. Dikaiakos, Distributed large-scale data collection in online social networks, in: 2016 IEEE 2nd International Conference on Collaboration and Internet Computing (CIC), 2016, pp. 373–380.

[32] A. Dwi Laksito, Kusrini, H. Sismoro, F. Rahmawati, M. Yusa, A comparison study of search strategy on collecting Twitter data for drug adverse reaction, in: 2018 International Seminar on Application for Technology of Information and Communication, 2018, pp. 356–360.

[33] D.M. Blei, A.Y. Ng, M.I. Jordan, Latent Dirichlet allocation, Journal of Machine Learning Research 3 (2003) 993–1022.

[34] P. Ray, A. Chakrabarti, Twitter sentiment analysis for product review using lexicon method, in: 2017 International Conference on Data Management, Analytics and Innovation (ICDMAI), 2017, pp. 211–216.

[35] K. Jitkajornwanich, C. Kongthong, N. Khongsoontornjaroen, J. Kaiyasuan, S. Lawawirojwong, P. Srestasathiern, S. Srisonphan, P. Vateekul, Utilizing Twitter data for early flood warning in Thailand, in: 2018 IEEE International Conference on Big Data (Big Data), 2018, pp. 5165–5169.

[36] S.H. Archana, S.G. Winster, Drugs categorization based on sentence polarity analyzer for Twitter data, in: 2016 Second International Conference on Science Technology Engineering and Management (ICONSTEM), 2016, pp. 28–33.

[37] T. Jagić, L. Brkić, Hot topic detection using Twitter streaming data, in: 2020 43rd International Convention on Information, Communication and Electronic Technology (MIPRO), 2020, pp. 1730–1735.

[38] R. Compton, C. Lee, T.-C. Lu, L. De Silva, M. Macy, Detecting future social unrest in unprocessed Twitter data: "emerging phenomena and big data", in: 2013 IEEE International Conference on Intelligence and Security Informatics, 2013, pp. 56–60.

[39] T. Mikolov, K. Chen, G. Corrado, J. Dean, Efficient estimation of word representations in vector space, arXiv:1301.3781, 2013.

[40] R.D. Perera, S. Anand, K.P. Subbalakshmi, R. Chandramouli, Twitter analytics: architecture, tools and analysis, in: 2010 - MILCOM 2010 Military Communications Conference, 2010, pp. 2186–2191.

[41] Q. Le, T. Mikolov, Distributed representations of sentences and documents, in: E.P. Xing, T. Jebara (Eds.), Proceedings of the 31st International Conference on Machine

Learning, in: Proceedings of Machine Learning Research, vol. 32, PMLR, Bejing, China, 2014, pp. 1188–1196, https://proceedings.mlr.press/v32/le14.html.

[42] P. Tatineni, B.S. Babu, B. Kanuri, G.R.K. Rao, P. Chitturi, C. Naresh, Post Covid-19 Twitter user's emotions classification using deep learning techniques in India, in: 2021 International Conference on Artificial Intelligence and Smart Systems (ICAIS), 2021, pp. 338–343.

[43] C. Wang, L. Marini, C.-L. Chin, N. Vance, C. Donelson, P. Meunier, J.T. Yun, Social media intelligence and learning environment: an open source framework for social media data collection, analysis and curation, in: 2019 15th International Conference on eScience (eScience), 2019, pp. 252–261.

[44] S. Fortunato, Community detection in graphs, Physics Reports 486 (3–5) (2010) 75–174, https://doi.org/10.1016/j.physrep.2009.11.002.

[45] Infomap - community detection, http://www.mapequation.org/code.html.

[46] X. Que, F. Checconi, F. Petrini, J.A. Gunnels, Scalable community detection with the Louvain algorithm, in: 2015 IEEE International Parallel and Distributed Processing Symposium, 2015, pp. 28–37.

[47] Documentation home | docs | Twitter developer platform, https://developer.twitter.com/en/docs.

[48] 2013 hyderabad blasts, https://en.wikipedia.org/wiki/2013_Hyderabad_blasts, Aug 2021.

[49] Sandy hook elementary school shooting, https://en.wikipedia.org/wiki/Sandy_Hook_Elementary_School_shooting, Oct 2021.

[50] Typhoon hagupit (2014), https://en.wikipedia.org/wiki/Typhoon_Hagupit_(2014), Aug 2021.

[51] 2013 North India floods, https://en.wikipedia.org/wiki/2013_North_India_floods, Oct 2021.

[52] G.A. Sandag, A.M. Manueke, M. Walean, Sentiment analysis of Covid-19 vaccine tweets in Indonesia using recurrent neural network (rnn) approach, in: 2021 3rd International Conference on Cybernetics and Intelligent System (ICORIS), 2021, pp. 1–7.

[53] C.M. Yoshimura, H. Kitagawa, Tlv-bandit: bandit method for collecting topic-related local tweets, in: 2021 IEEE 4th International Conference on Multimedia Information Processing and Retrieval (MIPR), 2021, pp. 56–62.

[54] Jain A. K, Murty M. N, Flynn P. J, Data clustering: a review, ACM Computing Surveys 31 (3) (1999) 264–323, https://doi.org/10.1145/331499.331504, http://doi.acm.org/10.1145/331499.331504.

[55] C.H. Lee, C.H. Hung, S.J. Lee, A comparative study on clustering algorithms, in: 2013 14th ACIS International Conference on Software Engineering, Artificial Intelligence, Networking and Parallel/Distributed Computing, 2013, pp. 557–562.

[56] A. Nsouli, A. Mourad, D. Azar, Towards proactive social learning approach for traffic event detection based on Arabic tweets, in: 2018 14th International Wireless Communications Mobile Computing Conference (IWCMC), 2018, pp. 1501–1506.

[57] S.-R. Sandra, V. Ana, D.R. Rebeca, P.-A. Jose, Comparing tag clustering algorithms for mining Twitter users' interests, in: 2013 International Conference on Social Computing, 2013, pp. 679–684.

[58] Kanungo Tapas, Mount David M, Netanyahu Nathan S, Piatko Christine D, Silverman Ruth, Wu Angela Y, An efficient k-means clustering algorithm: analysis and implementation, IEEE Transactions on Pattern Analysis and Machine Intelligence 24 (7) (2002) 881–892, https://doi.org/10.1109/TPAMI.2002.1017616.

[59] M.P. D, M.T. Brendan, Model-based clustering of microarray expression data via latent Gaussian mixture models, Bioinformatics 26 (21) (2010) 2705–2712, https://doi.org/10.1093/bioinformatics/btq498, arXiv:/oup/backfile/content_public/journal/bioinformatics/26/21/10.1093/bioinformatics/btq498/2/btq498.pdf.

[60] Tetko Igor V, Livingstone David J, Luik Alexander I, Neural network studies. 1. Comparison of overfitting and overtraining, Journal of Chemical Information and Computer Sciences 35 (5) (1995) 826–833, https://doi.org/10.1021/ci00027a006, arXiv:https://pubs.acs.org/doi/pdf/10.1021/ci00027a006.

[61] Petrovskiy M I, Outlier detection algorithms in data mining systems, Programming and Computer Software 29 (4) (2003) 228–237, https://doi.org/10.1023/A:1024974810270.

[62] E. Zhou, S. Mao, M. Li, Z. Sun, Pam spatial clustering algorithm research based on cuda, in: 2016 24th International Conference on Geoinformatics, 2016, pp. 1–7.

[63] K. Ari, M. Nicholas, K. Akshay, M. Andrew, A hierarchical algorithm for extreme clustering, in: Proceedings of the 23rd ACM SIGKDD International Conference on Knowledge Discovery and Data Mining, KDD '17, ACM, New York, NY, USA, 2017, pp. 255–264, http://doi.acm.org/10.1145/3097983.3098079.

[64] D. Manoranjan, P. Simona, S. Peter, Efficient parallel hierarchical clustering, in: D. Marco, V. Marco, L. Domenico (Eds.), Euro-Par 2004 Parallel Processing, Springer Berlin Heidelberg, Berlin, Heidelberg, 2004, pp. 363–371.

[65] S. Das, A. Abraham, A. Konar, Automatic clustering using an improved differential evolution algorithm, IEEE Transactions on Systems, Man and Cybernetics. Part A. Systems and Humans 38 (1) (2008) 218–237, https://doi.org/10.1109/TSMCA.2007.909595.

[66] S. Guha, K. Shim, R. Rastogi, Rock: a robust clustering algorithm for categorical attributes, in: Proceedings 15th International Conference on Data Engineering (Cat. No. 99CB36337), 1999, pp. 512–521.

[67] S. Guha, R. Rastogi, K. Shim, Cure: an efficient clustering algorithm for large databases, Information Systems 26 (1) (2001) 35–58, https://doi.org/10.1016/S0306-4379(01)00008-4, http://www.sciencedirect.com/science/article/pii/S0306437901000084.

[68] Z. Tian, R. Raghu, L. Miron, Birch: an efficient data clustering method for very large databases, SIGMOD Record 25 (2) (1996) 103–114, https://doi.org/10.1145/235968.233324, http://doi.acm.org/10.1145/235968.233324.

[69] Kaufman L, Rousseeuw P. J, Finding Groups in Data: an Introduction to Cluster Analysis, Wiley, 1990.

[70] S. Vivek, H.N. Bharathi, Study of density based algorithms, International Journal of Computer Applications 69 (2013) 1–4.

[71] R. Prabahari, D.V. Thiagarasu, Density based clustering using Gaussian estimation technique, in: Density Based Clustering Using Gaussian Estimation Technique, vol. 2, 2015, pp. 4078–4081.

[72] H. Mark, F. Eibe, H. Geoffrey, P. Bernhard, R. Peter, W.I. H, The WEKA data mining software: an update, SIGKDD Explorations 11 (1) (2009) 10–18.

[73] L. Yanchi, L. Zhongmou, X. Hui, G. Xuedong, J. Wu, Understanding of internal clustering validation measures, in: Proceedings of the 2010 IEEE International Conference on Data Mining, ICDM '10, IEEE Computer Society, Washington, DC, USA, 2010, pp. 911–916.

[74] Jain Anil K, Dubes Richard C, Algorithms for Clustering Data, Prentice-Hall, Inc., Upper Saddle River, NJ, USA, 1988.

[75] Davies David L, Bouldin Donald W, A cluster separation measure, IEEE Transactions on Pattern Analysis and Machine Intelligence 1 (2) (1979) 224–227, https://doi.org/10.1109/TPAMI.1979.4766909.

[76] U. Maulik, S. Bandyopadhyay, Performance evaluation of some clustering algorithms and validity indices, IEEE Transactions on Pattern Analysis and Machine Intelligence 24 (12) (2002) 1650–1654, https://doi.org/10.1109/TPAMI.2002.1114856.

[77] H. Cui, K. Zhang, Y. Fang, S. Sobolevsky, C. Ratti, B.K.P. Horn, A clustering validity index based on pairing frequency, IEEE Access 5 (2017) 24884–24894, https://doi.org/10.1109/ACCESS.2017.2743985.

[78] R. Xu, J. Xu, D.C. Wunsch, A comparison study of validity indices on swarm-intelligence-based clustering, IEEE Transactions on Systems, Man and Cybernetics. Part B. Cybernetics 42 (4) (2012) 1243–1256, https://doi.org/10.1109/TSMCB.2012.2188509.

[79] R. Peter, Silhouettes: a graphical aid to the interpretation and validation of cluster analysis, Journal of Computational and Applied Mathematics 20 (1) (1987) 53–65, https://doi.org/10.1016/0377-0427(87)90125-7.

[80] M. Mai, H. Katsuhiro, N. Akira, Xie-beni-type fuzzy cluster validation in fuzzy co-clustering of documents and keywords, in: Y.I. Cho, E.T. Matson (Eds.), Soft Computing in Artificial Intelligence, Springer International Publishing, Cham, 2014, pp. 29–38.

[81] S. Dutta, S. Ghatak, M. Roy, S. Ghosh, A.K. Das, A graph based clustering technique for tweet summarization, in: Reliability, Infocom Technologies and Optimization (ICRITO) (Trends and Future Directions), 2015, pp. 1–6.

[82] M. Blei David, Y. Ng Andrew, I. Jordan Michael, Latent Dirichlet Allocation, Journal of Machine Learning Research (2003) 993–1022.

CHAPTER 10

Conclusion and future directions

10.1 Introduction

The primary objective of the research in this chapter is to develop effective algorithms for information filtering and information organization on social microblogging sites [1–3]. This concluding chapter summarizes the contributions of the chapter and indicates possible directions for future research [4].

10.2 Summary of contributions

In this chapter, the major focus areas are:

(i) attribute selection for spam filtering in social networks, especially filtering out spam tweets [5,6], and

(ii) clustering and summarization of tweets to reduce information overload on users.

Different data mining techniques are investigated. Data mining has an important role for understanding different events represented in several datasets by transforming data into useful knowledge [7]. Data mining research should focus on developing scalable algorithms to handle high-dimensional dataset efficiently and effectively [8–10].

Spam (information) filtering

Spam filtering on social microblogging sites needs to be accurate as well as very fast, since hundreds of millions of microblogs need to be filtered every day [11,12]. To address the real-time spam classification problem on online social media, attribute selection plays an important role. In this work, a rough set theory-based algorithm is proposed for attribute selection, and the algorithm is applied to the task of spam classification on online social media [13]. Experiments are carried out on five different datasets, demonstrating that the proposed methodology selects a subset of attributes which is smaller than what is selected by several baseline attribute selection methodologies, but which leads to better classification performances [14].

Information organization

The huge amount of redundant information posted on social microblogging sites leads to information overload among the users. To address this

Data Analytics for Social Microblogging Platforms
https://doi.org/10.1016/B978-0-32-391785-8.00023-8

problem, methodologies for summarization and clustering of microblogs are developed [15]. The ideas is to organize the information by grouping similar posts, so that it is sufficient for a user to read a summary of a few selected tweets or some representative tweets from every group [16].

Another issue highlighted in the chapters is information organization in terms of summarization and clustering. As microblogging sites have become important sources of real-time information, summarization of microblogs (tweets) has become an important problem.

Several text summarization algorithms are already available that can be used for microblog summarization. In this book, rather than trying to devise a new summarization algorithm, off-the-shelf summarization algorithms have been combined to produce better-quality summaries. To this end, two ensemble summarization algorithms are proposed – an unsupervised scheme and a supervised scheme – that can combine the outputs of multiple base summarization algorithms to produce summaries that are better than what is obtained from any of the individual base algorithms [17].

With respect to clustering, several clustering approaches are proposed in the book, such as graph-based clustering, genetic algorithm-based clustering, feature selection-based clustering, and dimensionality reduction-based clustering. A comparative study of the algorithms is carried out [18].

Information organization is particularly important during specific events such as emergencies, e.g., natural and man-made disasters. During such events, thousands of tweets are posted per hour, and since time is critical, it is necessary for the responders (e.g., relief workers) to get a quick overview of the information posted. Keeping this requirement in mind, the summarization and clustering algorithms developed in this chapter are applied on microblogs posted during several emergency situations. The experiments demonstrate the effectiveness of the proposed approaches [19,20].

It can be noted that the works in this chapter have used a wide variety of methodologies from various disciplines, including rough set theory, complex network analysis, evolutionary algorithms, ensemble algorithms, and other mathematical and statistical approaches [21].

10.3 Future research directions

There are several ways in which the works in this chapter can be extended:
- The attribute selection algorithm developed in Chapter 3 focuses on social media data that consist of discrete/categorical attributes only. In the future, the attribute selection algorithm can be generalized for

different types of data. Also, the methodology can be extended to continuous attributes.

- The ensemble summarization algorithms developed in Chapter 4 are meant for extractive base summarization algorithms in particular. In the future, the ensemble schemes can be extended to abstractive summarization algorithms by considering different text fragments (instead of whole tweets) selected by abstractive algorithms for generating the ensemble summaries [22].

- The clustering and summarization algorithms developed in this book consider a static set of tweets. In reality, tweets come in a continuous stream, and clustering and summarization need to be performed periodically in a dynamic setting. It is a challenging future direction to extend the summarization and clustering methods to dynamic data streams [23,24].

- The clustering and summarization methods developed in this book have considered only tweets in English. They can be extended so that they can process both tweets in English and non-English languages, and even code-mixed tweets (where multiple languages are used in the same post) [25].

- There is a practical need for developing Web-based/mobile systems for organizing social media data posted during emergency events, e.g., systems which will extract critical information and then summarize the information, or systems which will identify the evolving news stories (which can be modeled as clusters of tweets). The algorithms developed in this book can be used to develop such systems [26].

References

[1] S. Goswami, A.K. Das, Determining maximum cliques for community detection in weighted sparse networks, Knowledge and Information Systems 64 (2) (2022) 289–324, https://doi.org/10.1007/s10115-021-01631-y.

[2] P. Das, A.K. Das, Convolutional neural networks-based sentence level classification of crime documents, in: A.K. Das, J. Nayak, B. Naik, S. Dutta, D. Pelusi (Eds.), Computational Intelligence in Pattern Recognition, Springer, Singapore, 2022, pp. 65–73.

[3] A. Mukherjee, S. Bhattacharyya, K. Ray, B. Gupta, A.K. Das, A study of public sentiment and influence of politics in COVID-19 related tweets, in: A.K. Das, J. Nayak, B. Naik, S. Dutta, D. Pelusi (Eds.), Computational Intelligence in Pattern Recognition, Springer, Singapore, 2022, pp. 655–665.

[4] A. Campan, T. Atnafu, T.M. Truta, J. Nolan, Is data collection through Twitter streaming api useful for academic research?, in: 2018 IEEE International Conference on Big Data (Big Data), 2018, pp. 3638–3643.

[5] A. Das, D. Pal, C. Mallick, A.K. Das, An unsupervised COVID-19 report summarizer for developing smart healthcare system, in: A.K. Das, J. Nayak, B. Naik, S. Dutta, D.

Pelusi (Eds.), Computational Intelligence in Pattern Recognition, Springer, Singapore, 2022, pp. 157–168.

[6] C. Mallick, S. Das, A.K. Das, Evolutionary algorithm based summarization for analyzing COVID-19 medical reports, in: J. Nayak, B. Naik, A. Abraham (Eds.), Understanding COVID-19: The Role of Computational Intelligence, in: Studies in Computational Intelligence, Springer International Publishing, Cham, 2022, pp. 31–58.

[7] S. Kumar, K.M. Carley, What to track on the Twitter streaming api? A knapsack bandits approach to dynamically update the search terms, in: 2019 IEEE/ACM International Conference on Advances in Social Networks Analysis and Mining (ASONAM), 2019, pp. 158–163.

[8] S. Chattopadhyay, T. Basu, A.K. Das, K. Ghosh, L.C.A. Murthy, Towards effective discovery of natural communities in complex networks and implications in e-commerce, Electronic Commerce Research 21 (4) (2021) 917–954, https://doi.org/10.1007/s10660-019-09395-y.

[9] M. Basu, S.D. Bit, S. Ghosh, Utilizing microblogs for optimized real-time resource allocation in post-disaster scenarios, Social Network Analysis and Mining 12 (1) (2021) 15, https://doi.org/10.1007/s13278-021-00841-0.

[10] P. Bhattacharya, S. Paul, K. Ghosh, S. Ghosh, A. Wyner, DeepRhole: deep learning for rhetorical role labeling of sentences in legal case documents, Artificial Intelligence and Law (2021), https://doi.org/10.1007/s10506-021-09304-5.

[11] K. Hazra, T. Ghosh, A. Mukherjee, S. Saha, S. Nandi, S. Ghosh, S. Chakraborty, Sustainable text summarization over mobile devices: an energy-aware approach, Sustainable Computing: Informatics and Systems 32 (2021) 100607, https://doi.org/10.1016/j.suscom.2021.100607, https://www.sciencedirect.com/science/article/pii/S2210537921000950.

[12] A. Mandal, K. Ghosh, S. Ghosh, S. Mandal, A sequence labeling model for catchphrase identification from legal case documents, Artificial Intelligence and Law (2021), https://doi.org/10.1007/s10506-021-09296-2.

[13] M. Basu, K. Ghosh, S. Ghosh, Information retrieval from microblogs during disasters: in the light of IRMiDis task, SN Computer Science 1 (1) (2020) 61, https://doi.org/10.1007/s42979-020-0065-1.

[14] R. Mandal, S. Dutta, R. Banerjee, S. Bhattacharya, R. Ghosh, S. Samanta, T. Saha, City traffic speed characterization based on city road surface quality, in: J.M.R.S. Tavares, P. Dutta, S. Dutta, D. Samanta (Eds.), Cyber Intelligence and Information Retrieval, Springer, Singapore, 2022, pp. 515–524.

[15] H. Efstathiades, D. Antoniades, G. Pallis, M.D. Dikaiakos, Distributed large-scale data collection in online social networks, in: 2016 IEEE 2nd International Conference on Collaboration and Internet Computing (CIC), 2016, pp. 373–380.

[16] A. Dwi Laksito, Kusrini, H. Sismoro, F. Rahmawati, M. Yusa, A comparison study of search strategy on collecting Twitter data for drug adverse reaction, in: 2018 International Seminar on Application for Technology of Information and Communication, 2018, pp. 356–360.

[17] P. Ray, A. Chakrabarti, Twitter sentiment analysis for product review using lexicon method, in: 2017 International Conference on Data Management, Analytics and Innovation (ICDMAI), 2017, pp. 211–216.

[18] K. Jitkajornwanich, C. Kongthong, N. Khongsoontornjaroen, J. Kaiyasuan, S. Lawawirojwong, P. Srestasathiern, S. Srisonphan, P. Vateekul, Utilizing Twitter data for early flood warning in Thailand, in: 2018 IEEE International Conference on Big Data (Big Data), 2018, pp. 5165–5169.

[19] S.H. Archana, S.G. Winster, Drugs categorization based on sentence polarity analyzer for Twitter data, in: 2016 Second International Conference on Science Technology Engineering and Management (ICONSTEM), 2016, pp. 28–33.

[20] T. Jagić, L. Brkić, Hot topic detection using Twitter streaming data, in: 2020 43rd International Convention on Information, Communication and Electronic Technology (MIPRO), 2020, pp. 1730–1735.

[21] R. Compton, C. Lee, T.-C. Lu, L. De Silva, M. Macy, Detecting future social unrest in unprocessed Twitter data: "emerging phenomena and big data", in: 2013 IEEE International Conference on Intelligence and Security Informatics, 2013, pp. 56–60.

[22] R.D. Perera, S. Anand, K.P. Subbalakshmi, R. Chandramouli, Twitter analytics: architecture, tools and analysis, in: 2010 - MILCOM 2010 Military Communications Conference, 2010, pp. 2186–2191.

[23] P. Tatineni, B.S. Babu, B. Kanuri, G.R.K. Rao, P. Chitturi, C. Naresh, Post Covid-19 Twitter user's emotions classification using deep learning techniques in India, in: 2021 International Conference on Artificial Intelligence and Smart Systems (ICAIS), 2021, pp. 338–343.

[24] C. Wang, L. Marini, C.-L. Chin, N. Vance, C. Donelson, P. Meunier, J.T. Yun, Social media intelligence and learning environment: an open source framework for social media data collection, analysis and curation, in: 2019 15th International Conference on eScience (eScience), 2019, pp. 252–261.

[25] G.A. Sandag, A.M. Manueke, M. Walean, Sentiment analysis of Covid-19 vaccine tweets in Indonesia using recurrent neural network (rnn) approach, in: 2021 3rd International Conference on Cybernetics and Intelligent System (ICORIS), 2021, pp. 1–7.

[26] C.M. Yoshimura, H. Kitagawa, Tlv-bandit: bandit method for collecting topic-related local tweets, in: 2021 IEEE 4th International Conference on Multimedia Information Processing and Retrieval (MIPR), 2021, pp. 56–62.

Index

Printed in the United States
by Baker & Taylor Publisher Services